A CO

BALTIMORE, ANNAPOLIS & THE CHESAPEAKE BAY

7TH EDITION

BALTIMORE, ANNAPOLIS & THE CHESAPEAKE BAY

A Great Destination

Allison Blake

The Countryman Press
Woodstock, Vermont

OPPOSITE: *An egret on a piling watches over a creek, a familiar Chesapeake sight.* Queen Anne's County
Department of Economic Development, Agriculture & Tourism

Baltimore, Annapolis & the Chesapeake Bay: A Great Destination

ISBN: 978-1-58157-112-7

Interior photographs by the author unless otherwise specified
Maps by Mapping Specialists, Ltd, and Erin Greb Cartography, © The Countryman Press
Book design by Bodenweber Design
Composition by Eugenie S. Delaney

Published by The Countryman Press, P.O. Box 748, Woodstock, VT 05091
Distributed by W. W. Norton & Company, Inc., 500 Fifth Avenue, New York, NY 10110
Printed in the United States of America

10 9 8 7 6 5 4 3 2 1

Recommended by *National Geographic Traveler* and *Travel + Leisure* magazines

A crisp and critical approach, for travelers who want to live like locals.—*USA Today*

Great Destinations™ guidebooks are known for their comprehensive, critical coverage of regions of extraordinary cultural interest and natural beauty. Each title in this series is continuously updated with each printing to ensure accurate and timely information. All the books contain more than one hundred photographs and maps.

Current titles available:

The Adirondack Book

The Alaska Panhandle

Atlanta

Austin, San Antonio
   & the Texas Hill Country

Baltimore, Annapolis & the Chesapeake Bay

The Berkshire Book

Big Sur, Monterey Bay
   & Gold Coast Wine Country

Cape Canaveral, Cocoa Beach
   & Florida's Space Coast

The Charleston, Savannah
   & Coastal Islands Book

The Coast of Maine Book

Colorado's Classic Mountain Towns

Costa Rica: Great Destinations
   Central America

Dominican Republic

The Finger Lakes Book

The Four Corners Region

Galveston, South Padre Island
   & the Texas Gulf Coast

Guatemala: Great Destinations
   Central America

The Hamptons

Hawaii's Big Island: Great Destinations
   Hawaii

Honolulu & Oahu: Great Destinations
   Hawaii

The Jersey Shore: Atlantic City to Cape May

Kauai: Great Destinations Hawaii

Lake Tahoe & Reno

Las Vegas

Los Cabos & Baja California Sur:
   Great Destinations Mexico

Maui: Great Destinations Hawaii

Memphis and the Delta Blues Trail

Michigan's Upper Peninsula

Montreal & Quebec City:
   Great Destinations Canada

The Nantucket Book

The Napa & Sonoma Book

North Carolina's Outer Banks
   & the Crystal Coast

Nova Scotia & Prince Edward Island

Oaxaca: Great Destinations Mexico

Oregon Wine Country

Palm Beach, Fort Lauderdale, Miami
   & the Florida Keys

Palm Springs & Desert Resorts

Philadelphia, Brandywine Valley
   & Bucks County

Phoenix, Scottsdale, Sedona
   & Central Arizona

Playa del Carmen, Tulum & the Riviera Maya:
   Great Destinations Mexico

Salt Lake City, Park City, Provo
   & Utah's High Country Resorts

San Diego & Tijuana

San Juan, Vieques & Culebra:
   Great Destinations Puerto Rico

San Miguel de Allende & Guanajuato:
   Great Destinations Mexico

The Santa Fe & Taos Book

The Sarasota, Sanibel Island & Naples Book

The Seattle & Vancouver Book

The Shenandoah Valley Book

Touring East Coast Wine Country

Tucson

Virginia Beach, Richmond
   & Tidewater Virginia

Washington, D.C., and Northern Virginia

Yellowstone & Grand Teton National Parks
   & Jackson Hole

Yosemite & the Southern Sierra Nevada

The authors in this series are professional travel writers who have lived for many years in the regions they describe. Honest and painstakingly critical, full of information only a local can provide, Great Destinations guidebooks give you all the practical knowledge you need to enjoy the best of each region.

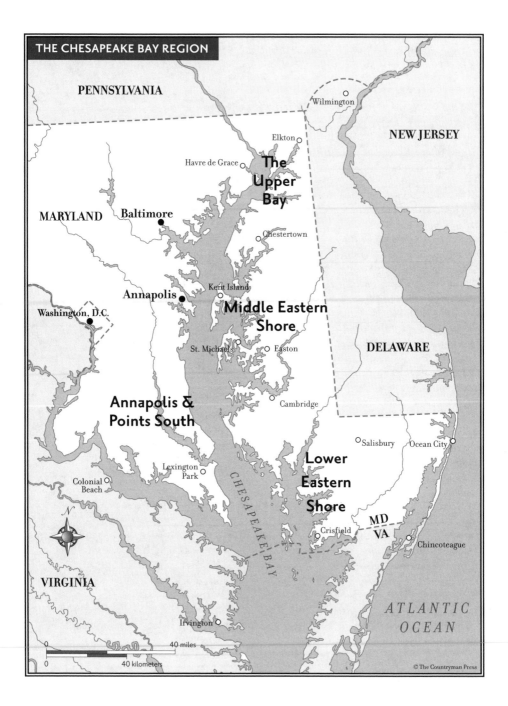

THE CHESAPEAKE BAY REGION

PENNSYLVANIA

Wilmington

NEW JERSEY

Elkton

Havre de Grace

The
Upper
Bay

MARYLAND   Baltimore

Chestertown

Kent Island

Annapolis

Middle Eastern
Shore

Washington, D.C.

St. Michaels   Easton

DELAWARE

Annapolis &
Points South

Cambridge

Salisbury   Ocean City

Lexington
Park

Lower
Eastern
Shore

Colonial
Beach

CHESAPEAKE BAY

Crisfield   MD
VA

Chincoteague

VIRGINIA

ATLANTIC
OCEAN

N

Irvington

40 miles

40 kilometers

© The Countryman Press

Contents

Acknowledgments

For this ongoing exploration of the Chesapeake Bay region, numerous talented people contributed their words and wisdom, or supplied photographs as needed.

Christine Stutz wrote the bulk of the Baltimore restaurant profiles (all but two, to be exact), lending her local knowledge and expertise. On the Middle Eastern Shore, Beth Rubin broke out her notebook on behalf of restaurants, while Fran Severn contributed restaurant, lodging, and shopping profiles on the Lower Eastern Shore. Eric Mills wrote about Chesapeake City and contributed restaurant profiles from the Upper Shore. Thanks to all of them.

Thanks also to Vanessa Parks, Sara Hisamoto at the Baltimore Convention and Visitor's Bureau, John Zeimann at the Sports Legends Museum, Pete Hilsee at the American Visionary Art Museum, Kjeld Lauritzen of the Living Classrooms Foundation, Peggy Wall at the National Park Service, Connie Yingling at the Maryland Office of Tourism, Susan Steckman at the Annapolis & Anne Arundel County Conference & Visitors Bureau, Bernadette Van Pelt in Kent County's tourism department, Julie Widdowson in Somerset County's tourism office, Amanda Fenstermaker in Dorchester County's tourism department, Debbie Dodson in Talbot County's tourism department, Annapolis gallery owner Cynthia McBride, John Neely Jr., and numerous kind and accommodating staff who showed me around numerous fascinating museums, inns, hotels, and other attractions. Thanks also to Joe Evans at *PropTalk,* Jeff Holland at the Annapolis Maritime Museum, along with many others.

Thanks, as always, to the fine folks at The Countryman Press and Kathryn Flynn, as well as Joshua and all the family.

Introduction

Crossing the eastbound span of the Chesapeake Bay Bridge is kind of like watching the orange slit of day break up ahead on a trans-Atlantic red-eye. The promise of adventure lies ahead.

"But you get that same feeling when you pull up to Point Lookout or arrive in Solomons Island," says my husband.

So you do. I even get excited tunneling under the Patapsco River when I take the Baltimore Harbor Tunnel route into the big city.

When it comes to the Chesapeake Bay and its endless network of tributaries large and small, you'll be making lots of crossings. You can even traverse a tended country draw-bridge, or take a ferry that's been running since the late 1600s. There's no mistaking the charm of Bay travel. Possibilities always exist on the other side.

THE WAY THIS BOOK WORKS

Organization

This book covers Baltimore city, Annapolis and points south to the Potomac River, the Upper Eastern Shore, the Middle Eastern Shore, and the Lower Eastern Shore to the Virginia border—in other words, the Maryland portion of the Chesapeake Bay plus Tangier Island, an iconic Bay island located in Virginia. Lodgings and restaurants are arranged geographically within each chapter, except in Baltimore, where restaurants and shops are arranged by neighborhood.The city's other offerings, including museums, are arranged alphabetically. Every effort was made to ensure the information in this book was correct as of publication time, but prices, hours, and policies change. It's always best to check ahead. (In particular, we suggest you check with your innkeeper for specific needs or requests, including those regarding children or handicapped access. Check their Web sites for specials, too.

Prices

Because prices change, we guide via price ranges. Lodging prices usually drop in the off-season, and are lower midweek than they are on weekends. The main place that guidance might not be firm is in Baltimore, where business travelers keep hotels busy during the week. Two-night minimums may apply on weekends at inns and B&Bs. Check their Web sites, which often offer specials and packages.

Restaurant prices are based on the cost of an entrée. In cases where a sandwich or large salad might reasonably be considered an entrée, we included those. The Chesapeake region varies in terms of price. Rural areas are often less expensive than the cities or even the tourism centers in the Middle and Upper shores.

Every effort was made to ensure the accuracy of these prices prior to going to press, but prices change. Always check with the establishment for current pricing.

Price Codes

	Lodging	Dining
Inexpensive	up to $75	$1–10
Moderate	$75–150	$10–20
Expensive	$150–225	$20–30
Very Expensive	Over $225	Over $30

1

History

"A Very Goodly Bay"

> There is but one entrance by Sea into this Country, and that is at the mouth of a very goodly Bay, 18 or 20 myles broad. The cape on the South is called Cape Henry, in honour of our most notable Prince. The North Edge is called Cape Charles, in honour of the worthy Duke of Yorke. Within is a country that may have the prerogative over the most pleasant places. Heaven and earth never agreed better to frame a place for man's habitation. Here are mountains, hills, plaines, valleyes, rivers, and brookes, all running into a faire Bay, compassed but for the mouth, with fruitful and delightsome land.
>
> Capt. John Smith, 1607

Archaeologists digging in this cradle of U.S. history have unearthed countless remnants of an even deeper past. Layered in sand and clay along Chesapeake Bay shores are oyster shells, some thousands of years old. The largest cache was a 30-acre Indian shell midden spread across Popes Creek, off the Potomac River. Long before Chesapeake watermen took up their tongs, the Bay was feeding her people.

The native inhabitants called her Chesapeake Bay, "the Great Shellfish Bay." In the 16th century, a Jesuit priest sailed through the Virginia capes described by John Smith and bestowed a second name: *La Bahía de la Madre de Dios*—the Bay of the Mother of God.

The Chesapeake has always looked after those who lived here. Just as the Native Americans thrived on Bay oysters, so early European settlers grew crops in rich Bay soil. As the indigenous peoples paddled canoes from encampment to encampment, so ferries linked later settlements.

Today, the waters of this ancient river valley fan out into a complex network of urban bridges and rural lanes. Here endures the heart of the modern Mid-Atlantic megalopolis and the soul of 19th-century fishing villages. U.S. history here is old; geological history is young.

The Chesapeake Bay is bookended by two major metropolitan areas in two states: Baltimore, Maryland's largest city, and Norfolk–Hampton Roads in Virginia's Tidewater. Both are major Atlantic ports. Near John Smith's Virginia capes, now spanned by the 17.6-mile Chesapeake Bay Bridge–Tunnel, Naval Station Norfolk presides over the Navy's strong Tidewater presence.

OPPOSITE: *Maryland's statehouse is the country's oldest in continuous use.* www.VisitAnnapolis.org

The Blackwater National Wildlife Refuge in Cambridge, Maryland, is home to the largest nesting population of bald eagles north of Florida. Mark D. Raab, photo courtesy Maryland Office of Tourism

Much of Maryland's Western Shore life looks to urban centers, as city dwellers willing to endure the hour-plus commute to Washington, D.C., or Baltimore have moved to Annapolis and nearby Kent Island, drawing these former Bay outposts into the region's suburbs. For their highway-bound hours during the week, these government types are repaid with long sails on the Bay or afternoons anchored in secluded "gunkholes," shallow coves where green or great blue herons fly from nearby marshes. On the Eastern Shore, fishing, farming, tourism, and the retirement business spur local economic life.

Up the Bay's major tributaries stand the region's major cities: Washington, D.C., on the Potomac; Richmond, Virginia, on the James; and Baltimore on the Patapsco. Maryland's capital, Annapolis, stands at the mouth of the Severn River, near where the William Preston Lane Jr. Memorial Bridge—better known simply as the Bay Bridge—links the Eastern and Western shores.

Even as the Chesapeake is defined by her waters, so she is defined by her history. A stop at the Maryland Statehouse in Annapolis, where George Washington resigned his Continental Army commission, is as integral to a Chesapeake Country visit as a charter boat fishing trip from Tilghman Island. In 1607, America's first permanent colonial English settlement was established at Jamestown, Virginia. The first Catholic settlers landed farther north, on the Potomac River, and established Maryland at St. Marys City in 1634. Washington and his peers used the Bay first to transport their tobacco, the region's first sizable cash crop, and then to their military advantage as they plotted their navigational comings and goings during the Revolutionary War.

For all of the Bay's history and navigability, however, she shares a problem with virtually every other heavily populated estuary. A confluence of pressures has threatened the health of her rich waters since European settlers first chopped down forests to create fields to farm. Soil from the fertile lands lining the Bay's shores has slipped into the water, silting in harbors and obscuring marshy invertebrate nurseries. Damage has been compounded by 20th-century wastes: fertilizers, air pollution, and sewage bring phosphorous and nitrogen, nutrients that damage the Bay.

Many say the magnificent Chesapeake is at the most crucial crossroads of her most recent geological incarnation. A massive assault against pollution has been under way since the late 1970s. Perhaps, like the estuary's flushing by fresh water from the north and by saltwater tides from the south, the diverse mix of urban and rural can find a balance in La Bahía de la Madre de Dios.

NATURAL HISTORY

Cargo ships journeying the 200-mile length of the Chesapeake Bay travel in a deep channel that more than 10,000 years ago cradled the ancient Susquehanna River. The mighty river flowed south to the ocean, drawing in the waters of many tributaries but for one independent soul: the present-day James River. Then came the great shift in the glaciers of the last Ice Age, when the thick sheets of ice that stopped just north of the Chesapeake region—in what is now northern Pennsylvania and New York State—began to melt under warming temperatures. As the Pleistocene Era ended, torrents of released water filled the oceans. The Susquehanna River valley flooded once, twice, and probably more, settling eventually within the bounds of the present-day Chesapeake Bay.

A 1980s discovery cast new light on evidence of an even earlier event that helped to shape the Bay. An asteroid or comet hurtling 50,000 miles per hour into the earth is thought to have left the mile-deep, 56-mile-wide Chesapeake Bay Impact Crater near what is now the mouth of the Bay, apparently the largest such crater in the United States.

An osprey sits near its distinctive nest on a Bay area channel marker.

The shifts of the earth and, perhaps, the remnants of space have left behind North America's largest estuary. Estuaries are duel bodies of water, mixing the fresh waters of inland mountain streams and rivers with salty ocean currents. The undulating brew of fresh and salt stirs a habitat that supports a huge range of creatures. Clams, crabs, oysters, American shad, striped bass (known hereabouts as rockfish), menhaden, and more have always thrived in these waters, living a solitary life in the deep as bottom dwellers, bedding down in the shallows, or navigating to the fresh water to spawn.

The Susquehanna River, supplying 50 percent of the Chesapeake's fresh water, flows into the head of the Bay. The Potomac River adds another 20 percent. Even the glacial-era renegade James River finally joined other Chesapeake tributaries, adding fresh water that helps to nourish the vast mix of species living in the Bay.

Solid evidence of a prehistoric past lies layered along the Western Shore of the Bay, per- haps most famously at Calvert Cliffs, located 53 miles south of Annapolis. In a swath trav- eling from here south to the Virginia side of the Potomac River, shark teeth and other fossils still wash up from time to time. These are 12- to 17-million-year-old forebears to the Bay's crabs, menhaden, and oysters that lived in a Miocene Era sea that stretched to present-day Washington, D.C. Crocodiles, rhinoceroses, and mastodons lived along the cliffs that were once the uplands of the ancient Susquehanna River valley.

Where Land and Water Meet

Consider the Chesapeake's considerable statistics: She is nearly 200 miles long with dozens of tidal tributaries and all manner of coves, creeks, and tidal rivers. Shoreline length for the Bay and tidal rivers equals 11,684 miles. The total system is filled by 18 *tril- lion* gallons of water, with the estuary's fresher water in the upper Bay and the saltier far- ther south.

The Bay's width ranges from 4 miles at Annapolis to about 35 miles at Point Lookout, Maryland, where the Potomac River meets the Bay and serves as the border between Maryland and Virginia. Despite the enormity of this expansive body of water, the Chesapeake is surprisingly shallow. Its average depth is 21 feet, although at the so-called Deep Trough off Kent Island, just over the bridge from Annapolis, depths reach 174 feet.

Beyond the waters of the Bay, within her six-state, 64,000-square-mile watershed, is geological diversity: the metamorphic rock of the Appalachian plateau, the weathered, iron-rich soil of the Piedmont, and the low-lying coastal plain.

A shoreline that seems to snake forever along marshes, creeks, and rivers provides ample habitat for thousands of species of resident or migratory wildlife and aquatic dwellers. Rookeries of great blue herons and colonies of terns nest on isolated islands, and even brown pelicans appear in—and even breed—the southern reaches of the Bay.

Overhead each fall come the migratory waterfowl—tundra swans, Canada geese, brants, and, of course, ducks: mallards, pintails, canvasbacks, and teals—all following the Atlantic Flyway. The mighty osprey is common, back from its severely depleted numbers after the insecticide DDT was banned in the early 1970s. Visitors can easily see osprey nests upon navigational markers and buoys throughout the Bay. And don't be surprised if that other distinctive raptor with a white head glimpsed near a marsh turns out to be a bald eagle. Numbers of the formerly endangered bird are so improved that it has been removed from the federal list of Endangered and Threatened Wildlife and Plants.

Deep on the Eastern Shore, in the lowlands of Dorchester County, the brackish marshes of the Blackwater National Wildlife Refuge welcome the red-cockaded woodpecker, peregrine falcon, and bald eagle, which breeds here. The great horned owl likewise nests in this marshy blackwater, and the rare Delmarva fox squirrel also makes this area its home. Secretive river otters can occasionally be spotted; more likely, you've seen a muskrat.

Just as it's a surprise to see the pelicans this far north, so it seems surprising that bald cypress exist this far north. Hikers in the mid-Bay region will spot cypress knees along some wetland trails. In Calvert County, Maryland—not far from the fossils of Calvert Cliffs—stands the Battle Creek Cypress Swamp, where a low boardwalk winds through this mysterious habitat.

But far more common are the Chesapeake's tidal wetlands, crucial creature nurseries once thought to be no more than mosquito breeding grounds. Saltwater grasses adapted to this habitat between land and sea once grew profusely, sheltering critters such as molting crabs and protecting the sea from the land.

Talk to a salty waterman who has worked the Bay and her rivers for a few decades, though, and he'll tell you the once-prolific underwater Bay grasses are nothing compared to what they once were. Bay environmentalists consider this "submerged aquatic vegetation," or SAV, a sort of clarity gauge of the Bay. Sediment and nutrients from pollution feed algal blooms, which then block the sunlight and prevent growth of the grasses. Efforts to bring back these protectors have been somewhat successful in recent years, helping to return an important nursery to young creatures such as rockfish and crabs.

A waterman heads out in search of crabs.   www.VisitAnnapolis.org

Officially, 350 species of fish live in Bay waters; only some of these create reliable fisheries. Finfish, including striped bass, bluefish, American shad, croaker, Atlantic menhaden, and alewives, are among those who live here. But most famed among the Bay's aquatic residents are the blue crab and the oyster. Both are the focus of considerable attention in the ongoing effort to restore the ecological health of the Bay. Unfortunately, their numbers are not what they once were.

Saving the Bay

Time and tide have sent shoreline crumbling into the Bay, and the debris of human development has followed, speeding the Bay's decline. In addition to chemical fertilizers from farms and suburban lawns throughout this vast watershed, waste discharged from even vastly improved, modern sewage treatment plants continues to flow in. Air pollution from cars and coal-fired power plants funnels more nitrogen into the Chesapeake.

Efforts to bring back the Chesapeake's historical health stretch back to 1977, when formal federal and state programs allied to launch a massive Bay research and cleanup program. Interestingly, in 1964 President Lyndon B. Johnson announced the federally supported start to a cleanup of the famed Potomac River, a Bay tributary. The $1 billion project is considered a great success story, inspiration to the many agencies now devoting millions of dollars and countless hours to a Baywide cleanup.

Research launched in 1977 culminated in a landmark agreement that established a nuts-and-bolts plan to renew the Bay's deteriorating habitat. This accord, the Chesapeake Bay Agreement of 1983, was signed by Maryland, Virginia, Pennsylvania, the District of Columbia, the federal Environmental Protection Agency, and the Chesapeake Bay Commission, a group of area legislators. When the agreement was launched, the focus was on cleaning up the Bay per se. After a long history of limited success, President Barack Obama in 2009 issued an order that puts the federal government at the cleanup's helm. He ordered the EPA to take the reins, and federal agencies are now charged with doing a better job. The EPA even has a pollution "budget," which means it can penalize states that don't meet set goals. Legislation also is in the offing to give the whole process sharper teeth. Will it improve the Bay? Time will tell.

The blue crab, mainstay of a Chesapeake summer diet, has become a source of concern. Over the years, both Maryland and Virginia have tightened harvesting regulations in an effort to ensure the continued future availability of this astronomically popular crustacean. This doesn't mean that blue crabs aren't available—tables fill at crabhouses throughout the Chesapeake all summer long—but do *Callinectes sapidus* a favor when dropping your crab net in the water: Take only as much as you'll need for dinner, and return the females to the water. (And don't be surprised if crabs are imported from North Carolina or the Gulf Coast at Memorial Day—the Chesapeake season while underway, really gets rolling over the ensuing weeks.

Perhaps signaling a brighter future for the crab are the success stories behind the return of the rockfish. Commercial fishermen once enjoyed steady rockfish catches of 5 million pounds annually, then watched as stocks dropped to 2 million pounds in the late 1970s. In 1985, Maryland put in place a temporary moratorium on rockfish harvesting. Virginia followed in 1989. Stocks were officially declared restored in 1995. Habitat restoration and the two fishing moratoria are given credit for bringing back the rockfish.

Visitors can expect to see continued development around the Chesapeake as subdivisions grow from former farmland. But they also can expect to see enthusiastic local support for the beloved Bay, as its residents participate in activities like organized SAV-planting canoe trips. Cars sport Chesapeake Bay specialty license plates, and in Maryland you can check off a box on your state tax return to give money to clean up the Bay.

Sailing and boating thrive; recreational fishers enthusiastically go after striped bass. The central effort for all Bay lovers and residents is to help restore the estuary and nurture it as the Mid-Atlantic region continues to grow. The balance, though tough to strike, is the fulcrum of efforts to bring back the Bay.

SOCIAL HISTORY

The first settlers of the Chesapeake region lived here during the last Ice Age. These Paleo-Indians were hunters, following mammoth and bison on their migrations. The melting of the glaciers marked the beginning of the Archaic period, when these forebears of the Piscataway and Nanticoke tribes convened in villages and began to eat oysters and other shell- and finfish from the Bay. About 3,000 years ago, they began to farm these shores, raising maize, ancestor to the stacks of corn found at farm stands throughout the region come August, and tobacco, which the English settlers later converted into the region's early economic foundation.

Early Settlers

Dutch and Spanish explorers of the 16th century were reportedly the first Europeans to sail into the Bay, although Vikings may have visited even earlier. The first Europeans to settle permanently, however, were the English. In 1607, Capt. Christopher Newport left England, crossed the Atlantic to the West Indies, then sailed north into the Bay. He navigated up what would come to be called the James River. Those aboard Newport's three-ship fleet, the 49-foot *Discovery,* the 68-foot *Godspeed,* and the 111-foot *Susan Constant,* settled Jamestown.

The new colony, chartered by the Virginia Company, proved to be a near disaster. Hostiles and disease either drove off or killed many of the original settlers. Among the survivors was Captain John Smith, by all accounts an adventurer. It was here that Smith's fabled rescue by the maiden Pocahontas took place—an event recorded in Smith's journal but questioned by scholars. As the story goes, the young captain was captured and taken to a village where the old "powhatan," or chief, was to preside over Smith's execution. Even as the warriors threatened with raised clubs, the chief's young daughter threw herself upon the English captain, thus saving him from a brutal fate.

Smith was also the first Englishman to explore the Bay, and indeed he charted it rather accurately. He set out on his exploration from Jamestown in 1608, accompanied by 14 men on an open barge. They sailed first up the "Easterne Shore," where sources of fresh water proved poor. While still in what came to be called Virginia, Smith wrote, " . . . the first people we saw were 2 grimme and stout Salvages upon Cape-Charles, with long poles like Javelings, headed with bone. They boldly demanded what we were, and what we would, but after many circumstances, they in time seemed very kinde." Smith learned from them "such descriptions of the Bay, Isles, and rivers, that often did us exceeding pleasure." The party then went on across the Bay to its western shore, sailing as fast as they could ahead of a fearsome storm. "Such an extreame gust of wind, rayne, thunder, and lightening happened, that with great danger we escaped the unmercifull raging of that Ocean-like water," Smith wrote.

Efforts to create a water trail tracing Smith's route are under way by the National Park Service following the successful tercentennial re-creation of Smith's voyages.

Early Jamestown survived as Virginia's colonial capital until the end of the 17th century. Meanwhile, English migration across the Atlantic continued. In 1631, William Claiborne established his trading post on Kent Island, mid-Bay, setting himself up to become arguably the first settler of Maryland. In ensuing years, on behalf of the Virginia Company, he provided ample rivalry for Maryland's "proprietors," or royal grant holders, the Calverts.

George Calvert, the first Lord Baltimore, hoped to settle his own Avalon. He first sought to establish a colony in Newfoundland but soon abandoned the harsh northern land. A second grant for a new colony passed to his son, the second Lord Baltimore, Cecil Calvert. The younger Calvert, a Catholic, knew that Virginia would not welcome the new settlement and feared that enemies in England would try to undermine his colony. He put his younger brother, Leonard, in charge of the settlers who boarded the ships *Ark* and *Dove* and sailed off to found Maryland, named in honor of Charles I's queen, near the mouth of the Potomac River at St. Clement's Island. Visitors can still take a weekend boat out to the island, now shrunk from 400 acres to about 40.

The 128 hardy souls aboard the two ships landed on March 25, 1634, after taking a route similar to that taken by Newport. Upon landing, Leonard Calvert, as governor, led a party of men up the river to meet the "tayac," or leader, of the Piscataways. The tayac gave the settlers permission to settle where they would; their village was to become Maryland's first capital, St. Marys City. These Native Americans also taught the English settlers how to farm unfamiliar lands in an unfamiliar climate.

Among the Marylanders' first crops was tobacco, soon to be a staple of the Chesapeake economy and already being harvested farther south along the Virginia Bay coast. In the years that followed, farmers would discover just how damaging tobacco proved to be in costs to both the land and humans. Because the crop sapped the soil's nutrients, without fertilizers a field was used up after a couple of seasons, so more land constantly had to be cleared and planted. This called for labor. While some Englishmen indentured themselves to this life in exchange for trans-Atlantic passage to the colonies, tobacco farming was nevertheless responsible for the beginnings of African slave labor along the Chesapeake. By the late 17th century, wealthy planters had begun to "invest" in slaves as "assets."

Up and down the Chesapeake grew a tobacco coast, fueled by demand from English traders. From its beginnings as a friendly home to new settlers, the Bay grew into a seago-ing highway for the burgeoning tobacco trade. Soon came fishing and boatbuilding.

A rural manorial society grew up around St. Marys City, which itself was never very large. Perhaps a dozen families lived within its 5 square miles. Planters raised tobacco, a fort was established, and government business eventually brought inns and stables. In 1650, a settlement named Providence was established about 100 miles to the north, near what is now Annapolis. In 1695, the new governor, Francis Nicholson, moved Maryland's capital to Annapolis, near the mouth of the Severn River. By 1720, St. Marys City was gone. That colony's heyday has been re-created, however, in a living museum complete with Ossabaw pigs. Archaeological work continues on the site as well. In the early 1990s, three lead coffins holding the remains of members of the Calvert clan were unearthed and authenticated.

The old Bazzell Church deep in Dorchester County on Maryland's Eastern Shore.

Nicholson's Annapolis, considered America's first Baroque-style city, remains evident to any visitor. Two circles, State Circle and Church Circle, form hubs from which the streets of today's Historic District radiate. Three statehouses have stood inside State Circle, the most recent begun in 1772. This was the building used as the national capitol during the period of the Articles of Confederation, and it is the nation's oldest state capitol in continual use. From the center of Church Circle rises the spire of St. Anne's Church, the third on the site since 1696.

Known also as "the Ancient City," Annapolis grew into a thriving late 17th- and 18th-century town, renowned as the social gathering spot for colonial gentlemen and ladies. Here, the provincial court and the legislature met. Planters "wintered" here amid fashionable society; among social clubs, the most famed included the witty men of the Tuesday Club, whose members, such as colonial painter Charles Willson Peale, gathered at the homes of its members for music and poetry.

Elsewhere along the Chesapeake, other settlements were emerging. Chestertown was established as a seaport and Kent County seat in 1706. Near the head of the Bay, "Baltimore Town" was first carved in 1729 from 60 acres owned by the wealthy Carroll family. Those who couldn't survive the fluctuations of the tobacco market turned to tonging for oysters, fishing for herring, or shipbuilding.

The Chesapeake in Wartime

During the Revolutionary War, Annapolis's central port location drew blockade-runners and Continental colonels alike. Both Americans and British used the Bay to transport troops. War meetings that included George Washington and the Marquis de Lafayette were held beneath the Liberty Tree, a 400- to 600-year-old tulip tree that stood on the campus of St. John's College until dealt a final blow by a hurricane in 1999.

Three Annapolitans—Samuel Chase, William Paca, and Charles Carroll of Carrollton—signed the Declaration of Independence in 1776; their colonial-era homes have been preserved and are open for public tours. The fourth Maryland signer, Thomas Stone, later took up residence here, too, in what is now known as the Peggy Stewart House. The war finally ended in 1781 at Yorktown, Virginia, near Jamestown. Reinforcements traveled south along the Bay to meet up with Washington's gathering troops, and the French Admiral de Grasse barricaded the mouth of the Bay. Lord Cornwallis, the British commander, surrendered.

In 1783, during a meeting of the Continental Congress in the Maryland Statehouse in Annapolis, George Washington resigned his Army commission; visitors can still see the chamber where this occurred. This is also where the Treaty of Paris was ratified in 1784, formally ending the war. Likewise, Annapolis itself saw an end to its glittery social role. The city soon fell quiet, awakened only by the 1845 establishment of the U.S. Naval Academy, which overshadowed much of city life for at least the next century.

Peace with the British after the Revolution was short-lived. Soon came the War of 1812, the final time hostile British troops reached the new nation's shores. The British established their operations center at Tangier Island, and many battles and skirmishes ensued upon the Bay. Visitors to the Virginia island will learn about the Methodist "Parson of the Islands," Joshua Thomas, who predicted defeat when he preached to the British before they sailed up the Bay to Baltimore.

The citizens of the young nation, including those at the shipbuilding center of St. Michaels, were not eager to bow to the British. Blockade-runners routinely left the Eastern Shore port, and hostility ran high. Late on the night of August 9, 1813, amid rumors of an impending British attack, the good citizens of St. Michaels blew out their lanterns. Just before dawn, the British attacked a nearby fort. The wily shorefolk were ready. They hoisted their lanterns into the treetops, the British fired too high, and the town was saved. For this, St. Michaels calls itself "The Town That Fooled the British."

A year later came the war's decisive battle. In September 1814, a man watched the fire of cannons and guns as the Americans successfully defended Fort McHenry, which guards the entrance to Baltimore Harbor. The next morning, that man, Francis Scott Key, saw a tattered U.S. flag flying and, inspired, penned the words to "The Star-Spangled Banner," thus creating what would become the U.S. national anthem in 1931.

19th-Century Life

Once this second war ended, the denizens of 19th-century Chesapeake Country turned to building their economy. Tobacco declined; shipbuilding grew. Smaller Chesapeake shore towns such as Chestertown and Annapolis lost commercial prominence to Baltimore, which grew into the Upper Bay region's major trade center. Steamships were launched, and the Baltimore & Ohio Railroad more speedily connected the region to points west. Eastern Shore—grown wheat and the watermen's catch of oysters, menhaden, and more were exported. By all accounts, there was no love lost between the landed gentry, who controlled the region, and the Chesapeake watermen. These scrappy individualists may have been one-time small farmers down on their luck or descendants of released indentured servants who had once served the wealthy class.

During this era, Chesapeake's shoals saw their first aids to navigation erected as lightships were sent out to warn passing ships of the worst sandbars. In 1819, Congress made provisions to set two lightships in Virginia waters. This experiment in safety was popular, and by 1833, 10 lightships stood sentinel at the mouth of the Rappahannock River and elsewhere in the Bay. The mid-19th century saw construction of the Chesapeake's distinctive screw-pile lighthouses, with pilings that could be driven securely into the muddy bottom of the Bay. Today, only three stand—two at maritime museums at Solomons and St. Michaels, Maryland, and one in action in the Bay just southeast of Annapolis, off Thomas Point. The Thomas Point Lighthouse was manned until automation came in 1986, and visitors can go there (see the tours offered by the Annapolis Maritime Museum in that city's chapter).

As the Bay became easier to travel, the people who spent the most time on the water discovered perhaps her greatest wealth. In the 19th century, demand increased for the famous Chesapeake oysters. Watermen went after them in an early ancestor to many Bay-built boat designs, the log canoe. Boats like the fast oceangoing schooners known as Baltimore clippers already were being built, but oyster dredging and tonging required boats that could skip over shoals, run fast, and allow a man to haul gear over the side. Log canoes have unusually low freeboard; crab pots and oyster tongs can be worked over their sides with relative ease. These successors to dugout canoes were given sails and

The exterior of a surviving slave cabin at Sotterley Plantation in St. Mary's County.

shallow-draft hulls so that they could navigate shoals. With their top-heavy sails and low sides, these log canoes now present one of a yachtsman's greatest challenges. Shifting their weight just ahead of the wind, sailors race them during the summer along the Eastern Shore.

The Bay's 120-year steamboat era arrived in 1813, seven years after packets first carried passengers on a ship-and-stagecoach journey from Baltimore to Philadelphia. The steamboat *Chesapeake* paddled out of Baltimore Harbor on June 13, 1813, bound for Frenchtown, Maryland, a now-extinct town at the head of the Bay. Within a week, a trip was offered to Rock Hall, on Maryland's Eastern Shore, for 75 cents. By 1848, the steamship company that came to be called the Old Bay Line ran the 200-mile length of the Bay, from Baltimore to Norfolk. Steamships ran in the Bay into the 1960s.

The Civil War and Slavery

Even as the Chesapeake Bay fueled a growing 19th-century economy, these were the years of growing North-South hostility. The Chesapeake region was largely slaveholding, although the nearby Mason-Dixon Line (the southern boundary of Pennsylvania) to the north beckoned many slaves to freedom.

The history of slavery here had started with tobacco farming in the late 1600s; by 1770, tobacco exports reached 100 million pounds in the Western Shore region. When the tobacco trade declined in the 19th century, the services of many slaves were no longer needed. Abolitionist Quakers living in the Bay area campaigned to free many slaves, and free blacks were not uncommon in Annapolis and Baltimore in the first half of the 19th century. Many Eastern Shore watermen were free blacks who mixed with white watermen in mutual contempt for the wealthy.

In 1817, abolitionist and writer Frederick Douglass was born into slavery in Talbot County, Maryland. As a boy, he worked at the Wye Plantation, owned by Edward Lloyd V, the scion of a political dynasty in Maryland. Following alternately civil treatment in Baltimore and brutal treatment as an Eastern Shore field hand, Douglass escaped to Philadelphia at age 21 and became a free man.

Because the upper reaches of the Bay were so close to freedom, the Underground Railroad thrived here. The best-known local conductor was Harriet Tubman, an escaped slave from Dorchester County, Maryland, who became known as "The Moses of Her People," as she led nearly 300 slaves north during her lifetime.

When the Civil War broke out in 1861, the Virginia half of the Chesapeake quickly turned to Richmond, located at the head of navigation of the James River. Maryland struggled over its political loyalties, and many Chesapeake families would be divided by North-South rivalries.

Naval warfare changed forever on the waters of the Civil War Bay, when the ironclads *Monitor* and *Merrimack* met at Hampton Roads. The *Merrimack*, having been salvaged, rebuilt as an ironclad, and renamed *Virginia* by the Confederates, had already rammed and sunk the Union *Cumberland* and disabled the *Congress*, which burned and sank. The next day, the ironclad *Monitor*, with her two guns protected in a swiveling turret, arrived to engage the *Merrimack's* fixed guns. Neither ship sank the other and neither side won, but the encounter was the first battle between armored battleships.

Ironically, when the Emancipation Proclamation went into effect in January 1863, slaves laboring on the Virginia shores of the Chesapeake were freed where federal law—via Union occupation—prevailed; slaves in Union Maryland were not. The proclamation freed only those in states "in rebellion against the United States." It wasn't until September 1864, when Maryland voted for its own new constitution, that those in bondage in the state were freed.

The Oyster Boom

In the years before the war, shrewd Baltimore businessmen had opened oyster-packing plants. With the war over, enterprising Chesapeake business was renewed. The fertile oyster bars of the Bay's famed shoals fueled a much-needed economic burst on the Eastern Shore.

Chesapeake oyster production peaked at 20 million bushels a year in the 1880s, the height of the great oyster boom that started after the Civil War. At the same time, the Eastern Shore Railroad snaked through the flatlands of the Lower Shore, where one John Crisfield, former Maryland congressman, set about capitalizing on it. At the head of Tangier Sound, where watermen dredged or tonged millions of oysters from the rich waters, Crisfield built his namesake town, which now calls itself "The Crab Capital of the World." The town was literally built upon millions of oyster shells. An enormous wharf stretched along Somer's Cove, and the railroad depot stood nearby. Shuckers and packers set to work once the daily catch was landed; the cargo was shipped out on the railroad line, and newly developed refrigeration techniques kept it fresh on its way deep into the nation's interior.

Both Maryland and Virginia have taken steps to protect the population of the region's famous blue crabs.
Maryland Office of Tourism

Like Crisfield, Solomons, Maryland, on the Western Shore, sprang from the oyster rush. Isaac Solomon came from Baltimore, taking his patented pasteurizing canning process to the tiny village, where he set up a successful packing plant.

From this gold mine grew greed, and the famed Chesapeake Oyster Wars ensued. Virginia and Maryland oystermen—the tongers and dredgers, known as "drudgers"—battled over rights to oyster beds. Tempers ran high, and shots were fired. Maryland authorities, already funding an "Oyster Navy" to maintain some measure of decorum on the Bay, were angered that Virginia was less than helpful when it came to keeping its watermen within its boundaries, wherever exactly they were.

The Oyster Wars proved to be the catalyst that finally forced Maryland and Virginia to define their disputed Bay border. Three years of negotiations at the federal bargaining table set the boundary in 1877 at about where it is today. The southern shore of the Potomac was always the boundary between the two states, but how far down that shore the river ended and the Bay began, from which point to draw the line east across the Bay, was subject to dispute. The two states agreed to draw the line across Smith Point to Watkins Point on the Eastern Shore's Pocomoke River. Today, the boundary has been further refined: Maryland extends to the low-tide line of the river on the Virginia shore.

Chesapeake Tourism

The late 19th century brought the first tourists to the Bay, lured by clever investors who built the first resorts. Vacationers from Baltimore and Philadelphia turned to the Chesapeake, staying at new hotels built at Betterton and Tolchester on Maryland's Eastern Shore. On the Western Shore, Chesapeake Beach, just south of the Anne Arundel–Calvert County line, was carved from the shore by businessmen from the Pennsylvania Railroad. A new train station built there gave easy access to people from Baltimore and Washington, D.C.

Until about 1920, the Bay and its tributaries were the region's highways. Ferries connected to railroad lines crisscrossed the network of water and land, and steamships traveled everywhere. Farming and fishing supported much of the rural Western and Eastern shores in both Maryland and Virginia. Following World War II, the Chesapeake region mirrored the rest of the country, as industry and shipping propelled Baltimore and Norfolk into a new prosperity.

The automobile, too, fueled change, and by the mid-20th century the time had come to span the Bay by highway. On October 1, 1949, construction of the Chesapeake Bay Bridge began. Less than three years later, on July 30, 1952, the $112 million, 4.3-mile bridge opened. Over the ensuing decades, travelers "discovered" the Eastern Shore as never before. As far south as Salisbury, Maryland, towns saw growth; Talbot and Kent counties in particular became home to many retirees from the cities or owners of second homes.

In 1964, the other end of the Bay was spanned. The spectacular Chesapeake Bay Bridge–Tunnel was more than three years in the making, at $200 million, and in the late 1990s its multimillion-dollar twin span was opened. Two mile-long tunnels and 12 miles of trestled roadway alternately soar above, then dive beneath, the Chesapeake Bay. Four constructed islands serve as supports between bridge and road, as the bridge-tunnel spans the entryway through which early explorers first found the Chesapeake.

What is the future of the Bay area? Apparently, it depends on the self-control of those who live here—and of those within the watershed that spreads all the way to upstate New York, as the debris of their lives ultimately trickles into the Bay. Annapolis is part of the

Baltimore and Washington, D.C. urban region, yet its Historic District maintains its colonial charm.

The Bay area still retains its rural places. On the Eastern Shore, for instance, the old shipbuilding port of Oxford still is a quiet, colonial-style village, counting among its residents many people who have escaped the city.

The first English settlers, Protestant and Catholic, brought diversity when they came to live among the Native Americans already here. So it is today, as city dwellers and those who fall in love with "the land of pleasant living" move in among the old families whose forebears long ago planted and fished along the Chesapeake Bay.

2

TRANSPORTATION

Of Ferries & Freeways

The history of Chesapeake transportation is intimately tied to this vast inland sea, plied in ancient days by dugout canoes, later by indigenous sail craft, and today by massive steel cargo ships and yachts. For centuries, native inhabitants—the Susquehannock, Wicomico, and Nanticoke—had the Bay to themselves. Soon after the vessels *Ark* and *Dove* delivered Maryland's first settlers in 1634, commerce drove the development of a ferry system across the Bay's rivers and creeks.

By the late 1600s, ferries crossed the South River south of present-day Annapolis to deposit traders at London Town, where they swapped furs for supplies. In 1683, what is now said to be the oldest privately operated ferry service in the country launched its run between Oxford and Bellevue on Maryland's Eastern Shore.

Later came the steamship era, ultimately symbolized by the Baltimore Steam Packet Company, known as the Old Bay Line, which launched in 1839 with wooden, then steel, paddle-wheelers and steamships that operated into the 1960s. Visitors will find museum exhibitions devoted to those days, especially in small towns formerly served by steamships.

Even as boat routes linking small towns spread across the Bay, ambitious plans connected the Chesapeake with the young nation's expanding interior. In 1850, the 184.5-mile Chesapeake and Ohio Canal opened after 20 years of construction. Just about the time this marvel of modern engineering opened, the first rails were laid for the Baltimore & Ohio Railroad.

The B&O was the first railroad to connect Chesapeake Country to the "outside," but others soon followed. Working in tandem with packet and steamship lines, railroads dramatically opened up the area. Passenger and freight stations ran deep on the Eastern Shore to places like Crisfield, which boomed as a result of oyster exports in the late 19th century.

A bridge didn't span the Bay until 1952, when the 4.3-mile William Preston Lane Jr. Memorial Bridge (known locally as the Bay Bridge) replaced a ferry. In 1991, a new bridge replaced an aging drawbridge at Kent Narrows, just east of the Bay Bridge, greatly easing beach-bound traffic over the busy Narrows.

OPPOSITE: *The Oxford-Bellevue Ferry is one of several ferries that still ply the waterways of the Chesapeake region. It's been in operation since 1683.* Tim Tadder, photo courtesy Maryland Office of Tourism

Soon after the Middle Eastern Shore was opened up to cars, a feat of engineering did the same at the mouth of the Bay, site of the Chesapeake Bay Bridge–Tunnel. The massive, 17.6-mile span alternates bridge and tunnel across four constructed islands to Cape Charles from the Virginia mainland, and not long ago a span opened headed in the other direction.

Today's travelers can reach the gateway cities to Maryland's Chesapeake region–Washington, D.C. and Baltimore–by air, bus, or train. Mass transportation outside the cities is limited, although some connections can be made. To get the most out of your visit, rent a car to explore the small towns and back roads of the often rural, rambling Chesapeake region. For a taste of local adventure, cross tributary creeks and rivers the same way European forebears did as early as the late 1600s: by ferry.

Getting to the Chesapeake Bay Area

Unless you plan to spend your entire visit in Baltimore or Annapolis, the area's country roads and tidewater lanes are best explored by car. Rent one at the airport, or tool into town in your own.

By Air

Three major airports serve the Baltimore-Washington region, and there's a regional airport on the Eastern Shore in Salisbury.

Baltimore-Washington International Thurgood Marshall Airport, aka "BWI" (410-859-7111 in the Baltimore area, 301-261-1000 in the Washington area, or 1-800-435-9294; www.bwiairport.com; P.O. Box 8766, BWI Airport, MD 21240) BWI lies an easy 25-mile drive north of Annapolis via Interstate 97, and less than 15 minutes from Baltimore's Inner Harbor with no traffic.

Ronald Reagan Washington National Airport (703-417-8000; www.metwashairports .com; Ronald Reagan Washington National Airport, Washington, DC 20001) Located at the edge of the city, with easy access to highways leading to Annapolis (and a Metro subway station).

Washington Dulles International Airport (703-572-2700; www.metwashairports.com; Washington Dulles International Airport, Dulles, VA 20101) Thirty miles to the west of D.C. in northern Virginia, Dulles is a hike from Baltimore and Annapolis and should be avoided during region's extended rush hour if possible. If not, leave lots of extra time for the drive.

Airport Ground Transportation

The airports' Web sites provide information on ground transportation and security. Among ground transportation options at all three airports is the **SuperShuttle**, which departs each airport every 15 minutes between 6 AM and 2 AM. Reservations are encouraged and fares are determined by ZIP code. For information, call 1-800-BLUEVAN, visit www.supershuttle.com, or check with the SuperShuttle representative at the airport. A newcomer to the scene is the **BayRunner Shuttle**, based in Salisbury, which provides shuttle service between BWI and Cambridge, Salisbury, Easton, Ocean Pines, Ocean City, and Kent Island. For online reservations and quotes, check out www.bayrunners.com or call 410-912-6000.

A sailboat heads up the Patuxent River at the Gov. Thomas Johnson Bridge at Solomons Island.

Travelers trying to get from Dulles to Washington may want to contact Washington Flyer at 1-888-WASHFLY or www.washfly.com. The company operates a shuttle that connects to the city's Metro subway system (202-637-7000; www.wmata.com) at the West Falls Church (Virginia) Metro station. From there, ride the Metrorail to Washington's Union Station, which has connections to Amtrak or, if you're Baltimore-bound, hop aboard the Maryland Area Rail Commuter (MARC) trains (410-539-5000 or 1-866-RIDE-MTA; www.mta maryland.com)

Finally, weekday travelers may want to use the commuter bus that takes city workers into Washington from Kent Island and Annapolis/Anne Arundel County in the morning and home in the evenings. For information, contact Dillon's Bus Service (410-647-2321 or 1-800-827-3490; dillonbus.com).

Regional Airports

COMMERCIAL SERVICE

Salisbury–Ocean City–Wicomico Regional Airport (410-548-4827; Airport Manager's Office, 5485 Airport Terminal Rd., Unit A, Salisbury, MD 21804) offers service to Washington and Philadelphia via US Airways Express.

PRIVATE PLANES

Pilots with their own planes can check out these regional airports:

Bay Bridge Airport (410-643-4364; www.baybridgeairport.net; 202 Airport Rd., Stevensville, MD 21666) Flight school, tie-downs, and repairs. Can arrange shuttles.

Cambridge-Dorchester Airport (410-228-4571; 5263 Bucktown Rd., Cambridge, MD 21613) Tie-downs and other support, including a restaurant.

Easton Airport (410-770-8055; www.eastonairport.com; 29137 Newnam Rd., Easton, MD 21601) Fuel, tie-downs, and charter service.

Freeway Airport (301-390-6424; www.freewayaviation.com; 3900 Church Rd., Bowie, MD 20721) Fuel, tie-downs, and maintenance.

Lee Airport (410-956-1280 or 410-956-4129; www.leeairport.org; Old Solomons Island Rd./P.O. Box 273, Edgewater, MD 21037). Tie-downs, fuel, and maintenance. No charter service.

By Rental Car

Three major airports clustered in the area means that rental car agencies may let you rent a car at one airport and drop it off at another without additional cost. Reservation phone numbers are:

Alamo (1-800-327-9633; www.alamo.com)

Avis (1-800-331-1212; www.avis.com)

Dollar (1-800-800-3665; www.dollar.com)

Hertz (1-800-654-3131; www.hertz.com)

National (1-877-222-9058; www.nationalcar.com)

Thrifty (1-800-847-4389; www.thrifty.com)

By Bus

Bus service to the Bay area is limited. Contact Greyhound (1-800-231-2222; www.grey hound.com) for schedule and fare information.

By Train

Amtrak's (1-800-USA-RAIL; www.amtrak.com) classic train stations operate in fully renovated pre–World War II elegance: in Baltimore, Pennsylvania Station (1500 N. Charles St.), and in Washington, Union Station (Massachusetts and Louisiana Aves.) Amtrak also operates a rail station at BWI Airport, a short ride from the terminal.

GETTING AROUND THE CHESAPEAKE BAY AREA

By Bus

The Washington, D.C., **Greyhound** terminal (1-800-231-2222; www.greyhound.com) is located at 1005 First St. N.E., less than a mile from Union Station and the closest Metrorail ("Metro") stop. To get to Annapolis, ride the Metro's Red Line to Metro Center, change to the Orange Line, and go to the New Carrollton stop. Monday through Friday, you can taken the Dillon's Bus Service commuter bus from either Union Station or New Carrollton into Annapolis (410-647-2321 or 1-800-827-3490; dillonbus.com).

Greyhound offers daily service from Baltimore and Washington, D.C., to towns around the Bay, with stops in Easton, Salisbury, and Ocean City. The Baltimore-to-Salisbury run operates twice a day in each direction. For information, call the bus station in Easton, 410-822-3333.

For a map of public bus service around Annapolis, check out www.ci.annapolis.md .us/info.asp?page=6763. Free service is offered in the Historic District; see page 103 for details.

Shore Transit operates in the Eastern Shore's four southernmost counties. This means you can get around Salisbury and travel to some of the smaller towns in its orbit. On Sundays, you can even go from Crisfield to Salisbury. All in all, a much-needed service in this generally rural (but growing) region. For info, try 443-260-2300 or www.shore transit.org.

Public Transportation Around Baltimore

Charm City Circulator was launching as we went to press. When fully up and running, this green and free service will operate three routes. The Orange Route operates from the B&O Railroad east to Harbor East. Also on deck: a north and south route between Penn Station and Federal Hill (the Purple Route), and a Green Route that runs from the Johns Hopkins Hospital area down to Fell's Point and then up President Street and beyond. Buses of a hybrid technology will stop every 10 minutes, and plans to track their travels to produce digital updates on personal technology devices are in the works. Until then, annual guides should be available around town to explain the system. For updates: www.charmcitycirculator.com.

Maryland Transportation Authority buses operate throughout Baltimore, Baltimore County, and even northern Anne Arundel County. Of particular note to visitors: the Hampden Shuttle Bug (Route No. 98), an easy way through the eclectic neighborhood. For maps, fares, and additional information: www.mtamaryland.com or call 1-866-RIDE-MTA.

Subway/MARC Service around Baltimore: Baltimore's Metro Subway runs from Owings Mills in Baltimore County into the city, where it terminates at Johns Hopkins Hospital. En route, the train stops at Lexington Market and the Shot Tower, among other stops near tourist destinations. Hours are 5 AM to midnight. Check www.mtamaryland.com or call 1-866-RIDE-MTA for schedules, fares, and additional information.

The Chesapeake Bay Bridge, a scenic link between Maryland's Eastern and Western shores.   www.VisitAnnapolis.org

In addition, a light rail service operates from Hunt Valley, a business district in Baltimore County, south through the city, where it terminates at BWI Airport or Glen Burnie, a town in northern Anne Arundel County. For maps, fares, and schedules, check www.mtamaryland.com or call 1-866-RIDE-MTA.

By Car

Travelers through Bay Country spend a lot of time on US 301 and US 50. Here are the details about each road that will smooth your ride.

US 301 runs north–south from the Potomac River to US 50 at Bowie, where it turns east with US 50. The northbound road becomes MD 3 to Baltimore. South of the Potomac toll bridge (aka the Harry W. Nice Memorial Bridge), US 301 traverses Virginia's northern Tidewater area to Richmond.

US 50 is the eastbound thoroughfare from Washington, D.C., toward Annapolis, and it picks up a US 50/301 designation at Bowie. Soon after crossing onto the Eastern Shore, the road splits. US 50 heads south, providing the Shore's major north–south artery, then turns east after crossing the Choptank River at Cambridge. North of the split, US 301 goes solo again through the far Upper Eastern Shore.

US 13 is the other major north–south highway on the Shore, running all the way up Virginia's Eastern Shore from the Chesapeake Bay Bridge–Tunnel at Kiptopeke, through the middle of Maryland's Lower Shore, and up the Delmarva Peninsula into Delaware.

US 13 and US 50 intersect at Salisbury.

By Rental Car

If you failed to pick up a car at the airport and need one once you arrive in Chesapeake Country, here are some local offices:

Annapolis/Western Shore

Budget (1-866-327-8225; 2002 West St., Annapolis)
Enterprise (in Annapolis: 410-268-7751, 1023 Spa Rd.; 410-224-2940, 913-A Commerce Rd.; or 410-897-0420, 1900 West St.)
Hertz (301-863-0033; 22711 Three Notch Rd., Lexington Park)

Lower Eastern Shore

Avis (Salisbury–Ocean City: 410-742-8566; Salisbury–Ocean City–Wicomico Regional Airport)
Hertz (Salisbury–Ocean City: 410-749-2235; Salisbury–Ocean City–Wicomico Regional Airport)
U-Save (410-957-1421; 1727 Market St., Pocomoke City)

By Ferry

The Chesapeake's 300-plus-year history of ferryboat transportation remains in this region of snaking rivers, creeks, and can't-get-there-from-here roadways. These days, however, a moseying motorist is more likely to clank aboard one of the small ferries than a wagon full of grain for market. Oh, well. Times change.

Follow your map (or, in a pinch, ask directions) if you get turned around trying to find one of these small ferries.

The Whitehaven Ferry crosses the scenic Wicomico River.

Middle Eastern Shore

Oxford–Bellevue Ferry (410-745-9023; www.oxfordbellevueferry.com) The oldest continuously operating private ferry in the country launched on November 20, 1683, and allowed easy access between Oxford and St. Michaels in Talbot County. Still does, in fact. The ferry operates daily from Apr. through Oct., 9 AM–sunset. From June 1–Aug. 15, the last trip leaves Oxford at 8:30 PM, and Bellevue at 8:45. In November, the ferry operates only Fri.–Sun. Rates are $10 one-way for a car and driver, $3 per pedestrian, $4 for a bicyclist (lots of cyclists use the ferry), $5 for a tandem, and $6 for motorcycles plus $1 per passenger. Round-trip and multiple trip discounts are available.

Lower Eastern Shore

The tiny **Whitehaven Ferry** crosses the scenic Wicomico River about 18 miles southwest of Salisbury on MD 352. Free. Open year-round, 6 AM–7:30 PM May 16–Sept. 15, 7 AM–6 PM the rest of the year. The **Upper Ferry** also crosses the Wicomico near Salisbury. Free. Open year-round, same hours as the Whitehaven. The ferry information hotline with info for both ferries is 410-543-2765.

Several ferries operate out of Crisfield to Smith and Tangier islands. For information on all of these, check full listings in the Smith and Tangier islands section of Chapter 7, "Lower Eastern Shore," Page 279. If you're visiting either island, be sure to arrange accommodations in advance if you intend to stay overnight.

3

BALTIMORE

A Charmer of a City

If you view Baltimore through the lens of a John Waters movie, you might be surprised to learn that the filmmaker's hometown is also home to the building that housed a new nation's first museum. Conversely, if the word "Baltimore" conjures only sepia visions of old Baltimore clippers, you might be surprised to find yourself at, say, the American Visionary Art Museum. This is the nation's flagship to alternative art made by people who aren't necessarily artists but create great work. If you don't understand it, don't fret. The world's largest Matisse collection is nearby at the Baltimore Museum of Art.

This is a city of old and new, and offbeat is OK.

Baltimore was first settled in 1729 and became the country's fastest-growing city in 1790. Its port, its shipbuilders and its captains at Fell's Point made and sailed those swift, trade-boosting Baltimore clippers, and thus fed commerce and industry. The city's thriving (and effective) trade fleet drew the notice of the British as they waged battle during the War of 1812, a significant chapter of which took place in the Chesapeake Bay. The new country, with no navy, had hired privateers to commandeer the high seas. Many came from Fell's Point, and they were making an impact on the enemy. Intent upon destroying the city's "den of pirates," the British sailed up the Patapsco River and famously shelled Fort McHenry. Attorney Francis Scott Key, aboard a British ship negotiating the release of an American taken prisoner, breathed a sign of relief when he saw the smoke from the shelling clear after an overnight battle. Indeed, the flag was still there. Key's "Star-Spangled Banner" became the national anthem in 1931.

Although Baltimore always had captains of industry, waves of ongoing immigration (the city at one time was second only to Ellis Island as a point of entry) and a large free black population fed the city's cultural mix from early on. Its industrial base, much of it along the water—whether the harbor or its "falls"—gave it jobs. From this emerged a city with a strong culture of neighborhoods, more than 250. This is part of the city's unique charm that draws visitors today.

Baltimore's most famous neighborhood may be the **Inner Harbor.** Starting in the 1960s, industry moved off and made room for icons that now define the skyline: the

OPPOSITE: *Baltimore's Washington Monument, Mt. Vernon Place United Methodist Church, and Lafayette statue crown Mt. Vernon Square.*

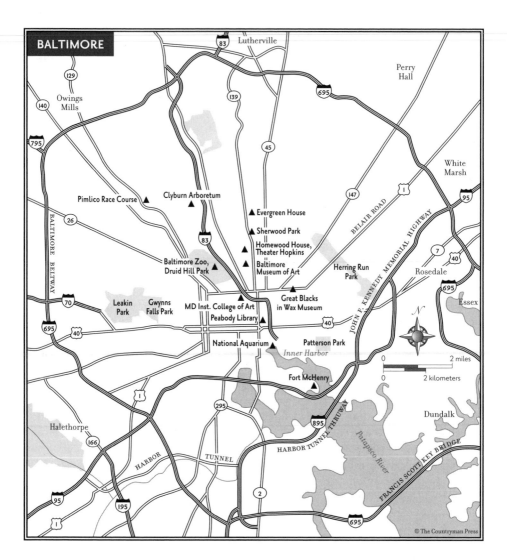

National Aquarium in Baltimore, for example, or the *USS Constitution.* For a fine introduction to the waterfront, do two things: Stop at the Seven Foot Knoll Lighthouse, located at Pier 5, for a free overview of the Inner Harbor's past working life. While you're there, appreciate that this is one of four extant Chesapeake icons, the cottage-style screw-pile light. This one is the oldest surviving, built in 1856; it stood at the mouth of the Patapsco for 133 years. Once you've peered into the past, head up 27 floors of the nearby World Trade Center for a rooftop view of the present-day skyline (Top of the World Observation Level; 410-837-VIEW; www.viewbaltimore.org; 401 E. Pratt St.; open daily in summer, Wed.–Sun. in fall, Fri.–Sun. in winter; $5 for adults, $4 for seniors, military; $3 for kids 3–12). From here you can see across to Federal Hill, now a green park, which Captain John Smith saw during his 1608 travels. When Maryland ratified the U.S. Constitution, a joyous crowd paraded to the hill, thus bestowing the name. Architecture in the **Federal Hill** neighborhood today ranges from 18th to early 20th century, and the townhouse-lined

South Charles and Light streets nurture a lively mix of small shops, bistros, grills, and taverns. One of the city's five markets that trace their lineage to pre-Revolution times, the Cross Street Market, still bustles. Farther east lies **Locust Point**, a gentrifying industrial waterfront neighborhood.

Back on the north side of the harbor, new glass towers rise to the east. This is **Harbor East**, which sits between the Inner Harbor and Fell's Point. Upscale hotels, shops, and restaurants, many of them trendy or boutique-sized chains, make this a popular place to go. The neighborhood also has made it easier to walk along the water from the Inner Harbor to **Little Italy** and its fabled restaurants right next door (and a few blocks inland), or to **Fell's Point**, where cobblestones still line the streets. Fell's Point is a must-stop on your Baltimore visit, for the city has lived and breathed here since it began. The neighborhood also has a good visitor center at 1724–1726 Thames St., which is open daily (410-675-6751; www.preservationsociety.com). One William Fell bought the point in 1726. This was the city's working deepwater port, with salty characters (there are a few left), historic old homes that survived the Great Baltimore Fire of 1904 that took out most of downtown, and some good stories. After Tropical Storm Isabel swamped the neighborhood in 2003, a staff member in the Admiral Fell Inn stayed in the lobby to man the phones while her colleagues went for dinner. She heard what sounded like a foot-stompin' party upstairs. It stopped the minute the others returned. Next night, same thing. The ghosts apparently were pleased to have their home to themselves.

A bit farther east, formerly industrial **Canton** has transformed itself into a happening neighborhood of young professionals who flock to the bistros of O'Donnell Square or head over to the waterfront developments to shop and dine.

North of the harbor, **Mount Vernon** announces itself even before you've made it up North Charles Street. Crowning the hill is the Washington Monument, the first such salute to the first president in the country to begin construction. It stands in the middle of a square surrounded by the Peabody Conservatory (home to the mustn't-miss George Peabody Library) and the parklike squares of Mount Vernon Place with its spectacular 19th-century homes. Now known as the Mount Vernon Cultural District, the neighborhood is home to the Meyerhoff Symphony Hall, the Walters Art Gallery, and the Maryland Historical Society. Artists and literary types who've called the square home include Gertrude Stein, F. Scott Fitzgerald, and Baltimore bard H. L. Mencken. Visit a museum here, have lunch in a café, and—if it's not Tuesday, when most stores are closed—walk over to North Howard Street to see the remaining antiques shops of the once-bursting Antique Row.

A bit farther north is the **Charles Village–Homewood** neighborhood, home to Johns Hopkins University. Nearby is the **Hampden** district, home of the beehive-wearing "Bawlmer hon," originally a mid-20th-century working gal but now an updated city icon. This neighborhood draws hipsters and shoppers to 36th Street, aka "The Avenue," and visitors curious to check it out will find it easiest to get there by taking a cab. Not far from here is **Woodberry**, the transformed old mill area; elegant **Bolton Hill** with its art students; and **Roland Park**, the upscale first suburb. Neighborhoods go on and on, and you are quite likely to hear of many as you explore.

To get around, it's best to take a cab if you're heading north from the waterfront or traveling after dark. Another option is the new Charm City Circulator, a free service, which was launching as we went to press. When fully operational, three routes will operate as follows: The Orange Route runs from the B&O Railroad east to Harbor East. The Purple Route

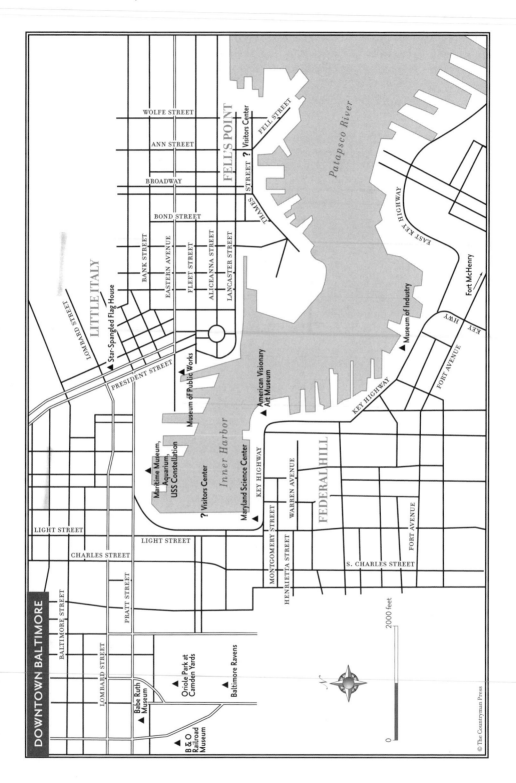

DOWNTOWN BALTIMORE

WOLFE STREET
ANN STREET
BROADWAY
BOND STREET
BANK STREET
EASTERN AVENUE
FLEET STREET
ALICEANNA STREET
LANCASTER STREET
THAMES STREET
FELL STREET
FELL'S POINT
? Visitors Center

LITTLE ITALY
LOMBARD STREET
Star-Spangled Flag House
PRESIDENT STREET

Patapsco River

EAST KEY HIGHWAY
Fort McHenry
KEY HWY
FORT AVENUE
Museum of Industry
KEY HIGHWAY

American Visionary Art Museum
Museum of Public Works
Inner Harbor
Maritime Museum, Aquarium, USS Constellation
? Visitors Center
Maryland Science Center
KEY HIGHWAY

FEDERAL HILL
MONTGOMERY STREET
HENRIETTA STREET
WARREN AVENUE
FORT AVENUE
S. CHARLES STREET

LIGHT STREET
LIGHT STREET
CHARLES STREET
PRATT STREET
BALTIMORE STREET
LOMBARD STREET

Babe Ruth Museum
Oriole Park at Camden Yards
Baltimore Ravens
B & O Railroad Museum

2000 feet
0

© The Countryman Press

will be a north and south route between Penn Station and Federal Hill, and a Green Route will run from the Johns Hopkins Hospital area down to Fell's Point and then up President Street and beyond. Stops will take place every 10 minutes. Pick up a free guide that explains the system. For updates: www.charmcitycirculator.com.

Also in the city is Ed Kane's Water Taxi, the go-to service that takes visitors around the harbor from Canton and Fell's Point to Locust and Tide Points, and numerous points in between. Stops are well-marked and concierges are well-versed in the water taxi schedule. For details: www.thewatertaxi.com.

Another option if you know your way through the city streets: Green Rider, a Vespa dealer that also has a rental service at 723 S. Broadway in Fell's Point. Call them at 410-522-5857 or check www.greenriderusa.com.

Light rail offers commuter service to the northern suburbs with key city stops at Woodberry (near Hampden, although it's a bit of an unscenic hike to Hampden's shops that is not advised at night), University of Baltimore/Mount Royal, Lexington Market, Camden Yards, and BWI Airport. Trains run more often during the week than on weekends, and service ends at 11 every night but Sunday, when trains run from 11–7. The schedule is available online at www.mtamaryland.com or free at kiosks around town. Call 410-539-5000.

And, alas, a note of caution. Like other old, large cities, Baltimore sees its share of crime. Use street smarts. Stay in the busy neighborhoods, take a cab after dark, and stay alert.

The Inner Harbor-based **Baltimore Visitor Center** (1-877-BALTIMORE; www .baltimore.org; 401 Light St., Baltimore) is convenient and easy to find. Call or visit the Web site for tourism information, including the latest calendar of events. Harborpass offers a discount ticket price on five of the city's leading attractions if visited over four days. These include the Maryland Science Center, National Aquarium in Baltimore, Top of the World Observation Level, Sports Legends at Camden Yards, and a choice between the American Visionary Art Museum or Port Discovery Children's Museum.

LODGING

Baltimore's hotels pay attention to detail—at least the ones we saw. Expect flat-screen TVs and ask if Fido's allowed to stay in your room. (Often, an additional charge is levied.) Also ask about daily fees for Internet service. The general trends seem to be free service, or it may be free in a business center but cost a fee in the guest rooms. In cases where we indicate a cost (or not), we are referring to in-room Internet service.

In addition, room prices tend to fluctuate widely depending on whether it's a weekday or weekend, in-season or off-season. Many hotels and inns run specials on their Web sites, so check for the latest price and don't be shy about inquiring about discounts. Here is our price range:

Inexpensive:	Up to $75
Moderate:	$75–150
Expensive:	$150–225
Very Expensive:	$225 and up

The luxe 1840s Carroll Inn is part of a historic complex in one of the oldest sections of Baltimore.

1840S CARROLLTON INN

410-385-1840
www.1840scarrolltoninn.com
50 Albemarle St., Baltimore, MD 21202
Price: Expensive to Very Expensive
Handicapped Access: Yes
Parking: Small lot next door, free; Dodge
Garage, $10 for 24 hours

Part of a historic complex that includes one of Charles Carroll's homes, the 1840s Carrollton Inn sits on a well-located and well-traveled street near the edge of Little Italy. This is a good location from which to get around the city. Brocades, swags, fine furniture, and lots of bathroom marble create the unmistakable whiff of luxury in the inn's 13 rooms, which feature flat-screened TVs, luxe bedding, gas fireplaces, and, in some cases, a double whirlpool tub. In the case of at least two suites, lights are inset into the bed canopy. Suites come with daybeds, which makes them a good option for traveling companions. Guests will find breakfast served on a brick courtyard patio during summer. Indeed, they'll be greeted at check-in with a breakfast menu on their door. Sound machines are in all the rooms, but if you're not accustomed to city living, ask for an interior room. The complex includes the former City Life Museum, some of whose exhibit panels have been incorporated into the event spaces. Internet service is free.

THE ADMIRAL FELL INN

410-522-7377; 1-866-583-4162 for reservations
www.admiralfell.com
888 S. Broadway, Baltimore, MD 21231
Price: Expensive to Very Expensive

Handicapped Access: Yes
Parking: Valet, $29 overnight

Long before the cult TV cop drama *Homicide: Life on the Street* put Fell's Point on the map, there was the Admiral Fell Inn, aptly named after the man responsible for this quaint part of Baltimore. This collection of seven buildings dates to the 1770s, but its hospitality business only goes back to 1889, when Christian ladies established lodging for seamen. Now, when the occasional guest complains of thumping in the room above, hotel staff know to shoo off resident ghosts Bitsy or Grady. This 80-room inn, located right in the midst of the Fell's Point action, embodies the neighborhood's Old World charm with Federal-style furnishings. Tempting Meli Patisserie & Bistro serves beautiful pastry, coffee, and meals. Packages are high on this company's list; check the Web site for specials and consider taking a ghost tour of the inn or have proper tea. Guests may use the Maryland Athletic Club in nearby Harbor East. Internet service is $9.95 per day.

BALTIMORE MARRIOTT INNER HARBOR CAMDEN YARDS

410-962-0202
www.marriott.com/bwiih
110 S. Eutaw St., Baltimore, MD 21201
Price: Expensive to Very Expensive
Handicapped Access: Yes
Parking: Adjacent garage, $24 overnight

At 524 rooms on 10 floors, the smallest (and oldest) of Marriott's Baltimore hotels completed a renovation in 2008, so your room will be stylish and new. It's also five blocks from the Inner Harbor. Located near the University of Maryland's Baltimore campus, the property offers 34 suites among the room menu (replete with comfy signature bedding), free wireless in the hotel's public areas ($12.95 in the rooms), a fitness center (but no pool), the on-site

Café Promenade, as well as The Yard, a sports bar that plays upon the hotel's location a mere block from the city's stadiums. The gift shop, with drinks and sandwiches, stays open until 10 PM.

BALTIMORE MARRIOTT WATERFRONT

410-385-3000 or 1-800-228-9290
www.marriott.com/hotels/travel/bwiwf-baltimore-marriott-waterfront
700 Aliceanna St., Baltimore, MD 21202
Price: Expensive to Very Expensive
Handicapped Access: Yes
Parking: Valet, $36 ; self-park, $25. Parking garages nearby

This high-rise hotel towers alongside the new Legg Mason building, and you can see the water from 70 percent of its 753 rooms. This is the heart of the newly developed Harbor East area, located between the Inner Harbor and Fell's Point and adjacent to Little Italy. Fall out the front door and you'll quickly find yourself amid high-end chain restaurants (Roy's, Oceanaire), shops, and, yes, the water. As for the hotel: Walk into a grand lobby with classic marble floors and vaulted ceilings. Off to the side of the relatively narrow lobby are wide, modern lounge areas and restaurants. Built in 2001, the hotel renovated its rooms in 2009 so they're pretty and contemporary with their design mix of neutrals. They also come with all the fine amenities, including a fridge by request as well as upgraded sheet thread counts (and, your author's personal fave, a selection of pillow types). Deluxe corner rooms offer blue-ribbon comfort and water views. The room count includes 21 suites that range up to the highest of high-end offerings. This Marriott consistently rates at the top of the company's own list for service, the fitness center is slated to double in size, and there's a pool. The hotel hosts Rigano's Bakery and Deli, Grille 700 for all three meals, and Kozmo's Lounge for all your cocktailing needs. Wireless access costs $9.95 per day.

CELIE'S WATERFRONT BED AND BREAKFAST

Innkeepers: Kevin and Nancy Kupec
410-522-2323 or 1-800-432-0184
www.celieswaterfront.com
1714 Thames St., Baltimore, MD 21231
Price: Moderate to Very Expensive
Handicapped Access: No
Parking: Nearby lot, $9

This oasis sits tucked amid the brick row house shops and taverns lining Thames Street, just across the cobblestone street from tugboats moored in the harbor. The three-story inn's nine attractive rooms and suites come with harbor or courtyard views and combine a contemporary touch with traditional style in keeping with the historic neighborhood. Rooms are available with king-sized beds, fireplaces, and whirlpool tubs. Two rooms have private balconies. All have TVs, coffeemakers, updated tiled baths, and Wi-Fi. Breakfast is "gourmet continental." There's a brick courtyard garden out back, and a rooftop deck offers views of the harbor and city. This is centrally located to the Fell's Point nightlife.

DOUBLETREE INN AND SPA AT THE COLONNADE BALTIMORE

410-235-5400
www.colonnadebaltimore.com
4 W. University Pkwy., Baltimore, MD 21218
Price: Moderate to Very Expensive
Handicapped Access: Yes
Parking: Valet parking with in and out privileges, $24; self-parking $20

This recently renovated hotel located across the street from the Johns Hopkins University campus is also near the Baltimore Museum of Art and comes with nice amenities, such as a small solarium pool and on-site spa. The latter offers a variety of services, and was closed for renovations at deadline (but perhaps will be reopened by the time you visit). As for your room, check into one of 125 rooms (31 junior or luxe suites included), and look for either queen or king beds with plush-top mattress and comfy linens, and an all-around updated look. Suites come with fridges and microwaves. A bistro called alizée serves all meals, including Sunday brunch in the space that once housed the city's popular Polo Grill. This hotel offers a good-looking opportunity to enjoy Baltimore's charms from a neighborhood point of view. A cab to the Inner Harbor costs about $10. Wi-Fi in the rooms is complimentary.

FAIRFIELD INN & SUITES

410-837-9900 or 1-800-228-2800
greenfairfieldinn.com
101 President St., Baltimore, MD 21202
Price: Moderate to Expensive
Handicapped Access: Yes
Parking: Valet, $27 overnight, $19 for the day; nearby garages available

This reasonably priced hotel recently opened on the site of the former Baltimore Brewing Company Bricks dating to the 1780 brewery even have been incorporated into the facade, making the hotel not just stylish but green. Indeed, the Fairfield boasts of being both Marriott's and Baltimore's first LEED-certified hotel, which means environmentally conscious elements are part of its design. If you've never used a low-flush toilet, here's your chance. The attractive hotel's 154 rooms include 30 suites (including "studio" suites and two-room "eco suites" that are allergen-free and come with a mountain bike) around a pretty courtyard that incorporates the brewing company's old silo. It's been repurposed to collect rainwater for irrigation. Rooms are contemporary and have body heat sensors that adjust the room temperature accord-

A pretty escape in the midst of the Fell's Point action.

ingly. Well-stocked suites with mini-fridges, microwaves, and pullout sofas are a good option for traveling families. The hotel is also well-located within easy walking distance of the Inner Harbor, Harbor East, and Little Italy. Continental breakfast and free Internet access are included in the room rate.

HAMPTON INN & SUITES
BALTIMORE INNER HARBOR
410-539-7888
www.baltimorehamptoninn.com
131 E. Redwood St., Baltimore, MD 21202
Price: Expensive to Very Expensive
Handicapped Access: Yes
Parking: Valet, $29; local garages and street parking nearby

Once the headquarters of U.S. Fidelity & Guaranty Company, this building was con-structed in 1906 after the Great Baltimore Fire of 1904 leveled most of downtown. Hampton Inns arrived in 2004 and installed a smart, 116-room hotel. Renovations to the rooms—half of which are suites—were completed in 2009. The standard rooms come with a mix of pillow choices, comfy king or queen mattresses, and minifridge. The hotel even offers a second-floor laundry facility. If it's a special occasion, check out the mahogany suite that once was the USF&G executive offices, replete with vaulted ceiling and hardwood floors. Internet connectivity and breakfast, served in a comfortable first-floor lobby, come with your room. There's also a fitness center, indoor pool large enough for lap swimming, and business center. Their use also comes with your room so, except for parking, you've paid what you need to pay once you've plunked down for your room.

HILTON BALTIMORE

443-573-8700
www.baltimore.hilton.com
401 W. Pratt St., Baltimore, MD 21201
Price: Expensive to Very Expensive
Handicapped Access: Yes
Parking: Self-parking, $26; valet, $34

Glide easily from the interstate to the sleek and modern Hilton, which opened at the Inner Harbor in August 2008. This is a good-looking hotel, with its huge lobby with its sophisticated accents. Cool sculptures suspended from the ceiling suggest waves in the harbor beyond. Of the meeting-ready hotels connected to the Baltimore Convention Center, this is the only one with a covered skybridge. It also appears to be the only one with wide windows along the upscale (especially for a hotel) fitness center that literally fronts Oriole Park at Camden Yards. Work out and watch the game—the view is breathtaking! Or step over to the lap pool with a full-time lifeguard. The hotel offers 757 contemporary rooms, including 20 suites with grand high-end offerings, $11.95 daily Internet access (an hourly rate's also available), signature beds with pillowtop mattresses, and direct HD signal to the flat-screen TVs for those so inclined. Basically, you're in the contemporary lap of luxury here at the Hilton. Pets are OK with prior arrangement (expect to pay a cleaning deposit), and the Diamond Tavern—as sleek as the rest of the hotel—serves buffet breakfast, lunch, and dinner as well as a few pregame cocktails. See our restaurant profile for more.

HOMEWOOD SUITES/HILTON GARDEN INN

410-234-0065
www.homewoodsuites.com; hiltongardeninn.hilton.com
625 S. President St., Baltimore, MD 21202
Price: Hilton Garden: Moderate to Expensive; Homewood Suites: Expensive to Very Expensive
Handicapped Access: Yes
Parking: $25 with in and out privileges, $22 without; some street parking available

A shared lobby and upper-tier management link these properties, giving visitors to the stylish Harbor East area a couple of Hilton choices. This first dual effort from the company opened in 2007. Here are the details: The Hilton Garden is a traditional hotel, with 183 rooms and one suite done up in pretty seafoam blue and neutral tans. Rooms come with all the amenities, such as flat-screen TVs, free Wi-Fi, plus a microwave and mini-fridge. Homewood Suites offers 165 suites that provide a lot for families, business travelers in town for a few days, or budget travelers. The suites include regular fridges, a complimentary "Welcome Home" reception from 5–7 PM Mon.–Thurs. that will more than suffice for the evening meal, and breakfast. They also provide a full kitchen, pullout sofas, flat-screen TVs, and on-site coin laundry. Grocery shopping service is available—all you pay for is the food. Dogs are allowed on one floor here, and Wi-Fi's free. The full-service Maryland Athletic Club is accessed through the second floor, and The Great American Grill is in the building.

HOTEL MONACO

443-692-6170
www.monaco-baltimore.com
2 N. Charles St., Baltimore, MD 21201
Price: Moderate to Very Expensive
Handicapped Access: Yes
Parking: Overnight valet, $36; garages also adjacent to property

Stylish Kimpton Hotels has come to Baltimore and renovated the circa-1906 B&O Railroad headquarters downtown. Its new Hotel Monaco breathes hip comfort and style into the stately marble-laden building, suffusing it with a "grand adventure" theme in keeping with the building's past. The 202 guest rooms (including 27 suites) have 12-foot ceilings and way-cool blue, goldish-neutral, and wood interiors to go with all the amenities you'd expect (the bathrobes are leopard print). High windows look out onto interesting downtown views. The occasional photo of a train, or a steamer trunk serving as a table, drive home the adventure theme. The Monaco doesn't have a lobby, it has a "living room" where the coffeepot's on early in the morning and the wine carafe comes out in the late afternoon. Guests will find free wireless in the living room ($9.95 in guest rooms), a fitness facility, in-room spa services, and the contemporary B&O American Brasserie serving breakfast, lunch, and dinner. Flexible meeting space couldn't be more attractive.

HYATT REGENCY BALTIMORE
410-528-1234
www.baltimore.hyatt.com
300 Light St., Baltimore, MD 21202
Price: Moderate to Very Expensive
Handicapped Access: Yes
Parking: Valet, $36; self-parking, $27

This was the first hotel built on the Inner Harbor, so it's easy to reach from incoming highways and you can take one of two skywalks over to the Baltimore Convention Center. You can also hang out at the hotel's rooftop pool overlooking the harbor, which seems like an invitingly cool idea on a pleasant summer day. The hotel's 488 rooms (including 26 suites) received a $20 million upgrade in 2006. They're dressed in a beautiful array of textured neutrals. Ask for one with a primo harbor view (although the city skyline views are lovely, too). The hotel's "Harborview" section even has glassed-in elevators (which, by the way, come with security keys for guests) so the harbor always can be seen. Rooms come with all the fine amenities, including deluxe beds. Fitness facilities include a

walking track, two tennis courts, and a basketball court in addition to the fitness center. Bistro 300 serves regional cuisine. In-room wireless Internet access is $9.95.

INN AT 2920
Owners: Warren Munroe and David Rohrbaugh
410-342-4450 or 1-877-774-2920
www.theinnat2920.com
2920 Elliott St., Baltimore, MD 21224
Price: Expensive
Handicapped Access: No
Parking: Free street parking

Aunt Fifi's fluffy B&B this is not. No, 2920 delivers contemporary style in a terrific location in the midst of Canton. This place has everything you need to be comfortable. A friendly fish even swims in a bowl in each room, keeping travelers company. Five rooms (one is a two-room suite) include TVs with movies, whirlpool baths, free wireless, and a very good-looking guest lounge where full breakfast is served from 7–9 during the week and 9–10 on weekends. The spacious suite, called the Gato Casa, even has a full kitchen and sofa bed, making it a great option for traveling companions. Canton's central O'Donnell Square, with all of its restaurants and pubs, is just around the corner and the B&B is two blocks from the water taxi.

THE INN AT HENDERSON'S WHARF
410-522-7777 or 1-800-522-2088
www.hendersonswharf.com
1000 Fell St., Baltimore, MD 21231
Price: Expensive to Very Expensive
Handicapped Access: Yes
Parking: The complex has a lot; parking included with room rate

Look for plantation shutters, vessel sinks, British Colonial-style furniture, genuine living plants, and maybe even exposed brick in your room in this rescued B&O Railroad tobacco warehouse that was fully renovated after Tropical Storm Isabel plowed through in 2003. The inn offers 38 rooms, some with water views. (Those with partial water views are also likely to take a good look at a nearby marina parking lot.) This really couldn't be a better-looking or more comfortable lodging. Coffee is available in the lobby all day, a lovely courtyard offers a respite, there's free parking, Wi-Fi, a 24-hour fitness center, deluxe continental breakfast, and even a printer/fax/copier /scanner—in your room—if need be. Did we forget the complimentary bottle of wine upon check-in? Indeed a gem, this inn is hidden at the end of a cobbled Fell's Point street. The Henderson's Wharf complex also includes condos and a 256-slip marina. The water taxi is a block away. Pets, by the way, are not allowed.

INTERCONTINENTAL HARBOR COURT BALTIMORE

410-234-0550
www.intercontinental.com/baltimore
550 Light St., Baltimore, MD 21202
Price: Expensive to Very Expensive
Handicapped Access: Yes
Parking: Overnight self-parking, $21; valet, $32

InterContinental Hotels now runs this Baltimore mainstay, a luxury hotel across Light Street from the Inner Harbor that offers plenty of Old English charm. Renovated in 2005, the hotel decor runs toward traditional, starting with the sweeping staircase in the lobby. Elephants and monkeys are painted on the murals in the British Colonial safari-inspired Explorer's Lounge. The hotel offers 195 guest rooms with harbor or courtyard views and 22 suites with which you're assured a water view. The hotel is shaped like a hollow square with the rooms facing out, so quiet is likely. The luxe rooms come with all the latest amenities and, in the suites, a second flat-screen TV in the bathroom. Beds come with a choice of pillows. There's an indoor pool, outdoor tennis courts, spa services, sauna, whirlpool, and a nice fitness center that even offers Pilates and yoga classes. Pretty Brighton's Orangerie Restaurant serves breakfast, lunch, dinner, Sunday brunch, and afternoon tea on Friday and Saturday. The hotel's Expresso Etc. supplies coffee and sandwiches. Wireless Internet access costs $12.95 per day.

PEABODY COURT

410-727-7101
www.peabodycourthotel.com
612 Cathedral St., Baltimore, MD 21201
Price: Moderate to Very Expensive
Handicapped Access: Yes
Parking: Valet, $29; some street parking available

Feel like staying outside the downtown hubbub? Head for the elegant Mount Vernon district, where the Peabody Court stands across from Mount Vernon Square and its Washington Monument. You'll feel like you're tucked away in your favorite Upper West Side hotel, or maybe the arrondissement of your choice. This small Clarion hotel is all about neighborhood charm. About three-quarters of its 104 rooms face the square and are decorated in pretty, traditional style. They're not brand-new, but the top-to-bottom marble bathrooms come with towel warmers, and the rooms offer free wireless Internet and a minifridge. Beds are triple-sheeted with a choice of pillows. Pets are allowed with prior discussion and a fee. George's serves breakfast, lunch, and dinner. There's also a 24-hour exercise room. Internet access is free.

PIER 5 HOTEL

410-539-2000
www.harbormagic.com
711 Eastern Ave., Baltimore, MD 21202
Price: Expensive to Very Expensive

Handicapped Access: Yes
Parking: Valet, $32.61; self-park, $20–30 at nearby lots and/or garages

Contemporary is the word for Pier 5, with its sometimes offbeat color combinations, curves—like in the furniture—and overall style. The hotel also sits right on the water in the midst of the Inner Harbor action and it's easy to walk to all the attractions. Guests find 65 rooms with harbor or city views, all the amenities you'd expect and some that you wouldn't—like "Crabby Hour" cooking demonstrations taking place during the traditional cocktail hour. Upscale suites are fun and can even include Murphy beds. (You get the vibe that fun is valued here.) The hotel is part of the Harbor Magic stable (as is the Admiral Fell Inn), and the group focuses on packages, so check the Web site to see if there's something for you. On-site restaurants include Ruth's Chris Steakhouse, McCormick & Schmick's, and Pizzazz Tuscan Grille. Guests also have the use of the Maryland Athletic Club in Harbor East. Internet access is free.

SCARBOROUGH FAIR
BED & BREAKFAST

Innkeepers: Barry Werner and Jeff Finlay
410-837-0010 or 1-877-954-2747
www.scarboroughfairbandb.com
801 S. Charles St. (entrance formerly 1 E. Montgomery St.), Baltimore, MD 21230
Price: Expensive to Very Expensive
Handicapped Access: No
Parking: Free passes available
Children: 12 and under welcome with prior discussion in certain rooms

Baltimore's own Edgar Allan Poe is celebrated at the Scarborough Fair B&B.

Well-located within walking distance of the Inner Harbor and the pubs and pleasures of Federal Hill, Scarborough Fair offers accommodating hosts (early risers, ask about a "grab and go" breakfast), a movie library, and complimentary drinks and goodies to go with its six rooms. The rooms may come with amenities such as gas fire-places or giant showerheads. Two down-stairs rooms have their own entrances, and two rooms have private hallway baths. Attractive, traditional decor means antique oak furniture or toile fabric may highlight your room. Change, however, is afoot, as one look at the lavender and gray Poe Suite attests. Here, a flair for the dramatic is tak-ing root (but isn't overtaking the space) and it couldn't be more fun: A gas fire flickers below the mantel, which features a tableau featuring a raven and, yes, a pallid bust of Pallas. Visitors in the coming years may find a literary theme wending its way through the red brick inn. Scarborough Fair is a member of Select Registry, Distinguished Inns of America. Free in-room wireless.

SHERATON INNER HARBOR HOTEL
410-962-8300 or 1-800-325-5353
www.sheraton.com/innerharbor
300 S. Charles St., Baltimore, MD 21201
Price: Moderate to Very Expensive
Handicapped Access: Yes
Parking: Garage, $24 for 24 hours

Located smack-dab in the midst of the Inner Harbor action, this Sheraton received a face-lift in 2008. It's also the official hotel of the Baltimore Orioles (which gives you an opportunity to purchase home game tickets), and many of its rooms overlook next-door Oriole Park at Camden Yards. Its 337 rooms (including 20 suites) offer sta-dium views, harbor views, city views, or perhaps a combination thereof. The hotel also links directly to the Baltimore Convention Center via skywalk. The comfy beds include white duvets, good pillows, and a pillowtop mattress. The hotel also has a small indoor pool, 24-hour fitness room, a Glatt-level kosher kitchen, and $9.99 per day in-room Internet service. The Orioles Grill serves breakfast, lunch, and dinner. There's meeting and event space, Morton's is the on-site steakhouse, and dogs are allowed with prior arrangement.

TREMONT PLAZA HOTEL
410-727-2222 or 1-800-TREMONT
www.tremonts.com
222 St. Paul Place, Baltimore, MD 21202
Price: Moderate to Very Expensive
Handicapped Access: Yes
Parking: Valet, $25 per day; public garage nearby, $10–15

Each of the 303 "rooms" at the 36-story Tremont Plaza, a former apartment build-ing set on a downtown hill, is a studio or suite. Free Internet access, a mini-fridge, microwave, and stylish wet bar are all part of the package in these clean and attractive spaces. Eleven high-end suites top out the luxury factor. There's an outdoor pool tucked into an urban courtyard and a fit-ness center. Attached to the hotel is the Tremont Grand, the former 1866 Freemason Lodge that's been renovated into 19 event spaces on five floors, which hotel guests are welcome to go see. They should. Grand it is, with vaulted ceilings, frescoes, stained glass, and even the nation's No. 2 "best restroom" (beating out Radio City Music Hall), according to Cintas Corporation, the office cleaning supply people. Check out the Corinthian columns, the chandeliers, and the marble. Magnifique! Also at the Tremont: the Plaza Deli, with overstuffed sandwiches, pastries, breads, and soups. Tugs is the in-house restaurant; light fare's available at Grand Café. Internet access is free.

RESTAURANTS

A distinctive food scene has taken root in Baltimore and is flowering with creations like Chef Spike Gjerde's Woodberry Kitchen and Chef Cindy Wolf's Charleston (and Cinghiale among others) climbing culinary heights to national recognition. Settle in and enjoy. If, however, all you're after is good pizza or barbecue in a local joint, we've got you covered. If you've come to Baltimore to crack crabs, plenty of local options suit your needs. We have focused on profiling Baltimore's local and independent restaurants, but high-end chains like Roy's can be found in Harbor East, and numerous chains can be found in the Inner Harbor, too. If you're in town in January and August, check www.baltimorerestaurant week.com to see if your visit coincides with the twice-annual week of restaurant deals throughout the city. Note that restaurants are arranged by neighborhood.

Here's the price range, based on entrées:

Inexpensive up to	$10
Moderate	$10–20
Expensive	$20–30
Very Expensive	$30 and above

The following abbreviations are used to denote meals served:
B = Breakfast; L = Lunch; D = Dinner; SB = Sunday Brunch

INNER HARBOR

DIAMOND TAVERN

443-573-8777
www.diamondtavern.com
401 W. Pratt St.
Open: Daily
Price: Moderate to Expensive
Cuisine: New American
Serving: L, D
Reservations: Accepted
Handicapped Access: Yes

The Diamond Tavern, which opened in 2009, is a great addition to the Inner Harbor dining scene. The main restaurant in the Baltimore Hilton is large, bright, and cheerful, with an open layout that provides excellent views of Oriole Park at Camden Yards. There's also a sizable bar with numerous flat-screen TVs. From 6 AM until midnight, Diamond Tavern's friendly and accommodating staff serves up New American cuisine. Breakfast offerings include brioche French toast, crabcake Benedict and vanilla yogurt parfait. Lunch, served from 11 AM–5 PM, consists of burgers and sandwiches, pastas like lobster and crab bucatini in a Parmesan cream sauce, and hearty salads topped with chicken, salmon, or steak. At dinnertime, choose from a variety of appetizers, including flash-fried calamari and sliders. The entrée selection is somewhat limited, but contains tempting items like scallops, bourbon-glazed salmon, and pan-seared crabcakes with risotto. If you're feeling decadent, end your meal with Grand Marnier crème brûlée and a spiked coffee, or a super-indulgent "dessert martini."

FRANK AND NIC'S WEST END GRILLE

410-685-6800
www.frankandnics.com
511 W. Pratt St.
Open: Daily
Price: Moderate
Cuisine: American
Serving: L, D

Reservations: Accepted
Handicapped Access: Yes

One of the newest restaurants in the Inner Harbor, Frank and Nic's seems to offer something for everyone. It has both a lively bar with energetic music and a more sedate dining room, and it offers pub food as well as more upscale fare, including some Asian-inspired dishes. The menu leans toward lighter, less-expensive fare: soups, salads, and sandwiches. Try the mango chicken noodle salad, BLT with fresh mozzarella and avocado, or pulled pork sandwich with house-made BBQ sauce. For entrées, choose from standard steaks, chops, and seafood prepared in interesting and flavorful ways, like pan-seared salmon drizzled with cilantro-ginger sauce. Located on the ground floor of an apartment building adjacent to Oriole Park at Camden Yards, Frank and Nic's is convenient for dining before a game or taking a break during an afternoon at the harbor. Kids are welcome and there are menu items—mac and cheese, burgers, etc.—just for them. And there's patio dining in good weather.

MISS SHIRLEY'S CAFE—DOWNTOWN
410-528-5373
www.missshirleys.com
750 E. Pratt St.
Open: Daily
Price: Moderate
Cuisine: Southern-style comfort food
Serving: B, L
Reservations: Not accepted
Handicapped Access: Yes

Miss Shirley's takes breakfast and elevates it to the level of haute cuisine. The gargantuan menu offers so much temptation, it's very difficult to narrow down the choices. The Southern influence is felt in dishes like chicken 'n' waffles, and blackened shrimp with grits and bacon. Fried green tomatoes and corn make frequent appearances. Yet there's also a New American approach to many entrées, such as the veggie egg tower, a magnificent mini-edifice of colorful veggies, a poached egg, and mozzarella that is almost too pretty to eat. Miss Shirley's makes it difficult to stick to a diet, too. From the pancakes to the croissant sandwiches to the omelets stuffed with crabmeat and cheese, this is a place for indulgence, not virtue. At lunch, the emphasis switches to salads and sandwiches. The horseradish Caesar is a favorite, and the sandwiches are packed with good things like yellow tomatoes, bibb lettuce, goat cheese, avocado, and roasted peppers. The decor is bright and cheerful, and a superbly trained staff ensures the experience is nurturing as well as nourishing.

Harbor East
CHARLESTON
410-332-7373
www.charlestonrestaurant.com
1000 Lancaster St.
Open: Mon.–Sat.
Price: Expensive to Very Expensive
Cuisine: Low-country Southern
Serving: D
Reservations: Recommended
Handicapped Access: Yes

Charleston has long enjoyed a reputation as Baltimore's best restaurant, by almost any measure. Food, service, wine, ambience—all reflect an almost fanatical attention to detail that is the hallmark of the local Cindy Wolf–Tony Foreman restaurant empire. The restaurant offers low-country South Carolina cuisine prepared using traditional French techniques. Chef Wolf bases her menu offerings on the quality and availability of seasonal ingredients, striving for simplicity to allow the flavors to shine. A typical summer menu might include shrimp and grits with andouille sausage, a curried lobster soup, pan-roasted duck breast with a white peach compote, and a grilled lamb chop infused with lavender

Get Your Steamed Blue Crabs

Many would argue that no visit to Baltimore is complete without sitting down to a huge pile of steamed crabs—preferably in a downscale eatery favored by locals for its knotty-pine familiarity and plentiful pitchers of icy beer.

Here's a list of popular crabhouses around Baltimore. Some of the most colorful spots are not in town but rather on the outskirts, and therefore only reachable by car. Call ahead or check online for prices and availability.

Bo Brooks (410-558-0202; www.bobrooks.com; 2780 Lighthouse Point, Baltimore) This busy Canton crabhouse offers waterfront dining with an outdoor deck.

Canton Dockside (410-276-8900; www.cantondockside.com; 3301 Boston St., Baltimore) More upscale than its brethren, Canton Dockside is relatively new. While situated near the water, there is not much of a waterfront view.

Costas Inn (410-477-1975; www.costasinn.com; 4100 N. Point Blvd., Dundalk) A friendly spot for crabs and beer, Costas is also known for its extensive seafood menu.

Crackpot Seafood Restaurant (410-828-1095; www.crackpotcrabs.com; 8102 Loch Raven Blvd., Towson) Longtime favorite in the suburbs northeast of the city.

Gunning's Seafood Restaurant (410-712-9404; www.gunningsonline.com; 7304 Parkway Dr., Hanover) This strip-mall crabhouse south of Baltimore is known for its fried pepper rings, which are dusted with powdered sugar.

L. P. Steamers (410-576-9294; www.lpsteamers.com; 1100 E. Fort Ave., Baltimore) Good prices and a rooftop deck with views of downtown make this Locust Point stalwart a favorite among the locals.

Mr. Bill's Terrace Inn (410-687-5994; 200 Eastern Blvd., Essex) Crisp, efficient service and customers who are serious about their crabs are the hallmarks of this unpretentious suburban outpost.

Nick's Fish House (410-347-4123; www.nicksfishhouse.com; 2600 Insulator Dr., Baltimore) Situated under the Hanover Street bridge in south Baltimore, Nick's offers a waterfront view of

working-class Baltimore you won't find in any tourist brochure. The rustic interior adds another element of charm.

Obrycki's Crab House and Seafood Restaurant (410-732-6399; www.obryckis.com; 1727 E. Pratt St., Baltimore) Long the grande dame of Baltimore crabhouses, Obrycki's lives up to its reputation with big, meaty crabs steamed in its secret, peppery spice blend.

Crabcakes and steamed crabs: It's what's cookin' in Chesapeake Country. www.VisitAnnapolis.org

and other Provencal herbs. Suggested wine pairings accompany each menu item. Guests are charged according to the number of courses they choose, or can select a prix fixe "Menu of the Moment," but any way you slice it the meal will be expensive. And probably one you'll remember for the rest of your life.

PAZO

410-534-7296
www.pazorestaurant.com
1425 Aliceanna St.
Open: Daily
Price: Moderate
Cuisine: Tapas
Serving: D
Reservations: Recommended
Handicapped Access: Yes

Baltimore has never been thought of as an uber-cool town, but with the arrival of Pazo a few years ago, we're a little closer to it. It's both restaurant and lounge in a cavernous two-story structure that has been carved into moody, intimate spaces for drinking and casual dining. The open kitchen dishes up small Mediterranean-style plates such as ceviche, lamb meatballs with mint, and wood-roasted mushrooms with lemon and rosemary. Salads, rustic breads, and Neopolitan pizzas round out the extensive menu. Desserts and specialty cocktails also dazzle. As the evening progresses, Pazo becomes more of a nightspot: The volume is turned up and floor space is cleared for dancing. Pazo is another successful Baltimore restaurant owned by the husband-and-wife team of Tony Foreman and Chef Cindy Wolf. Also in Harbor East is their latest venture, Cinghiale, featuring Italian cuisine and wine.

CANTON
JACK'S BISTRO

410-878-6542
www.jacksbistro.net
3123 Elliott St.
Open: Wed.–Sun.
Price: Moderate
Cuisine: Eclectic
Serving: D
Reservations: No
Handicapped Access: Yes

Innovation and fun are the hallmarks of this Canton eatery. Renowned for its sous-vide dishes and inventive cocktails, Jack's is the place to try something new and different. Known as a hangout for Baltimore's best chefs, Jack's is among a handful of Baltimore restaurants using molecular gastronomy on a regular basis. Menu items range from playful—macaroni and cheese with Belgian chocolate—to divinely inspired—Guinness-braised filet mignon served with smoked Gouda-bacon-jalapeño grits. The restaurant is small but cozy. An exceptional beer list, including numerous Belgian ales, and daily specials, including Sunday entrée specials, make Jack's a great place to linger with friends.

NACHO MAMA'S/MAMA'S ON THE HALF SHELL

410-675-0898
www.nachomamascanton.com
2907 O'Donnell St.
Open: Daily
Price: Moderate
Cuisine: Tex-Mex
Serving: L, D
Reservations: Not accepted
Handicapped Access: Yes

Nacho Mama's is exactly the sort of irreverent, kitschy spot that attracts young people looking for cheap beer and spicy Tex-Mex. There's an Elvis theme and a sports theme, and sometimes they even overlap (is that the King in a Baltimore Colts uniform?). The food is typical Tex-Mex fare: quesadillas, nachos—even a margarita served in a hubcap. The wait for a table can be long, as Nacho Mama's doesn't accept reservations, and service can be spotty when the place is packed. Sister restaurant Mama's on the Half Shell, nearby at 2901 O'Donnell St., takes a similar approach to seafood. The food and atmosphere are slightly more sophisticated, however, and the oyster is given the respect it deserves.

FEDERAL HILL
ABBEY BURGER BISTRO
443-453-9698
www.abbeyburgerbistro.com
1041 Marshall St.
Open: Daily
Price: Moderate
Cuisine: Burgers
Serving: L, D
Reservations: Not accepted
Handicapped Access: Yes

Abbey Burger Bistro is a great little place to grab a burger and a beer—but not just any burger, and not just any beer. Abbey customers can order from an inventive array of burger choices, or build their own from a menu of meat—and nonmeat—options, toppings, and buns. The possibilities are just about endless, with options like peanut butter burger, foie gras burger and lamburger. Abbey uses Roseda beef, made from locally raised Black Angus that are hormone-free, grass-fed and grain-finished. For the kids, plain burgers, hot dogs and grilled cheese are available. For dessert, enjoy treats made with ice cream from Gifford's of Washington, D.C. For the grown-ups, Abbey's makes shakes spiked with liqueurs. Now, let's talk about the beer selection. A dozen varieties are on tap at any given time, including Belgians, Germans, and the best American craft brews. Another 60 beers are stocked in cans or bottles.

REGI'S AMERICAN BISTRO
410-539-7344
www.regisamericanbistro.com
1002 Light St.
Open: Daily
Price: Moderate
Cuisine: Bistro fare
Serving: L, D
Reservations: Accepted
Handicapped Access: No

If you're looking for a comfortable, casual spot with an eclectic menu, Regi's is the place. It's narrow and cozy, with lots of exposed brick, a marble fireplace, and hardwood floors. Enter through the low-lit bar to one of two small dining rooms, or, in decent weather, grab a sidewalk table. Like any good bistro, Regi's is big on sandwiches and wraps. Try the salmon club with applewood bacon and a red pepper aioli, or the La Jolla chicken wrap, in which roasted corn, black beans, guacamole, and salsa share the tortilla with a grilled chicken breast. For heartier appetites, Regi's has meatloaf and mashed potatoes, pork chops finished with Chinese mustard sauce, and pecan-encrusted rainbow trout. Regi's also features cocktails made from fresh ingredients, such as sweet tea vodka with housemade lemonade, cucumber margaritas, and fresh lemonade with blueberry vodka.

RYLEIGH'S OYSTER
410-539-2093
www.ryleighs.com
36 E. Cross St.
Open: Daily
Price: Moderate
Cuisine: Oysters and seafood
Serving: L, D
Reservations: Accepted
Handicapped Access: Yes

If oysters make you squeal with delight, Ryleigh's must be on your list of places to visit. First off, it's a beautiful place with the feel of a really cool New York tavern. During a recent renovation, touches such as a slate raw bar and red oak wine bar were added to provide subtle elegance. Oysters are a standout, of course, and are offered raw, steamed, grilled with an herb butter and

Parmesan cheese, or fried and served with an adobo aoili. Other kinds of seafood are available, too, such as pan-seared scallops with a carrot-ginger sauce, seared Ahi tuna, and Maryland crabcakes. The menu is chock-full of tempting offerings, from sun-dried tomato and lobster pasta to a sandwich made with roasted turkey breast, prosciutto, and bacon. Ryleigh's happens to be located on a major bar-hopping strip, so a quiet dinner is best had in the early evening. In warm weather, Ryleigh's opens its café-style doors for open-air dining. One of the best ways to experience Ryleigh's is on a lazy weekend afternoon, before the bar crowd descends.

LOCUST POINT
HARBORQUE
410-685-PORK (7675)
www.harborque.com
1421 Lawrence St.
Open: Tues.–Sun.
Price: Inexpensive to Moderate
Cuisine: Pizza, risotto, sandwiches
Serving: L, D
Reservations: Not accepted
Handicapped Access: No

If good barbecue is what you're after, a visit to HarborQue will not disappoint. Serving up Carolina pit BBQ, HarborQue is a winner when it comes to selection, quality, and location. Meats are slow-cooked over a hickory fire. The menu features mouthwatering chicken, pulled pork, ribs, ham, beef, and turkey—even smoked Polish sausage. Side dishes include the usual baked beans, coleslaw, and potato salad, plus a few more. The corn bread, baked on the premises, is moist and buttery. An array of house-made flavored pound cakes are available for dessert. In good weather, take your tray out to the deck and enjoy a view of the Inner Harbor. Customers are even allowed to bring their own beer or wine.

THE WINE MARKET
410-244-6166
www.the-wine-market.com
921 E. Fort Ave.
Open: Daily
Price: Moderate
Cuisine: New American
Serving: L, D
Reservations: Recommended
Handicapped Access: Yes

The Wine Market is a popular spot for casual, upscale dining, cocktails, and good wine. The setting is simple, with lots of exposed brick and blond wood. Choose from their wine list, or browse in the adjacent wine shop and bring in your own selection for a small corkage fee. The food here represents the best of contemporary American cuisine: fresh ingredients and assertive flavors in surprising combinations. A cheese plate is enhanced by a dollop of quince paste and cardamom-spiced almonds. A simple organic chicken is encrusted with potato, then pan fried and served with a split pea polenta cake, Swiss chard, and chicken and golden raisin sausage. And a kobe sirloin steak gets a colorful pick-me-up from tomato ceviche, white asparagus, and an avocado mousse. Servers at The Wine Market are friendly and intent on maximizing the diner's experience. And the enthusiasm of the entire kitchen staff is reflected in the food.

PATTERSON PARK
MATTHEW'S PIZZA
410-276-8755
www.matthewspizza.com
3131 Eastern Ave.
Open: Daily
Price: Inexpensive
Cuisine: Pizza
Serving: L, D
Reservations: Not accepted
Handicapped Access: No

Matthew's Pizza has been named Baltimore's Best Pizza by various publications more than 39 times, or about as long as these awards have existed. And the basic recipe has not changed in the six decades it has been open, making its legion of fans very happy. Plan to wait in line at Matthew's, as the dining room is small, but your reward will come in the form of a doughy crust topped with fresh tomato sauce and hand-grated Italian cheeses. The decor is cheerfully luncheonette, the waitresses folksy and efficient. Besides a variety of pizzas, Matthew's serves spaghetti, subs, and salads. Desserts include sorbet, cheesecake from The Cheesecake Factory, and cannolis from Vaccaro's Bakery in Little Italy. They also serve beer, wine, and liquor.

SALT TAVERN

410-276-5480
www.salttavern.com
2127 E. Pratt St.

Open: Mon.–Sat.
Price: Moderate to Expensive
Cuisine: New American
Serving: D
Reservations: Accepted
Handicapped Access: Yes

When it opened in 2006, Salt was a welcome addition to the Patterson Park community, which lacked upscale restaurants. Occupying a corner building in a residential neighborhood, Salt is small but lively. The bar, with its Day-Glo green lighting, dominates the scene and generates the vibe. Despite its size, the unpretentious Salt is as packed with energy as the food is packed with flavor. Consider an appetizer of grilled quail with fig molasses, foie gras and dried cherries, or the entrée whimsically called Cheek to Cheek: a spicy hoisin veal cheek paired with a seared halibut cheek, served over edamame purée with a scallion rice cake. A twist on the classic Reuben

A painted screen in Baltimore's Patterson Park neighborhood.

sandwich uses tuna pastrami and comes with a side of tempura horseradish chips. Chef-owner Jason Ambrose wasn't joking when he named his eatery Salt: His dishes are richly seasoned. Savor the bold flavors with a tasty cocktail, or choose from a good selection of wine and craft beer.

FELL'S POINT
JIMMY'S
410-327-3273
801 S. Broadway
Open: Daily
Price: Inexpensive to Moderate
Cuisine: Breakfast, sandwiches
Serving: B, L, D
Reservations: Not accepted
Handicapped Access: Yes

Jimmy's is our favorite greasy spoon, and we say that with genuine affection. It's full of Baltimore characters, perhaps nursing hangovers, and cuts across all demographic lines. Longshoremen sit next to college students, who sit next to (presumed) ladies of the evening or pols or cops. They come—often waiting as long as 30 minutes to be seated—for the strong coffee, pancakes, and scrapple served up by gum-snapping waitresses under fluorescent lights. Doors open at 5 AM, making Jimmy's an interesting crossroads for early risers filling the tank for a busy day and all-night partiers who have run out of gas. Drink in the local color with your caffeine and melted butter, and you'll get a glimpse of Baltimore that escapes most visitors. Cash is preferred, although they take Visa and MasterCard.

KALI'S COURT
410-276-4700
www.kaliscourt.com
1606 Thames St.
Open: Daily
Price: Moderate to Expensive
Cuisine: Mediterranean, seafood
Serving: D

Reservations: Recommended
Handicapped Access: Yes

Entering Kali's Court is a real treat. The brick-walled front patio has been transformed into a lush garden with a gurgling fountain, abundant tropical plants, and tables topped with white market umbrellas. Balconies with intimate seating overlook the terrace. The decor is sleek and romantic, with soft lighting and comfortable seating. Service is professional but unobtrusive. No wonder couples have come to Kali's to celebrate anniversaries and other special occasions for more than a decade. Kali's is first and foremost a seafood restaurant, so expect to find little else on the menu. Calamari, octopus, and scallops stand out on the appetizer menu, and the most popular entrées include a grilled whole bronzini, bouillabaisse, crabcakes, and wild striped bass served over polenta. For dessert, try the chocolate chunk crème brûlée. Kali's also has two sister restaurants nearby: Mezze, featuring Mediterranean-style small plates, and Meli, a honey-focused patisserie and bistro.

ZE MEAN BEAN CAFE
410-675-5999
www.zemeanbean.com
1739 Fleet St.
Open: Daily
Price: Moderate
Cuisine: Eastern European
Serving: L, D, weekend brunch
Reservations: Accepted
Handicapped Access: Yes

You have to forgive Ze Mean Bean for having a split personality. It seems to debate being a coffeehouse or a white-tablecloth restaurant, and whether it specializes in Eastern European cuisine or New American. But that's quite all right, for Ze Mean Bean is utterly charming in its dichotomy. The downstairs is cozy and relaxed, with comfy couches and tables tucked into nooks. Upstairs, seating and service are somewhat more formal. An ambitious menu brings together traditional Slavic dishes like borscht, pierogies, and stuffed cabbage with trendy Western fare like goat cheese salad, lamb rubbed with rosemary pesto, and seared scallops with pomegranate sauce. There's even an attempt to make worlds collide in one dish, the Krupnik crabcake: two jumbo lump crabcakes topped with a spicy Polish honey vodka sauce. The wine list is nothing short of adventurous and well worth exploring. Recommended wine pairings are thoughtfully included under each entrée as well.

LITTLE ITALY
CAFÉ GIA
410-685-6727
www.cafegias.com
410 S. High St.
Open: Daily
Price: Moderate
Cuisine: Italian
Serving: L, D
Reservations: Accepted
Handicapped Access: Yes

This charming Little Italy gem started small and found its niche before expanding, buying a liquor license, and adding a full-time chef, all in 2009. The walls, inside and out, are covered with cheerful murals of Sicilian street life that impart an Old World ambience. Two levels of cozy dining rooms are supplemented by an upstairs balcony with open-air seating. Led by the mother-daughter ownership team (both are named Gia), service is friendly and accommodating. The menu offers a pleasing array of traditional Italian dishes, such as rigatoni in vodka sauce, tortellini alla rosa, shrimp fra diavolo, and chicken marsala. Price points are on the low side for Little Italy. Desserts are limited to cannolis and tiramisu, but Gia's does offer cappuccino

and espresso drinks. Special dinner menus are available for groups of 15 or more.

DELLA NOTTE
410-837-5500
www.dellanotte.com
801 Eastern Ave.
Open: Daily
Price: Expensive
Cuisine: Italian
Serving: L, D
Reservations: Accepted
Handicapped Access: Yes

Della Notte is one of the most beautiful restaurants in the downtown area. A massive tree at the center of the dining room sparkles with white lights. The coolness of the classical decor, with antique columns and marble statuary, is offset with warm wood fixtures and rich golden fabrics. The kitchen blends traditional Italian cooking with an occasional modern twist. Pasta dishes include pappardelle with Bolognese sauce, and bucatini with wild mushrooms, pancetta, mascarpone cheese, and truffle oil. Seafood dishes, which can be pricey here, include crabcakes topped with a basil vinaigrette and red snapper with anchovy butter. A standout among the meat entrées is a pine nut–crusted lamb loin served with an eggplant caponata. Free parking and a knockout wine list add to the appeal of this Little Italy mainstay, whose atmosphere works for a romantic dinner or the family's observance of Grandpa's birthday.

LA SCALA
410-783-5949
www.lascaladining.com
1012 Eastern Ave.
Open: Daily
Price: Moderate to Expensive
Cuisine: Italian
Serving: L, D
Reservations: Accepted
Handicapped Access: Yes

It's not every restaurant—or even every
Italian restaurant, for that matter—that can
boast of having its own bocce court right
inside the restaurant. How it enhances the
dining experience is unclear, but fortunately the food at La Scala doesn't need to
rely on gimmicks to satisfy. The menu is
extensive and the offerings rich.
Prosciutto, pancetta, butter, cream, and
cognac are used in abundance in the thick
sauces that adorn huge helpings of pasta,
veal, chicken, and seafood. On the lighter
side, try an appetizer of artichokes topped
with crabmeat and capers and served in a
lemon-butter sauce, or veal francese,
sautéed veal with a simple sauce of lemon,
butter, and white wine. Service at La Scala
is quite attentive, and the atmosphere is
suitable for a business dinner or a romantic
evening for two. The wine list is exceptional, focusing on Italy, as expected, but
including notable wines from all over the
world as well. There is also a good selection
of wines by the glass.

MOUNT VERNON
THE BREWER'S ART
410-547-6925
www.thebrewersart.com
1106 N. Charles St.
Open: Daily
Price: Moderate
Cuisine: New American
Serving: D
Reservations: Accepted
Handicapped Access: No

A visit to The Brewer's Art can be a totally
casual experience or an elegant one.
Housed in a high-ceilinged, 19th-century
town house trimmed in mahogany and
marble, The Brewer's Art is carved into a
series of intimate spaces, each with a different attitude. The bar in front feels
relaxed but energetic, and the dining rooms
become slightly more formal as you move
toward the rear of the restaurant. One big
reason people flock to The Brewer's Art is

their amazing Belgian-style beer, brewed
right on the premises. But the menu shines
on its own, offering seasonal dishes based
on locally sourced ingredients and tempting comfort food like pork carnitas with
corn bread pudding, baked polenta with
ratatouille, and the always popular grilled
sirloin with rosemary garlic fries. If beer is
not your thing, fear not: The wine list is
excellent. And desserts are house-made, so
try the vanilla and goat cheese cheesecake
or the chocolate torte made with the restaurant's own Proletary Ale.

THE HELMAND
410-752-0311
www.helmand.com
806 N. Charles St.
Open: Daily
Price: Moderate
Cuisine: Afghan
Serving: D
Reservations: Encouraged
Handicapped Access: Yes

The Helmand remains one of the city's
most popular restaurants because it consistently offers tasty, interesting food at reasonable prices. Afghan cooking can be
described as a cross between Indian and
Mediterranean cuisines, featuring rice,
lamb, onions, and tomatoes, and season-
ings such as garlic, mint, and yogurt. Some
of the more interesting items on the menu
include Kaddo Borawni, a pan-fried baby
pumpkin served with a yogurt and garlic
sauce, and the popular aushak, which are
leek ravioli served on yogurt and topped
with ground beef and mint. Many of the
offerings are vegetarian as well. Service is
friendly and efficient, but as tables are
placed very close together this might not be
the spot for an intimate tête-à-tête. It's a
wonderful spot, however, for small-group
dining or a relatively quick meal before or
after heading to the theater or symphony
hall.

SOTTO SOPRA

410-625-0534
www.sottosopra.us
405 N. Charles St.
Open: Daily
Price: Moderate to Expensive
Cuisine: Northern Italian
Serving: L, D (D only on Sun.)
Reservations: Recommended; highly
recommended for the weekend
Handicapped Access: Yes

There's something very grand about this
colorful and contemporary dining room,
even though the 19th-century town house it
occupies is not huge. A sweeping curtain
separates the front dining room from the
bar area. The mirrors lining one wall go
three-quarters of the way to the 22-foot-
high ceiling, and they reflect huge, colorful
murals on the facing wall. Amid the drama
comes your meal. Pastas and salads, carne y
pesce get fresh face-lifts. Try the sesame-
seared scallop with asparagus corn relish. A
beef carpaccio salad one hot day gave us
hope we'd get through the day, but the pis-
tachio crème brûlée gave us reason to live.
Check their Web site for terrific specials.
Maybe the Mon.–Fri. $25 three-course
meal will be offered, or you can nab a
reservation for a monthly Opera Night,
replete with arias between the six courses
for $58. Molto favoloso!

HAMPDEN
CAFÉ HON

410-243-1230
www.cafehon.com
1002 W. 36th St.
Open: Daily
Price: Inexpensive to Expensive
Cuisine: Comfort food
Serving: B, L, D
Reservations: Accepted
Handicapped Access: Yes

For a truly authentic Baltimore experience,
visit this restaurant with someone who

remembers the Hampden neighborhood
from its blue-collar heyday in the 1950s.
When your companion orders an omelet
with Hon potatoes, he can confirm that they
are, indeed, cooked like hash browns were
back in the day. Retro burgers, shakes, pies,
and a cuppa joe that fully meet present-day
expectations can be found here, where
owner Denise Whiting gave rebirth to the
"Hon" craze. It's all about the working
ladies in beehive hairdos (and their
accents) who created this neighborhood
back in the day—what you might call a certain "Balmer-ness." However, since this is,
after all, a restaurant for those in the here
and now, look also for good seafood and a
variety of sandwiches, salads, and entrées
that include items like Cuban-style black
beans and brown rice for $10.95. Blue plate
specials are served from 4–6.

WOODBERRY KITCHEN

410-464-8000
www.woodberrykitchen.com
2010 Clipper Park Road (Woodberry, near
Hampden)
Open: Daily
Price: Moderate to Expensive
Cuisine: Farm to table
Serving: D, Sunday brunch
Reservations: Strongly recommended
Handicapped Access: No

When chef-owner Spike Gjerde opened
Woodberry Kitchen in late 2007, the farm-
to-table concept, emphasizing locally
sourced, sustainable ingredients, was not
yet common parlance as it is now. Yet the
risk paid off, and WK quickly became the
most popular place in town. It consistently
tops Open Table's list of most-booked
Baltimore restaurants, and *Bon Appetit*
named WK one of the country's hottest
restaurants in 2009. Part of the magic definitely comes from the setting, a former
foundry that has been rehabbed with a
warmly rustic feel, despite the fact that it's

essentially one huge open space. Crumbling brick, rough-hewn wood, and subdued lighting help contain the high energy of this whirring beehive. The menu changes often, depending on what's available locally, but expect to find excellent cheeses, interesting salads, and an array of small plates like baked clams and flatbread with squash pesto and goat cheese to whet your appetite. Entrées lean toward comfort food, such as rib-eye steaks, chicken and waffles, and braised short ribs. Add an amazing wine list, enthusiastic servers, innovative cocktails, and memorable desserts, and it's no wonder WK's on everyone's short list.

Station North
JOE SQUARED
410-545-0444
www.joesquared.com
133 W. North Ave.
Open: Daily
Price: Moderate
Cuisine: Pizza, risotto, sandwiches

Serving: L, D
Reservations: Not accepted
Handicapped Access: Yes

As a cornerstone of the fledging midtown Station North Arts District, Joe Squared has brought more than great pizza to the community. Chef-owner Joe Edwardsen features live music most nights and lets local artists display their work in his cozy and eclectic eatery. Diners come for the thin-crust, sourdough pizza baked in Maryland's only coal-fired pizza oven, but they soon discover gems like the scallop and tomato risotto and the lamb cheese steak made with Asiago cheese and mint grown in Edwardsen's rooftop herb garden. Substantial salads, hearty pastas, and above-average desserts round out the surprisingly extensive menu. Joe Squared also has an extensive rum selection, so try a Cuba Libre made with real cane sugar cola, or ask for a guided tasting. The beer selection is also very good, with multiple selections available on tap.

Food Purveyors

Looking for a quick bite or a tasty treat? Howzabout a decent cup of coffee? Try these:

Attman's Delicatessen (410-563-2666; www.attmansdeli.com; 1019 E. Lombard St.) Open since 1915 along Baltimore's waning "Corned Beef Row," this old-fashioned Jewish deli features lots of corned beef, brisket, pastrami (New York's finest hot pastrami sandwich, $6.29), knockwurst, liverwurst, beef tongue ("no lip"), salami, chopped liver, whitefish salad, and a famous Reuben sandwich. You get the idea. The business started in 1915, when Marc Attman's grandparents sold sandwiches in brown paper bags for a nickel. By the '20s they were doing mail-order, in Yiddish, to Virginia and North Carolina. Now, Attman's is one of the city's enduring legends. The food is cooked fresh daily, there's free parking, and you can eat for less than $10. What's not to like?

Baltimore Farmers' Market & Bazaar. This is the city's biggie, held on Sundays from early May until December downtown at Saratoga Street between Holliday and Gay streets (under the Jones Falls Expressway viaduct). Hours are 8 AM to noon. For info: www.bop .org, then click under "Seasonal Events and Festivals."

Bonaparte Breads (410-342-4000; 903 S. Ann St., Fell's Point) A good spot to enjoy an alfresco table by the water in Fell's Point, some good coffee, and a tasty lunch. The breads and pastries are pretty much to die for.

Broadway Market (www.bpmarkets.com; 1640–1641 Aliceanna St.) At deadline, plans for a renovation were in the works at Fell's Point's public market, which dates to 1797. It's

open Mon.–Sat. from 7–6, and you
should stop in to see what's happening
if you're in the neighborhood.

Cake Love (410-522-1825; www.cake
love.com; 2500 Boston St., Suite 4B,
in the American Can Company complex, Canton) Former attorney and
food network "Sugar Rush" host
Warren Brown has moved into
Baltimore from Washington, D.C.,
with his cakes. Stop in for cupcakes
(try the red velvet!) and cookies.

Cross Street Market
(www.bpmarkets.com; 1065 S. Charles
St.) Get your flowers, produce, freshly
cut meat, seafood, sandwiches, or
maybe a beer and raw oysters at Nick's
(410-685-2020) here at the busy
Federal Hill market.

Dangerously Delicious Pies (410-522-
PIES; www.dangerouspies.com; 1036
Light St.) The Food Network found its
way to the savory pies here in Federal
Hill: steak mushroom, onion and
gruyere, perhaps, or pulled pork BBQ.
The sweet pies include the usuals plus
specialties like a "Baltimore Bomb," a
vanilla chess pie topped with the city's
much beloved Berger cookies (themselves notably topped with chocolate).
Pies range from $25–31.50, but slices
and minipies are available.

*Neighborhood markets like the Cross Street Market
in Federal Hill have served Baltimore for hundreds
of years.*

Dominion Ice Cream (410-243-2644; www.dominionicecream.com; 3215 N. Charles St.)
You've had fruit in your ice cream. Why not veggies? Spinach is the vanilla-tasting best-
seller among Donna Calloway's uncooked, veggie-filled ice creams that take on surprising tastes once the spices and flavors are added. Try sweet potato, carrot, and tomato,
which apparently tastes a bit like strawberry. The idea is to promote nutrition and
healthy eating even if it's a 99-calorie scoop of ice cream with more nutrition than the
usual (and 3 grams of saturated fat). Typical flavors from Hershey are also available.

Evergreen Café (410-235-8118; 501 W. Cold Spring Ln., Roland Park) Popular coffee shop
with plenty of seating, sandwiches, and such.

Lexington Market (410-685-6169; www.lexingtonmarket.com; 400 W. Lexington St.)
Named for the Battle of Lexington, this market has stood at this very spot since 1782.
The gleaming renovation you see today was completed in 2002, and vendors inside
include the famous Faidley Seafood, home of the fabled crabcake. They're open 9–5
Mon.–Sat.; 410-727-4898 or www.faidleyscrabcakes.com. The market is open 8:30 AM
to 6 PM Mon.–Sat.

Piedigrotta Italian Bakery & Pastry Shop (410-522-6900; www.piedigrottabakery.com; 1300 Bank St., Little Italy) Get breakfast (by 6:30 AM), lunch, or dinner at this well-liked and friendly bakery-café, its case brimming with tempting torte, pane and dolci like torta di fragola and pane dolce. Owner Carminantonio Iannaccone was born near Naples, and his offerings are authentic.

Pitango Gelato (410-702-5828; www.pitangogelato; 802 S. Broadway, Fell's Point) This small, Baltimore-based chain has spread into D.C. with its all-natural gelato made from grass-fed organic milk, organic fruits, and nuts. Try the chocolate noir. Also serving European-style hot chocolate and Zeke's coffee.

Roland Park Bagel Company (410-889-3333; www.rolandparkbakery.com; 500 W. Cold Spring Ln., Roland Park) Voted "best bagels" by Baltimore *City Paper*, with 13 varieties (jalepeño to onion), breakfast sandwiches, and a lunch menu featuring soups, salads, and deli sandwiches. Open 6:30 AM during the week, and 7 AM on weekends.

Rosina Gourmet (410-675-9300; www.rosinagourmet.com; 2819 O'Donnell St., Canton; second location downtown, 410-244-1885, 300 E. Lombard St.) Terrific spot on O'Donnell Square, with a menu that includes fancy gourmet sandwiches, desserts, coffees and teas, and even capicola ham on one of the breakfast sandwiches.

Soup's On! (410-366-SOUP; soupsonhampden.com; 842 W. 36th St.) A cute neighborhood eatery with tables on the front porch in good weather and great soups like white bean and sausage with tomato and summer herbs.

Spro (410-243-1262; www.sprocoffee.com; 851 W. 36th St., Hampden) Serious coffee and pastries brought to you by world-renowned barista and barista competition judge Jay Caragay who, at deadline, was slated to open a new shop on The Avenue in Hampden. Enjoy offerings from six different roasters brewed eight different ways.

Vaccaro's Italian Pastry Shop (410-685-4905; vaccarospastry.com; 222 Albemarle St., Little Italy; second location in the Light Street Pavilion at Harbor Place, 410-547-7169) Family owned since 1956, this old line, Little Italy-based institution offers a range of yummy pastry, including cool little mini cannolis.

Zeke's Roastery (410-917-1496; www.zekescoffee.com; 3003 Montebello Terrace) Pretty much Baltimore's homegrown coffee of choice, Zeke's is in coffee shops, restaurants, and farmer's markets. You can also stop by the roastery to pick up a pound, or for one of their Sunday tastings during winter. The biggie: kopi luwak, in January.

Nightlife

Two things you need to know: Baltimore's neighborhoods support a thriving tavern scene, and the local *City Paper*, which is free, gives up-to-the-minute advice on what's hot. It's at stands all around the city.

In Fell's Point, it's easy to find a place to grab a drink, hear music, or get in some quality people-watching. Prominent among local taverns are the **Cat's Eye Pub** (410-276-9866; www.catseyepub.com; 1730 Thames St.) with live local music; **Kooper's Tavern** for a burger (410-563-5423; www.koopers.com; 1700 Thames St.); and **The Wharf Rat** with its Oliver Ales (www.thewharfrat.com; 801 S. Ann St. and near Camden Yards at 206 W. Pratt St.). For a major beer selection: **Max's on Broadway** (formally called Max's Taphouse) at 737 S. Broadway; 410-675-MAXS; www.maxs.com.

O'Donnell Square, northeast of Fell's Point in Canton, is rimmed with taverns and cafés. **Nacho Mama's** (410-675-0898; www.nachomamascanton.com; 2907 O'Donnell St.) is popular and profiled in our restaurant section. Also popular: The **Claddagh Pub &**

Restaurant (410-522-4220; www.claddaghonline.com; 2918 O'Donnell St.), with live music.

On the southern side of the Inner Harbor is Federal Hill. **Mother's Federal Hill Grille** (410-244-8686; www.mothersgrille.com; 1113 S. Charles St.) is a popular stop, as is **Ryleigh's Oyster** (410-539-2093; www.ryleighs.com; 36 E. Cross St.), which is profiled in our restaurant section. This is also home to **The 8X10** (410-625-2999; www.the8x10.com; 10 E. Cross St.), a small space that books bands like New Orleans standard bearers Bonerama, Galactic, and Papa Grows Funk. For something different, consider **Illusions Magic Bar & Lounge** (410-727-5811; www.illusionsmagicbar.com; 1025 S. Charles St.), operated by magician Spencer Horseman, the son of two Ringling Bros. clowns. He's a globe-trotter who's played Vegas with David Copperfield and takes the stage of his speakeasy-style supper club when he's in town. The lights go up on a one-hour comic magic show every Friday and Saturday night at 10 PM, and if Horseman's not in town, the show goes on with a different performer.

At the Inner Harbor, groove to the music at **Power Plant Live!** (www.powerplantlive .com, with links to all of its establishments; 34 Market Place), a huge, multiestablishment venue housed inside the city's former brick power plant. It's popular with young singles. Eight clubs and bars (and one art gallery) light up the night. Try the **Havana Club** for upscale offerings, **Howl at the Moon** and its two busy baby grands, or **Luckie's Tavern** for all your beer-drinking and sports-watching needs. Or see who's playing at **Rams Head Live!** (410-244-1131, tickets; 410-244-8854, office; www.ramsheadlive.com). This three-story venue has seen 'em all: from Yonder Mountain String Band to the Tragically Hip, from Jay-Z to Lucinda Williams. The 26,000-square-foot space has five bars, and tons of video monitors and lights. The calendar's on their Web site. And if it's summer, check who's playing at **Pier 6 Concert Pavilion** (410-659-7100; www.piersixpavilion.com; 731 Eastern Ave.), with its plein air music under the tent against the backdrop of the Inner Harbor. Major acts ranging from Anita Baker to The Goo Goo Dolls have performed, and concerts end by 11 PM.

Deeper into the city, in the Hampden neighborhood, the **13.5% Wine Bar** (410-889-1064; 13.5winebar.com; 1117 W. 36th St.) has been gaining notice. Food is served late, four wine flights are available, and so are Tuesday night tastings.

CULTURE

Commercial art galleries are included in the shopping chapter, although there's no question they contribute to the city's culture.

Arts Centers & Colleges

CREATIVE ALLIANCE AT THE PATTERSON
410-276-1651
www.creativealliance.org
3134 Eastern Ave. (Highlandtown)

The Highlandtown neighborhood's renovated former movie theater now operates as a unique multiarts center. Catch a performance (Hank Williams tribute, flamenco, films), take a class (life drawing, West African cooking), or check out exhibitions in the Main Gallery, the Amalie Rothschild Gallery, or tiny "Minstallation" gallery for miniature work.

Look for a focus on Baltimore and Maryland artists. Film is also on deck, with the Creative Alliance MovieMakers, aka CAmm, screening film and videos produced around the region. The theater even has a bar and popcorn. This is a cool place where something's always going on.

MARYLAND ART PLACE
410-962-8565
www.mdartplace.org
8 Market Place, Suite 100 (Power Plant Live!)

Two options: Catch the visual artists at the Power Plant Live! space in the Inner Harbor, where new shows open six or so times per year. Or, catch a cab over to the second location at 218 W. Saratoga St. for an evening performance at The 14Karat Cabaret, an artist-run space where you can see dance, film, video, music—or a hybrid. Drinks are cheap, and it's $6 at the door. Call 410-220-0706.

MARYLAND INSTITUTE COLLEGE OF ART GALLERIES
410-669-9200
www.mica.edu
1300 Mount Royal Ave.
Galleries: Meyerhoff and Decker galleries, Brown Center, 1301 W. Mount Royal Ave.;
Pinkard Gallery, Bunting Center, 1401 W. Mount Royal Ave. Several other galleries on campus; check Web site for more
Open: Mon.–Sat. 10–5; Sun. noon–5

The students at this top-notch school come from around the world, and opportunities to see (and maybe buy) their work occur during the year. The MFA students in graphic design, painting, sculpture, photographic and electronic media show from late March through early May. In early May comes the Commencement Exhibition, highlighting about 400 emerging artists graduating in every media you can imagine. The college's permanent galleries, hallways, classrooms, and open spaces are transformed into one expansive gallery space. (Check the Web site for details on the preview party, called ArtWalk.) In addition, the annual MICA Art Market the second week in December takes place in the campus's Brown Center. Finally, the school's new Gateway building hosts free artist's lectures and performances. Check it out. Parking tips: two hours in posted Bolton Hill streets; the 1100 block of Mount Royal Avenue has metered parking that lasts 10 hours. You can also take the Light Rail to the University of Baltimore/Mount Royal Station.

Cinema
Plein air cinema has caught on in Baltimore. In the summer, go to the **Little Italy Open-Air Film Festival** showing free films at 9 PM Friday nights in July and August and drawing upward of 2,000 viewers. The season always opens with *Moonstruck* (and the audience always recites with Cher: "Snap out of it!") and closes with *Cinema Paradiso*. Check the schedule at www.littleitalymd.com/openair.htm. In addition, the **American Visionary Art Museum** at 800 Key Hwy. offers alfresco movies during the warm season. For info, go to www.avam.org or call 410-244-1900. The **Maryland Film Festival** in May (www.mdfilmfest.com; 410-752-8083) is held at venues around town.

THE CHARLES THEATER

410-727-FILM
www.thecharles.com
1711 N. Charles St.

This is the city's art movie house in Mount Vernon. The theater also screens operas—
including simulcasts from La Scala—and ballets. Cinema Sundays is a film club with gatherings that include coffee and speakers.

LANDMARK THEATRES

www.landmarktheatres.com
645 S. President St.

Seven screens well-located in Harbor East showing first-run fare. This theater offers digital projection and stadium seating, and is convenient to many downtown hotels.

SENATOR THEATER

410-433-0755 or 410-779-3837
www.senator.com
5904 York Rd.

The grand old Senator was in flux as we headed to deadline, but this we know: A range of movies and live music will continue to play as the theater's performing arts future (and there will be one) is determined. Don't miss the Walk of Fame in the sidewalk in front of the theater that salutes Baltimore film notables.

Major Attractions, Museums, and Historic Sites

AMERICAN VISIONARY ART MUSEUM

410-244-1900
www.avam.org
800 Key Hwy.
Open: Tues.–Sun. 10–6
Admission: Adults $14, seniors 60 and older $10, students and children 7 and older $8

If you visit no other museum in Baltimore (or even, dare we say, Washington, D.C., or New York City), make time to see this one. "Visionary art" is loosely defined as work by self-taught artists, primitive artists, and other such appellations. Let's just call them people who simply want to make art, do so, and produce thought-provoking—even huge—results. From Southerners with religious or otherwise apocalyptic visions to guys who

The American Visionary Art Museum is home to thought-provoking pieces in unique exhibits. Photo courtesy of American Visionary Art Museum, Baltimore

Poe's City

Baltimore inspired one-time resident Edgar Allan Poe, and what the mystery giant left behind certainly has inspired Baltimore. The city even named its pro football team after his fabled poem, "The Raven." This was Poe's father's hometown, and he lived in what is now the Edgar Allan Poe House and Museum at 203 Amity St. (www.eapoe.org) from approximately 1832 to 1835. In the small building lived his aunt and future mother-in-law, Maria Clemm, along with her daughter—his future wife, Virginia—who was 10 at the time. Today, you can tour the house, see Poe artifacts, and learn about his life. Poe departed the Clemm household, but returned to Baltimore some years later. As the story goes, he spent his fair share of time in Fell's Point at the waterfront pub now called The Horse You Came In On Saloon. Rumor has it that he once was found in a gutter, the street, or some similarly disreputable spot not far from the saloon—and not far from death. Indeed, after he died in 1849 he was buried at Westminster Hall & Burying Ground (410-706-2072; www.westminsterhall .org; 515 W. Fayette St.). First, he was interred in an unmarked grave in the family plot. In 1865, he was moved to the marquee spot near the front gate where today you can easily find the grave of Poe, as well as his wife and mother-in-law. You shouldn't have any trouble finding the marble monument inside the cemetery at West Fayette and Greene streets.

retired from their jobs and decided to make art, this place is full of amazing pieces. A reproduction *Lusitania* made of 193,000 toothpicks and a seven-panel vision reminiscent of Bosch for the modern era are among the pieces in the small permanent collection. In addition, the museum hosts wonderful annual exhibitions of 11 months or so. To wit: a Holocaust survivor who recalls her childhood loss of family and survival in the innocent medium of quilt panels. The artists' stories are told in full, and they're at least as interesting as the work. The creative Mr. Rain's Fun House (purple yam soup, prawns, and pheasant) is open Tues.–Sun.

BABE RUTH BIRTHPLACE MUSEUM

410-727-1539
www.BabeRuthMuseum.com
216 Emory St.
Open: Daily 10–5; until 7 when the Orioles play; closed Thanksgiving, Christmas, and New Year's Day
Admission: Adults $6, seniors $4, children 3–12 $3

George Herman Ruth Jr. was born here at his grandparents' house on Feb. 6, 1895, a day that warmed up to 11 degrees. Visitors can see the re-created room where the Babe was born, check out his baseball card from his rookie season with the 1914 Orioles, and even see the bat he got from Shoeless Joe Jackson. This small but well-done museum is a must for baseball aficionados, and you can get here from Oriole Park at Camden Yards by following the giant baseballs painted on the street. The museum is affiliated with Sports Legends Museum at Camden Yards. In addition to being sister (or brother) museums, the two have another connection: Babe's father's bar stood right between where second and third bases stand today.

BALTIMORE MUSEUM OF ART
410-396-7100 or 443-573-1700
www.artbma.org.
10 Art Museum Dr.
Open: Wed.–Fri. 10–5, Sat.–Sun. 11–6
Admission: Free

Maryland's largest art museum also claims the world's largest and most significant collection of works—at 500—by Henri Matisse, courtesy of two Baltimore sisters who visited
their friend (and former Johns Hopkins student), Gertrude Stein, in Paris. Claribel and
Etta Cone returned home with a newfound love of work by their new acquaintances,
Matisse and Pablo Picasso. Highlights of the BMA's Cone Collection include Matisse's well-
known *Seated Odalisque, Left Leg Bent, Ornamental Background and Checkerboard* and *Purple
Robe and Anenomes.* The collection also includes numerous other modern works by
Cezanne, Miro, and Gris. Also at the museum: Warhol, deKooning, Motherwell, and other
contemporary masters. The BMA's collection goes back to Botticelli and Rembrandt, and
includes art of Africa, Asia, and ancient Americas, as well as textiles from around the
world in the Jean and Allan Berman Textile Gallery. The sculpture gardens are a must, featuring Calder, Rodin, and Henry Moore. Enjoy them from Gertrude's, the restaurant operated by Chesapeake celebrity chef John Shields. A relatively recent development is a great
bonus: Admission to the museum is now free.

BALTIMORE MUSEUM OF INDUSTRY
410-727-4808
www.thebmi.org
1415 Key Hwy.
Open: Tues.–Sat. 10–4, Sun. 11–4; closed Memorial Day, Thanksgiving Day, Christmas Eve
and Christmas
Admission: Adults $10, seniors and children $6, kids under 4 free

Come learn about Baltimore industry's many firsts: the first disposable standard bottle
cap, the first gas street lamps (circa 1816), the world's first portable electric drill with a
hand grip (partners Mr. Black and Mr. Decker had been working on a pistol for Mr. Colt),
and the birthplace of the commercial umbrella. If you look around your own house—or
think back to what was in your childhood home—you must agree that's a good list of indis-
pensables. And it isn't complete, as you'll find when you visit the museum, part of which
was once an oyster cannery. Among the museum's marquee exhibits is Dr. Bunting's
Pharmacy, where you'll find out how his effort to find a sunburn cream turned into the
product we know as Noxzema.

B&O RAILROAD MUSEUM
410-752-2490
www.borail.org
901 W. Pratt St.
Open: Mon.–Sat. 10–4, Sun. 11–4 (last admission 30 minutes prior to closing); closed on
major public holidays
Admission: Adults $14, children 2–12 $8, seniors 60 and older $12

This is considered the birthplace of American railroading, the very spot where the first train left the station (so to speak). It was Independence Day 1828 when Charles Carroll—one of the Free State's signers of the Declaration of Independence—laid the first stone. A year later, the so-called "Mount Clare Shops" came into being, and what was built from that includes the very roundhouse, circa 1884, that forms a critical museum display place. You see, the old B&O also had the foresight to amass what turned out to be the world's largest collection of locomotives. Included is the 1856 locomotive you might have caught in movies such as the *Wild Wild West* that came out in 1999. Recently added technology means you can hear the sound of a steam engine, or find out about the impact of railroads on society. This is a very interesting museum where you'll learn as much about the building of the nation as you will of the railroad. Because, after all, the railroad helped build the nation.

BALTIMORE PUBLIC WORKS MUSEUM
410-396-5565
www.baltimorepublicworksmuseum.org
751 Eastern Ave.
Open: Tues.–Sun. 10–4
Admission: Adults $4; seniors, students, and active military $3; children under 6 free

Enter the elegant Beaux Arts building affixed to the 1912 pumping station that circulates two-thirds of the city's wastewater for a look at public works. The circa 1912 Eastern Avenue Pumping Station can be toured after you've had a look around the museum proper, which shares such basic exhibits as the circa 1790 white oak water drain that once helped keep the predecessor of present-day Pratt and Light streets dry. Learn about the garbage operations that have kept Baltimore clean since 1872 and other basics of public works—which, as you'll see, is one darn basic necessity. The museum is located near Pier 7 at the Inner Harbor, and is part of a recent $26 million overhaul to the building. Look for the lights at night.

BASILICA OF THE NATIONAL SHRINE OF THE ASSUMPTION OF THE BLESSED VIRGIN MARY
410-727-3564
www.baltimorebasilica.org
408 N. Charles St.
Open: Mon.–Fri. 7–4:30, Sat. and Sun. 7 until 5:30 Mass ends

Baltimore is home to the nation's first Roman Catholic cathedral, built between 1806 and 1821. A recent renovation returned the church to its original Benjamin Henry Latrobe design (as envisioned by John Carroll, the country's first bishop). Visitors are allowed until 4:30 every day, and guided tours take place Mon.–Sat. at 6 AM, 11 AM, and 1 PM, and Sun. at noon. Due to weddings, check ahead on Saturday visits and please don't plan a touring visit during Mass.

CONTEMPORARY MUSEUM
410-783-5720
www.contemporary.org
100 W. Centre St.
Open: Wed.–Sat. noon–5

Admission: Suggested adults $5, students $3

Although it's located near the Walters Art Museum, the Contemporary offers a completely different view of art. Recent exhibitions have included "FAX," in which a cross-section of artists submitted their drawings via fax machine, or "Where Do You Live" by Baltimore artist Soledad Salamé, in which Google maps are part of her Maryland coastline.

DR. SAMUEL D. HARRIS NATIONAL MUSEUM OF DENTISTRY
410-706-0600
www.dentalmuseum.com
31 S. Green St.
Open: Wed.–Sat. 10–4, Sun. 1–4
Admission: Adults $7; youths, senior citizens, and students with I.D. $5; children 3–18 $3

One genuine set of George Washington's dentures is exhibited here, made from hippopotamus ivory and displayed in a case that includes copies of the other four extant sets of George's fake teeth. This is, after all, the national dental museum. It's also located here at the University of Maryland, the nation's first dental school, and it's quite interesting. A "Tooth Jukebox" plays old commercials that will be familiar to visitors of a certain age; an old-timey dental office reminds visitors that there's a lot less to fear from the dentist now than there once was; and Queen Victoria's Baltimore-trained dentist's instruments can be examined. This museum is good for all ages.

FLAG HOUSE & STAR-SPANGLED BANNER MUSEUM
410-837-1793
www.flaghouse.org
844 E. Pratt St.
Open: Tues.–Sat. 10–4
Admission: Adults $7, seniors and military $6, K–12 $5, under 6 free

In 1806, Mary Pickersgill moved to this circa-1793 house with her daughter and her mother, who was a flag-maker from her Revolutionary War days in Philadelphia. Mary famously made the enormous flag that flew over nearby Fort McHenry when the British shelled the city during the War of 1812. Francis Scott Key watched the battle from a British ship in the Patapsco, and wrote "The Star Spangled Banner" the next morning. Not only can you learn about life in the house during the Pickersgill era, but you can learn about the British blockade of the Chesapeake during the war. The museum also has a Discovery Gallery for kids.

FORT McHENRY NATIONAL MONUMENT & HISTORIC SHRINE
410-962-4290
www.nps.gov/fomc/index.htm
2400 E. Fort Dr.
Open: Daily 8 AM–5 PM; fort and visitor center close at 4:45. Extended summer hours mean the park is open until 8 PM, the star fort until 6:30 PM, and the visitor center until 5 PM
Admission: Adults 16 and older $7 to enter the fort; entrance to the park itself is free

It's easy to get choked up here, where a new nation gained new world standing after the brave soldiers of Fort McHenry stood up to British attack on Sept. 13–24, 1814. Attorney

Francis Scott Key was anchored out in the Patapsco River aboard a British vessel as he tried to pay ransom for a prominent Upper Marlboro doctor taken by the British. After a tense night of shelling, the flag literally was still there after the smoke cleared, flying over the unique five-pointed "star fort," and an inspired Key penned "The Star Spangled Banner." You'll learn the story of our national anthem here, where a new 17,000-square-foot visitor center is slated to open in late 2010 or early 2011. Don't miss the free movie that tells the story of that fateful battle. After you explore the exhibits, spend as much time as you can walking the old fort. The brick barrack depicts a soldier's life, the flag pole stands at the verifiable spot where THE star-spangled banner flew, and the cannons still point toward the river with its present-day maritime industry on the far shore. Fort McHenry was built in 1805 and remained an active military post

Fort McHenry on the Patapsco River, where the star-spangled banner flew over a young country.

into the 20th century. A mile-long walk circles the park along the water, and food and drinks are available for purchase. Check the Web site for special events. As for the new visitor center? Once open, three galleries will tell of the war in the Chesapeake, the development of the anthem and flag as major U.S. symbols, and you'll even learn about versions of the anthem ranging from a Civil War version to the electric version by Jimi Hendrix.

FREDERICK DOUGLASS ISAAC MYERS MARITIME PARK

410-685-0295, Ext. 252
www.douglassmyers.org
1417 Thames St.
Open: Tues.–Fri. 10–5
Admission: Adults $8, seniors $7.50, students 6–18 $7, children 5 and younger free; tours available

Maryland has produced numerous African American history-makers, Frederick Douglass prominent among them. The abolitionist and suffragist, born a slave on the Eastern Shore, spent a chapter of his life in Baltimore. His story is told here near the Fell's Point docks where he once worked. Also explored here is the life of freedman Isaac Myers, whose shipyard once stood nearby and was an early post-Civil War success among black-owned businesses. Douglass reportedly helped to back the venture. The Chesapeake Railway and Dry Dock Marine operated until 1884. The Sugar House (or Coffee House) is an old brick building that is part of this two-structure museum that survived the Great Baltimore Fire of 1904, some years after the round-edged building reportedly became a beacon for escaping slaves who could spot its distinctive shape. Those rounded edges allowed for easier cleanup and less spoilage of dry goods, too. This museum also succinctly shares the high and low points of life as a free black in Baltimore, where threats to their safety from attacks and the city's active slave market made for a dubious double standard. The park includes a boatworks—located in the Sugar House—where experts and youngsters in a learning program perform rehab work for the affiliated *USS Constellation*. The café serves organic food.

Historic Houses & Towers

Bromo Seltzer Arts Tower (443-874-3596; 21 S. Eutaw St.) Constructed in 1911 by Bromo Seltzer inventor Capt. Isaac Emerson to accompany his heartburn tonic plant, the replica of the Palazzo Vecchio in Florence, Italy, is a true city icon. Now artists' studios, the tower occasionally is open to the public.

Carroll Mansion (410-605-2964; www.carroll museums.org; 88 E. Lombard St.) Tour this old Carroll family manse, the winter home of Charles Carroll of Carrollton. Open Sat.–Sun. noon–4.

Mount Clare Museum House (410-837-3262; www.mountclare.org; 1500 Washington Blvd.) This is the Patapsco River-side plantation home of Charles Carroll the Barrister, a major player in Colonial Maryland, and the state's first museum house.

It's 228 steps to the top of Baltimore's Washington Monument at Mount Vernon Square.

Phoenix Shot Tower (410-605-2964; www.carrollmuseums.org; 801 E. Fayette St.) Built in 1828 as a lead shot manufacturing facility, this 234-foot structure was the nation's highest until the Washington Monument in Washington, D.C., came along.

Washington Monument And Museum (410-396-0929 info; 410-396-1049; www.baltimore museums.org/washington.html; 699 N. Charles St.) Climb the 228 steps up the nation's first monument to George Washington to be started (a rustic cousin in Western Maryland is the first one completed). It's a great view from the monument in this pretty square with its grand old mansions, all built on land once owned by Col. John Eager Howard. He was once one of Washington's officers.

Described as a "cathedral of books," the George Peabody Library's five-tier, cast iron stack room houses a 300,000-volume collection that reflects the scholarly interests of the 19th century. Norm Baker, photo courtesy The Sheridan Libraries, Johns Hopkins University

THE GEORGE PEABODY LIBRARY

410-659-8179
www.peabodyevents.library.jhu.edu
17 E. Mount Vernon Place
Open: Tues.–Fri. 9–5
Admission: Free

This is a glorious room, and one you should visit. Ironwork railings lining the stacks climb for five stories, and you can see them all from the center of the room. It's a breathtaking sight. So are the glimpses of history, like the small plaque on the wooden table holding a card catalog computer monitor that indicates John Dos Passos wrote here. The library, located just inside the front door of the Peabody Conservatory, has an exhibition space displaying manuscripts and book treasures. The institution was born when industrialist George Peabody gave the library to the city in 1857. At the time, it was one leg in the four-part Peabody Institute that established culture in Baltimore with a lecture series, an art collection, and a conservatory. The library is now part of the Sheridan Libraries Special Collections at Johns Hopkins University.

GEPPI'S ENTERTAINMENT MUSEUM

410-625-7060
www.geppismuseum.com
301 W. Camden St. (second floor of historic Camden Station)

Open: Tues.–Sun. 10–6

Admission: Adults $10; seniors 55 and older $9; students 5–18 $7; kids under 4 free

This is a clever pop culture museum full of artifacts from childhoods dating from the late 19th century to the present. The former includes Palmer Cox's Brownies, little creatures based on different jobs, like a policeman, or ethnicity, such as Irish, that appeared in games and books and were intended to teach kids good morals. The museum marches down the eras that followed, including those identified with Mickey Mouse, Howdy Doody, G. I. Joe and Fred Flintstone. Museum founder Stephen A. Geppi founded Diamond Comic Distributors, and his collection shown here includes the debuts of Superman in 1938 and Batman in 1939. You can also see some of the earliest exploits of Captain America and Wonder Woman. All in all, this is a fascinating look at pop culture and its vast influence on our society and, indeed, our own lives. It's located upstairs from the Sports Legends Museum at the old Camden Station.

HISTORIC SHIPS IN BALTIMORE including the USS *CONSTELLATION*

410-539-1797

www.constellation.org

Pier 1, 301 E. Pratt St.

Open: Hours change seasonally; check Web site for latest

Admission: Tickets are priced according to how many of the museum's ships you visit. For one ship, adults pay $10, seniors $8, kids 6–14 $5. For two ships, make that $13, $11, and $6, respectively. To visit four ships, adults pay $16, seniors $13, and kids 6–14 $7. Military personnel with I.D. and kids 5 and younger are free.

A retired submarine, the USS Torsk, *contrasts with Baltimore's city skyline.*

The last all-sail warship built by the U.S. Navy, the 1854 USS *Constellation,* is the marquee attraction in this collection of ships that gives visitors a strong taste of the city's maritime heritage. She arrived in Baltimore in 1955 after an illustrious career that, no kidding, saw action during the Civil War. The sloop-of-war remains the only active-duty ship from that war that's still afloat. Visitors can check out 22 cannons, 60 hammocks, the captain's state-room, the officers' quarters, and the hospital on her four decks. In addition to Civil War duty, she fought the African slave trade. Artifacts of life aboard ship can be examined, and specialized group tours include the "Powder Monkey" tour that tells of the boys who served as powder monkeys during the Civil War. The museum also operates tours of the nearby *Lightship 116 Chesapeake* and submarine USS *Torsk* at the Inner Harbor's Pier 2, the USCGC *Taney* on Pier 4, and the Seven Foot Knoll Lighthouse, which is at Pier 5. All are within a comfortable few blocks of one another, and all are well worth a stop.

JEWISH MUSEUM OF MARYLAND
410-732-6400
www.jewishmuseummd.org
15 Lloyd St.
Admission: Adults $8, students $4, children under 12 $3
Open: Sun., Tues.–Thurs. noon–4

German Jews arrived early in Baltimore, and the circa-1845 Lloyd Street Synagogue, the state's first synagogue, is now a cornerstone of the Jewish Museum of Maryland. Its stained glass Star of David window is thought to be the first architectural rendering of the star on a public building in America. (And it stayed put even during a Catholic congregation's own-ership of the building.) The recently renovated synagogue is one of two that bookend the modern museum building. Come learn about Baltimore's Jewish history, and find out about immigrant life in the process. "Voices of Lombard Street" shows tenement living in East Baltimore, which was a melting pot in the 19th century. Exhibits are set up so kids can touch some items, such as food from a dining table. Exhibits include both temporary and contemporary, such as the recent "Drawing on Tradition: The Book of Esther," which tells her tale via graphic comics. The 1876 B'nai Israel Synagogue, which still has a congrega-tion, rounds out the museum's buildings. Guided tours of the synagogues available at 1 and 2:30 PM on days the museum is open.

MARYLAND HISTORICAL SOCIETY
410-685-3750
www.mdhs.org
201 W. Monument St.
Open: Thurs. noon–8, Sat. 9–5
Admission: Museum, adults $4, seniors and students $3, children under 12 free, free for all on first Thurs. of each month; library, $6 includes museum admission

Founded in 1844, the MdHS is truly the state's attic. You just can't go wrong in a place that houses the Peale family's paintings and the original manuscript of "The Star Spangled Banner." The latter was, of course, composed by Maryland son Francis Scott Key after watching the British shell Fort McHenry. Permanent exhibits include "Nipper's Toyland," which tells of Maryland-made toys such as the Ouija Board (invented in Baltimore in 1925)

Johns Hopkins University Museums:

EVERGREEN MUSEUM & LIBRARY

410-516-0341

www.Museums.jhu.edu

4545 N. Charles St.

Open: Tues.–Fri. 11–4, Sat.–Sun. noon–4

Admission: Adults $6; seniors $5; students with ID, children 6 and older, and JHU alumni and retirees $3 ($1 discount if you buy tickets to both JHU museums)

Prepare to be dazzled. If the Dufy paintings, the Modigliani, the Tiffany glass lit up overhead and in display cases, or the theater designed by Ballet Russes' set designer Leon Bakst don't do it for you, perhaps the 23K gold-leaf toilet seat will. This 1857 Italianate mansion was owned by the Garretts of B&O Railroad founding fame (not to mention a namesake Maryland county), and no expense or whim appears to have been spared. Showstopping furniture includes a Thebes chair from, well, Thebes, as well as Dutch marquetry pieces, and apparently any other Arts and Crafts or heavy Renaissance piece that struck the fancy of the two generations who lived here. Toscanini was here. The house's excellent library (including pre-Gutenberg illuminations) includes collections that scholars use today, particularly the architecture books. Devotees of Baltimore silver will want to see the Kirk serving dishes, and anyone who's renovated a kitchen will marvel at the cabinets in the butler's pantry. Mere mortals did not live here, as the numerous collections attest. The grounds are lovely. Owned by Johns Hopkins University, the museum hosts lectures, music, and other events. Check the Web site for schedule. Museum shop; free parking.

HOMEWOOD MUSEUM

410-516-5589

www.museums.jhu.edu

3400 N. Charles St.

Open: Tues.–Fri. 11–4, Sat.–Sun. noon–4; tours every half-hour until 3:30 PM

Admission: Adults $6, seniors $5, students and children 6 and older $3 ($1 discount if you buy tickets to both JHU museums)

Visiting this five-part Palladian, Federalist home provides a nice opportunity to stroll the tree-lined Hopkins campus which, as our "Hopkins Man" tour guide pointed out, is technically located on the Homewood Farm. That's the spread where this building went up in 1802, a wedding gift from Charles Carroll, the signer of the Declaration of Independence, to his son, Charles Carroll of Homewood. The green and yellow paint on the walls is authentic to the period and reflects the family's affluence. Fan windows over doorways were set to filter light in the pre-gas days. Furnishings are of the time, although only one black chair is believed to (possibly) be authentic to the home. The book collection was the Carroll's second-most valuable possession behind the wine collection. The building itself encountered a number of uses—including a chapter as office to JHU President Milton Eisenhower, the U.S. president's brother—prior to being converted to a museum in the late 1980s. Indeed, it influenced the architecture of campus buildings. Visit the museum shop, located in the old brick kitchen. Parking is available on campus.

or "Served in Style: Silver Collections of the Maryland Historical Society." If you haven't
been polishing Grandmother's silver candlesticks lately, you may not be aware of local
manufacturers such as Kirk. A recent temporary exhibit looked at the notable Baltimore
Album Quilts, famous for their distinctive appliquéd blocks.

MARYLAND SCIENCE CENTER
410-685-5225
www.mdsci.org
601 Light St.
Open: Tues.–Fri. 10–5, Sat. 10–6, Sun. 11–5. Memorial Day–Labor Day, open Sun.–Wed.
until 6 PM and Thurs.–Sat. 10–8
Admission: Adults $14.95–24.95, children $10.95–18.95, seniors 60 and older
$13.95–23.95

Spend hours exploring the inner workings of the human body, the mysteries of dinosaurs,
and even stop off at "Newton's Alley" at the major galleries in this Inner Harbor landmark.
("Newton's Alley" is a hands-on activity space where visitors experiment with physics,
gravity, sight, sound, and light.) Opened in 1976 and expanded by $35 million and 40,000
square feet in 2002, the center is considered one the region's premier places to spend an
afternoon, and many hands-on activities will keep kids (and their parents) fascinated. In
addition to the main galleries, the center has an IMAX Theater, the Davis Planetarium, an
observatory, and even a Kids Room designed for youngsters from infancy through age 8.
A café's on-site. Prices are charged according to how many attractions you view.

MARYLAND ZOO IN BALTIMORE
410-366-5466
www.marylandzoo.org
Druid Hill Park
Open: Mar. 15 through Dec. 15, daily 10–4; closed Thanksgiving, Christmas Day and the
second Fri. in June
Admission: Adults $15, seniors 65 and older $12, children 2–11 $10

The 161-acre zoo opened in 1876, making it the nation's third oldest. Go on an African
Journey, where the lions, lemurs and giraffes roam; the Polar Bear Watch, replete with
genuine "Tundra Buggy"; and the acclaimed Children's Zoo, a walk-through, interactive
display of Maryland's habitats and species, like river otters and eastern box turtles. Recent
additions include prairie dogs and a baby dik-dik—although he'll probably be grown up by
the time you read this. Ride the train and check it out!

NATIONAL AQUARIUM IN BALTIMORE
410-576-3800
www.aqua.org
501 E. Pratt St.
Open: Hours change with the season; check Web site for latest
Admission: Adults $24.95–29.95; seniors, $23.95–28.95; children 3–11, $14.95–19.95

Get caught in the mist in the Tropical Rain Forest at the Inner Harbor's popular National
Aquarium. Or check out the Coral Reef, where a winding, downward path takes you up

The National Aquarium at Baltimore takes visitors from Maryland to the coral reefs.

close to a huge tank containing the reef, with its sharks, tortoises, and other colorful inhabitants. The Amazon River Forest re-creates a section of a blackwater Amazon River tributary, where visitors can spy schools of dazzling tropical fish, giant river turtles, and a giant anaconda. The Marine Mammal Pavilion features dolphins that perform several times daily. While the show costs a fee in addition to admission, there's a window alongside the tank where you can see the dolphins swim—and you should. "Animal Planet Australia: Wild Extremes" anchors a second building, replete with a 35-foot waterfall and a range of flora and fauna native to this land of extremes. Through 2011, jellyfish species star in an exhibit that reflects their differences—sometimes under a black light. And the 4-D IMAX theater is not to be missed (although it's perhaps a tad too realistic for very small children). The aquarium's biggest drawback is its crowds. Lines start forming early on the weekends, and the crush of people can make viewing the exhibits a bit uncomfortable. Try visiting after 3 PM, be in line when the aquarium opens, or buy tickets online in advance.

Tips for visiting the aquarium with kids

- The buildings are not designed to accommodate strollers, so they aren't permitted. You can check them, and the aquarium provides free backpacks.
- Before 10 AM and after 3 PM may be less crowded.
- The last ticket is usually sold at 4 PM, and the building closes 1½ hours later. Consider advance ticket sales, including online, in summer.

NATIONAL GREAT BLACKS IN WAX MUSEUM

410-563-3404
www.greatblacksinwax.org
1601–1603 E. North Ave.
Open: Mar.–June and Sept., Tues.–Sat. 9–6, Sun. noon–6; July–Aug. and Feb., Mon.–Sat.
9–6, Sun. noon–6; Oct. 15–Jan., Tues.–Sat. 9–5, Sun. noon–5
Admission: Adults $12; seniors, college students, and children 12–17 $11;
children 3–11 $10

Meet the movers and shakers of African American history from across the spectrum of
life's accomplishments and challenges, more than 100 figures rendered in wax. This is a
unique museum. Among the highlights: a full-model slave ship depicting the Atlantic slave
trade. You'll also see Marylanders such as Underground Railroad conductor Harriet
Tubman, musician Eubie Blake, or NBA star Reggie Lewis.

PORT DISCOVERY

410-727-8120
www.portdiscovery.org
35 Market Place
Open: Memorial Day–Labor Day, Mon.–Sat. 10–5, Sun. noon–5; rest of the year, Tues.–Fri.
9:30–4:30, Sat. 10–5, Sun. noon–5; closed Thanksgiving and Christmas
Admission: $12.95 for adults and children 2 and older

Ranked in the top five among the nation's children's museums, Port Discovery beckons
with a three-story, interactive wonderland for the 2-through-10 set. Kids can slide, jump,
and swing through an "urban treehouse"; travel back in time to the land of the pyramids to
search for a lost pharaoh's tomb; and learn to make healthy choices at the Royal Farms
Convenience Store and Fill'er Up Station.

REGINALD F. LEWIS MUSEUM OF MARYLAND AFRICAN AMERICAN
HISTORY & CULTURE

443-263-1800
www.AfricanAmericanCulture.org
830 E. Pratt St.
Open: Wed.–Sat. 10–5, Sun. noon–5, Thursdays until 8 PM June–Aug.
Admission: Adults $8, seniors and students $6, children 6 and younger free

This good-looking, modern museum is the East Coast's largest African American museum,
and offers a wide-ranging look at black life in Maryland and beyond. Temporary exhibitions that change twice annually fill the second-floor gallery space. You may see slices of
local life, such as the recent "East Side Stories: Portraits of a Baltimore Neighborhood," or
explore broader themes such as "381 Days: The Montgomery Bus Boycott Story." The permanent third-floor gallery focuses on three themes: African American labor (such as that
exerted by Chesapeake watermen); community and arts; and intellect. You can learn about
(and take a listen to) Maryland musicians including Cab Calloway, Ethel Ennis, Eubie
Blake, and Billie Holliday, or find out how local barbershops illuminate African American
life in the Old Line State. Additional facilities include a 200-seat theater, oral history lis-
tening and recording studio, gift shop, and café. Ongoing programming includes lectures,

poetry, workshops, and music such as the recent First Fridays series. Check the Web site for schedule.

SPORTS LEGENDS MUSEUM AT CAMDEN YARDS

410-727-1539
www.sportslegendsatcamdenyards.com
301 W. Camden St.
Open: Oct.–Mar., Tues.–Sun. 10–5; Apr.–Sept., 10–5 daily except Orioles game days, when the museum's open until 7 PM
Admission: Adults $8, seniors $6, children 3–12 $4

This is sports fan heaven, especially if you love Maryland sports and, particularly, those hailing from Baltimore. What other town would even think to acquire the bed Johnny Unitas was born in? This is only one of many interesting bits of sports history at this museum located on the first floor of the old Camden Station, the 1856 terminus of the B&O Railroad (which, as the country's first commercial railroad, gives it some history itself). Your author would be remiss if she failed to note that the championship ball from the 1958 NFL win by the Baltimore Colts is displayed here. This was a pre-Super Bowl win of epic proportions, and now the subject of lore in this old port city. The museum is located alongside Oriole Park at Camden Yards, and is affiliated with the Babe Ruth Birthplace— which you can reach by following the baseballs painted on the street.

THE WALTERS ART MUSEUM

410-547-9000
www.thewalters.org
600 N. Charles St.
Open: Wed.–Sun. 10–5; the Hackerman House is only open Sat.–Sun.
Admission: Free

Three buildings knit together by the art of architecture contain the Walters's eclectic collection of nearly 34,000 pieces that range from the treasures of Islam to suits of armor and mail. You can also see a mummy. This is one of only a few museums worldwide to present a history of art from the third millennium B.C. to the early 20th century. The Walters also

The treasures of The Walters Art Museum include its Chamber of Wonders. Courtesy The Walters Art Museum, Baltimore, photography by Patrick O'Brien

boasts a fine collection of ivories, jewelry, enamels, and bronzes, and a fine reserve of medieval and Renaissance illuminated manuscripts. Also featured: highly regarded collections of Egyptian, Greek and Roman, Byzantine, Ethiopian, Medieval, Renaissance, and Asian works. In addition to traveling exhibitions there are permanent ones, such as the intriguing "Palace of Wonders: The Galleries of Renaissance and Baroque Art." This was the museum's 100th birthday present to itself, and depicts the marvels that might have been displayed by a 17th-century nobleman from the southern Netherlands. By that, we mean stuffed curiosities of the highest order, like a trophy crocodile. The museum's Sculpture Court is a replica of the 17th-century Palazzo Balbi in Genoa. Free activities for kids take place on Sat. and Sun.

Performing Arts

AN DIE MUSIK
410-385-2638
www.andiemusiklive.com
409 N. Charles St.
Tickets: $10–20

This is an intimate, concert hall–style space that seats 75 audience members who've come to hear local to international classical or jazz musicians. Violinist Hilary Hahn has even taken the stage. The bar is set up with beer, wine, and soda for jazz shows; head downstairs for a wine reception after classical performances. Also a CD store.

BALTIMORE SYMPHONY ORCHESTRA at the
JOSEPH MEYERHOFF SYMPHONY HALL
Box office: 410-783-8000; 1-877-BSO-1444
www.bsomusic.org
1212 Cathedral St.

With a classical maestra and a pops conductor on deck, the Grammy Award-winning BSO might perform Tchaikovsky with guest pianist Lang Lang, or the best of Judy Garland with Broadway star Linda Eder. Or, perhaps you'll be lucky enough to catch soprano Kathleen Battle backed by the Morgan State University Choir. Founded in 1916, the BSO performs a diverse, 100-concert season at its notable Baltimore home. Known locally as "The Meyerhoff," the symphony hall opened in 1982 and is noted for its acoustics made possible by the building's unique architectural curves. There are no obstructed views in the 2,443-seat hall. Family concerts and an annual *Messiah* are among the schedule's offerings, which are posted on the BSO's Web site. A variety of ticket options are available. If you're willing to let the symphony choose for you, a $20 unreserved, best-available-seat option is available.

CENTERSTAGE
Box office: 410-332-0033
www.centerstage.org
700 N. Calvert St.

Baltimore's major professional theater company produces its own shows, which in recent years have included Tony Kushner's *Caroline, or Change,* Thornton Wilder's *The Matchmaker,* and August Wilson's *Ma Rainey's Black Bottom.* In addition to full-length productions, CENTERSTAGE performs short works, concert readings, and a cabaret series. Ticket discounts may be available; see the company's Web site for options including day-of-show discounts. Performances are held in the 541-seat Pearlstone Theater or the flexible space of The Head Theater.

EVERYMAN THEATRE

410-752-2208
www.everymantheatre.org
1727 N. Charles St.

This midsized professional company performs classic American theater such as Wilder's *Our Town,* but also takes chances such as a recent Baltimore premiere of playwright David Lindsay-Abaire's *Rabbit Hole.* The resident company currently performs in a 175-seat theater, but expects to move into new digs at 315 W. Fayette St.—across from the Hippodrome Theatre—in 2011. Tickets generally range between $18 and $40.

FRANCE-MERRICK PERFORMING ARTS CENTER
HIPPODROME THEATRE

410-837-7400; 410-547-seat for tickets
www.france-merrickpac.com
12 N. Eutaw St.

Broadway comes to Baltimore at the restored Hippodrome Theatre, a Thomas Lamb—designed movie and vaudeville palace first opened in 1914. Later came acts like Bob Hope, Benny Goodman, and a young Frank Sinatra performing with the Tommy Dorsey Orchestra. Today, catch *Dreamgirls, Stomp,* or *Phantom of the Opera* during their multiweek stops beneath the elegant proscenium. The box office is open Mon.–Fri. 11–3 and show days from 11 AM–curtain.

The lights go up on a beautiful stage at the Hippodrome Theatre.   Keith Weller, photo courtesy of the Hippodrome Theatre

LYRIC OPERA HOUSE

410-685-5086
www.lyricoperahouse.com
140 W. Mount Royal Ave.

Opera is imported to Charm City, and Broadway, comedy, and music play here, too. Check the Web site for the very latest. This is circa-1894 music house, former home to the late Baltimore Opera Company.

PEABODY CONSERVATORY OF MUSIC PERFORMANCES

Box office: 410-659-8100, Ext. 2
www.peabody.jhu.edu
1 E. Mount Vernon Pl.

If life were fair, we could all live on Mount Vernon Square and stroll over to this world-class conservatory to enjoy its numerous concerts, recitals, and perhaps even a dance performance, some of which are free. More than 80 major public concerts are performed each year, from the Peabody Symphony Orchestra to the Peabody Concert Orchestra to the Peabody Chamber Winds, the Peabody Jazz Orchestra, and the Peabody Opera Theatre. There's even a Peabody Latin Jazz Ensemble. That distinguished list doesn't include individual recitals or choral performances by the talented students and faculty. Performances take place in settings both grand and intimate, such as Friedberg Hall with a proscenium arch, or Griswold Hall, which overlooks Mount Vernon Square. Check www.peabody.jhu .edu/events for the calendar and ticket prices (which tend to be modest). Some free performances may require advance tickets.

SINGLE CARROT THEATRE

443-844-9253
www.singlecarrot.com
120 W. North Ave. (appended to Load of Fun)

A group of students from the University of Colorado at Boulder graduated and went looking for a place to call their theatrical home. They found it in Baltimore, and now stand at the vanguard of the local guerilla theater movement. The 10-member ensemble performs five shows per season, 16 performances each. Recent shows have included *Richard II*, an update on the story of Eurydice, and a percussion- and dance-inspired *Illuminoctem*. The company's name, by the way, comes from a Cezanne quote: "The day is coming when a single carrot, freshly observed, will set off a revolution."

Seasonal Events and Festivals

For the latest on Baltimore festivals, including parades celebrating Martin Luther King Jr. Day, St. Patrick's Day, and July Fourth, check www.baltimore.org. In addition, get information on the June through October "Showcase of Nations" ethnic festivals. It's a unique series of festivals that celebrate Baltimore's diverse cultures.

American Craft Council Baltimore Fine Art Show, the nation's largest juried indoor craft show, draws more than 700 artisans of every type to the Baltimore Convention Center in February. For info: www.craftcouncil.org/baltimore.

Annual Black Heritage Art Show in February draws visual an[d] ... around the country to the Baltimore Convention Center. Em[...] also held. For info: www.blackheritageartshow.com.

Maryland Film Festival, which runs early to mid-May at venues including the Charles Theater, is a showcase that brings filmm[...] info: www.md-filmfest.com.

Kinetic Sculpture Race, first Saturday in May. Artists and enginee[rs] and would-be engineers) called kinetinauts launch their kinetic [...ocky] Horror Picture Shoe") across the starting line for a zany tour through Baltimore via land and sea. Who will win the coveted Next-to-Last-Award? Fifi, the giant pink tulle poodle, represents the race's sponsor, the American Visionary Art Museum. For information, check www.avam.org/kinetic/index.html or www.kineticbaltimore.com, or call 410-244-1900.

Flowermart dates to 1911. Go down to Mount Vernon Square in the springtime and get your potted seedlings. Kids from the '50s recall a peppermint stick in a lemon, and the tradition lives on. Pet parade, booth decorating contest, food, and more. See www.flowermart.org.

Preakness Stakes. This day at Pimlico Race Course is a treasured Maryland tradition, as spectators cheer the second jewel in horse racing's famous Triple Crown on the third Sunday in May. The celebration also includes a prerace parade, a kid-friendly "Pee Wee Preakness" race, and a Preakness Balloon Festival and Crab Derby. "InfieldFEST" takes care of infield festivities. See www.preakness.com.

HonFest started as a backyard beauty contest behind Café Hon on 36th Street—aka "The Avenue"—in 1994 and has grown into a two-day neighborhood extravaganza drawing 50,000 folks that you can learn all about at www.honfest.net. Here's your chance to celebrate the era of the working class "hons" of Baltimore, the gals who made industrial Baltimore so Bawlamer. Among the events: the crowning of Baltimore's "Best Hon."

African American Heritage Festival is the largest African American heritage festival on the East Coast and features a range of activities such as well-known entertainers; ethnic food; interactive children's activities; an Arts, History and Education Village with exhibits from local institutions; and the Health Village, where private screenings are provided. The multiday festival takes place in July. For more: www.aahf.net.

Artscape is the nation's largest free arts festival and fans out for blocks. Live concerts on four stages; performing arts including opera, dance, fashion, classical music, film and theater; three street theaters; food and drink; children's entertainers; and more than 120 arts and craftspeople from around the country. The festival takes place in mid-July. For more: www.artscape.org.

Maryland State Fair is a late-summer celebration of the Old Line State's way of life at the state fairgrounds just north of Baltimore in Timonium. For more: www.marylandstatefair.com.

Baltimore Book Festival is a biggie, held in September and showcasing more than 150 authors. Readings, kids' activities, food, live music, food, and cooking demos by celebrity chefs. For more: www.baltimorebookfestival.com.

Annual Defenders Day Celebration. Head for Fort McHenry to commemorate Baltimore's successful September 1814 defense against British invaders in the Battle of Baltimore during the War of 1812. For more: www.nps.gov/fomc.

n Festival. This outdoor street festival in October is Fell's Point's major fest,
stages, music, dancing, arts and crafts, a flea market, and food. If you come by
, reserve dockage early. For more: www.preservationsociety.com.

vy Metal: Big Truck Day. Sponsored by the Baltimore Museum of Public Works, this
October event features the 20-truck Truck Trail Game that allows humans to map their
way across the truck trail, visiting a fire and rescue boat, a Bureau of Solid Waste Street
Sweeper, and a police helicopter. For information, call the museum at 410-396-5565.

Hampden's Miracle on 34th Street. Residents on two sides of one block slather their
homes with lights and holiday kitsch (Natty Boh beer can angels, Rudolphs) that's a
huge holiday season draw throughout the region. The lights are even strung across the
street between the houses. For info: www.christmasstreet.com.

Night of 100 ELVISes. Bite into a fried peanut butter and banana sandwich or catch a surf
guitar version of "Love Me Tender" at this early December extravaganza, which is far
more than guys in white jumpsuits. On three stages over two nights, bands of all types
interpret The King's music, although Elvis impersonators also perform. Food, drink,
and many Elvis-inspired sartorial elements. A shuttle operates from a downtown hotel.
For info: www.nightof100elvises.com.

A Monumental Occasion is the name of the celebration in which the Washington
Monument is lit up with holiday lights. In addition, there's entertainment, refreshments, and fireworks. For more: www.bop.org.

Baltimore Parade of Lighted Boats sees craft festooned for the holidays parade through
the Inner Harbor and Fell's Point. Check www.fpyc.net for info.

Tours

Tickets for many tours can be obtained at the Inner Harbor-based Baltimore Visitor
Center, 401 Light St., Baltimore, MD 21202. Call 1-877-BALTIMORE, email vc@baltimore
.org. Open daily 9–5 in Mar. and Oct.; daily 9–6 Apr.–Sept.; Wed.–Sun. 10–4 Nov.–Feb.
For the latest: www.baltimore.org.

Baltimore Ghost Tours (410-522-7400; www.baltimoreghosttours.com) This popular
touring outfit can take you through Fell's Point, which has as salty a history as you're
likely to find, as well as literary Mount Vernon. A PubWalk in Fell's Point is also available, as are group tours. Check the Web site for dates and prices.

Baltimore Sightseeing Tours (410-254-TOUR; www.baltimoresightseeingtours.com) This
90-minute tour is a good get-acquainted option, pointing out city highlights from the
Little Italy neighborhood to fabled Fort McHenry. Pick up tickets at the city Visitor
Center on Light Street or call 1-877-BALTIMORE. Tickets are $22.95 for 13 and older,
$14.95 for ages 6–12.

Clipper City Brewing Company (410-247-7822; www.ccbeer.com; 4615 Hollins Ferry Rd.,
Suite B) Taste-test one of 18 beers on three Saturdays per month during a 45-minute
brewery tour. For $5, pick up a souvenir pint glass and tokens to trade for samples, and
sip your way from the tasting room to the brewing and packaging operations. The brewery also sponsors four festivals per year with bands and area restaurants, such as
"Pyrates, Pigs and Pints," a bacon-themed gathering held in Sept.

Heritage Walk (443-984-3089; 401 Light St.) Tour more than 20 city landmarks from
Little Italy to the USS Constellation at 10 AM daily, May 1–Nov. 1.

Oriole Park at Camden Yards Tour (410-547-6234; www.orioles.mlb.com; Oriole Park at
Camden Yards) Did you know that 52 home runs landed in the street outside Oriole

Named for the Chesapeake's alleged sea monster, the Chessie paddleboats are an Inner Harbor tradition.

Park by the end of the '09 season? Go see where, as well as the bullpen, the dugout, and the control room behind the JumboTron. You might even get to see the nearby Camden Station that Abe Lincoln traveled through to Gettysburg. Ninety-minute tours are offered daily Mar.–Nov. and group tours can be arranged year-round. Adults $9, seniors and kids 14 and younger $7, kids 3 and younger free.

Preservation Society of Fell's Point and Federal Hill tours (410-675-6750; www .preservationsociety.com; 1732 Thames St.) See the city's oldest surviving urban residence, learn about the salty neighborhoods, take an immigration tour, and don't forget to find out about the Fell's Point ghosts. Tours are held daily or weekly; the annual Historic Harbor House Tour takes place on Mother's Day.

Star-Spangled Trails (www.starspangledtrails.org) As the anniversary of the War of 1812 draws nigh (even though the fabled Fort McHenry battle occurred in 1814), take time to see the pivotal role Baltimore and the Chesapeake played in this war that established a new country's strength. The Baltimore City Heritage Area Association's Web site tells you about these self-guided trails, and you can pick up a brochure at the Visitor Center on Light Street.

RECREATION

Boating

Chessie Paddleboats (410-385-2733; Baltimore Waterfront Promenade in front of Harborplace Pratt Street Pavilion; 301 E. Pratt St.) Head out on an iconic paddleboat in the form of "Chessie," the Chesapeake seamonster. A total of 45 paddleboats (not all are Chessies) are available. Chessies are $17 per hour, regular boats are $10, minors must be accompanied by an adult, and boats hold up to four people. Open Mar.–Oct.

Downtown Sailing Center (410-727-0722; www.downtownsailing.org; 1425 Key Hwy.)
Take a private lesson for $50 for one hour ($30 per person per hour after that) and tool
around the Inner Harbor. The nonprofit community outreach sailing center is located
in the same parking lot as the Baltimore Museum of Industry.

Getaway Sailing School (410-342-3110; www.getawaysailing.com; 2700 Lighthouse Point
#905) Kick off a nice weekend with Fri. evening social sails. Gather at 5:15 PM to rig
boats and sail until sunset for $35—which means nearly three hours on the water in
high summer. Learn a bit about sailing or kick back with your cooler's contents.
Getaway also offers sailing instruction, charters, and rentals.

Spirit Cruises (1-866-312-2469; www.spiritcruises.com/bc/bridge.jsp) Take a lunch or
dinner cruise, or get a 75-minute narrated cruise of the Inner Harbor. Check the Web
site for details, prices, and tickets.

Watermark Cruises (www.watermarkcruises.com) This Annapolis-based touring company also operates in Baltimore's Inner Harbor, and takes visitors out for a 45-minute
cruise aboard *Annapolitan II*. View the city's landmarks from the water. Adults $15, chil-
dren 11 and younger $6. Cruises operate 11–4 during the week and 11–7 on weekends
and holidays May–Oct. Departs from near the Visitor Center.

Cycling

Light Street Cycles (410-685-2234; www.lightstcycles.com; 1124 Light St.) Rent from this
Federal Hill cycling shop's changing inventory. One-day rates are $25 for hybrids, $40
for mountain bikes and road bikes.

Monumental Bike Tours (monumentalbiketours.com) Join local cycling enthusiast Ron
Brown for one of his occasional Sunday morning tours around the city or, perhaps, out
to an organic farm. The bakery tour is most popular (held Saturday morning), and Ron
points out the passing history. Even though you're riding in the city, Ron tries to schedule the trips for light traffic times.

Fitness

Canton Club Health & Fitness (410-276-5544; www.cantonclub24.com; 2780D
Lighthouse Point East) Classes are included in the $10 daily pass price to work out at
this fitness club with panoramic views of the water and the city. Open 4 AM–11 PM.

Charm City Yoga (1-800-336-YOGA; www.charmcityyoga.com) Stay balanced for $15 per
drop-in class at one of three centers within the city limits. Guests are asked to arrive
15 minutes early to tour the facility, register, and inform the teacher about past/present
injuries. Forgot your mat? The studios rent them for $2 per class. Other props are free.
All studios except Federal Hill have showers (towel rental, $2). Check the Web site for
schedules. Locations: Midtown, 107 E. Preston St.; Fell's Point, 901 Fell St.; Federal
Hill, 37 E. Cross St.

Maryland Athletic Club (410-625-5000; www.macwellness.com; 655 President St.)
Great-looking full-service club in the Harbor East district offers short-term memberships for visitors who'll be in town several days, or a $20 per-visit guest fee.

Golf

Clifton Park Golf Course (410-243-3500; www.bmgcgolf.com; 2701 Saint Lo Dr.) The
circa-1915 Clifton Park is an 18-hole public course operated by the Baltimore Municipal
Golf Corporation. It claims some of the area's best putting.

Mountain Branch Golf Course (1-877-588-1492; www.mountainbranch.com; 1827 Mountain Rd., Joppa) Located north of the city in Harford County, this 18-hole course offers public play as well as memberships. Instruction, restaurant.

Natural Areas, Gardens and Parks

Cylburn Arboretum (410-367-2217; www.cylburnassociation.org; 4915 Greenspring Ave.) This 207-acre property recently has undergone a yearlong face-lift, so come see the public gardens full of roses, dahlias, and a storied Japanese maple collection dating to the turn of the last century. There are 3½ miles of trails and a green 10,000-square-foot Visitor's Orientation and Education Center that will have maps of what's in bloom and will become the headquarters for the Federated Garden Clubs of Maryland and the Horticultural Society of Maryland. Also on the grounds is Cylburn's Mansion, an 1860s Renaissance Revival home.

Druid Hill Park (410-396-6106; 2700 Madison Ave.) This 746-acre city park dates to 1860 and was developed in grand style. Druid Hill Lake, constructed starting in 1863, has fitness equipment installed around it and is a good place to jog. The park also has 17 tennis courts, athletic fields, picnic pavilions, and a good playground. This is home to the Maryland Zoo and also its plant conservatory, replete with historic palm house and orchid room.

Gunpowder Falls State Park (410-592-2897; www.dnr.state.md.us/publiclands/central /gunpowder.html; 2813 Jerusalem Rd.) Fly-fishers are well aware of Gunpowder Falls, nearly 18,000 acres north of the city in Kingsville. Numerous trails (100 miles) as well as two marinas, paddling, playgrounds, swimming, boat launch, and boat rentals are among the facilities and activities you'll find. Get out of the city and go play in nature for a day.

Jones Falls Trail (410-261-3515; www.jonesfalls.org/trail.htm) Hike and bike along this trail that runs alongside the Jones Falls. The trail currently extends from Druid Hill Park to Penn Station and will someday extend 12 miles from the Inner Harbor to Lake Roland. The easiest way for visitors to find out about the trail is to check out the map on the Web site.

Leakin Park/Gwynns Falls (www.gwynnsfallstrail.org; 4921 Windsor Mill Rd.) At 952 acres, Leakin Park is one of the largest undisturbed wooded parks inside a city, and it has a greenway running through it. It also has pavilions, ball fields, and a nature center. The 15-mile Gwynns Falls Trail starts at the park and stretches through west and south-west Baltimore, following the falls to the Middle Branch of the Patapsco, then to the Inner Harbor. It's very urban from the Inner Harbor for several miles.

Patapsco Valley State Park (410-461-5005; www.drn.state.md.us/publiclands/central /patapscovalley.html; 8020 Baltimore National Pike) Located west and south of the city in Ellicott City, this park covers a 32-mile area along the river that once hosted settlements. Hike, mountain bike, fish, paddle, and canoe the area, which covers 14,000 acres. In the park is the Thomas Viaduct, a modern wonder when built in 1835 that remains in use and is the world's longest multiple-arched stone railroad bridge.

Patterson Park (410-276-3676; www.pattersonpark.com; 27 S. Patterson Ave.) The park has a lake, athletic fields, two playgrounds, a famous structure called The Pagoda designed by Benjamin Latrobe, and one of the city's two ice rinks. You can download a running map at the Web site.

Spectator Sports

The **Baltimore Orioles** (baltimore.orioles.mlb.com; 333 W. Camden St.) play at Oriole
Park at Camden Yards in a retro-modern stadium that caused a sensation when it
opened in 1992. The O's opening day sells out, big crowds show up for Yankees and Red
Sox matchups, but with 81 games per season you're likely to get tickets. Tours of the
park take you from the dugout to the press box, and fans will be intrigued to know that
Baltimorean and one-time Oriole Babe Ruth's father operated a bar between what is
now second and third base. The family lived above the bar, which is why his mother
went over to her parents' house two blocks away to give birth (visit the Babe Ruth
Birthplace; details under "Major Attractions, Museums, and Historic Sites"). The stadium stands on a former railroad yard, and the East Coast's longest building, the
1898–1905 B&O Warehouse, stands beyond right field.

Baltimore Ravens (410-261-RAVE; www.baltimoreravens.com; 1101 Russell St.)
Baltimore's NFL football team plays at M&T Bank Stadium, just a stone's throw from
Oriole Park at Camden Yards. They arrived in 1996, eons after the much-booed departure of the city's beloved Colts, named themselves for Baltimore resident Edgar Allan
Poe's famous "The Raven," and have proceeded to make black and purple the most popular colors in town—at least during the fall and winter football season. Regular season
tickets tend to be sold out, but if you want to catch the fever, head over to the stadium
anyway. An outdoor Fan Festival with big-screen TV, kids' activities and food (even
crabcake sandwiches) takes place outside the stadium. You can't miss it. Stadium tours
also are available for those who want to get down to that field. And, if you want to try for
tickets, buying through the Ravens' site seems to be the most secure way to go.

*The old brick B&O Warehouse—the East Coast's longest building—stands at the back of the beautiful
retro-modern Oriole Park at Camden Yards.*   Todd Olszewski, Baltimore Orioles

Pimlico Race Course (410-542-9400; www.pimlico.com; 5201 Park Heights Ave.) Come bet on the ponies April through early June, when racing's typically held Thurs.–Sun. And make time for the Preakness Stakes, the third jewel in horse racing's Triple Crown and the biggest single-day sporting event in Maryland. It's held the third Saturday of May.

SHOPPING

We're betting that you'll be rummaging through Baltimore's shops by neighborhood rather than dashing from neighborhood to neighborhood in search of the perfect belt. We could be wrong, but in case we're not we've arranged this section by neighborhood. A tip for those who want to spend a day shopping: From the Inner Harbor, it's an easy walk to either Federal Hill or Harbor East.

INNER HARBOR

Harborplace and The Gallery (410-332-4191; www.harborplace.com; 200 E. Pratt St.) One of the Inner Harbor pioneers, Harborplace, with its Pratt and Light Street pavilions, is a restaurant/entertainment/shopping complex. Look for a variety of shops ranging from bebe, Banana Republic, and Urban Outfitters to local stores like Eastern Shore Outfitters. This is also the place to grab an easy lunch or snack at the numerous café/food court-style offerings, from Auntie Anne's pretzels and Lee's Ice Cream to Johnny Rockets and M&S Grill, McCormick & Schmick's family-oriented offering. Open Mon.–Sat. 10–9, Sun. 11–7.

Power Plant (410-752-5444; 601 E. Pratt St.) Check out Barnes & Noble, work out at Gold's Gym, or take your sports enthusiast to the ESPN Zone for a meal.

FEDERAL HILL

Artesanos Don Bosco (410-563-4577; www.artsanosdonbosco.com; 828 S. Charles St.) Young men in the Peruvian countryside go to school for several years to learn to create these breathtaking pieces of wood furniture with hand-chiseled details or bent rockers. The program, founded by a Salesian priest from Italy named Father Ugo De Censi, keeps the young men employed. The prices are amazingly good for such handcrafted work.

Babe (a BOUTIQUE) (410-244-5144; www.babeaboutique.com; 910 S. Charles St.) Look for premium denim jeans in the fall and a thumbs-up selection of summer dresses in prices ranging from $40–190, and never astronomical. Also look for Betty, the black Yorkie poo.

The Book Escape (410-576-8885; www.thebookescape.com; 805 Light St.) More than 60,000 books spill from packed shelves here in Federal Hill, where you can find new and regional books amid the old books.

Ladybugs & Fireflies, (410-244-0472; www.ladybugsandfireflies.com; 1049 S. Charles St.) Operated by neighborhood mom Andrea Sommer, this little shop stocks a wide range of toys and kid stuff—from locally made burp rags to educational toys—and none of it costs a fortune. Ergo, other neighborhood moms stop by on their strolls and sometimes pick up a goodie, and you should too.

Lucky Lucy's Canine Café (410-837-2121; www.luckylucyscaninecafe.com; 1126 S. Charles St.) Fido's food is here, but so are his peanut butter cookies, fancy collars, and other doggie (and some kitty) doodads.

Antique Row, North Howard Street

The nation's oldest Antique Row has dwindled from its heyday, but Baltimore's North Howard Street still offers much to admire. Located at the edge of the Mount Vernon district, Antique Row traces its lineage to 1840, when major local furniture-makers like William Camp and John Needles refurbished and resold furniture here. Back about 1910, 35 dealers worked in the city, and 24 operated from Howard Street. Now there are far fewer, but they're still fun to shop. Most are closed on Tuesday, and you can find out more about them at www.shopantiquerow.com. Highlights include **Dubey's Art & Antiques** (410-383-2881; 807 N. Howard St.), which specializes in Chinese export pottery and pre-1840 American furniture. Philip Dubey's company also owns the next-door **Antique Row Stalls** (410-728-6363; 809 N. Howard St.), where more than 20 dealers—vetted by Dubey himself—sell a range of select antiques. The delightful **Drusilla's Books** (410-225-0277; www.drusillasbooks.com; 817 N. Howard) not only remains open even on Tuesday, but offers the kind of browsing book-lovers dream about. Children's books are among the specialties and first-edition Beatrix Potter tomes are just the start. **Richard Sindler Fine Art of Antiques** (410-225-2727; 833 Howard St.) is the place to go for antiquities and bronzes, but with 2,000 objects there's plenty of eclecticism to be found. And look for your mission and Arts and Crafts finds as well as mahogany pieces and chandeliers at **Weber's Mission Gallery** and **Weber's Antiques** (410-383-0811; 867 N. Howard). In a nutshell: mostly furniture and lighting.

Drusilla's Books has been part of Baltimore's fabled Antique Row for more than 25 years.

Whimsey/Reason (410-234-0204; www.whimsyreason.com; 1033 S. Charles St.) Ladies' clothes downstairs at Whimsey (fun stuff, like a good salmon clutch) and gentlemen upstairs at Reason, where blue and white regimental ties were spotted not far from a hip black leather trilby.

FELL'S POINT

aMuse (410-342-5000; www .amusetoys.com; 1623 Thames St.) A very well-considered store full of thoughtful toys and other stuff for children, such as Putamayo kids' CDs. Look for purposeful items with clean design. Haba is among the European brands offered.

The Antique Man (410-732-0932; www.theantiqueman.com; 1806 Fleet St.) An attraction as much as an antique shop, The Antique Man harbors the giant ball of string from Baltimore's famous Haussner's Restaurant ($8,900 at auction after the restaurant closed in 1999), a two-headed mummy, a shrunken head, and a stuffed four-legged chick. Check out these carny-style oddities

Unique handmade furniture for sale in a Federal Hill shop.

while browsing through the antiques at this genuinely lovely shop, which is open 1–5 on weekends or by appointment.

Brassworks Company (1-877-97-BRASS; www.baltimorebrassworks.com; 1641 Thames St.) Brass and copper restoration services as well as a wide array of brass home and maritime items, from door knockers to weather instruments. Gifts, too.

Killer Trash (410-675-2449; 602 S. Broadway) Retro and vintage dresses and clothing from the '20s to the '80s. Good for Halloween parties.

Poppy and Stella (410-522-1960; www.poppyandstella.com; 728 S. Broadway) "Every-thing but the clothes" reads this accessory boutique's tagline, and folks around Baltimore know they're especially talking about cute shoes.

Ten Thousand Villages (410-342-5568; baltimore.tenthousandvillages.com; 1621 Thames St.) Part of a chain, which we generally don't cover, but who can resist plugging a fair-trade emporium filled with goods from Third World artisans?

Scent-sational

Theresa Cangialosi mixed her first elixir of organic essential oils 20 years ago, and she's watched small miracles occur ever since. Scars may heal and nausea may abate from the potions she mixes with the oils, which are stronger than herbs because they're distilled from the plants themselves. For a more lighthearted experience, belly up to her aromatherapy bar at **SoBotanical** in Federal Hill (410-234-0333; www.sobotanical.com; 1130 S. Charles St.) and enjoy the process of creating your own scent. Custom perfumes typically cost $50–150 per blend. You can even get a natural "copy" (more or less) of Chanel No. 5 if you want. Or, tap into the beautiful handmade soaps, milk baths, skin creams, and facial care products here, where you can, as the shop says, "stop and smell life." SoBo Essentials is Cangialosi's signature line, also available online.

Special soaps are available at SoBotanicals in Federal Hill.

HARBOR EAST

Amaryllis Jewelry (410-576-7622; www.amaryllisjewelry.com; 612 S. Exeter St.) Formerly located in the Gallery at Harborplace, Amaryllis has moved over to the other side of the harbor with its stock of artist-made jewelry. You can pay more than $50–400, but that's the typical price range. In business since 1985.

Benjamin Lovell Shoes (410-244-5359; www.blshoes.com; 618 S. Exeter St.) This Philly-based company has brought its first Maryland store to Harbor East, where shoppers with tired feet will find fine, comfortable brands like Naot, Thierry Rabotin, Clarks, and Mephisto.

MOUNT VERNON AND POINTS NORTH

A People United (410-727-4451; apeopleunited.com; 516 N. Charles St.) A photo of smiling kids in the front of this shop shows where some of the profits go: toward scholarships for Nepalese children. Clothes designed here are made in Nepal or India at a fair wage. They're great, too, as is the basement full of Indian furniture.

A. T. Jones & Sons (410-728-7087; 708 Howard St.) You'll feel like you've stepped back a century—at least—if you visit this costume shop, which has been here since 1950 but in business since 1868. Although owner George Goebel primarily oversees a costume-making operation for productions around the country, customers can make an appointment. Next door is a theatrical makeup store, which is open during general business hours, aka Mon.–Fri. 9–5.

The Dollhouse Boutique (443-874-7900; 525 N. Charles St.) This is a showcase for local designers, including owner Natalie Graham's Ragdolls line. One-of-a-kind pieces may come with lots of exposed zippers, or ruffled crinolines may include leather camo, denim, and silk all in the same garment. Image consulting available; open daily.

Gian Marco Menswear (410-347-7974; www.gianmarcomeanswear.com; 517 N. Charles St.) What could be classier than fine Italian linen in summer? This is a terrific shop full of Italian menswear near Mount Vernon Square. We're still gloating over our $50 sale purchase of a gorgeous white linen shirt that regularly cost $175.

Salamander Used Books (410-290-2323; 519 N. Charles St.) When he's not out in the field, photographer Michael Cantor oversees his well-considered selection of books on art, politics, philosophy, and more. This shop recently moved from Hampden to Mount Vernon.

The Store Ltd. (410-323-2350; 24 Village Square in The Village of Cross Keys) Streamlined Nordic flair highlights many of the home items in this shop, also the home of Baltimore modernist jeweler Betty Cooke's work. At it for decades, Cooke's architectural work has been recognized twice with Beers Diamond awards, and she had a retrospective at MICA. Ebony, wood, and beach pebbles may be inset as easily as a diamond.

Woman's Industrial Exchange (410-685-4833; www.womansindustrialexchange.org; 333 N. Charles St.) Welcoming baby to Baltimore with a handmade item from The Exchange is a time-honored local tradition. Back in 1889, the exchange purchased this circa-1850 building for its shop and tea room. This was part of a national movement that began prior to the Civil War to help women discreetly earn an income. The tea room is gone, but in its place is Plates, operated by the nonprofit Kitchens for Change, and another restaurant, Sofi's Crepes. The exchange is still helping people support themselves with dignity (and is one of the few places you can buy a genuine sock monkey).

HAMPDEN

Atomic Books (410-662-4444; www.atomicbooks.com; 3620 Falls Rd.) A Baltimore mainstay for nearly two decades, Atomic Books has a tagline: "Literary finds for mutated minds." Alternative and underground lit, self-published zines, underground comics, art books, graphic novels, fiction tending toward the Beats, true crime, and monster lit.

Avenue Antiques (410-467-0329; www.AvenueAntiques.com; 901 W. 36th St.) This place is big and packed: painting, clothing, and furniture—including a lovely baby grand, last time we were in.

breathe books (410-235-READ; www.breathebooks.com; 810 W. 36th St.) A wide variety of New Age books, gifts, and CDs, as well as an endless array of events, workshops, and other opportunities to b-r-e-a-t-h-e. If you're around on Dec. 25, stop by for "Jewish Christmas," replete with Chinese food and movies.

Doubledutch Boutique (410-554-0055; www.doubledutchboutique.com; 3616 Falls Rd.) A local media "best of" favorite, this boutique offers a wide variety of independent designer clothing and accessories.

Form (410-889-3116; www.formtheboutique.com; 1115 W. 36th St.) Graphic designer Aimee Bracken brings her eye to fashion. Sophisticated lines such as Catherine Malandrino and Diane Von Furstenberg—as well as lesser-known but no less interesting designers—draw Baltimore's creative professionals who might otherwise look to New York. Check out Bracken's jewelry.

Hometown Girl (410-622-GIFT; 1001 W. 36th St.) Baltimore-oriented mugs, books, photos, cards, and gifts on "The Avenue." Get them here!

In Watermelon Sugar (410-662-9090; 3555 Chestnut Ave.) This lovely-smelling boutique, one of current-day Hampden's pioneers, offers cool home items such as small Haitian bird sculptures painted aqua and frames made from reclaimed boat wood in the Caribbean.

K Staton Boutique (410-258-5166; www.kstatonboutique.com) Tucked behind Lynn's Gifts, this shop gives women who aren't stick thin stylish opportunities to show off their curves.

Ma Petite Shoe (410-235-3442; www.mapetiteshoe.com, 832 W. 36th St.) Specializing in chocolate and shoes—is that inspired, or what? We couldn't help but covet the cowboy boots with handmade Guatemalan cloth insets. Stop in for First Friday chocolate samplings.

Minás (410-732-4258; www.minasgalleryandboutique.com; 815 W. 36th St.) This is an inspired boutique, with everything from retro CDs ("The Best of Johnny Mercer"), jack-in-the-boxes for kids, and hipster T-shirts. The upstairs gallery shows local artists monthly.

Mud and Metal (410-467-8698; www.mudandmetal.com; 1121 W. 36th St.) Open since 1995, this shop offers handmade functional home accessories ranging from switch plates to a garden turtle created from a helmet painted red. The media of choice tend to be—you guessed it—mud or metal.

Red Tree (410-366-3456; www.redtreebaltimore.com; 921 W. 36th St.) A terrific home store where the metal pendant you're eyeing may be as fabulous as the perfect upholstered chair for your living room. Two floors include distressed furniture from Indonesia.

Shine Collective (410-366-6100; www.shopshinecollective.com; 1007A W. 36th St.) Open since 2002 and a reliable stop for a selection of clothing and accessories, including some vintage jewelry. This is a very fun place to check out.

Wild Yam Pottery (410-662-1123; www.wildyampottery.com; 863 W. 36th St.) Four potters keep their working studio busy here on "The Avenue." The wheel is on the first floor, so you may catch them at work while browsing the shop's wares, which can be surprisingly affordable.

Galleries

Art Gallery of Fells Point (410-327-1271; www.fellspointgallery.org; 1716 Thames St.) This is a cool little co-op located right across the cobblestone street from the harbor. It's just the kind of place where you might find a gem of a painting for a price you can afford (assuming you aren't a zillionaire). Fifty artists; most are from Baltimore.

Canton Gallery (410-342-6176; www.cantongallery.com; 2935 O'Donnell St., Canton) Located on Canton's magnetic square, this gallery offers contemporary artwork, custom framing and—if you're lucky—perhaps a square of Baltimore's famous screen painter's work, a dying art. Closed Sun., open Mon. by appointment.

C. Grimaldis Gallery (410-539-2229; www.cgrimaldisgallery.com; 523 N. Charles St.) The city's oldest contemporary gallery is situated only a block from The Walters Art Museum. High-profile and big-name artists are among those represented, including Baltimore master Grace Hartigan and Elaine deKooning.

Robert McClintock Studio Gallery (410-814-2800; 1809 Thames St.) The painter's regional work is on exhibit.

Steven Scott Gallery (410-902-9300; www.stevenscottgallery.com; 808 S. Ann St., Fell's Point) In 2009 longtime local art dealer Scott moved his gallery into Fell's Point, where contemporary works by 20 painters and artists from both regional and more distant points show their work. Exhibitions change about every two months; the space is open and, yes, contemporary.

4

Annapolis & Points South

A Capital Destination

On a clear day in early September, station yourself near City Dock and look out to the harbor, where white sails catch the wind on a gentle breeze. Or go out to Sandy Point State Park to watch sailboats, powerboats, or huge container ships pushing through the Bay's main channel. For all the historic charm of this 300-year-old capital city, its downtown clustered with good restaurants, fun shops, and, no doubt, the house you wish you owned, it's these sparkly days that make folks fall in love with Annapolis.

Two circles located up a hill from the harbor help to define the Historic District of Maryland's state capital. St. Anne's Episcopal Church stands in the midst of Church Circle, which is nearly adjacent to State Circle. There, the first colonial capitol building was constructed in 1699, soon after royal governor Francis Nicholson moved the seat of government north from St. Marys City on the Potomac to this town along the Severn River. He built the Baroque-style streets that colonists would still recognize.

From these early beginnings spring tales of patriots passing through Annapolis, where Maryland's four signers of the Declaration of Independence owned homes that still stand. For a brief time—November 1783 to August 1784—Annapolis served as the new nation's capital city. In the current statehouse, George Washington resigned his commission from the Continental Army and patriots signed the Treaty of Paris, which ended the Revolutionary War.

Evidence of the city's colonial and post-colonial Golden Age remains. St. John's College, the intellectual home of the "Great Books" program, descends from King William's School, founded in 1696. This makes St. John's the nation's third-oldest school, after the College of William and Mary and Harvard University. Benjamin Franklin sent cousin Jonas Green from Philadelphia to become the city's printer in 1738. His home still stands, and is considered one of the two oldest houses in this city of old houses, where Colonial Georgian, Federal, and even Greek Revival structures line the streets. By 1845, the U.S. Naval Academy was established, renewed by stunning Beaux Arts buildings after the Civil War, during which the academy and St. John's College were taken over as hospitals.

Across the Spa Creek Bridge from the Historic District sits the city's maritime district called Eastport, giving working credence to the city's claim of being "America's Sailing

OPPOSITE: *The Maryland statehouse dome is one of Annapolis's best-known landmarks.*

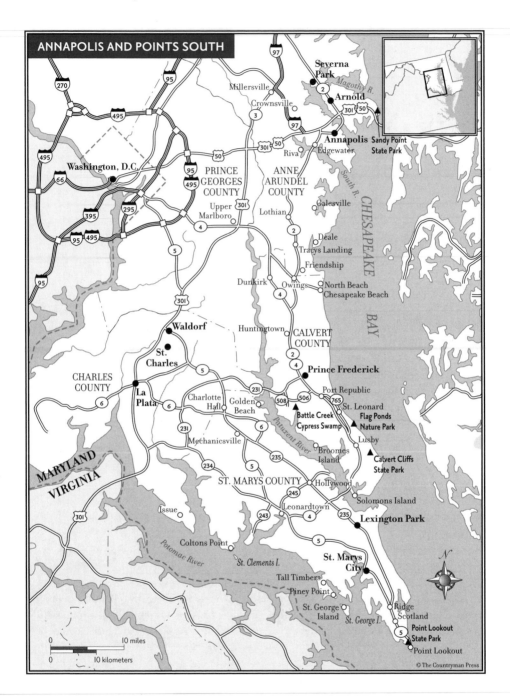

ANNAPOLIS AND POINTS SOUTH

Capital." The city annexed this former workingman's neighborhood decades back, and from yacht brokers and other boating industry businesses has sprung a fine group of restaurants—perhaps the city's reliably best. Take a tour of Eastport or the Historic District to learn more about the city which has grown outward from its colonial Severn River nexus.

Parking in the Historic District can be difficult. (These are, after all, narrow Baroque-style streets created back when horses and human feet were the primary modes of transportation). Feed the parking meters, don't exceed the nonresident time limit in the neighborhoods, and check http://annapolis.gov/info.asp?page=8305 to see all of your parking garage (six) and parking lot (five) options in the Historic District.

It's easy to get into the district without taking your car. After turning onto Rowe Boulevard from US 50, turn right into Navy-Marine Corps Memorial Stadium. Satellite parking is available for $5. It's a pleasant mile-long walk into the Historic District. Or, Annapolis Transit runs free shuttles downtown every five to 10 minutes during rush hour, midweek, and on the half-hour every day. The "State" shuttle operates continuously from 6:30 AM–8 PM during the week, and until 10:30 PM during the legislative session Jan. through mid-Apr. The "Navy Blue" shuttle operates on the hour and half hour, 9–6 Mon. through Fri. and 10–6 weekends. For information, call 410-263-7964 or visit www .annapolis.gov/transport.

If you board and exit within the Historic District's "free fare zone," you can catch the city bus for free. Boundaries: Compromise Street on the Annapolis side of the Eastport Bridge to Westgate Circle, out West Street.

If you want to travel by boat, the City Dock–based Jiffy Water Taxi (410-263-0033; www.watermarkcruises.com) crosses Spa (or Back) Creek. The former is the small creek separating the Historic District and Eastport. Water taxis operate from March through late October from 9:30 AM–11 PM weekdays. On weekends, it's 9 AM to 1 AM. Visitors to Annapolis also should check Chapter 6, "Middle Eastern Shore," for ideas for nearby explorations, including Kent Island. Although it's officially part of the Eastern Shore, the island has essentially become a suburb of Annapolis. It's just a quick hop across the Chesapeake Bay Bridge. For additional info on Annapolis, visit www.visitannapolis.org, or stop by the Visitor Center at 26 West St. (within the first block after Church Circle) or the seasonal information booth at City Dock.

LODGING

Annapolis offers an excellent range of B&Bs located within the walkable historic areas (or even slightly outside), as well as many chain hotels. B&B guests can take advantage of a discount deal for parking in city garages that tops out at half-price. You can't come and go without repaying, but it's easier to walk the Historic District and Eastport anyway. Although many good B&Bs are not members of Annapolis Bed and Breakfast Association (annapolisbandb.com), those that are make referrals to member establishments.

Lodging prices may vary according to day of the week and time of the year. In general, prices peak during high season and are higher on weekends than during the week. (In Annapolis, high season includes October weekends when the city hosts popular boat shows and U.S. Naval Academy home football games.) But lodgings often offer specials on their Web sites, and price flexibility may be available during slow times. It's worth asking.

Lodgings with more than two rooms are taxed at 13 percent, which we do not include in our lodging rate range. Other considerations when booking a room: Check to see whether lodgings have two-night minimums or cancellation policies. Their Web sites may provide information about these and changing specials or packages. Our rates cover the range you're likely to encounter.

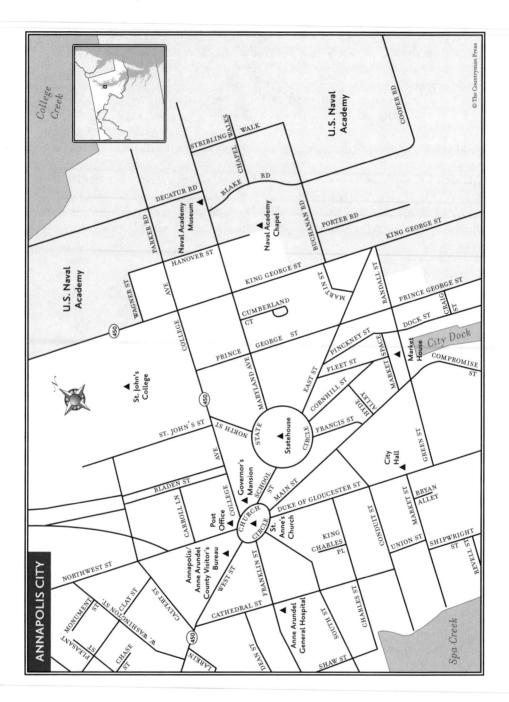

ANNAPOLIS CITY

College Creek

© The Countryman Press

U.S. Naval Academy

U.S. Naval Academy

STRIBLING WALK
CHAPEL WALK
DECATUR RD
BLAKE RD
Naval Academy Museum
Naval Academy Chapel
BUCHANAN RD
PORTER RD
KING GEORGE ST
PARKER RD
HANOVER ST
WAGNER ST
COLLEGE AVE
KING GEORGE ST
MARTIN ST
RANDALL ST
PRINCE GEORGE ST
CRAIG ST
CUMBERLAND CT
PRINCE GEORGE ST
DOCK ST
PINCKNEY ST
Market House
City Dock
COMPROMISE ST
St. John's College
MARYLAND AVE
EAST ST
FLEET ST
CORNHILL ST
MARKET SPACE
ST. JOHN'S ST
NORTH ST
STATE CIRCLE
Statehouse
FRANCIS ST
HYDE ALLEY
GREEN ST
City Hall
BLADEN ST
Governor's Mansion
SCHOOL ST
MAIN ST
City Hall
CARROLL LN
COLLEGE AVE
CHURCH CIRCLE
Post Office
St. Anne's Church
DUKE OF GLOUCESTER ST
MARKET ST
BRYAN ALLEY
CONDUIT ST
UNION ST
SHIPWRIGHT ST
NORTHWEST ST
Annapolis/ Anne Arundel County Visitor's Bureau
WEST ST
FRANKLIN ST
KING CHARLES PL
CHARLES ST
REVELL ST
MONUMENT ST
PLEASANT ST
W. WASHINGTON ST.
CLAY ST
CALVERT ST
CATHEDRAL ST
Anne Arundel General Hospital
SOUTH ST
Spa Creek
CHASE ST
LARKIN
DEAN ST
SHAW ST

Lodging rates are as follows:

Inexpensive: Up to $75
Moderate: $75–$150
Expensive: $150–225
Very Expensive: $225 and up

1908 WILLIAM PAGE INN

Innkeeper: Robert Zuchelli
410-626-1506
www.williampageinn.com
8 Martin St., Annapolis, MD 21401
Price: Expensive to Very Expensive
Handicapped Access: No
Restrictions: No children under 12

Well located on a quiet street just around the corner from the Historic District's hustle and bustle, this 1908 cedar-shingled house offers five rooms and an innkeeper with oodles of experience. The rooms are neutral, straightforward, and anticipate the guest's needs. They include the Marilyn Suite on the top floor, with a big sitting area and television. On the second floor, two rooms share a bath (named for *Charlotte's Web's* Wilbur and Charlotte). Two others have their own baths, including one with a whirlpool. For a treat, ask for the private Fern Room, which opens onto the wraparound porch. Zuchelli, long active in the local tourism industry, opened the inn in the mid-1980s and knows how to run a classy operation, providing luxury, privacy, and in-the-know recommendations without a fuss. Full breakfast. Off-street parking.

ANNAPOLIS INN

Innkeepers: Joe Lespier and Alex De Vivo
410-295-5200
www.annapolisinn.com
144 Prince George St., Annapolis, MD 21401
Price: Very Expensive
Handicapped Access: No
Restrictions: No guests under 18

It's hard to overstate the upscale level of Cupid-and-Psyche romance at this renovated 1770s home. Gilded rosette moldings crown the downstairs salons, and etched-glass doors separate bedroom from sitting room in an upstairs suite. King-sized beds are dressed up in the finest cotton linens; tapestries hang from walls; and French and English reproductions or antiques furnish the house. The three accommodations include the Murray Suite, which has a heated marble bathroom floor, and the Rutland Suite on the third floor, with its bath of three kinds of marble, a remote-controlled whirlpool tub, and easy access to the roof deck. This onetime home to a doctor to Thomas Jefferson fills a top-tier niche in this luxe city's diverse selection of B&Bs and lodgings. Plan to tuck in to a pampered good time. Breakfast starts at 8 AM.

ANNAPOLIS MARRIOTT WATERFRONT

410-268-7555; reservations 1-800-336-0072
www.annapolismarriott.com
80 Compromise St., Annapolis, MD 21401
Price: Very Expensive
Handicapped Access: Yes
Parking: Valet, $19

This hotel offers an Annapolis commodity: the Historic District's only waterfront rooms, with views over mast-filled Spa Creek and out to the Severn River. The 150 rooms—which were renovated in 2008—include water and city views, and come with all the amenities. Room rates are based on whether there's a water view. Suites, king-sized beds, a small on-site fitness room, and concierge service are available. Visitors also will find a fine location for a cold one at the hotel's Pusser's Landing, a pub right on the waterside edge of Ego Alley, so named for the parade of boaters showing off their crafts.

Waterside B&Bs offer tranquil spots to relax along the Bay.

THE BARN ON HOWARD'S COVE

Innkeepers: Graham and Mary Gutsche
410-266-6840
www.barnonhowardscovebandb.com
500 Wilson Rd., Annapolis, MD 21401
Price: Moderate to Expensive
Handicapped Access: No
Special Features: Pets allowed with prior discussion

Ordinarily, we skip lodgings that offer only two rooms—even if one is a suite. However, The Barn on Howard's Cove is a great find for many reasons. You can bring the kids (even infants!), park easily just 2 miles outside the Historic District, and, best of all, put a canoe or kayak in a Chesapeake tributary on the property. Your hosts have renovated this waterside 1850s barn to ensure a lovely year-round view of Howard's Cove, and the rooms, with quilts and floral wallpaper, are very comfortable. There's one large room, one suite with sitting room and deck, gardens and, perhaps best all, kayaks so you can head out into the cove and creek. An excellent choice for families. Full breakfast is served in the solarium in winter.

BUTTERFLY FIELDS B&B

Innkeepers: Lynda and Dan Ells
410-271-1433
www.butterfly-fields.com
320 Frank Moreland Rd., Lothian, MD 20711
Price: Expensive
Handicapped Access: Partial; call for details

Once their eight kids grew up, Lynda and Dan Ells found themselves with a big, empty, passive solar house tucked amid six-plus acres south of Annapolis. What to do?

They opened a B&B. The result is three spacious and comfortable guest rooms with queen-sized beds and adjoining, recently constructed baths in a true getaway environment. Maybe you'll hear sheep and horses in the pasture. A deck rings the house and gardens spill forth. The guests' orderly public areas include a big, round table to play backgammon or Chinese checkers on; a business desk with fax, computer, and printer; and another big, round table with a big lazy Susan for their big farm breakfasts. Guests also can plug into the home's wireless Internet. But forget about TV. Take a walk around the property's mown path instead. If the raspberries aren't in season, maybe the apples are. Guests are asked to leave their shoes at the front door when they enter the house.

FLAG HOUSE INN

Owners: Charlotte and Bill Schmickle
410-280-2721 or 1-800-437-4825
www.flaghouseinn.com
26 Randall St., Annapolis, MD 21401
Price: Expensive to Very Expensive
Handicapped Access: No
Restrictions: No children under 13

Located across the street from the U.S. Naval Academy's main gate, the Flag House offers a central location and sociable innkeepers who have sent a son through the academy. The Schmickles have redone this five-guest-room gem, where guests will find the rooms quite comfortable, with king-sized beds, televisions, and European-style split bathrooms in some. Ask for the room wallpapered in gorgeous purple toile or the room done up in red toile. A two-room suite can accommodate up to three people. A friendly industriousness seems to be at work here; once when we pulled out of the driveway, Bill was adjusting the clever irrigation system he'd created for the plants that hang from the wide front porch, where the state or national flag of each guest in residence flies. Full breakfast is served in the dining room downstairs. Off-street parking.

HARBOR VIEW INN

Innkeepers: Andrea and Chuck Manfredonia
410-626-9802
www.harborviewinnofannapolis.com
1 St. Mary's St., Annapolis, MD 21401
Price: Expensive to Very Expensive
Handicapped Access: No
Restrictions: No children under 14

A wide-open contemporary home hides behind the gray siding and bright green shutters of this downtown B&B. The architectural detail here is terrific. An oculus—an oval opening—cuts through the ceiling of the tiled foyer leading to a second-floor guest room, allowing even more light to filter downstairs. Three rooms are available, two with patios. A room highlighted in cobalt blue is a favorite, with a built-in wainscoted "headboard" and a deck looking toward the water. The gardens out back change with the seasons, and you can hide from life in a hammock tucked into a far, shaded corner. A change from much of what you'll find in the Historic District, the Harbor View harbors nary an Oriental rug. Full breakfast and off-street parking.

HISTORIC INNS OF ANNAPOLIS

Owner: Remington Hotels
410-263-2641 or 1-800-847-8882
www.historicinnsofannapolis.com
58 State Circle, Annapolis, MD 21401
Price: Moderate to Expensive
Handicapped Access: Yes
Special Features: Valet parking; includes the Maryland Inn, Governor Calvert House, and Robert Johnson House

With three inns set on two circles, the Historic Inns has a unique setup. No matter where you're staying, you'll check in at the

Historic Maryland Inn dates to colonial times and still draws visitors today. www.VisitAnnapolis.org

Governor Calvert House on State Circle, directly across from the Maryland statehouse. Management does its best to efficiently shepherd guests through the process, down to a valet in a minivan to take you to your room. Guests may request a favorite inn, although it's possible the inns may not be able to comply. In all, 124 rooms are available, and each is different. The most modern of the three is the Governor Calvert House, part of which dates to the 18th century. During a 1983 renovation/construction project, archaeologists discovered a 1730 hypocaust, a central heating system originally engineered by the Romans that is now preserved in a Plexiglas-covered floor. The 1773 Robert Johnson House, also set on State Circle across from the statehouse, is probably the quietest inn. The Maryland Inn, part of which dates to the Revolutionary era, started life as an inn early on and remained so until a post–World War I hiatus as an office/apartment complex. The Maryland Inn is a sentimental favorite among many Annapolitans and visitors, with its intimate brick-walled Treaty of Paris restaurant and Drummer's Lot tavern. Renovations in 2006 have given the inns' rooms a fresh look, including renovated baths.

THE INN AT 30 MARYLAND AVENUE

Innkeeper: Robert Dunn
410-263-9797
www.30maryland.com
30 Maryland Ave., Annapolis, MD 21401
Price: Expensive to Very Expensive
Handicapped Access: No
Special features: Prefers children 10 and older

Location, location, location—this is a good one for exploring the Historic District. Maryland Avenue radiates from State Circle, but it's set apart from the nightlife scene elsewhere in the district and there-

fore quieter. Chef Robert Dunn, formerly of Baltimore, discovered this Victorian with wife Michelle and converted the house to a comfortable five-bedroom guest house in 2004. His background means guests choose breakfast from a daily menu, sit at individual tables, enjoy continental breakfasts if they're early birds up before the organic menu breakfast is served, and generally find an operation well run by a pro. "You can see me as much or as little as you want to," says Robert. The inn is stately and unfussy, with decor running to Oriental-style rugs, high ceilings, door transoms, and chandeliers. It also provides guests with a bistro for coffee, snacks, ice buckets, and such. Lodgings include two suites with daybeds, and options for king- and queen-sized beds—all in rooms with recently installed bathrooms.

INN AT HORN POINT

Innkeepers: Corey and Carol Bonney
410-268-1126
www.innathornpoint.com
100 Chesapeake Ave., Annapolis, MD 21403
Price: Expensive to Very Expensive
Handicapped Access: Full ADA room
Special features: Prefers children 13 and older

Between its red-hot location in laid-back Eastport and its bubble gum pink parlor, the Inn at Horn Point offers something a bit different. This was a little workingman's house and tiny grocery with no plumbing before the Bonneys started swinging the crowbar. Now, five stylish guest rooms (all named for the Trumpy yachts once built nearby) include four upstairs that range from small to quite large. One even has a small balcony, and you may find exposed brick in your room along with the inn's amenities such as TV and Wi-Fi. (Rooms are wired with HD cable, and TVs are available upon request.) Downstairs is a spacious room that is fully handicapped accessible. Guests can look forward to an all-natural or organic, heavy continental breakfast with three kinds of juices. Corey, a former manager at two of the city's major hotels, knows his way around the city and the hospitality business. Check or cash payment is preferred to credit cards.

LOEWS ANNAPOLIS HOTEL
410-263-7777 or 1-800-526-2593
www.loewshotels.com
126 West St., Annapolis, MD 21401
Price: Expensive to Very Expensive
Handicapped Access: Yes
Special Features: Pet rooms available
Parking: Valet, $22 per night

Considered one of the city's finest hotels, Loews provides all of the amenities in a brick courtyard-style hotel located just blocks from the Historic District. The hotel has undergone renovations in recent years. In 2007, 216 guest rooms and suites were renovated so visitors will find a regatta theme of blues and reds with amenities ranging from hypoallergenic pillows and pillowtop mattresses cloaked in 300-thread-count cotton sheets to high-speed Internet. The hotel restaurant, called Breeze, serves regional cuisine. In addition, the fitness room has undergone an expansion and the Commodore Lounge was scheduled for an update as of deadline. Visitors can also book appointments with the on-site Annapolis Day Spa. Hotel services include child care, and kids under 18 stay in their parents' room for free. Lovely meeting and party spaces include those in the complex's brick Powerhouse Conference Center. Ideal for visitors seeking well-located lodgings with all the amenities.

O'CALLAGHAN HOTEL ANNAPOLIS
410-263-7700 or 1-866-782-9624
www.ocallaghanhotels-us.com/annapolis

174 West St., Annapolis, MD 21401
Price: Moderate to Expensive
Handicapped Access: Yes

The Annapolis outpost of this small Irish hotel chain is well located within walking distance of the city's hubbub. The dark-paneled lobby has a traditional feel to it, and the 120 guest rooms (including two suites) are furnished in typical hotel style. Eight have balconies along West Street. The pubby and clubby John Barry Restaurant and Bar sits off the lobby. The hotel has a free fitness room, too. Look for room service, high-speed Internet, and a shuttle that operates in the Historic District. Internet access is free.

SCHOONER *WOODWIND*
410-263-7837 or 410-263-1981
www.schoonerwoodwind.com
P.O. Box 3254, Annapolis, MD 21403
Price: Very Expensive
Handicapped Access: No
Restrictions: No children under 16; available Sat. only, early May through late Sept.

Sleep aboard the schooner *Woodwind* and see what it's like to wake up with the sun peeking through the porthole. The boat stays docked at its berth alongside the Annapolis Waterfront Marriott through the night, and a captain stays on board. Guests will share heads (aka bathrooms), and those in the two forward-most cabins can even open the hatch. Double berths; breakfast on deck. A two-hour sunset sail goes along with your stay.

TWO-O-ONE BED & BREAKFAST
Innkeepers: Graham Gardner and Robert A. Bryant
410-268-8053
www.201bb.com
201 Prince George St., Annapolis, MD 21401
Price: Expensive to Very Expensive
Handicapped Access: No

Restrictions: No children
Parking: On-site parking available

This elegant Georgian home, furnished with English and American period antiques, also comes with a surprisingly large yard for the Historic District. Your hosts have beautifully landscaped this back area, creating garden rooms large enough to offer a measure of privacy to their guests. Expect this same sensibility to extend to the guest rooms, which are spacious and comfortable and come with enough towels to last the weekend. The four suites include two with whirlpool tubs. All have refrigerators. Fun antique finds include a Beau Brummel, which is, essentially, a vanity for gentlemen of a certain era; this one came from Pickfair. This well-located B&B offers a full breakfast. A dog lives here as well.

WESTIN ANNAPOLIS

410-972-4300
www.westin.com/annapolis
100 Westgate Circle, Annapolis, MD 21401
Price: Expensive to Very Expensive

Handicapped Access: Yes
Special Features: Restaurants in the complex include Morton's steakhouse, Fadó Irish Pub, and Carpaccio Tuscan Kitchen and Wine Bar

The Westin Annapolis anchors Park Place, a trendy $250 million mixed-use development on West Street outside the Historic District. The upscale chain hotel, with its pretty, modern lounge, offers 225 sleek rooms that have either king or double beds. The beds come dressed up with Westin's signature 10-layer "heavenly bed," triple-sheeted with a thick duvet. Dual shower-heads and big tubs come in the bathrooms. The hotel also has a pool, a nice fitness center, a shuttle that goes downtown, and top-notch conference facilities with flexible technology. Starbucks operates mornings in the lobby, a lounge opens up as the day goes on, and Morton's steakhouse is the signature restaurant. The hotel is also affiliated with a spa across the plaza. Wireless is free in common areas and $9.95 per 24 hours in guest rooms.

RESTAURANTS

From the colonial taverns ringing City Dock to more adventurous Pacific Rim cuisine in well-appointed eateries, diversity reigns among Annapolis restaurants. Steak lovers hungering for a New York strip in a clubby atmosphere won't be disappointed, hearty Irish fare is easily available, and good sushi is at the ready. While crabcakes aplenty, crab imperial, and crab dip (best served on French bread) show up on local menus, those with a hankerin' for hard-shell crabs spilled across brown-paper-lined tables will find their best bets are just outside of town.

Price ranges based upon dinner entrée price range—which includes sandwiches or salads if appropriate—are as follows:

Inexpensive	Up to $10
Moderate	$10–20
Expensive	$20–30
Very Expensive	$30 and above

The following abbreviations are used to denote meals served:
B = Breakfast; L = Lunch; D = Dinner; SB = Sunday Brunch

ANNAPOLIS
49 WEST COFFEEHOUSE, WINEBAR & GALLERY
410-626-9796
www.49westcoffeehouse.com
49 West St.
Open: Daily
Price: Inexpensive to Moderate
Cuisine: French-influenced; light American
Serving: B, L, D
Reservations: For six or more or for musical performances
Handicapped Access: Yes

This is a favorite luncheon spot, where side dishes run to celery root salad instead of coleslaw. Great salads and sandwiches that don't require a post-meal cholesterol check are the luncheon fare; dinner sees the sandwiches (by request) and the salads, but also moves on to entrées like mojito-glazed chicken or "The Devil You Know," chipotle shrimp over pasta. The drinks are just as cheerfully named, what with a "Mist Opportunity" (Stoli with Irish Mist) in the chorus line of martini options. If spirits, wines, and beers aren't your thing, lucky you: The coffees are good and the sodas includes a pear-apple option. Monthly artist exhibits are hung and nightly music of all sorts (including much jazz) can be heard in this cozy bistro, which stays open late. All in all, 49 West comes off like a Florentine café-bar. It has outdoor seating, and sells wine retail.

BOATYARD BAR AND GRILL
410-216-6206
www.boatyardbarandgrill.com
400 Fourth St., Eastport
Open: Daily
Price: Inexpensive to Moderate
Cuisine: Seafood, casual American
Serving: B, L, D, weekend brunch (as well as the day after major holidays)
Reservations: No

Handicapped Access: Yes

A casual, yachty restaurant with an Annapo-Caribbean vibe, the Boatyard is a good place to get great raw oysters or discover the pleasures of smoked crabcakes without spending a fortune. For that, give it a big thumbs-up. It's also the heart of the extended Eastport neighborhood whose denizens include boaters, fishers, and all-around Bay lovers from near and afar. For that, you gotta check it out. Say you want to meet some sailors. Settle in at the bar and note that your drink is, literally, pint-sized. If it's a summer Wednesday night, the just-completed sailboat races will be replaying on the flat screen overhead. Say you want to find out what's biting. Head for the back room, where trophy fish caught by local anglers line the walls along with black and white photos of the Chesapeake and Cuba. This dining room is also quieter than the front, and it's convenient to the raw bar. The light-filled main dining room with its sail art–lined walls bustles with locals, visitors, and families. The menu is extensive, with everything from creative seafood to a daily chili, fancy pizza and panini, cool salads and sandwiches, and steaks. Somehow the Boatyard manages to be a lot of things to a lot of people, and it works. One percent of sales go to Bay-related conservation groups, and the restaurant's Web site details their four annual fundraisers, including the big rockfish opening day tournament on the third Saturday in April. Check it out.

CAFÉ NORMANDIE
410-263-3382
185 Main St.
Open: Daily
Price: Inexpensive to Expensive
Cuisine: French
Serving: B (Sat.–Sun.), L, D
Reservations: Recommended on weekends, during special events, and for the Jan.

Blue crabs, a Chesapeake staple. www.VisitAnnapolis.org

through mid-Apr. legislative session
Handicapped Access: Yes

Long before the word "Provence" started appearing in many best-seller titles, Café Normandie was delivering country-French style on upper Main Street. Wood-backed booths downstairs look to a fireplace, and a row of tables upstairs peers out over the street. The menu caters to different tastes, offering higher-priced entrées (filet mignon, veal) for serious appetites and a good selection of moderately priced meals for those who want less. Portions are plentiful. The Caesar salad here is one of the city's best, and the crepe selection is legendary, created in regular or buckwheat batter and served with a good-sized side salad. A 23-year specialty predates the popularity of dietary antioxidants: salmon with blueberries in a light burre blanc sauce. You can, of course, order the burre blanc on the side. An early dining menu is available from 5–6:30 PM.

CANTLER'S RIVERSIDE INN

410-757-1311
www.cantlers.com
458 Forest Beach Rd.
Open: Daily
Price: Moderate to Expensive
Cuisine: Seafood
Serving: L, D
Reservations: Weekend reservations accepted Nov.–Mar. 31
Handicapped Access: Limited; not to bathrooms.

Cantler's, reached via a twisting ride out of town, is the area's premier crab-picking spot. Located on scenic Mill Creek, it rakes in awards year after year. Crabs come every which way hot from the pot and laden with spices, as a soft-shell sandwich, mixed with seasoning and filler in a crabcake (sandwich or platter), or stuffed in your favorite fish. Despite scanty harvests and escalating prices (up to $50 for a dozen large in 2009), visitors from all over the world hunker down with mallet and knife at these famed paper-covered tables, both indoors and out. Which explains the backup waiting to get into the parking lot. You'd think this place was a religious shrine. For many, it is. And, for the few who don't eat crabmeat, there's fresh fish, fried shrimp and chicken, light fare, even hamburgers and hot dogs. Also note that updated culinary trends are not ignored: butternut squash and crab soup appears on a fall menu, while a crab caprese shows up in summer. If you have kids in tow, walk down to the dock to see the peeler crabs and turtles. To avoid the crowd, come on a weekday or at off hours on weekends. For directions, check the Web site.

CARROL'S CREEK WATERFRONT RESTAURANT

410-263-8102
www.carrolscreek.com
410 Severn Ave., Annapolis City Marina, Eastport
Open: Daily
Price: Moderate to Expensive
Cuisine: Contemporary American, seafood
Serving: L, D, SB
Reservations: Recommended Fri. night, Sat., and Sun.; Wed. in summer, especially for larger parties
Handicapped Access: Yes
Special Features: Waterside deck and view

Here's your blue-ribbon view of Spa Creek, from the comfort of a contemporary dining room. We recommend you reserve a table, then sit back and enjoy the treats this kitchen has been creating for years. While the main menu changes about every six months, the cream of crab soup remains legendary and the rockfish, crabcakes, and scallop dishes are recommended. Fancy sandwiches join entrées on the lunch menu, while dinner features contemporary American takes on seafood, beef, and poultry. The lengthy wine list offers something

for every budget, and the outdoor deck offers primo sunset watching. There's even parking for those who aren't strolling to Eastport across the Spa Creek Bridge from the Historic District. (You also can take the water taxi.)

CHICK & RUTH'S DELLY

410-269-6737
www.chickandruths.com
165 Main St.
Open: Daily
Price: Inexpensive to moderate
Cuisine: American, kosher
Serving: B, L, D
Reservations: No
Handicapped Access: Limited

Check out the Formica decor and dip into the kosher pickles at this centrally located Annapolis institution where state politicians, locals, and out-of-towners all come to sample the diner food, reasonable prices, and ambience that hasn't changed a whit since Chick & Ruth's opened in 1965. "Comfort" is the operative word here, as in *comfort* food served in *comfort*able surroundings, replete with celebrity photos blanketing the walls. Fall into the delly for the breakfast platters, served all day, with delly fries. The peppery, onion-laden potatoes (actually home fries) are among the best we've ever tasted. Come here also for the homemade soups, hamburgers, and generous sandwiches named for state lawmakers. When in doubt, go for the No. 1, the Main Street—corned beef, coleslaw, and Russian dressing on rye. Either that, or the tuna on wheat toast. The soda fountain drinks are treats, the waitstaff is pleasant, and kid-sized portions with appropriately adjusted prices are available for rugrats. You should be able to eat for less than $10. Expect a line on weekends, especially for breakfast, when locals join owner Ted Levitt in the Pledge of Allegiance at 9:30 AM; weekdays, make that 8:30.

DAVIS' PUB

410-268-7432
www.davispub.com
400 Chester Ave., Eastport
Open: Daily
Price: Inexpensive to Moderate
Cuisine: Seafood, pub fare
Serving: L, D
Reservations: No
Handicapped Access: Yes

Davis' Pub is a classic, anchoring the working Eastport maritime scene with blackboard specials and plenty of beer. What's not to like? When last we lunched here, three of our party of four—the regulars—pounced on the turkey Reuben special. The fourth ordered her usual, the crabcake sandwich, and the server even subbed green beans for the usual fries or onion rings. Davis's burgers, sandwiches, combos, and platters taste mighty fine and don't cost a fortune. Picnic tables along the sidewalk offer a sunny-day spot alongside the legendary pub's green awning.

GALWAY BAY IRISH RESTAURANT AND PUB

410-263-8333
www.galway2006.com
61–63 Maryland Ave.
Open: Daily
Price: Moderate to Expensive
Cuisine: Authentic Irish
Serving: L, D, SB
Reservations: Recommended on weekends
Handicapped Access: Yes

This is no prefabricated, faux-Irish eatery concocted to capitalize on Celtic chic. Owners Michael and Fintan Galway are émigrés from Erin's lovely shore, and their restaurant has garnered both regional awards and a devoted following. Its popularity can be attributed to both atmosphere and cuisine. The feeling is inviting and evocative: exposed brick walls, a high ceiling, vintage Irish art, and soft strains of Irish music. The menu sports a handsome array of Hibernian fare, both no-frills and fancy. Starters include Oysters O'Reilly (a flavorful way to enjoy a regional favorite), or cockles and mussels. The potato and leek soup is therapeutic, and the soda bread is homemade from coarse whole-meal flour imported from Ireland. Entrées feature Irish favorites—corned beef and cabbage, shepherd's pie, Irish stew, fish and chips—that are prepared here in expert fashion. Also here: higher-end entrées (pork, steak) and Miss Peggy's crabcakes, a menu holdover from the long-gone decades when this was the fabled Little Campus Inn. Tuesday night is trivia quiz night for charity, and a crab-ball eating contest takes place in September.

HARRY BROWNE'S RESTAURANT

410-263-4332
www.harrybrownes.com
66 State Circle
Open: Daily
Price: Moderate to Very Expensive
Cuisine: New American, regional
Serving: L, D, SB
Reservations: Recommended
Handicapped Access: Yes
Special Features: View of statehouse; outdoor dining (at sidewalk tables)

For a fine-dining experience, it doesn't get much better than Harry Browne's. The ambience is intimate and formal, the service attentive and unobtrusive. When making a reservation, request a window table for a picture-postcard view of the Maryland statehouse. Bathed in moonlight, it's something to write home about. The clubby Grill Room is open for wine pairing dinners. The main menu changes seasonally, and the kitchen seldom, if ever, takes shortcuts. We like to start with the Oysters Annapolitan (topped with—what else?—crabmeat), Caesar or mixed green salad, or cream of crab soup. Fresh fish and seafood shine here, as do the beef, duck, and lamb. The rack of lamb is another winner. Entrées are between $25 and $32. If you have room, try the rum raisin bread pudding, bananas Foster, crème brûlée, or homemade ice cream. Lunch is memorable, with a host of reasonably priced soups, salads, sandwiches, and hot entrées. Sunday, line up for the brunch buffet ($17) or choose from the à la carte menu ($9–14). Both include a glass of champagne or wine or a mimosa. The outside patio offers pleasant alfresco dining along State Circle.

JOSS CAFÉ & SUSHI BAR

410-263-4688
www.josscafe-sushibar.com
195 Main St.
Open: Daily
Price: Moderate

Cuisine: Japanese
Serving: L, D
Reservations: No
Handicapped Access: Yes

This is the granddaddy of Annapolis sushi restaurants and never disappoints. Two intimate dining rooms add to a social atmosphere that starts upon entering, when the sushi chefs behind the bar shout out "Irasshai," Japanese for "welcome." Tuck into a corner table and start with a terrific sesame-tinged seaweed salad. Follow with any type of sushi you can imagine; our household favorite is the rainbow roll with salmon, tuna, and flounder topping avocado, all rolled in roe. Lovers of Japanese food also will find tempuras, teriyakis, sukiyakis, and other traditional favorites on the menu. A tip for the dinner crowd: Get there at 5:30, because a line is likely to spill

Annapolis's City Dock area is busy with boats and visitors, restaurants and shops. Patrick Soran, photo courtesy the Maryland Office of Tourism

from the tiny waiting vestibule onto the street as the evening progresses. Expansion plans, however, are on the horizon. Joss also has opened a location at 413 N. Charles St. in Baltimore, which focuses on small plates.

LEMONGRASS
410-280-0086
www.kapowgroup.com
167 West St.
Open: Daily; D only on Sun. starting at 4 PM
Price: Inexpensive to Moderate
Cuisine: Thai
Serving: L, D
Reservations: Priority seating if you call ahead
Handicapped Access: Yes

Brought to you by the folks who delivered Tsunami to inner West Street, popular Lemongrass can be counted on for well-priced Thai cuisine. The crispy string beans are tempura'd, reasonably priced, and border on addictive. The ginger beef is good, the green curry awesome. The signature lemongrass pork has been known to require a fire extinguisher, but perhaps that's just a matter of taste. The small West Street restaurant has street-level patio dining, and its lime green dining room comes with a long, elevated central table that promotes camaraderie. It's an element repeated at Lemongrass's slightly larger location on the city's western outskirts at 2625-A Housley Rd., in the back of a large shopping center. The phone number there is 410-224-THAI.

LEWNES' STEAKHOUSE
410-263-1617
lewnessteakhouse.com
401 Fourth St., Eastport
Open: Daily
Price: Expensive to Very Expensive
Cuisine: Steakhouse
Serving: D
Reservations: Strongly recommended
Handicapped Access: Yes

Lewnes' has the look of a New York or Chicago steakhouse: spare and clubby. We go for the fork-tender prime-aged steaks and generous sides of salad, potatoes, and vegetables. Arrive with an appetite and full wallet. Entrées are $16.95 (grilled double breast of chicken) to $32.95 (porterhouse steak). Leave your caloric cheat sheet and cholesterol counter at home. The beef is cooked to perfection and served with a bit of melted butter. At your request, the kitchen will forgo the butter or add more. Trust us, it adds to the flavor. The salads serve two unless your appetite equals Henry VIII's. We favor the mashed or hash brown potatoes and sautéed mushrooms with a New York strip, leaving with half the meat for a midnight snack or lunch the next day. Nearby on-street parking may be scarce, so if you're up to it, park in the Historic District and enjoy the 10- to 15-minute walk. Go over the Spa Creek Bridge, turn left at Severn Avenue, and continue two blocks to Fourth Street. The after-dinner walk aids digestion—so maybe you'll have room for ice cream.

MCGARVEY'S SALOON & OYSTER BAR
410-263-5700
www.mcgarveys.net
8 Market Space
Open: Daily
Price: Moderate to Expensive
Cuisine: American, seafood, pub fare
Serving: L, D, SB
Reservations: Not accepted on weekends or holidays
Handicapped Access: No

Longtime Annapolis favorite McGarvey's offers polished wood, brass, and Tiffany-style lamps that create a welcoming atmosphere in the usually packed and noisy bar area. We prefer the less frenetic, natural-light-filled back room. Start with half a dozen oysters, steamed clams, or spiced shrimp from the raw bar. Pub fare shines here; it includes a smoked turkey Reuben; soft-shell crab sandwich with coleslaw and fries; and good hamburgers. Monday's Oyster Night from Nov. 1 through Apr. 15, with a dozen raw for a mere $6. Thursdays mean deals on turkey dinners or mussels. Kick back with an Aviator, the house lager, or Old Hydraulic root beer. (Owner Mike Ashford's passion for biplanes creates the connection between airplanes and beverages.) At dinner, we often find the beef and fish entrées reasonably priced. Service is friendly and reliable.

MIDDLETON TAVERN

410-263-3323
www.middletontavern.com
2 Market Space
Open: Daily
Price: Inexpensive to Very Expensive
Cuisine: Seafood, American, tavern fare
Serving: L, D, weekend B
Reservations: Only on major holidays; "priority seating" offered for those who call ahead
Handicapped Access: No

Located at City Dock, barn-red Middleton Tavern lays authentic claim to tavernhood dating to 1740. Ye olde place predates George Washington, who was once grounded off Annapolis in a ferry operated by Middleton's owner. Today, diners will find a dining room suitable for ladies' luncheons and a comfy bar in back known for its $1.50 "oyster shooters," in which the consumer drowns an oyster in cocktail sauce, then downs it and chases it with beer. Seafood is the menu's focus, with rockfish, crabcakes, and even seafood crepes along with salads and pasta dishes. The wide front porch, a great people-watching spot, is almost as much a city landmark as the Naval Academy chapel dome.

MIKE'S RESTAURANT & CRAB HOUSE

410-956-2784
www.mikescrabhouse.com
3030 Riva Rd., Riva
Open: Daily
Price: Inexpensive to Very Expensive
Cuisine: Seafood
Serving: L, D
Reservations: For large parties only
Handicapped Access: Yes
Special Features: Outdoor waterside deck and tiki bar; dockage

We like Mike's and have for years. Located on the outskirts of town, it's an easy place to meet friends coming from out of town without having to explain how to navigate Annapolis's sometimes confusing Historic District. It also comes with parking, overlooks the South River, and serves great hard-shell crabs and big seafood platters. It's a lively scene on the outdoor deck in midsummer. Even into Oct., the deck stays open if the weather is good. Boats dock alongside, mallards paddle in, and, with everybody cracking crabs, it's the consummate Chesapeake scene in full glory. The cavernous indoor dining room is as full as the parking lot during summer crab season, but if you come early, during the week, or in the off-season, you should have no problems. The menu has plenty of fresh fish, steak and rib entrées should make the beef eaters happy, and a fresh if utilitarian salad bar is offered alongside the bar, where bands gather and folks boogie on the small dance floor. A popular place, and owned by the same family since 1954.

O'LEARYS

410-263-0884
www.olearysseafood.com
310 Third St., Eastport
Open: Daily
Price: Expensive to Very Expensive
Cuisine: Seafood, nouveau
Serving: D

Reservations: Recommended
Handicapped Access: Yes

O'Leary's has long been considered a top
contender (if not the top contender) for the
city's best seafood restaurant. The dining
room lets the food take center stage,
although it's always fun to gaze at paintings
lining the mustard yellow walls. The menu
changes seasonally, and promises creative
executions of a range of seafood. The crispy
grouper is done with a whole-grain mustard barbecue sauce over black beans and
rice. Rockfish topped with crab also gets
the mustard treatment, this one a sherry-
Dijon sauce. The wine list includes a fairly
extensive list of half-bottles, a civilized way
to go. Located in the Eastport maritime
district, the restaurant resides in the former home of a waterman who ran a fish
market on the property. Seafood-loving
visitors to Annapolis would be remiss if
they didn't finagle a reservation at this
popular establishment, noticed by regional
reviewers from *The Washington Post* to
Baltimore magazine.

OSTERIA 177

410-267-7700
www.osteria177.com
177 Main St.
Open: Daily
Price: Moderate to Very Expensive
Cuisine: Italian-Mediterranean
Serving: L, D
Reservations: Recommended, especially on
weekends, and requested one business day
in advance
Handicapped Access: Yes

This Italian-Mediterranean restaurant
dwells in the old building that once housed
a Burger King. Now, crystal chandeliers
hang from the HVAC ducts and leather
placemats adorn the polished tables. Such
style! But Osteria hardly ignores substance.
The food here is light on its feet yet heavy
on the grace notes. Consider the handmade
pasta stuffed with pear, ricotta, and gorgonzola cheese. Yes, pear. Once the chef has
added the creamy porcini sauce, you will
feel like you've died and gone to heaven.
The menu includes a wide range of meat
and seafood dishes alongside an amazing
pasta list. Admittedly, most of us don't regularly pay $19–28 for a dinner pasta, but
the pear-filled Sacchetti di Pasta al Porcini
($24) will not crumble in memory's dustbin
any time soon. If you're looking to spend
less, consider a two-course lunch for $15.
The restaurant even provides throw pillows
to cushion the booth-sitters.

RAMS HEAD TAVERN

410-268-4545
www.ramsheadtavern.com
33 West St.
Open: Daily
Price: Inexpensive to Expensive
Cuisine: American, pub fare
Serving: L, D, SB
Reservations: Not necessary
Handicapped Access: Yes
Special Features: Outdoor dining, on-site
performance space

Locals remember back when the Rams
Head was a basement hole-in-the-wall
where Naval Academy midshipmen and
locals packed the closet-size brickskeller to
munch burgers and drink their way through
300-plus brands of beer. My, how times
have changed. After several expansions, the
Rams Head couldn't be more happening.
Depending on their mood and the weather,
diners can opt for the cozy, paneled Tea
Room, the dining room (with mostly
booths), the bustling bar area, or, weather
permitting, the New Orleans–style patio.
The food is hearty and eclectic.
Hamburgers, sandwiches, soups, salads
("The Spicy Pom Greeney" with dried cherries, sweet and spicy cashews, goat cheese,
and red onion topped with pomegranate

vinaigrette), and seafood dishes anchor the menu. The award-winning chili is just what the doctor ordered on a nippy day or night. Consider Sunday brunch in the brick courtyard. The beer menu comes from the related Fordham Brewery in Dover, Del., which outgrew its space here in the tavern. A $4.95 sampler of six is offered. (See the "Nightlife" section later in this chapter for details about shows in the adjacent performance space.) The staff is generally attentive, enthusiastic, and personable. No wonder repeat patrons pack the Rams Head. The company also operates the Rams Head Roadhouse west of town at 1773 Generals Hwy., 410-849-8058. In addition, the company operates Rams Head Live, a music venue you can read about in the Baltimore "Nightlife" section.

SKIPPER'S PIER RESTAURANT & DOCK BAR
410-867-7110
www.skipperspier.com
6158 Drum Point Rd., Deale
Open: Daily in spring/summer season; closed Mon. in fall/winter
Price: Inexpensive to Expensive
Cuisine: Seafood
Serving: L, D, SB
Reservations: Recommended
Handicapped Access: Yes
Special Features: Wide deck and separate dock bar; dockage for patrons

Long a waterside crab-cracking deck, Skipper's Pier, located about 20 minutes south of Annapolis in Deale, has taken a big step up the culinary ladder. Chef John Kozik, a local who went to Scottsdale Culinary Institute and then worked in prominent Washington restaurants, has come home. His cream of crab soup is light, with the sherry whispered into the cream. He doesn't just serve coleslaw, he serves gingered coleslaw. That said, don't feel shy about digging into a mess of hard-shell crabs here along Rockhold Creek. The back deck still has its picnic tables on the water and the dock bar still has the ring-toss game. Doors open wide from the patio/dining room area onto the deck. The menu's emphasis is seafood and Southern food (although Ipswich clams make an appearance) with good salads and a "Meat Board" for the carnivores. When your friends want to get away to try some crabs and seafood someplace new and/or different, bring them here. A light and airy face-lift was planned for the dining room at deadline. Consider the Fri. night seafood buffet for $22.99, and check the Web site for directions.

TSUNAMI
410-990-9868
www.kapowgroup.com
51 West St.
Open: Daily
Price: Inexpensive to Very Expensive
Cuisine: Asian fusion
Serving: L, D; D only Sat.–Sun.
Reservations: Recommended
Handicapped Access: Yes
Special Features: Sushi bar open until 1 AM; lounge open until 2 AM

Tsunami brought the Asian-fusion trend to Annapolis in the early 2000s. It remains one of the city's most visibly hip restaurants, with spare decor anchored by royal blue walls, top-notch food, and affable service. Fusion fare includes but a single nod to the Chesapeake (and that's on the sushi menu): an Annapolis roll with crab and Old Bay. Otherwise, plan on Asian touches like the New York strip (burnt sugar chili with foie gras port reduction) or the Chilean sea bass (mustard glazed, served with braised leeks). This is also a late-night gathering spot; think martinis, and don't be surprised if a crowd has gathered well into a weekend night. Live music's on tap from time to time.

REYNOLDS TAVERN

410-295-9555

www.reynoldstavern.org

7 Church Circle

Open: Daily

Price: Inexpensive to Expensive

Cuisine: English, regional Chesapeake, and light fare

Serving: L, D Wed.–Sun.

Reservations: Recommended

Handicapped Access: Yes

There must have been Tories in colonial Annapolis and their spirits must be pleased with the proper English tea at colonial-era Reynolds Tavern. A portrait of Queen Elizabeth and Prince Philip even hangs in the dining room. High tea can be a full meal served in the afternoon, but Reynolds offers a lovely lunch menu as well. With nods to British culinary taste—shepherd's pie and bangers and mash—crabcakes, quiche, and upscale sandwiches or salads are the lunch menu's focus. Six types of tea are served at a

Stop in for proper English tea at Reynolds Tavern, an old-fashioned colonial tavern.

per-person price, so you can order a basic "cream tea" with a pot of tea and your choice of two scones ($7.90), or the colonial high tea, with your choice of soup, salad, or slice of quiche to go along with a pot of tea, scone, finger sandwiches, savory tarts, and tea cakes ($19.95). A word about the tea selection: It's extensive and includes blooming teas. (And the strawberry preserves and cream that accompany the scones? Luxurious.) Fine dining takes over the white-clothed tables at dinner Wed.–Sun., and travelers can stay upstairs in one of two suites or one bedroom dressed in traditional style, albeit with new bathrooms and modern beds. The brick tavern, a beloved Church Circle fixture, was built soon after 1737. It was the city library from the mid-1930s to the 1970s. In the building's lower level is a separate business, the Sly Fox Pub, which, in addition to its bar area, has popular alfresco drinking and dining on its brick patio in clement weather.

THE WILD ORCHID CAFÉ

410-268-8009

www.thewildorchidcafe.com

909 Bay Ridge Ave.

Open: Daily

Price: Moderate to Expensive

Cuisine: Farm to table

Serving: L, D, SB

Reservations: Recommended, especially for dinner

Handicapped Access: Yes

Special Features: Garden patio

The Wild Orchid Café calls itself a contemporary coastal American restaurant. Although its habitués will find neither sandy beach nor cattail-studded marsh on view outside the window-lined dining room, they are likely to gasp with pleasure over the café's butternut squash–crab soup.

This is not your mama's crab soup. Or even yours, unless you're a genius. This dish truly is that delectable, so if your Chesapeake cuisine dream includes finding a crab soup without tomatoes or thick starch, this one's for you. The café itself is an appealing converted bungalow with buttery yellow walls and hardwood floors, and has been delighting diners for years with fresh takes on local cuisine with the occasional whiff of French provencal. Consider the $39 prix fixe for dinner, and enjoy it one balmy night on the backyard patio. Lunch entrées $6–13; light-fare dinner available.

Nightlife

Nighttime around 'Naptown offers variety. At City Dock, places that are quaint colonial taverns at lunchtime open their doors to the music and tourist scene at night. Summer weekends can be mobbed, but even locals try to slip in one night downtown to soak up the warm breezes off the water. West Street, up the hill from City Dock, is home to the area's best live music. And over the Spa Creek Bridge lies Eastport, a hotbed of sailors and some good places to grab a drink.

Pubs ring City Dock, and many offer live music. **Armadillo's** (410-280-0028; www .armadillosannapolis.com; 132 Dock St.) hosts bands and DJs. **McGarvey's Saloon & Oyster Bar** (410-263-5700; www.mcgarveys.net; 8 Market Space) brings an uptown saloon flavor, with mirror-backed, heavily polished, dark wood bars that are often crowded on weekends; it serves late. **O'Brien's Oyster Bar & Restaurant** (410-268-6288; www .obriensoysterbar.com; 113 Main St.) offers a dance floor and nightly entertainment. By far the hottest live music ticket is **Rams Head On Stage** on inner West Street (410-268-4545; ramsheadtavern.com; 33 West St.), the locally grown venue now also bringing music to Baltimore and nearby Kent Island. Acts ranging from Little Richard to Joe Sample to Alan Parsons may take the stage. Performance packages include deals on dinner or a drink. The attached Ram's Head Tavern is known for good happy hour specials. A couple of doors up stands **49 West Coffeehouse, Wine Bar & Gallery** (410-626-9796; 49westcoffeehouse.com; 49 West St.), a European-style café with regular art openings and jazz or classical guitar music. Martinis? Try **Tsunami** (410-990-9868; www.kapowgroup.com; 51 West St.), which has long worn the crown of hip local nightspot—and serves sushi until 1 AM. For a nice outdoor patio, try **Stan and Joe's Saloon** 410-263-1993; www.stanandjoessaloon.com; 37 West St.), which also has live music. Another first-rate patio: the **Sly Fox Pub** (443-482-9000; www.slyfoxpub.com) in the basement of Reynolds Tavern on Church Circle.

For drinks on the water, cross the Spa Creek Bridge to Eastport and try the Chart House (410-268-7166; www.chart-house.com; 300 Second St., Eastport). Big windows onto the water give a great view of Annapolis Harbor. Other waterside options include Carrol's Creek Waterfront Restaurant (410-263-8102; www.carrolscreek.com; 410 Severn Ave.), with a wide waterside deck. Across the street stands the Boatyard Bar & Grill (410-216-6206; www.boatyardbarandgrill.com; 400 Fourth St.); it's not on the water, but it's where the sailors hang out. Cross back to the Historic District side of Spa Creek to find the city's only drinking/dining spot directly on the water. Pusser's Landing at the Annapolis Marriott Waterfront Hotel (410-268-7555; www.pussersusa.com; 80 Compromise St.) comes with its outdoor deck and a full view of the boating scene.

Irish bars draw their fans. Grab a brew and catch some music at **Castlebay Irish Pub** (410-626-0165; www.castlebayirishpub.com; 193 Main St.) with its own Three Nuns Ale, and popular **Galway Bay** (410-263-8333; www.galwayayannapolis.com; 61–63 Maryland Ave.), with its Tuesday night "pub quiz" for charity and music from time to time. **Fadó**, the chain, operates in the Park Place complex out West Street at Westgate Circle (410-626-0069; www.fadoisrishpub.com/annapolis). Grab a drink on the patio, or catch the British & Irish Lions' rugby match via satellite.

Food Purveyors

Sitting down for a fine meal is no problem in Annapolis and environs, but sometimes you're on the run. Here are some local food purveyors who'll do right by you. Stop in for ice cream or pick through the world's best sweet corn before heading to the seafood market for hard-shell crabs.

Capital Teas (410-263-TEAS; www.capitalteas.com; 6 Cornhill St.) This tiny shop in an odd tricorner store smells like a dream and has definitely caught the tea wave. The most expensive leaves cost $25 an ounce, for a special organic smoked tea called Tong Mu Phoenix. Or, try something less pricey, like the $6 for two ounces of lemongrass ginger.

Market House (25 Market Space at City Dock) A market has stood on this location since the 18th century, and you can still find sandwiches (Atwater's, Baltimore's fabled Jewish deli), sweets (Vaccaro's, Baltimore's fabled Italian bakery), and, hopefully by the time you read this, much more. For the latest: www.markethouseannapolis.com.

Coffee Bars, Cafés, and Delis

City Dock Cafe (410-269-0961; www.citydockcoffee.com; 18 Market Space) Bright and often packed, this is the flagship for the homegrown coffee emporium with four locations. Get your espressos and sumatras here, along with sandwiches, fat cookies, and pastries. Front windows and sidewalk tables offer a fine people-watching spot. Open Sun.–Thurs. 6:30 AM–10 PM, Fri.–Sat. 6:30 AM–midnight. Just up the hill is a second Historic District City Dock Café at 71 Maryland Ave., 410-263-9747, open Mon.–Sat. 6:30–6:30 and Sun. 8 AM–6:30 PM. Free wireless at both cafés.

Giolitti Delicatessen (410-266-8600; www.giolittideli.com; 2068 Somerville Rd.) A bit outside of the usual tourist loop, but well worth knowing about, Giolitti creates excellent Italian food available for takeout or lunchtime eat-in; and a good selection of wines, cheeses, desserts, and other tasty Italian delights. The shop closes at 6 on weekdays, 5 on Sat., 4 on Sun.

Great Harvest Bread Company (410-268-4662; 2–8 Ridgely Ave.) Tucked into the West Annapolis neighborhood, Great Harvest bakes a daily menu of specialty breads and killer cookies, brownies, and scones. They even serve a pepperoni roll for lunch on Tues.–Thurs.

Hard Bean Coffee & BookSellers (410-263-8770; www.beansandbooks.com; 36 Market Space) A coffee-books-and-light-lunch emporium, Hard Bean also sells pastries, and there's a nice wireless work area, too. This has also become a bit of a local meeting spot, with a good bulletin board to check for local happenings.

Farmer's Markets

Anne Arundel County Farmer's Market (Harry S. Truman Pkwy. off Riva Rd.; aacofarmers market.com) This popular market dates to 1981 and operates on Sat. and Tues. from 7 AM–noon with a wide variety of produce and goods. The Sat. market runs Apr.–Dec., while the Tues. market runs June–Oct. Plan to look for those delectable Anne Arundel County tomatoes and corn come Aug.

Pennsylvania Dutch Farmer's Market (410-573-0770; padutchfarmmarket.com; 2472 Solomons Island Rd., Annapolis Harbour Center) Stalls here are filled with everything from subs to fresh produce, meat to top-quality baked goods. Amish quilts, furniture, and the on-site Dutch Market Restaurant (410-573-0771) serving good old-fashioned Pennsylvania Dutch food. The market is open Thurs.–Fri. 9–6 and Sat. 8:30–3.

Ice Cream and Sweets

Annapolis Ice Cream Company (443-482-3895; www.annapoliceicecream.com; 196 Main St.) One mom I know delights in this old-fashioned ice cream shop because they not only let kids cobble together their scoops from more than one flavor, the jimmies are free! Thirty-six flavors rotate daily with flavors like apple pie.

Ben & Jerry's (410-268-6700; 139 Main St.) The Vermont icon is located within sight of City Dock.

Nostalgia Cupcakes (410-280-0600; www.nostalgiacupcakes.com; 1888 Main St., Suite 102) Peanut butter oozing from decadent chocolate cake, key lime, or coconut are among the delicious concoctions.

Storm Bros. Ice Cream Factory (410-263-3376; 130 Dock St.) This longtime family-owned City Dock resident serves 46 flavors of ice cream (with four types of sherbet included) as well as shakes and sundaes. This is a popular, well-located stop with a line out the door on many summer evenings. Open late during the summer, but open year-round.

Natural/Whole Foods

Sun and Earth Natural Foods (410-266-6862; 1933 West St.) This beloved old health and whole foods shop stocks all of the necessities, including Green Goddess sandwiches and oolong tea by the big box. Look for second-day sandwiches for a bargain. Open Mon.–Sat. 9:30–6:30, Sun. noon–4.

Whole Foods (410-573-1800; 200 Harker Pl., Suite 100) Not that this whole foods giant needs a plug from us, but the locals so filled the aisles that the store moved to a new location and doubled in size, to 56,000 square feet. Now located at the Annapolis Towne Centre, the store's prepared foods mean ready-made takeout for a day on the Bay. The coffee roaster breakfast bar opens at 7 AM daily, the entire store is open at 8 AM. Closing time is 10 PM except on Sunday, when the doors shut at 9.

Seafood Markets

Annapolis Seafood Market (410-269-5380; www.annapolisseafoodmarket.com; 1300 Forest Dr.) Longtime popular seafood market, beautifully organized from in-season sweet corn to the line at the crab and spiced-shrimp counter to the excellent takeout sandwiches and platters for folks on the go. Other locations include the Park Plaza shopping center on Ritchie Highway (MD 2) in Severna Park; 3105 Solomons Island Rd. (MD 2) in Edgewater; and US 301 in Waldorf. Check the Web site for directions and the takeout menu.

CULTURE

Annapolis offers an array of attractive options for those interested in culture. For visual arts, stroll the city's galleries or head for St. John's College and its Mitchell Gallery, where you're quite likely to see works by masters. Performing arts? Start at Maryland Hall for the Creative Arts. If it's a walk into the past you're after, this city is perfect with its collection of brick Georgian buildings.

Cinema

Bow Tie Cinemas operate Annapolis's two commercial movie houses: **Harbour 9** (410-224-1145; Annapolis Harbour Center, 2474 Solomons Island Rd.), with nine screens, and **Bow Tie Annapolis Mall 11** (410-224-1145; Westfield Annapolis, 1020 Annapolis Mall Rd.), showing first-run fare. Check schedules and buy tickets online at www.bowtie cinemas.com/harbour-9.html and www.bowtiecinemas.com/annapolis-mall.html.

Galleries

Annapolis is home to numerous commercial fine arts and craft galleries. Learn more about them in the "Shopping" section. The area's thriving arts scene also supports Paint Annapolis, an annual plein air competition that draws artists from around the country. You can see painters at work throughout the city during this mid-September event. For info: www.mapapa.org/PAINTANNAPOLIS.

ELIZABETH MYERS MITCHELL ART
410-626-2556
www.stjohnscollege.edu/events/AN/art/main.shtml
Mellon Hall (attached to the Francis Scott Key auditorium lobby), St. John's College, 60 College Ave.
Open: Tues.–Sun. noon–5, Fri. 7–8 during school year; Tues.–Sun. noon–5 in summer during exhibitions

Your best chance in Annapolis to see major works by major artists. Visiting shows often are curated elsewhere by groups like the Smithsonian Institution's Traveling Exhibition Service or the American Federation of Art in New York. Recent shows have spotlighted "A Century on Paper: Prints by Art Students League Artists," Milton Avery, and Louise Nevelson. Lectures, gallery talks, and group tours are held in conjunction with exhibitions. Check www.sjca.edu for schedules.

MARYLAND FEDERATION OF ART CIRCLE GALLERY
410-268-4566
www.mdfedart.org
18 State Circle
Open: Tues.–Sun. 11–5

Originally built in the mid-1800s as a storage loft for the Jones and Franklin General Store, this gallery's exposed brick walls serve as backdrop for changing shows, which include paintings, sculpture, wearable art, and photographs by the federation's nearly 400-member roster. Two gallery spaces host monthly exhibitions, which often feature small group shows. This is a good place to look for a well-priced piece from an unknown artist.

Museums, Historic Buildings, and Sites

Visitors interested in the city's history may want to start at the city's old Customs House, now called **HistoryQuest** (410-267-6656; www.annapolis.org/index.asp?pageid=44; 99 Main St.). This City Dock–side attraction is a history orientation center operated by the city's main historic preservation group, the Historic Annapolis Foundation (www .annapolis.org). Peruse exhibits that tell of the city's Golden Age as a colonial cultural center, or buy tickets for tours. Audio walking tours are also available. Hours are Mon.–Sat. 9:30–5 and Sun. 11–5.

For 50 years, Historic Annapolis has worked to preserve and restore the city's architectural and historic gems. The foundation operates historic sites, including its flagship William Paca House and Garden (described below), as well as the "Hogshead" at 23 Pinkney St., where you might catch a tavern keeper or a colonial frontiersman doing living history interpretations. Nearly next door is the Waterfront Warehouse at 4 Pinkney St., and The Shiplap House near Hogshead is the foundation's headquarters. As you walk the city's streets, note the historic markers indicating the age of the houses, from green for "17th-century vernacular" (1681–1708) to ochre for "20th-century distinctive" (1901–1938). The eight designations include solid bronze for Georgian Buildings of National Importance. In addition, visitors to town are well advised to check the foundation's online calendar at www.annapolis.org for all kinds of activities, such as yoga in the William Paca Garden or lectures on architecture.

ANNAPOLIS MARITIME MUSEUM

410-295-0104
www.amaritime.org
723 Second St.
Open: Thurs.–Sun. noon–4

It's been more than 20 years since workers shucked the last oysters at McNasby's Oyster Company, but the old packing plant's still operating. Only now, it's fully renovated into a museum focused on the lives of the people who once made their living from the Bay. A permanent exhibit called "Oysters on the Half Shell," being installed as of deadline, reminds folks that not every boat berthed at City Dock has been a pleasure craft. Tongers went out into the Chesapeake, got the oysters, then brought them back here for sale and processing. Visit for a glimpse of Annapolis life gone by. As well as the Bay's: a living oyster reef in the exhibit shows how oysters clear water on a daily basis, which is a huge argument on behalf of bringing oysters back to the Bay. This is also your headquarters for tours out to Thomas Point Shoal Lighthouse, a five-star opportunity to get on the water and see inside the cottage-style light that was inhabited until the 1980s. A variety of events, art exhibits, and other activities seem to always be under way here, so check their Web site to see what's up when you're in town.

BANNEKER-DOUGLASS MUSEUM

410-216-6180
www.bdmuseum.com
84 Franklin St.
Open: Labor Day–Memorial Day, Tuesday–Saturday 10–4; Memorial Day–Labor Day, Wed. 10–4, Thurs. 10–7, Fri.–Sat. 10–4, Sun. 1–5
Admission: Free (donations welcome)

The old McNasby's oyster packing plant has become the Annapolis Maritime Museum, celebrating the old working waterman life. Photo courtesy of Annapolis Maritime Museum

Victorian Mount Moriah African Methodist Episcopal Church was built in 1874 and stands amid what was the Historic District's black neighborhood dating to the mid-19th century. Now it's a museum celebrating Maryland's African American life, and is named for prominent black Marylanders Frederick Douglass, born in the Eastern Shore's Talbot County, and Benjamin Banneker, who helped survey Federal City, now Washington, D.C., in the 1790s. In addition to the permanent exploration of black life in Maryland dating to the 1630s there are revolving exhibits such as the recent "Forty Blossoms from the Bouquet," an artist's portrait of nearby Calvert County's women.

CHARLES CARROLL HOUSE OF ANNAPOLIS
For private tours, 410-269-1737
www.charlescarrollhouse.com
107 Duke of Gloucester St.
Open: Sat.–Sun. noon–4 from mid-May through Oct. or by appt. year-round
Admission: Free

Four Marylanders signed the Declaration of Independence; all of them, at least for a time, owned homes in Annapolis. This was the birthplace and boyhood home of Charles Carroll of Carrollton, the only Roman Catholic to sign the Declaration. Located on the grounds of St. Mary's Church, his home housed a chapel in which Catholics worshiped during the mid-18th century, when the religion was forced underground. Archaeological digs in the formal gardens have turned up artifacts, likely from a tavern that once operated on the property. Construction of the original family house began in 1721; later additions came in the 1770s and 1780s. Carroll's grandfather purchased the property, then with a frame house, in 1706. The Redemptorists, an order of Catholic priests, purchased the property in the 1850s. Their additions included an underground wine cellar.

CHASE-LLOYD HOUSE

410-263-2723
22 Maryland Ave.
Open: Mar.–Dec., Tues.–Sat. 2–4
Admission: $4; children 8 and under free

Samuel Chase, yet another Annapolitan to sign the Declaration of Independence, started this house in 1769, before he became one of the new nation's first Supreme Court justices. Later, he sold the home, unfinished, to Edward Lloyd IV, member of a prominent Maryland political dynasty. The brick mansion is most noted for the spectacular "flying" stairway, which has no visible means of support.

GOVERNMENT HOUSE

410-260-3930
State and Church circles
Open: By appt. only; tours available Mon., Wed., Fri. 10:30–noon

Three statehouses have stood inside State Circle, the most recent begun in 1772. www.VisitAnnapolis.com

The official residence of Maryland's governors is an 1870 Georgian-style mansion filled with Maryland arts (including works by painters Joe Sheppard, a contemporary master, and Revolution-era Charles Willson Peale) and antiques. Current residents Gov. Martin O'Malley and his wife, Katie, are also making the mansion greener—look for the highly nonperiod solar panels on the roof.

HAMMOND-HARWOOD HOUSE

410-263-4683
www.hammondharwoodhouse.org
19 Maryland Ave.
Open: Apr.–Oct., Tues.–Sun. 10–5, last tour at 4; Nov.–Mar., closed except for group tours, school groups, and select weekends. Call for info (Ext. 16)
Admission: Adults $6, children $3, students $5.50

Widely considered one of the nation's finest remaining examples of Georgian architecture, this 1770s center-block house, preserved as a museum since 1926, boasts two wings connected by two hyphens. This is a Palladian style that was very popular in England back in the day. The symmetry is meticulous: False doors balance actual entrances. Inside hang portraits by onetime Annapolitan Charles Willson Peale and furniture by noted Annapolis coffin- and cabinetmaker John Shaw. Intricately carved ribbons and roses mark the front entrance. Gift shop and exhibitions, and an architecture tour at 10 AM on the second and fourth Sat. of every month for $15. Reserve online, and check the Web site for special events such as the Secret Garden Tour in early June.

HISTORIC LONDON TOWN AND GARDENS
410-222-1919
www.historiclondontown.com
839 Londontown Rd., Edgewater (Take MD 2 south from Annapolis; 1 mile past the South River Bridge, turn left onto Mayo Rd. (MD 253); after 1 mile, turn left onto Londontown Rd.)
Open: Mar.–Dec., Wed.–Sat. 10–4, Sun. noon–4. Tours of historic area at 10, noon, and 2; William Brown House tours at 11, 1, and 3. Jan.–Feb., grounds are open Wed.–Fri. 10–4
Admission: Adults $10, seniors 62 and older $9, youth 7–18 $5; children under 7 free. Jan.–Feb. reduced admission. Additional fee for audio tours.

Cross the South River Bridge to visit this 18th-century Georgian tavern on the riverbank, site of a once-booming town. It's now a beautiful riverside retreat on 23 acres, and eight of those are gardens you'll want to stroll. An ongoing archaeological dig brings the past to light and you'll see remnants in the visitor center, such as a blue mermaid plate that's become a Londontown icon. Visitors also will find the house-turned-tavern built by William Brown about 1760. Traveling colonial-era men of limited means once shared beds upstairs; traveling gentleman professionals—an itinerant dentist, for example—had their own rooms while they stayed in town to do business.

MARYLAND STATEHOUSE
410-974-3400
www.msa.md.gov/msa/mdstatehouse/html/home.html
100 State Circle
Open: Mon.–Fri. 9–5, Sat.–Sun. 10–4; call for group tour information or arrange smaller tours at the statehouse Visitor Center. Tours aren't available on Thanksgiving, Christmas, and New Year's.

The first statehouse was built on this hill in 1699; the current building is the third. Fire, the scourge of so many colonial-era buildings, destroyed the first building, which was replaced in 1705. The second lasted until 1766, when the government decided to build a more architecturally distinguished capitol. Marylanders now boast that theirs is the country's oldest state capitol building in continuous use. From Nov. 26, 1783, to Aug. 13, 1784, the building served as the capitol to a new nation. The Old Senate Chamber where George Washington resigned his commission in the Continental Army in 1783 remains, and you can see a bronze plaque on the floor where he stood. You can also see a copy of the letter he wrote—the real article is owned by the state. And the Treaty of Paris, which officially ended the Revolutionary War, was ratified here in 1784. This room is undergoing historical investigations, so furniture and Charles Willson Peale's portrait of Washington with Marylander Tench Tilghman and the Marquis de Lafayette at Yorktown may still be in storage during your visit. You can, however, see the exposed, original brick walls. The General Assembly convenes here for the annual 90-day legislative session from winter into spring, and a visitor's center in the first-floor lobby offers abundant state travel information. Security measures mean you'll need a photo ID to enter and will have to pass through a metal detector.

NATIONAL SAILING HALL OF FAME & SAILING CENTER

877-295-3022
www.nationalsailinghalloffame.org
67–69 Prince George St.

If you're standing at City Dock while reading this, you may be looking at a cool classic boat bearing a "National Sailing Hall of Fame" sign: the reproduction John Smith voyage shallop, perhaps, or a sleek old wooden yacht. These are the hall's displays, but what you may not see is the $20 million hall itself. As of deadline, the first-rate facility was still in development. When built, it will stand on the water at City Dock alongside the U.S. Naval Academy, and interactive exhibits will show people of all ages about the romance of wind in the sails and the science of coaxing the perfect amount of wind into those sails. However, nobody has to wait for the building to get bit by the sailing bug. The hall of fame, in conjunction with other organizations, hosts activities including free sailing on Sunday afternoons from spring until fall. All you have to do is preregister at www.annapolis communityboating.com and be prepared to spend the first 30–45 minutes of your afternoon learning safety and basics, then head out for a two- to three-hour sail. In addition to sailing, the hall hosts salty movies alfresco—and free—at City Dock on Wed. evenings in July and Aug. (*Pirates of the Caribbean* alongside a full moon, *Moby Dick*). And the hall's Web site gives its viewers a fine idea of what's to come when they'll be able to explore exhibits like the "Science of Sailing" (cartography, weather), the "Spirit of Sailing" (Homer and Eakins painted the sport), or "Sailing and the Environment" (how wind, water, and people impact seas). You should also check the Web site to find out what sailing activities—like team racing demonstrations—the hall is sponsoring.

ST. ANNE'S EPISCOPAL CHURCH

410-267-9333
www.stannes-annapolis.org
Church Circle (Parish House, 199 Duke of Gloucester St.)
Open: Tours by appointment

This is the third church built on this hallowed Annapolis site. The first, built between 1696 and 1704, took on official duties in the colony after the legislature donated money to its construction and pews were set aside for the governor. Fire destroyed much of the second (1792–1858), but parts of the old building were incorporated when the new church went up in 1859. Many graves in the old churchyard were moved when Church Circle was widened years ago, but the graves of Annapolis's first mayor, Amos Garret, and Maryland's last colonial governor, Sir Robert Eden, remain. Inside is a silver communion service given by King William III and dating from the 1690s. It's a beautiful building that includes a Tiffany window. The church presents the St. Anne's Concert Series, including Handel's *Messiah* during the holidays; check the Web site for information.

ST. JOHN'S COLLEGE
410-263-2371; for events, check the Web site
www.sjca.edu
60 College Ave.

"Johnnies," as students at St. John's College are called, study only the Great Books during their years here, where intellect is greatly valued and humor tends toward plays on Greek or Latin phrases. The college, descended from King William's School in 1696, claims to be the nation's third oldest. The oldest building on campus, McDowell Hall, houses the venerable Great Hall, where a banquet was tossed for the aging General Lafayette in 1824 and a hospital was set up during the Civil War. The 1934 Maryland Archives building now houses the college library. Visitors interested in the school's history should join a tour by an organized tour group (see the "Tours" section later in this chapter, or pick up a copy of the college's tour guide available around town).

UNITED STATES NAVAL ACADEMY
410-293-8687
www.usna.edu; www.navyonline.com (for visitor information)
Armel-Leftwich Visitor Center, 52 King George St.
Open: Visitor Center open Mar.–Dec., daily 9–5; Jan.–Feb. daily 9–4
Admission: Free to enter and see visitor center, museum, and grounds. Call for daily guided walking tour rates. (Tours are not held on Thanksgiving, Christmas, and New Year's Day).

The beautiful and recently renovated U.S. Naval Academy Chapel.   www.VisitAnnapolis.org

Security: Enter the academy grounds at Gate 1, located at the foot of King George St. Those 16 and older must show photo ID. The visitor center is nearby. No visitor parking is available (only vehicles with U.S. Department of Defense stickers permitted to enter the grounds).

Special note: Visitors are asked to remember that the Academy is, after all, a school, and they are subject to its schedule and rules. These may include Chapel closures for weddings or funerals, and noon formation cancellations due to weather. Also please remember that the 4,400-member student body, known as the Brigade of Midshipmen, is busy with its academic and other obligations.

Additional contact info: 1-800-US4-NAVY or www.navysports.com for sporting events.

For many people around the world, "Annapolis" and "U.S. Naval Academy" are synonymous. Locals who know their city's rich heritage might beg to differ, but none would disagree that the U.S. Naval Academy has been—and remains—a great influence on the city. Founded in 1845 at old Fort Severn, the Academy's long history includes its notable move from Annapolis to Newport, R.I., during the Civil War, prompted by the Maryland city's overwhelming Southern sympathies. During the war, both the Academy and nearby St. John's College became military hospitals and staging grounds for Union troops defending Washington, D.C. Upon their return, naval officers found the campus in great need of military spit-shine. So commenced plans for a "new Academy," the collection of Beaux Arts buildings designed by architect Ernest Flagg that visitors now see, constructed between 1899 and 1908.

The beautiful academy chapel's rotunda, subject of a recent $3 million facelift, was built in 1904. The nave was added in 1940. Tiffany windows line the aisle. In the basement stands the magnificent crypt of John Paul Jones, America's first naval war hero. Jones was finally entombed here in 1913 after a fantastic journey. He was buried in Paris in 1792, but his grave was lost in the turmoil of the French Revolution as the cemetery, owned by the House of Bourbon, was seized, sold by the Revolutionary government, and later developed. After a concerted search, Jones's tomb was rediscovered 100 years later by the administration of Teddy Roosevelt. Following much politicking, it was determined that the admiral should be laid to rest in the Academy chapel—then still under construction. The casket arrived at the Academy in 1906 but spent seven years beneath the grand staircase

Visit the U.S. Naval Academy Museum at Preble Hall to view spectacular ships' models. The museum has recently been renovated. www.VisitAnnapolis.org

leading to Memorial Hall from the giant Bancroft Hall. To see the spectacular marble sarcophagus, enter from the outside, beneath the chapel. The names of the seven ships that Jones commanded are inscribed in the floor encircling the tomb.

Bancroft Hall, the largest dormitory in the U.S., looks like a European palace with its mansard roof and small turret. Visitors may not wander the building, but will see grand Memorial Hall at its entrance. A sample midshipman's spartan room is also on view. Noon meal formations by the Brigade of Midshipmen at full military attention occur at Tecumseh Court most weekdays during the school year at 12:05, weather permitting.

Lovers of ships and naval history should not miss the recently renovated U.S. Naval Academy Museum at Preble Hall. The Class of 1951 Gallery of Ships at the museum is fabulous for its breadth of ship's models. Notable is the spectacular Henry H. Rogers Collection of more than 100 models, including some that are well over 300 years old. In addition, the museum shows "dockyard" models of ships built by order of the British Royal Navy and exquisite ships' cases dating to the Jacobean, William and Mary, and Queen Anne periods. And don't miss the world's largest collection of bone models, carved from leftovers of beef rations given French prisoners of war, generally from 1756 to 1815.

WILLIAM PACA HOUSE AND GARDEN
410-263-5553
www.annapolis.org
186 Prince George St.
Open: Mon.–Sat. 10–5, Sun. noon–5. Tours begin on the half-hour. Jan., Feb., weekends only
Admission: Adults $8; children $5

William Paca, three-time colonial governor of Maryland and signer of the Declaration of Independence, built his magnificent Georgian mansion between 1763 and 1765. Here he entertained during the era known as Annapolis's golden age. During meticulous renovations in the 1960s and 1970s, X-rays revealed that two architectural styles found in the main staircase dated to the same era, a mixing and matching apparently chosen by Mr. Paca himself. First-floor antiques date to Paca's residency; the second floor is decorated to reflect the Paca era of 1765–1770. In 1965, high-rise apartments were slated to replace the building, which was a hotel at the time. The Historic Annapolis Foundation bought the house and, in six weeks' time, convinced the Maryland General Assembly to buy the 2-acre garden site in back. Archaeologists set about reconstructing the gardens and knew that they had hit pay dirt when they uncovered an original pond—it promptly refilled from a spring beneath. A must-see for any gardener, the formal, terraced Paca Gardens boast a reconstructed pavilion and Chinese-style bridge, creating a favorite respite in the middle of town. Watch for a variety of special events, from music to special plant sales. The Historic Annapolis Foundation, which owns the Paca House, also operates other historic buildings around town; check the Web site for information.

WORLD WAR II MEMORIAL
MD 450, north side of U.S. Naval Academy Bridge
Open: Dawn to dusk

Come here for a spectacular view of the U.S. Naval Academy, downtown Annapolis, and the juncture of Spa Creek and the Bay, and to pay your respects to the veterans of World War II.

Performing Arts

Annapolis Chorale (410-263-1906; www.annapolischorale.org; headquartered at
   Maryland Hall for the Creative Arts, 801 Chase St.) This ambitious 150-voice chorale,
   which has performed at Carnegie Hall, has brought the smaller Annapolis Chamber
   Orchestra and Annapolis Youth Chorus together under the umbrella Live Arts
   Maryland. The chorale remains the centerpiece (often backed by the chamber orches-
   tra) of a healthy season of performances held at Maryland Hall or historic St. Anne's
   Church. The ever-popular annual *Messiah* is a must. Tickets: Adults $34 (discounts for
   students); $42 for Christmas concert.

Annapolis Opera (410-267-8135; www.annapolisopera.org; headquartered at Maryland
   Hall for the Creative Arts, 801 Chase St.) In addition to a major annual production and
   a children's opera, the company can be creative in its fall-through-spring offerings,
   including sampler delights such as "Very Verdi" or "Opera Lite" featuring lighter work.
   The opera also sponsors an annual vocal competition, and the finals are open to the
   public.

Annapolis Summer Garden Theatre (410-268-9212; www.summergarden.com; 143
   Compromise St.) This blacksmith shop near City Dock dates from 1696 and may even
   have housed George Washington's horses out back—right where the audience sits today.
   Established in 1966, the theater offers musicals and comedies under the stars, with
   three productions per season from Memorial Day through Labor Day. Recent productions have included Shakespeare's *The Taming of the Shrew* and the award-winning
   musical *Gypsy.*

Annapolis Symphony Orchestra (For tickets, 410-263-0907; for administration, 410-
   269-1132; www.annapolissymphony.org; headquartered at Maryland Hall for the
   Creative Arts, 801 Chase St.) Ambitious, multiconcert fall-spring seasons have
   included performances of music from Brahms, Mozart, Beethoven, and Bartok. Call
   early for tickets; the best go to subscribers. A holiday pops concert is held each
   December, and an annual family concert is held as well. Summer concerts are held outdoors; typical venues may include Anne Arundel Community College in Arnold or Quiet
   Waters Park in Annapolis.

Ballet Theatre of Maryland (410-263-8289; www.balletmaryland.org; headquartered at
   Maryland Hall for the Creative Arts, 801 Chase St.) This regional company, with its own
   school and principal dancers, performs a four-show Maryland Hall season that generally includes a modern production and updated classics. The annual *Nutcracker* is a holiday sellout (matinee tickets go first).

The Bay Theatre Company (410-268-1333; www.baytheatre.com; 275 West St.) This small
   professional theater company, founded in 2002, performs a season of contemporary
   and classic works in its West Street theater. Works range from Shepard's *True West* to
   Shaw's *Candida,* with fun like *The Fantasticks* for good measure.

Colonial Players (410-268-7373; www.cplayers.com; 108 East St.) Dating back to 1949,
   this 180-seat theater-in-the-round is known for the breadth of its seven-play performance schedule and well-priced tickets. Colonial Players does everything from
   comedies to modern classics, like *The Lion in Winter,* A. R. Gurney's *Sylvia,* or new plays
   like *The Violet Hour.*

Maryland Hall for the Creative Arts (410-263-5544; www.marylandhall.org; 801 Chase
   St.) The artistic and cultural hub of the city, Maryland Hall attracts a wide and diverse
   audience to performances by touring acts (Bruce Hornsby, Ralph Stanley, George

Winston) as well as resident companies the Annapolis Chorale, Opera, and Symphony, and the Ballet Theatre of Maryland. All are housed in this former high school building that bustles with creative activity daily. Classes in the performing and visual arts for babies to seniors run the gamut, from creative movement and rumba lessons to photography and painting. Galleries with changing exhibitions by students, teachers, and professional artists (some of whom have studios here) and a café featuring author talks and poetry readings have helped put this Annapolis gem on the map. Check the online schedule for the latest.

Naval Academy Musical Performances (For tickets, 410-293-TIXS; for information, 410-293-2439; www.usna.edu/Music; U.S. Naval Academy Music Department, Alumni Hall) From Glee Club concerts to world-class symphonies, the Naval Academy offers a broad variety of musical performances at venues throughout the campus. Don't pass up a chance to hear an organ concert in the exquisite Academy Chapel, particularly the Halloween concert by Juilliard-trained organist Monte Maxwell, replete with a laser light show. The annual *Messiah* is a holiday favorite. In addition, the Distinguished Artists Series brings in five productions a year by international groups such as the Russian National Ballet Theatre or the Dublin Philharmonic, plus a choral concert by the academy's Glee Club and the Annapolis Symphony Orchestra. These are held in the Bob Hope Performing Arts Center in Alumni Hall. The academy's annual winter musical, such as Sondheim's *Into the Woods,* is much anticipated. Call early; tickets are heavily subscribed with priority for the Brigade of Midshipmen. Also keep an eye out for concerts by the Academy's Gospel Choir and the Women's Glee Club. Check the music department's Web site for schedules and details.

Summer Concerts

The **Annapolis Maritime Museum** presents two summer concert series. The Summertime Lunchtime Maritime Concert Series takes place at City Dock at noon Thurs. in July and Aug., and features artists with seafaring ties. Then, at 7 PM, Chesapeake artists perform at the museum in Eastport. For the schedule, check www.amaritime.org or call 410-295-0104.

Quiet Waters Park, located out on the Annapolis peninsula about 3 miles from City Dock, at the entrance to the Hillsmere community, offers Sat. concerts from mid-June to early Sept., often featuring jazz, blues, and rock, or on occasion classical groups. For info: www.friendsofquietwaterspark.org or 410-222-1777 for the schedule.

The **Summer Serenade Concert Series,** held at 7:30 PM most Tues. from the second week in July through the third week in Aug., features the U.S. Naval Academy Band and guest performers at City Dock. Bring a chair. Call 410-293-0263 or check www.usna.edu /USNABand for the schedule.

Seasonal Events and Festivals

A couple of easy rules: oysters in the "R" months and crabs all summer long. Keep an eye peeled for the many festivals, church suppers, and volunteer firemen's association events that include a chance to chow down on these Chesapeake delicacies. For current information about local happenings, check the calendars at the Maryland Office of Tourism Development (www.visitmaryland.org) or the Annapolis and Anne Arundel County Conference and Visitors Bureau (www.visitannapolis.org).

The **Kunta Kinte Festival,** now more than 20 years old, celebrates African American life here in the city, where writer Alex Haley of *Roots* fame learned that his ancestor,

Kunta Kinte, stepped off a slave ship at Annapolis City Dock. Three days of events typically take place mid- to late September. For more information: 443-336-1043 or www.visit annapolis.org.

Held since 1975 at the private Roedown Farm southwest of Annapolis in Davidsonville, the early April **Marlborough Hunt Races** draw hundreds to watch the thoroughbred point-to-point timber race. For information, contact the Annapolis and Anne Arundel County Conference and Visitors Bureau (410-280-0445) or check www.marylandsteeplechasing .com/main/mhr/datetime.htm.

A newer city tradition comes at the time of the spring equinox. Head over to the Annapolis Maritime Museum for the **Burning of the Socks**. It's quite simple: Spring has come, your toes long for freedom, and the bonfire needs fuel. For info: www.amaritime.org.

Also in April, on the first day of rockfish season, comes the big **Boatyard Opening Day Rockfish Tournament** hosted by the Boatyard Bar and Grill and others for charities. The catch-and-release event draws all ages. Check it out: www.boatyardbarandgrill.com.

If the thought of a gut-busting, all-you-can-eat seafood session leaves you salivating, move the **Annapolis Rotary Crab Feast** to the top of your summer must-do list. *National Geographic* has even covered this event, which has taken place for more than 60 years. It's generally held the first Fri. of Aug. at Navy–Marine Corps Memorial Stadium. For more information, check www.annapolisrotary.com.

From its start on the weekend before Labor Day, 16th-century England is the order of nine consecutive weekends at the **Maryland Renaissance Festival**, held just west of Annapolis in Crownsville. You'll find bearded men wrestling in the mud, lovely ladies working the crowd, and a roving band of jesters, crafters, jugglers, magicians, and minstrels may be seen. Admission. For information, call 410-266-7304 or visit www.renn fest.com.

The **Maryland Seafood Festival** (410 626-8922; www.mdseafoodfestival.com) features lots of different music, lots of seafood, and a crab-eating contest. Generally held the weekend after Labor Day at Sandy Point State Park near Annapolis, it includes kids' activities and a popular crab soup cook-off.

Every mariner for miles around attends Columbus Day weekend's **U.S. Sailboat Show** at Annapolis's City Dock. The very latest in sailboat designs, from racing to cruising vessels, is found in the water along with every imaginable service or sailing gimcrack. In-town parking will be a challenge (try the shuttle from Navy–Marine Corps Memorial Stadium), but expect bargains, deals, and celebrations among the restaurants and bars. Admission fee. The following weekend, check out the **U.S. Powerboat Show** at the same location. Here's your chance to see the newest boats for work or play in the water, from yachts to inflatables. Admission fee. For information, call 410-268-8828 or visit www.usboat.com.

In November, it's time for Historic Annapolis Foundation's annual **Annapolis by Candlelight**, your opportunity to glimpse inside some of the city's historic buildings. For info: 410-267-8146 or www.annapolis.org.

Also in mid-November is the Maritime Republic of Eastport's fabled **Tug-of-War** challenge to the denizens of the Historic District (more or less). It's a huge tug of war across Spa Creek with proceeds going to local charities. For info: www.themre.org.

In mid-December comes the **Eastport Parade of Lights**, in which boats dressed up in their best holiday lights parade down Spa Creek. This is well worth seeing (and well worth making dinner reservations weeks in advance at Spa Creek-side restaurants). For info: www.eastportyc.org.

During the holidays, boats deck the halls (or their decks, as the case may be) for a festive parade through Annapolis Harbor and Spa Creek. www.VisitAnnapolis.org

Throughout December, the city's historic houses are decked out for the season. The **Paca House** and the **Hammond-Harwood House** should be on your holiday must-visit list.

Tours

The Annapolis and Anne Arundel County Conference and Visitors Bureau at 26 West St., its seasonal satellite at City Dock, and HistoryQuest, located at 99 Main St., are easy places to get information about tours—many of which depart from these locales—and possibly tickets, too. HistoryQuest is an orientation center to the city's history operated by Historic Annapolis Foundation, which offers four audio tours of this 300-year-old city's history: Revolutionary Annapolis, Civil War, an African American history tour, and one tour that looks at city highlights. Guides are available at HistoryQuest, or you can reserve online through www.annapolis.org. Special walking tours are held throughout the year, such as the recent Civil War walking tour. Ghost tours take place from spring to fall. For additional information, call 410-267-6656, visit www.annapolis.org, or stop by HistoryQuest.

Other tours operators include:

Annapolis Carriage (www.annapoliscarriage.com; 410-267-6656) Take a narrated 25- or 50-minute tour of the colonial capitol, held daily in summer, long weekends in fall (through Dec.), and spring (starting mid-Mar.). Pick up tickets at HistoryQuest, 99 Main St.

Capital City Colonials (410-295-9715; www.capitalcitycolonials.com) offers a terrific set of creative tours. High on your list should be the food and history tour, which combines exercise (walking between venues), food (a cup of coffee here, a sampler of crab there), and historic tidbits at the houses, taverns, and restaurants you'll visit—including the Sands House, said to be one of the two oldest houses in the city (both are privately owned). Numerous other tours, including one by Segway, are offered.

Discover Annapolis (410-626-6000; www.discover-annapolis.com) takes visitors for one-hour trolley tours, departing the city's visitor's center at 26 West St. Or, take a 40-minute tour, leaving from HistoryQuest at City Dock. Check the Web site for more info. This is a good way to get a quick overview of town.

Watermark (410-263-5401; www.watermarkjourney.com) Well-trained guides in colonial dress lead groups through city streets and the U.S. Naval Academy, point out the highlights, and disclose tales that you'd otherwise miss. Take the Four Centuries Tour, the African American Heritage Tour and, during fall, the Haunted Ghost Tour. Many tours leave from the city's information booth at 1 Dock St. For all the info, check the Web site.

RECREATION

Bicycling

It's easy to get around Annapolis by bike, thanks to the Free Wheelin' program that runs June–Oct. 1 from the Harbormaster's office at City Dock. You need to be 18 to sign out a bike, available 9 am–8 pm daily. You also need to show a valid driver's license, a credit card, and sign a waiver. For details: http://annapolis.gov/info.asp?page=10943 or 410-263-7964, Ext. 6003.

A friendly heads-up to cyclists: You can't cross the William Preston Lane Jr. Memorial Bridge—aka the Bay Bridge—on a bike. Officially, you're on your own to arrange transportation, like a taxi.

Places to cycle include the 13.3-mile **Baltimore & Annapolis Trail** from town: Cross the Severn River via the U.S. Naval Academy Bridge (MD 450). Continue on MD 450 to a left turn at Boulters Way. The trail, on your left, is built along the old railroad bed and travels north to Glen Burnie. You'll share it with inline skaters and walkers. For information, call 410-222-6244, or see www.dnr.state.md.us/greenways/ba_trail.html.

Another local favorite for family cycling is **Quiet Waters Park** (600 Quiet Waters Park Rd.) on the south side of town off Hillsmere Drive. Paved trails of just under 6 miles wind through woods and open parkland, and end overlooking the South River. For information, call 410-222-1777; closed Tues. Bike rentals are available at the park via Paddle or Pedal, 410-271-7007.

Bike Rentals

Capital Bicycle Center (410-626-2197; 300 Chinquapin Round Rd.) Cruiser rentals, ladies' rides, and repairs are available in addition to bicycle sales.

Pedal Pushers (410-544-2323; www.pedalpushersmd.com; 546 Baltimore Annapolis Blvd., Severna Park) Located right at the 5-mile mark of the Baltimore & Annapolis Trail, this is the place to rent bikes. Year-round.

Bird-Watching

Situated along the Atlantic Flyway, Sandy Point State Park offers good year-round birding, but provides particular treats in winter and spring. Northern waterfowl (loons, grebes, and gannets) and all owl species have been spotted in winter. Breeding birds, many of them songbirds, have been spotted in spring in the Corcoran Tract, sizable acreage behind the park. Check at the park office (410-974-2149; 1100 E. College Pkwy.) to get a map. The park itself also offers fine bird-watching.

Boating

Deck shoes are de rigueur and masts fill Spa Creek in the middle of America's Sailing Capital, where everybody can talk a little boat talk. On Wednesday evenings in summer, the Annapolis Yacht Club hosts races on Spa Creek—the starting gun goes off at approximately 6 PM. To watch, stake out a spot at the Eastport bridge, or visit a creekside restaurant to see the start or finish. Or, see if you can get a berth aboard the Schooners Woodwind, which compete during the last race.

Charters, Cruises, and Boat Rentals

Here are some options for getting out on the water, either by yourself or with a captain.
Annapolis Bay Charters (1-800-991-1776; www.annapolisbaycharters.net; Port
    Annapolis Marina, 7080 Bembe Beach Rd., Suite 211) This is a top chartering company
    in the area. Boats in the fleet range from 30 to 50 feet, and include sail (including

The starting gun goes off Wednesday evenings for the popular summertime sailboat races in Annapolis.
www.VisitAnnapolis.org

monohulls and catamarans) and power. Two-day charters are the typical minimum; group day charters (typically an event) can be arranged on large power boats or old-fashioned schooners. Or go on a fishing charter with a certified captain.

Annapolis Small Boat Rental (410-268-BOAT; www.asmallboatrental.com; 808 Boucher Rd.) Walk to Sarles Boatyard in Eastport to rent a small craft like a Boston whaler. Prior experience required.

Pirate Adventures (410-263-0002; www.chesapeakepirates.com; 311 Third St.) Shiver me timbers! Kids pull on their eye patches and sail out under the Jolly Roger aboard *Sea Gypsy* on this creative cruise that operates from spring through fall, six times daily during the summer, weekends only after Labor Day. $18 per person, $10 under age 3. Reservations highly recommended.

Schooner Woodwind (410-263-7837; www.schoonerwoodwind.com; Annapolis Marriott Waterfront dock, 80 Compromise St.) Twin 74-foot wooden *Woodwind I* and *II* ply Annapolis Harbor. This company is creative when it comes to your touring options. Take one of four daily two-hour cruises, catch local musicians on Thursday, or, even better, find a seat onboard as the twin schooners race one another during the traditional Wednesday night sailing races hosted by the Annapolis Yacht Club. Other cool touring options (like the Tuesday beer sampling) also are available. Try a destination cruise—for crabs, maybe. Or perhaps dinner aboardship? Rates for a two-hour tour are $34 for adults, $22 for kids under 12.

Watermark Cruises (410-268-7601; www.watermarkjourney.com; Annapolis City Dock) This longtime city business includes tours by foot, too, and is well-known for its 40- and 90-minute cruises of Annapolis Harbor and the Severn River aboard the old-fashioned steamboat *Harbor Queen,* or trips across the Bay to St. Michaels. Add pirate cruises, lighthouse cruises, and even Baltimore Harbor cruises to the list. They operate various vessels as well as the ever-popular water taxis around the harbor and Spa and Back creeks. Specialty cruises range from moonlit wine cruises to music cruises offered in conjunction with local radio station WRNR. Head for City Dock to find out more.

Edgewater

South River Boat Rentals (410-956-9729; www.southriverboatrentals.com; Gingerville Yachting Center, 2802 Solomons Island Rd.) Rent a 24- to 37-foot sailboat or a 21- to 26-foot powerboat for a half or whole day—or even longer if you like. Open mid-Mar. through mid-Nov.

Suntime Rentals of Annapolis (410-266-6020; 2820 Solomons Island Rd.) Powerboats (19-footers), Jet Skis, water skis, wakeboards (and their kin) are available just south of Annapolis on the South River at the foot of the South River Bridge. There are certain requirements for operating some of the equipment. Hourly or half-day options unless it's a boat, in which case you can rent for the day, too. Open daily May 1–Sept. 30.

Galesville

Hartge Chesapeake Charters (410-867-7240; www.hartge.com; 4881 Church Lane) Charter fleet includes sailboats from 28 to 36 feet. Located south of Annapolis. All bareboat. Also, fishing charter available aboard the 37-foot *Dancer.*

Landings and Boat Ramps
The state of Maryland makes things easy for anyone looking for a boat ramp. Go to the

Department of Natural Resources Web page, www.dnr.state.md.us, and click on "Find a Boat Ramp" in the column to your right.

Marinas

In Annapolis, try the following: **Annapolis City Marina** (410-268-0660; www.annapolis citymarina.com; 410 Severn Ave.), right in the midst of the city bustle. Laundry, showers, fuel, and pump-out station. The **Annapolis Landing Marina** (410-263-0090; www .annapolismarina.com; 980 Awald Rd.) on the city's Back Creek has fuel, showers, laundry, café, pump-out station, and swimming pool. **Annapolis Yacht Basin** (410-263-3544; www.yachtbasin.com; 2 Compromise St.) offers fuel, showers, Wi-Fi and laundry. **Bert Jabin's Yacht Yard** (410-268-9667; www.bjyy.com; 7310 Edgewood Rd.) is one of the biggest marinas in the area, complete with a huge yard with all services. **Chesapeake Harbour Marina** (410-268-1969; www.chesapeakeharbourmarina.com; 2030 Chesapeake Harbour Dr. E.) has bathhouses, pump-out, laundry, a good restaurant, and two pools. **Mears Marina** (410-268-8282; www.mearsmarinas.com; 519 Chester Ave.) is the Annapolis branch of this marina, which you'll find elsewhere around the Bay. Call in advance. Pool, tennis courts, headquarters of Severn River Yacht Club. **Port Annapolis** (410-269-1990; www.portannapolis.com; 7074 Bembe Beach Rd.) has bikes, a pool, a café, laundry, shuttle, and pump-out. No fuel.

South of Annapolis, at Friendship and Tracey's Landing, is **Herrington Harbour** (www.herringtonharbour.com). Herrington Harbor North (1-800-297-1930; 389 Deale Rd., Tracey's Landing) and Herrington Harbor South (1-800-213-9438; MD 261, Friendship) both have dining, plenty of amenities, and hundreds of slips.

Sailing and Powerboat Schools

Annapolis Sailing School (410-267-7205 or 1-800-638-9192; www.annapolissailing .com; 601 Sixth St., Annapolis) Classes of all sorts are offered by this venerable, reputable school. Experienced instructors teach courses ranging from "Become a Sailor in One Weekend" to "Coastal Navigation." Rentals of 24-foot Rainbow daysailers are available. Also home to KidShip, where sailors as young as 5 learn to tack and jibe. Bytes are 12 feet; Americans and Barnetts are 14 feet. Also, the companion Annapolis Powerboat School offers two- and five-day courses.

Chesapeake Sailing School (1-800-966-0032; www.sailingclasses.com; 7080 Bembe Beach Rd., Annapolis) This well-established school offers a wide range of sailing courses on vessels ranging from 8-foot Optis for children to Tanzer 22s for older folks. Also offers the "Kids on Boats" program for families, and private classes also are available. The school's "Tiller Club" allows members to sail all summer.

J World (410-280-2040; www.jworldannapolis.com; 213 Eastern Ave., Annapolis) Begun in Annapolis in the early 1990s, this sailing school offers weekend programs for folks who want to learn to sail or improve their skills, as well as five-day classes that can mix and match skills. Courses available for those interested in racing, cruising, or simply getting started.

Womanship (1-800-342-9295; www.womanship.com; 137 Conduit St., Annapolis) This reputable school was started by women for women and now has spread to numerous locations. Classes of varying duration and topic.

Fishing

Charter Fishing Boats

CD Outdoors (410-991-8468; www.tacklecove.com) Specializing in light tackle and fly-fishing, Capt. C. D. Dollar operates up and down the Bay with his 23-foot center console. He's also an outfitter, so see him for nature trips or kayak rentals, too.

Deale Captains Association (www.dealecaptains.com) An association of numerous captains operating out of Rockhold Creek and other areas around Deale, which is in southern Anne Arundel County and easily reached from Annapolis or Washington, D.C. Fish from the Bay Bridge south to Cove Point at the mouth of the Patuxent River.

Golf

Annapolis Golf Club (410-263-6771; 2638 Carrollton Rd., Annapolis) Nine holes. Local course; semiprivate. Located in the Annapolis Roads community.

Bay Hills Golf Club (410-974-0669; www.bayhillsgolf.com; 545 Bay Hills Dr., Arnold) 18 holes; semiprivate. Located north of Annapolis. Pro shop, restaurant.

Dwight D. Eisenhower Golf Course (410-571-0973; www.eisenhowergolf.com; 1576 Generals Hwy., Crownsville) 18 holes. Popular public course located just outside Annapolis; book online up to eight days in advance.

Golf Club at South River (410-798-5865 or 1-800-SO-RIVER; www.mdgolf.com; 3451 Solomons Island Rd., Edgewater) Challenging 18-hole public course. Driving range, putting green. Earned 4½ stars in *Golf Digest*'s 2000–2001 "Places to Play."

Natural Places: Parks and Sanctuaries

Jug Bay Wetlands Sanctuary (410-741-9330; 1361 Wrighton Rd., Lothian) Located on the Patuxent River. Seven miles of uncrowded trails; limited hours. If you're lucky, you might—and we mean might—catch a glimpse of the elusive river otter. Open Mar.–Nov., Wed., Sat., and Sun. Call for reservations and winter hours.

Quiet Waters Park (410-222-1777; www.friendsofquietwaterspark.org; 600 Quiet Waters Park Rd., Annapolis) Located down Annapolis Neck south of the Historic District area, the pretty park along the South River offers good walking and cycling, and you can also rent a small boat. Summer concerts take place, and there are two art galleries, too.

Sandy Point State Park (410-974-2149; www.dnr.state.md.us/publiclands/southern/sandypoint.html; 1100 E. College Pkwy., Annapolis) More than 780 acres located on US 50 near the last exit before the Bay Bridge. It's fun to hang out here and watch what goes on in the Bay—from passing scows and barges to the crisp white sails of the yachting set in summer. Plus, there's an up-close-and-personal view of the Bay Bridge. Beach for swimming, fishing, bird-watching, crabbing; marina for boating (rowboats and motorboats for rent), windsurfing; 22 boat ramps; bait, tackle, fuel, and fishing licenses. Costs vary depending on date and season.

Paddling

Getting out on the water is wonderful, but you must be safe about it. Check on weather before heading out: Is a windy storm due later in the day? Do you have proper gear for the weather? How about your water bottle? And check on conditions. Do you know how to handle your boat? Have you ever kayaked? Do you know the depth of the stream you're about to canoe—and will its depth change today because it's tidal? Outfitters and charter operations are an excellent choice for getting out into unfamiliar waters no matter how experienced you are. And check on stream conditions at local parks or marinas. The Maryland Department of Natural Resources may have more information you can use: www.dnr.state.md.us.

Jug Bay Wetlands Sanctuary (410-741-9330; www.jugbay.org; 1361 Wrighton Rd., Lothian; open Wed., Sat., and Sun. 9–5; closed Sun. Dec. through Feb.)Wild rice grows with midsummer abandon along Jug Bay, a suburban outpost along the Patuxent River west of Annapolis. Three centuries ago, this was a deepwater harbor, but time, siltation, and an old railroad bed have conspired to create a quiet paddler's paradise, studded by marshmallows and home to kingbirds, territorial red-wing blackbirds, and largemouth bass and perch. This is a limited-access sanctuary, but check to see if you can join one of the guided paddles that are offered here from time to time. Check the Web site for more.

Sandy Point State Park (410-974-2149; www.dnr.state.md.us/publiclands/southern/sandypoint.html; 1100 E. College Parkway, Annapolis) Small craft launch good for kayaks. Rent powerboats (15 feet with 6 hp) and a couple of rowboats.

Outfitters

Annapolis Canoe and Kayak (410-263-2303; www.annapoliscanoeandkayak.com; 311 Third St.) Located in Eastport, this is the city's only canoe and kayak shop on the water, and you can rent single or tandem kayaks for $15 or $20. The shop closes at 6:30 PM during the week. Weekend hours are 10–5; winter hours are Mon.–Sat. 11–5.

Kent Island Kayaks (1-877-KIKAYAK; www.kikayaks.com; 100 Channel Marker Way, Suite 100, Grasonville) Cross the Bay Bridge to Wells Cove Marina to rent a kayak. Please reserve first; owner C. D. Dollar can deliver to your location, too.

Paddle or Pedal (410-271-7007; operates at Quiet Waters Park, 600 Quiet Waters Park Rd., Annapolis) Rent kayaks, canoes, rowboat, pedal boats, sailboats, or paddleboards and get out on Harness Creek.

Spectator Sports

The **Washington BayHawks**, the region's professional lacrosse team, suits up in Annapolis for its seasons through 2011. Play takes place at Navy-Marine Corps Memorial Stadium, which is very easy to reach. Take the Rowe Boulevard exit off US 50 and you'll soon reach it on your right at Taylor Avenue. For the May–Aug. game schedule: washington bayhawks.com.

Sporting Goods and Camping Supply Stores

Angler's Sport Center (410-757-3442; 1456 Whitehall Rd., Annapolis) The dean of local sporting goods. Hunting and fishing licenses, fishing gear, decoys, outdoor clothing, supplies for crabbing and hunting. Located between Annapolis and the Bay Bridge, Exit 30 off US 50, east of Cape St. Claire.

Marty's Sporting Goods (410-956-2238; 95 Mayo Rd., Edgewater) Everything for fishing. Some hunting supplies. Licenses.

Swimming

Arundel Olympic Swim Center (410-222-7933 or 301-970-2216; www.aacounty.org
/RecParks; 2690 Riva Rd., Annapolis) Olympic-sized pool operated by the Anne
Arundel County Recreation and Parks Department. Nominal entrance fees. Open
Mon.–Thurs. 6 AM–10 PM, Fri. 6 AM–9 PM, Sat. 8 AM–4 PM, Sun. 10 AM–6 PM. Walk-in fee
is $4 for kids and $6 for seniors.

Sandy Point State Park (410-974-2149; www.dnr.state.md.us/publiclands/southern
/sandypoint.html; 1100 E. College Pkwy., Annapolis) One of the few sandy beaches on
the Bay. Costs vary according to season. Take the last exit off US 50 before the Bay
Bridge.

Tennis

In Anne Arundel County, 45 county parks have tennis courts; eight have lights for nighttime play. Visitors to Annapolis, where court time is harder to find, may want to use courts
in nearby towns in less-congested central or rural south county. For information, contact
the Anne Arundel County Department of Recreation and Parks at 410-222-7300.

SHOPPING

If you like to shop, Annapolis is your spot. You can go to the Historic District or West
Annapolis for unique small shops (mostly), or to Westfield Annapolis mall or Annapolis
Towne Centre at Parole for chains large and small (mostly).

The Historic District is where you'll find the City Dock and Main Street shops. Up the
hill, off State Circle, boutique-lined Maryland Avenue stretches east toward the Naval
Academy. Radiating west from the city's other fabled circle—Church Circle—is West Street.
It's seen quite the renaissance in recent years, with art galleries tucking in among the
restaurants and businesses.

For an off-the-beaten-path shopping opportunity, consider the West Annapolis neighborhood, home to specialty shops on Annapolis St. There's easy street parking here, and
it's about a mile away from the Historic District and parallel to Rowe Blvd.

For the full-on mall experience, go to the giant **Westfield Annapolis** (forever known
locally as "Annapolis Mall"; westfield.com/annapolis), which has more than 240 stores
selling just about anything you can imagine. This includes Nordstrom and Lord & Taylor.
It's located near the intersection of Bestgate Road and Generals Highway in Parole. Not far
away, **Annapolis Towne Centre at Parole** (www.visitatc.com) has come on the scene, with
its 39 shops and restaurants. Here you'll find upscale chains like Sur la Table, Coldwater
Creek, and lucy—as well as the local Target. The smaller **Annapolis Harbour Center** (410-
266-5857; MD 2 and Aris T. Allen Blvd.) is home to Office Depot, Barnes & Noble, Old
Navy, and many specialty stores. North of the city near BWI Thurgood Marshall Airport is
Arundel Mills (410-540-5100; www.simon.com; 7000 Arundel Mills Cir., Hanover, MD
21076), a massive mall with 17 anchors and more than 225 specialty stores and restaurants.
All but Annapolis Towne Centre count movie theaters among their tenants.

Antiques

Bon Vivant Antiques (410-263-9651; www.bonvivantantiques.com; 104 Annapolis St.,
West Annapolis) A stalwart on the West Annapolis shopping corridor; a wonderful
antiques shop full of china, silver, and jewelry treasures. Well worth a stop.

Evergreen Antiques (410-216-9067; 69 Maryland Ave.) Here's a shop that echoes the days when Maryland Avenue was lined with antique shops. There's a mix here that includes antique and vintage items, with interesting porcelains/ceramics and lots of silver and jewelry.

Then . . . & Again (410-573-0313; www.thennagain.com; 2009 West St.) Look for a "Lucky Bag"—the U.S. Naval Academy yearbook—or similar memorabilia among the stands here at this 30-vendor antique/collectible mall. There's a lot here.

West Annapolis Antiques (410-295-1200; 103 Annapolis St., West Annapolis) The women tee-heeing over the fabulous hats they found in this browsable shop were worth the stop here one day. Home furnishings and jewelry are among the specialties.

Art and Craft Galleries

American Craftworks Collection (410-626-1583; www.americancraftworkscollection .com; 189B Main St.) Excellent selection of fine contemporary crafts. Always fun to browse.

Annapolis Collection Gallery (410-280-1414; www.annapoliscollection.com; 45 West St.) A nice gallery that celebrates "six Annapolis masters." These are portraitists Moe Hanson and Ann Munro Wood, illustrator Sally Wern Comport, painters Greg Harlin and Roxie Munro, and Yoo Mi Yoon, who practices the Chinese fine art of paper cutting. You also can find work by the late photographer Marion Warren.

The Annapolis Pottery (410-268-6153; www.annapolispottery.com; 40 State Cir.) A well-loved local institution offering a wide array of stoneware and porcelain pieces, from handy pitchers to art platters to bird feeders. Watch potters work in back.

ARTFX (410-990-4540; artfxgallery.org; 3 Church Cir.) Mix of styles and media include pottery and prints and treats like folk art paintings of all Eastern Shore rivers by artist Jimmy Reynolds.

Aurora Gallery (410-263-9150; auroragallery.net; 67 Maryland Ave.) Paintings by local or locally affiliated artists and fine crafts in various media. Great jewelry, too. This shop is high on the browsability list and a longtime Maryland Avenue resident.

Easy Street (410-263-5556; www.easystreetgallery.com; 8 Francis St.) Among the best and most enduring of the city's upscale craft and gift galleries. Specializes in terrific blown glass and art glass pieces.

La Petite Galerie (410-268-2425; www.la-petite-galerie.net; 39 Maryland Ave.) Paintings from the 19th and 20th centuries; generally traditional, representational works.

Main Street Gallery (410-216-7166; www.mainstreetfineart.com; 216A Main St.) Nice space showing a mix of work by local, regional, and some international artists.

Maria's Picture Place (410-263-8282; www.mariaspictureplace.biz; 45 Maryland Ave.) A small gallery with a good frame shop showcases local and regional pieces, including a dwindling few printed by the late, famed Annapolis-based Chesapeake photographer Marion Warren. Look here for work by other regional photographers.

McBride Gallery (410-267-7077; www.mcbridegallery.com; 215 Main St.) Longtime local gallery hosts a variety of artists, many from Virginia and Maryland, and many with a maritime or shoreside appeal. For the exhibit schedule, check the Web site.

West Annapolis Gallery (410-295-6880; www.westannapolisgallery.com; 108 Annapolis St., West Annapolis) Colorful limited-edition prints and watercolors by Liz Lind, plus a frame shop.

Bustling Main Street, topped by the spire of St. Anne's Episcopal Church. www.VisitAnnapolis.org

Books

The Annapolis Bookstore (410-280-2339; www.annapolisbookstore.com; 68 Maryland
Ave.) Cozy and independent, with used, rare, and new books. This is a good place to
find sailing and maritime history books.

Barnes & Noble (410-573-1115; www.barnesandnoble.com; Annapolis Harbour Center,
MD 2 and Aris T. Allen Blvd.) Huge and popular, as one might expect. But it also has a
knowledgeable selection of regional and local books ranging from Bay histories and
watermen's tales to literature penned by local writers.

Borders (410-571-0923; www.borders.com; Westfield Annapolis, Jennifer and Bestgate
Rds. off US 50) The popular chain is located in a huge two-story emporium in
Annapolis's main mall. Books and much more.

Children

Be Beep-A Toy Shop (410-224-4066; www.bebeepatoyshop.com; Festival at Riva
Shopping Center, 2327C Forest Dr.) Quality toys.

The Giant Peach (410-268-8776; www.thegiantpeachonline.com; 17 Annapolis St., West
Annapolis) Probably the most venerable children's clothing shop in town.

Clothing

Brown Eyed Girl (410-990-GIRL; www.browneyedgirlannapolis.com; 234 Main St.)
Super cute surfer style for girls of all ages. Billabong, Rip Curl, and Scott Hawaii sandals
are among the brands tucked near the top of Main Street. Look for the hibiscus-
slathered surfboard.

Diva (410-280-9195; www.modiva.com; 30 Market Space) Designers well-known (Nicole Miller, Alice & Olivia) and less so can be found at this trendy boutique by City Dock.

Gina Fitz (90 Maryland Ave.; 410-280-9090) Big thumbs-up to this women's boutique, where professionals and sophisticates can find nice pieces that aren't cookie-cutter. Reversible jackets from Winding River are a hit with the legislative set.

Hats in the Belfry (410-268-6333; www.hatsinthebelfry.com; 103 Main St.) Something of an impromptu performance space, because everybody tries on hats: felt hats, straw hats (including genuine Panamas), funky hats, sporty hats, Easter bonnets, gardening hats, and more.

Paradigm (410-626-6030; www.shopparadigm.com; 179 Main St.) Trendy women's clothing boutique.

Jewelry

La Belle Cezanne (410-263-1996; www.labellecezanne.com; 186 Main St.) One of the best windows to shop in Annapolis. Some unique items.

Tilghman Company (410-268-7855; www.tilghmanjewelers.com; 44 State Cir.) The fine old Maryland name of this business tells you that this is a traditional jewelry store featuring classic gold and silver pieces and pearls, plus Lenox, Waterford, and fine sterling. In business since 1928; on State Circle since 1948.

W. R. Chance Jewelers (410-263-2404; www.wrchance.com; 110 Main St.) From traditional to contemporary work; fine service and well-located at City Dock. In business more than 50 years.

Zachary's (410-266-5555; www.zacharysjeweler.com; 100 Main St.) Beautiful shop full of intriguing jewelry.

Marine Shops

The chain marine stores are well represented in and around Annapolis. In addition to these, the city's spawned a couple of local institutions.

Bacon Sails and Marine Supply (410-263-4880; www.baconsails.com; 116 Legion Ave.) Nifty place for used equipment; noted for a broad array of secondhand sails. In business since 1959. Open during the week only, except Sat. 9:30 AM–12:30 PM Apr. through Aug.

Fawcett Boat Supplies (410-267-8681; www.fawcettboat.com; 919 Bay Ridge Rd.) Fawcett has been a local institution for 50 years, though the store recently moved from its venerable City Dock location. A good source of local boating supplies and information, and they carry a good selection of nautical books, too.

Specialty & Gift Shops

A. L. Goodies General Store (410-269-0071; www.algoodies.com; 112 Main St.) The resident, multistory five-and-dime in the trendy City Dock area. Racks and racks of greeting cards, brass weather vanes, even peanut butter cookies. Good for souvenirs.

Annapolis Country Store (410-269-6773; www.annapoliscountrystore.com; 53 Maryland Ave.) Upscale general store featuring Winnie-the-Pooh, Crabtree & Evelyn, numerous luxury bath items, and lots of great gifts and cards.

Art Things (410-268-3520; www.artthingsinc.com; 2 Annapolis St., West Annapolis) Great art supply shop where the employees are perennially helpful and cheerful. Paints, brushes, papers, and more.

Avoca Handweavers (410-263-1485; www.avoca.ie; 141-143 Main St.) Avoca has been doing business in Ireland since 1723 and continues to make a splash in the Annapolis Historic District. Exquisite handiwork. Wools, linens, and clothing, as well as Irish glass and pottery.

The Black Dog (410-263-4771; www.theblackdog.com; 117 Main St.) This is the non–New England (primarily Cape & Islands) outpost of this Labrador-inspired shop. Get your T-shirt, your golf glove, even your baby's onesie, here, all decked out with signature black Lab.

Dragonfly Garden (410-295-5677; www.dragonflygardendecor.com; 1888 Main St.) A great place to hunt for that cool metal garden sculpture or fun accent to set amid the posies.

Historic Annapolis Foundation Museum Store (410-268-5576; www.annapolis.org; 77 Main St.) Classic museum-quality gifts as well as a good selection of Chesapeake books in a restored 18th-century warehouse.

Mary & Blanche (410-280-8891; www.maryandblanche.com; 78 Maryland Ave.) This is a highly amusing stop for offbeat gifts, cards, and the like.

Mixed Greens (410-216-9830; 48 Randall St.) Great little earth-friendly gift shop operated by two local sisters offers everything from jewelry to candle sconces to sculptures to paper recycled from the oddest things.

Paws (410-263-8683; www.pawspetboutique.com; 64 State Circle) Get your gourmet dog goodies right here, including lovely prints and dinner bowls.

Pepper's (410-267-8722; www.navygear.com; 133 Main St.) Navy T-shirt and sweatshirt central.

Plat du Jour (410-269-1499; www.platdujour.net; 220 Main St.) Filled with tempting French and Italian ceramics and fine linens. Among the most unique shops in the Historic District.

Re-Sails (42 Randall St.; www.resails.com; 410-263-4982) Sails are recycled into bags at this small green shop tucked around the corner from the City Dock.

Vie Necessary Luxuries (410-269-6100; 86 Maryland Ave.) As the store itself says—"necessary luxuries." We once purchased a tea towel with a sorcerer on it for a gift that did, indeed, seem necessary. Reproductions, home items.

SOUTH OF ANNAPOLIS

CALVERT COUNTY

South of Annapolis is waterside countryside mixed with commuting neighborhoods. For complete tourism information, check www.co.cal.md.us/visitors. Otherwise, head for the Anne Arundel–Calvert County line to kick back in two small Bay-side towns there that offer some good rummaging. North Beach's small boardwalk can be fun to stroll, and check out nearby Nice & Fleazy Antique Center at Seventh St. and Bay Ave. (410-257-3044). Next door is Chesapeake Beach with its showcase destination, the **Chesapeake Beach Resort and Spa** (410-257-5596 or 1-866-312-5596; www.chesapeakebeach resortspa.com; 4165 Mears Ave., Chesapeake Beach, MD 20732). The 72-room hotel, located right on the water, comes with three restaurants, a marina, and fishing. Fishermen know this as the decades-old Rod 'N Reel complex, founded in 1946. Charter fishing for rockfish, bluefish, and whatever else is biting remains a time-honored sport here. For info and a rundown of charter boats and captains, check under the Rod & Reel portion of the resort's Web site.

The area offers some excellent parks well worth your time:

Battle Creek Cypress Swamp (410-535-5327; www.calvertparks.org; Gray's Rd. off MD 506 in Prince Frederick) A mix of habitat throughout the county means good bird-watching (herons, kingfishers, American woodcocks, and bald eagles can be seen), hiking, and even beach time. Visit the 100-acre site to stroll the boardwalk running through this unique (for this part of the world) habitat. Closed Mon.

Breezy Point Beach & Campground (410-535-0259 May–Oct., otherwise 301-855-1243; office: 175 Main St., Prince Frederick, MD 20678) is south of Chesapeake Beach. Nets off the beach help protect swimmers from sea nettles. You also can fish, crab, or camp here. Open May–Oct., 6 AM–dusk. Fee.

Flag Ponds Nature Park (410-586-1477; www.calvertparks.org; open 9–8 daily Memorial Day–Labor Day, 9–5 weekends the rest of the year; Calvert County residents $4, others $6) is one of the larger Bay beaches you're likely to see, along with a fishing pier, fossil hunting, a visitor's center, and a friendly nod to the property's life as a pound-net fishing station from the early 1900s to 1955. See the restored Buoy Hotel, where watermen once stayed for weeks at a time.

Jefferson Patterson Park and Museum (410-586-8500; www.jefpat.org; 10515 Mackall Rd.; open mid-Apr.–mid-Oct., Wed.–Sun. 10–5) is headquarters for much of the state's archaeological work. This is a cool place that on June 26, 1814, was the site of a War of 1812 battle called the Battle of St. Leonard Creek. It's also believed Capt. John Smith was here (or nearby) during his famous explorations. The 400-acre park features a visitor's center highlighting the Chesapeake's past, and easy trails through fields and along the Patuxent River. The old barn has been transformed into a broad picnic pavilion. Check the Web site for events.

SOLOMONS ISLAND

The 19th-century oystering village of Solomons Island, where the Patuxent River empties into the Chesapeake Bay, led a quiet life for decades. It's discovered now and easily is the tourism center of the Chesapeake's Western Shore region south of Annapolis. Fishermen looking to head out should contact the **Solomons Charter Captains Association** (1-800-450-1775; via www.fishsolomons.com) or **Bunky's Charter Boats** (410-326-3241; www.bunkyscharterboats.com; 14448 Solomons Island Rd. S.). If you just want to get out on the water for some fun, rent smaller craft from **Solomons Boat Rental** (410-326-4060; www.boat-rent.net). For complete tourism info, check www.ecalvert.com/content/tourism/index.asp and stop by the Solomons Information Center at 14175 Solomons Island Rd. S.; 410-326-6027. Here are some of the village's key highlights:

Annmarie Garden (410-326-4640; www.annmariegarden.org; 13480 Dowell Rd.; open daily 10–5 year-round; Arts Building and gift shop open Tues.–Sun. 10–5) Turn in at the colorful ceramic porcelain gates topped by the sculpted echo of waves along Dowell Rd. at the northern edge of town. This is "The Gateway," the entrance to this 30-acre sculpture garden on St. John Creek. A bronze oyster tonger (an oysterman using tongs, a cross between scissors and a pair of long-handled rakes) greets visitors. Amid the well-landscaped woods, find *The Council Ring* by B. Amore and Woody Dorsey quietly inviting reflection, or *The Surveyor's Map* by Jann Rosen-Queralt and Roma Campanile, an aluminum "boardwalk" into (and even over) the woods. Other sculptures are on loan from The

As part of a visit to the Calvert Marine Museum in Solomons, the William B. Tennyson discharges her passengers at the Drum Point Lighthouse, one of only three remaining screw-pile lights.

Hirshhorn Museum in Washington, D.C. Indoor exhibitions in the Arts Building run the gamut, such as the recent "Wild Things" in which artists from around the country showed their takes on wild animals. ArtsFest is held in mid- to late Sept.; check the Web site for other events.

Calvert Marine Museum (410-326-2042; www.calvertmarine museum.com; 14150 Solomons Island Rd.; open daily 10–5; adults $7, senior citizens $6, children 5–12 $2) is located at the town's Patuxent River-side entrance. Here, the tale of the Patuxent River and Chesapeake marine life is told in all its chapters, down to the prehistoric crocodile jaws and mastodon teeth dug from nearby Calvert Cliffs. Kids love the tanks full of Chesapeake critters like blue crabs and sea horses, and river otters play in a tank here, too. Take a spin through the post-war recreational boating scene and view leisure craft built by Solomons's M. M. Davis & Sons Shipyard, or check out "Secrets of the Mermaid's Purse" featuring skates and rays. ("Mermaid's purse" refers to the four-cornered skate egg case you've likely seen along Atlantic beaches.) Also on the grounds: Drum Point Lighthouse, one of only four remaining screw-pile lights. Forty-three of these distinctly Chesapeake sentinels once stood in the Bay's soft bottom, warning mariners off dangerous shoals. This is one of three screw-pile lights stationed at Bay-area museums (the others are at the Chesapeake Bay Maritime Museum in St. Michaels and along Baltimore's Inner Harbor), and kids like them in part because it feels fairly safe to climb their ladderlike steps to the first floor. They're also a bit like doll-houses. This one is a cozily re-created lighthouse keeper's home put together with help from the memory of a former keeper's granddaughter, Anna Weems Ewald. Down the street, the 1934 **J. C. Lore Oyster House** shows how oysters moved from tongers' boats to gourmets' plates. You can also take a one-hour ride around Solomons's Back Creek and into the Patuxent River aboard the William B. Tennison, a turn-of-the-19th-century "bugeye," one of the indigenous oystering craft. Her sail rig was removed in the early 1900s and an engine installed so she could do duty as a "buyboat," motoring among the oyster dredgers to purchase their catch. Cruises are held May–Oct., Wed.–Sun. at 2 PM; there are additional cruises at 12:30 and 3 PM on weekends in July and Aug. Adults $7, children 5–12 $4.

Fishing for Fossils

If you're interested in learning about the prehistoric sharks that swam here, the Calvert Marine Museum has lots of fossils and information about them. You can also look for them in nearby parks although digging for shark teeth is prohibited. Try **Flag Ponds Nature Center** (410-586-1477; 10 miles south of Prince Frederick on MD 2/4, look for the sign on your left); **Calvert Cliffs State Park** (301-743-7613; 14 miles south of Prince Frederick off MD 2/4 in Lusby; www.dnr.state.md.us/public lands/southern/calvertcliffs.html), or, further north, try **Bay Front Park** (410-257-2230; about half a mile south of Chesapeake Beach). A thin beach widens noticeably at low tide; we found seven shark teeth in an hour one afternoon!

Lodging options include:

Back Creek Inn B&B (410-326-2022; www.backcreekinnbnb.com; 210 Alexander Ln.; Solomons, MD 20688) This is a longtime B&B on the water with gorgeous gardens and a deepwater dock. Quartered in an 1880s waterman's house, the inn has four rooms in the original house, a newer addition with two suites, and a cottage. They're all named for herbs. Handicapped accessible. Room rates range from $105–220, with lower prices midweek.

The gardens are a treat at Back Creek B&B on the water in Solomons.

Blue Heron B&B (410-326-2707; www.blueheronbandb.com; 14614 Solomons Island Rd., Solomons MD 20688) This is a handsome contemporary waterfront inn with four guest rooms on two floors and a CIA- and Cordon Bleu-trained chef serving as host. Guest rooms provide deck space along the water and great waterfront views. Gourmet breakfast and, upon request, perhaps a fine dinner, too. Room rates range from $179–249.

Holiday Inn Solomons Conference Center & Marina (410-326-6311; www.solomonsmd.hiselect.com; 155 Holiday Dr., Solomons, MD 20688) More than 326 rooms include 50 suites, plus the hotel has a health and fitness center, on-site laundry, and outdoor pool.

Zahniser's Yachting Center (410-326-2166; www.zahnisers.com; 245 C St./P.O. Box 760, Solomons, MD 20688) Amenities include pool, bar and grill, bathhouse, and Wi-Fi. Transient slips available (reservations recommended). Also home to the fine Dry Dock Restaurant.

Restaurant options include:

The C. D. Café (410-326-3877; www.cdcafe.info; 14350 Solomons Island Rd.) This comfortable 11-seat restaurant serves creative fresh cuisine, so look for a cornmeal-crusted catfish salad or a healthy salmon dish. Since it takes no reservations, you and yours can wait in the Next Door Lounge in the same building where the café has been delighting the locals for years.

The Dry Dock (410-326-4817; Zahnizer's Yachting Center, 245 C St.) Serving lunch and dinner daily in fine-dining style from a waterside seat at this popular marina.

Popular **Stoney's** seafood restaurants include **Solomons Pier** (410-326-2424; solomonspier.com; 1457 Solomons Island Rd. S.), which you can't miss because it juts into the Patuxent, serving crab imperial, fried oysters, and Stoney's signature crabcakes. Almost directly across the street at 14442 Main St. is **Stoney's Kingfisher Grill** (410-394-0236; www.stoneysseafoodhouse.com), which has a nice, bright dining room and alfresco tables lined up across a back deck. FYI: Stoney's has a great seasonal crab-cracking deck and restaurant to the north at Broome's Island (410-586-1888) and, if you're passing through farther north, a restaurant on MD 2 in Prince Frederick (410-586-1888).

St. Mary's County

Maryland's first colonists stepped ashore in rural St. Mary's County, at St. Clement's Island in the Potomac River. Now preserved as a state park, the peaceable island sits out in the river upstream from St. Marys City, site of the colony's first capital and location of a village that re-creates the original, which is being excavated. It's an easy daytrip from Annapolis, Washington, D.C., or Baltimore to St. Mary's County via MD 235, 5, or 2/4. For complete tourism info, check tour.co.saint-marys.md.us.

Historic St. Marys City (240-895-4960 (administration), 240-895-4990 (visitor's center) or 1-800-762-1634; www.stmaryscity.org; 18559 Hogaboom Lane. Open mid-Mar.–Nov. In spring, open Tues.–Sat. (call for hours); summer and fall, Wed.–Sun. 10–5. Adults $10, seniors $8, students $6, ages 6–12 $3.50, ages 5 and under free) Near the southern tip of the county stands Maryland's re-created 1634 colonial capital. The original capital city was abandoned when state government moved to Annapolis and dismantled by 1720, but it's still the subject of extensive archaeological work. Among tantalizing discoveries: three lead coffins found in the early 1990s. After NASA finished testing the air to see whether it dated to the 17th century, researchers concluded that the remains inside likely belonged to members of the state's founding Calvert family. Visit active excavations during summer. At four living history sites, costumed interpreters explain the re-created elements of the city, from a Yaocomaco Indian village with sleeping furs inside the grass witchotts, or dwellings, to Godiah Spray's tobacco plantation populated with cows, chickens, and Ossabaw pigs, a species that first roamed here 300 years ago. The square-rigger *Maryland Dove* (a big hit with kids), a typical period representation of the two vessels that brought early settlers, docks in the St. Marys River. Also here: a 1934 reproduction of the statehouse. A brick chapel being re-created on an original 1667 foundation is open as construction allows and symbolizes the founding place of the Roman Catholic religion and freedom of conscience in English America. The St. John's Site Museum preserves one of the most important historic sites in the state and illustrates how archaeology helps us understand the past. Stop at the visitor's center for an overview, picnic at the riverside tables, and find snacks at the Shop at Farthing's Ordinary.

Point Lookout State Park (301-872-5688; www.dnr.state.md.us/publiclands/sourthern/pointlookout.html; 11175 Point Lookout Rd., Scotland) Once a Revolution-era lookout and later a Civil War–era Confederate prison camp, Point Lookout is located at the end

Interpreters alongside the re-created statehouse at Historic St. Mary's City. Photo courtesy of Historic St. Mary's City

of MD 5, where the Potomac River meets the Chesapeake Bay. Sun yourself on the beach or surf cast from a pier. Swim in designated areas. Hike back along the beach to the reconstruction of the Civil War's **Fort Lincoln** and, at the park's tip, check out its lighthouse. Grills, picnic area, and camping. The Civil War Museum/Marshland Nature Center, located in the campground, is open seasonally.

Scheible's Fishing Center (301-872-5185; www.scheibles.homestead.com; 48342 Wynne Rd.) This is the longtime charter fleet that takes anglers in search of striped bass or bluefish. Half- or full-day charters. Restaurant, lodge.

Trails, outbuildings, and special events tell the fascinating story of Sotterley Plantation in St. Mary's County.

Sotterley Plantation (301-373-2280 or 1-800-681-0850; www.sotterley.org; 4430 Sotterley Ln. off MD 235, Hollywood) is an architectural treasure and colonial grande dame that weathered many generations in relative obscurity. That, despite an intriguing group of owners that includes early Maryland governor George Plater III, who corresponded from here with his friend, George Washington. In addition, U.S. troops mustered here during the War of 1812, and Confederate sympathizers were here during the Civil War. Among the remaining relics of the plantation is a rare, small slave cabin—where 19 to 24 people slept—dating to the 1830s. Visitors can tour the manor house, and the grounds are lovely. Special events are held throughout the year; check the Web site for details. The plantation is located 9 miles east of Leonardtown on MD 245.

St. Clement's Island Museum (301-769-2222; www.stmarysmd.com/recreate/museums; 38370 Point Breeze Rd., Colton's Point; open late Mar. through Sept., daily 10–5; winter, Wed.–Sun. noon–4; $1 for ages 12 and up) can be reached by following brown history-marker signs on back roads from MD 5. The small but well-considered museum offers a fine review of early Maryland history, saluting its English settlers, who arrived just across the channel at St. Clement's Island in 1634. Among the museum's exhibits is a room that details the beginnings of the Church of England's separation from the Catholic Church. Learn all about the Calverts, successive Lords Baltimore, and Maryland's founders. The park is a great destination—even for folks who aren't Maryland history buffs—with riverfront picnic tables, a fishing pier (licenses required), and, best of all, a summer weekend water taxi shuttling guests to the 40-acre island, which features mown paths, narrow beaches, picnic tables, and multitudinous osprey. There's even a recently re-created lighthouse to replace one that burned decades back. The boat runs Memorial Day–Oct., Sat.–Sun. 12:30–4. Call 301-769-2222.

For lodging and fine weekend dining, try **The Brome-Howard Inn** (301-866-0656; www.bromehowardinn.com; 18281 Rosecroft Rd./P.O. Box 476, St. Marys City, MD 20686). Beautiful fine dining and rooms are available at this inn situated on 30 acres of farmland along the St. Marys River near Historic St. Marys City. Three rooms and one suite cost $125–185. Serving dinner Thurs.–Sun., and Sunday brunch. If you're arriving via boat, try **Point Lookout Marina** (301-872-5000 or 1-877-384-9716; www.pointlookoutmarina .com; 16244 Miller's Wharf Rd., Ridge, MD 20680) off the Potomac River on Jutlan and Smith creeks. Spinnakers Restaurant is on-site, serving steaks, seafood, and pasta.

5

The Upper Bay

Decoys, Docks & Lazy Days

CHESTERTOWN AND ROCK HALL AROUND THE HEAD OF THE BAY TO HAVRE DE GRACE

Fields of corn and soybeans go on forever as the countryside starts to roll north of the Chesapeake Bay Bridge on the Eastern Shore, en route to the stately brick buildings of Chestertown, a major 18th-century port, and on to crossroads towns beloved by antiquers and marinas alongside rivers named Chester, Sassafras, and Bohemia. Rounding the head of the Bay, the traveler salutes the Chesapeake & Delaware Canal at Chesapeake City, a recovered Victorian gem where plaques on the front of each colorful home announce the name of its 19th-century founder. Past Elkton and North East (and the top-of-the-Bay Elk and North East rivers), one finally crosses high above the mighty Susquehanna River. Here is the prehistoric forebear to the Bay, a wide river whose nearby towns include churches and mansions built of granite from its shores at nearby Port Deposit. Tougher stuff than you'll find in the southern Bay.

Look to the river as you cross to see the Susquehanna Flats, which once drew U.S. presidents and captains of industry to partake in the sportsman's "gunning" life. Here, the Northeast is coming on; travelers headed north on Interstate 95 will find themselves on the New Jersey Turnpike in less than an hour. They'd do well to stop where the river meets the Bay, in Havre de Grace, "Decoy Capital of the World" and a growing tourist town north of Baltimore. From many points in town, you can see the water.

This part of Bay Country tends to look more to Philadelphia or Baltimore than, say, Washington, D.C., but nowhere in Chesapeake does one escape colonial U.S. history. George Washington passed through the Upper Shore as he went about his Revolution-era duties.

Chestertown, with its abundant restored 18th-century buildings, sits snug alongside the Chester River. Cross the bridge into this college town, a royal port of entry that dates to 1706. Now, shops and restaurants line the streets. The Victorian-style Imperial Hotel and Colonial-era White Swan Tavern, famed restorations, hold court across High Street from one another. Washington College dates to 1782 and provides a cultural center for the town.

OPPOSITE: *Tall ships gather for Downrigging Weekend in Chestertown, when the sails come down from the schooner* Sultana. Photo courtesy of Sultana Projects

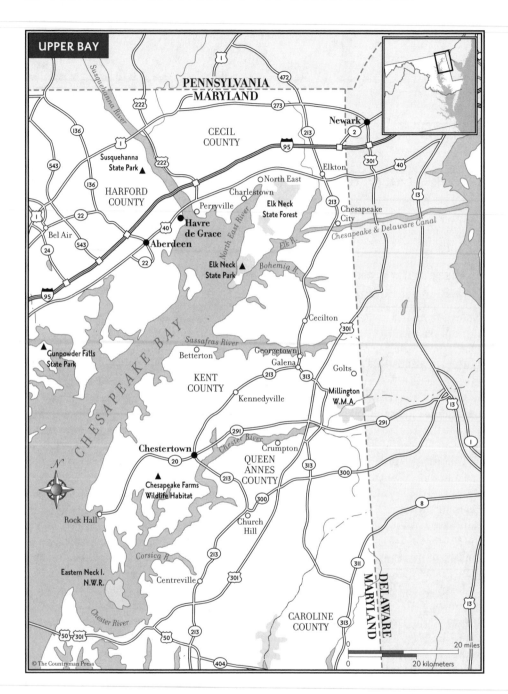

With its concentration of terrific lodgings, restaurants, and other amenities, Chestertown makes a central headquarters for exploring the Upper Eastern Shore area.

From here, you can head straight for the Bay, down MD 20 to **Rock Hall**. This little watermen's town is also port to numerous pleasure boaters who dock their craft at multitudinous marinas or stay in its pretty B&Bs. A ferry here transported Revolution-era

The boardwalk promenade at Havre de Grace.

travelers (Washington, Jefferson, Madison) to and from Annapolis, including the fabled Marylander Tench Tilghman, who carried news of the colonial troops' victory at Yorktown as he passed through en route to Philadelphia, where the Continental Congress was meeting. Plan to visit Eastern Neck National Wildlife Refuge, an island hugging the Eastern Shore's left bank past Rock Hall. Walk out on a boardwalk and look over the water for shorebirds in summer, or for the famed tundra swans that arrive as cooler days signal the coming of winter.

Not far away is **Crumpton,** home of Dixon's Furniture and its notable Wednesday auction that spans 30 acres.

The War of 1812 saw combat here in Kent County with the Battle of Caulk's Field in 1814. The house where the British commander purportedly died is now a B&B, the Inn at Mitchell House. In addition, just up MD 213 from Chestertown, the famed Kitty Knight stood up to the marauding British troops at Georgetown. The Kitty Knight House—saved from fire—also is now an inn.

Farther on up MD 213 stands **Chesapeake City,** famous for the 14-mile long Chesapeake & Delaware Canal that links the Bay with the Delaware River, as well as the Bayard House, a fine dining establishment whose physical rebirth may be as significant as its food. It was restored in the mid-1980s as this Victorian town's renaissance was under way. Bring your binoculars, since watching the major ships pass through the canal is a prime Chesapeake City activity. At the edge of town is the C&D Canal Museum.

Havre de Grace, less than an hour west of here across the tip of the Bay, has built a lot for visitors to enjoy over the past two decades. Along the Susquehanna River waterfront wends a lovely boardwalk that was rebuilt after Tropical Storm Isabel in September 2003. The community has also built a maritime museum that sits near its decoy museum—the latter saluting the local folk art that makes this the Decoy Capital of the World. The town's name is believed to derive from the Marquis de Lafayette, who compared this with Le

Havre in his own France. Dating to 1658, Havre de Grace still feels like a hometown despite changes along the waterfront. Along Washington Street, for instance, antique shops have moved into old department stores. Visitors of a certain age will recognize the feel of old downtowns from childhood.

The Kent County Visitor Center in Chestertown is well-located at the Cross St. and MD 213; it's open during the week 9–5, and Sat. and Sun. 10–4 during the summer; Sat. and Sun. 10–2 during the winter. In Havre de Grace, the Office of Tourism & Visitor Center at 450 Pennington Ave. is open Mon.–Fri. 9–5, Sat. 11–4 and, from Apr.–Dec., Sun. 11–4.

LODGING

The villages and crossroads towns of the Upper Bay region offer B&Bs and small inns that may be reproduction Georgians or old Victorians. Have tea on a brick patio during summer afternoons, or grab binoculars as the giant vessels transit the Chesapeake & Delaware Canal. Prices are highest during high-season weekends and tend to drop midweek and in the off-season. Of course, they are subject to change. Check cancellation policies and don't be surprised if your inn has a two-night minimum, especially in high season. Check lodging Web sites for other policies or for specials.

Rates

Lodging rates fall within this scale:

Inexpensive:	Up to $75
Moderate:	$75–150
Expensive:	$150–225
Very Expensive:	$225 and up

HAVRE DE GRACE

LA CLE D'OR GUESTHOUSE
Proprietor: Ron Browning
410-939-6562 or 1-888-HUG-GUEST
www.lacledorguesthouse.com
226 N. Union Ave., Havre de Grace, MD 21078
Price: Moderate to Expensive
Handicapped Access: No
Restrictions: Call to make arrangements for children under 12

La Cle D'or looks sturdily prosperous from the outside, but check out the crystal chandeliers and shiny gold wallpaper in the parlor! The 1868 brick house, once owned by members of the Johns Hopkins family, is surprisingly luxurious, and host Ron Browning knows a thing or two about antiques. Guest rooms retain a French flair—this is, after all, Havre de Grace, the "Harbor of Grace" named by Lafayette—right down to the Napoleonic wallpaper. The Rochambeaux Room comes with an antique double bed and a bath around the corner. Next door find the pleasant DeGrace Suite, rented only with the Rochambeaux, making a nice accommodation for traveling couples willing to share a hall bath. Then there's the Lafayette Suite, with a queen-sized bed and a window-lined sitting room overlooking the home's secluded walled garden. Each room comes with a television and VCR or DVD. Full breakfast.

SPENCER-SILVER MANSION
Innkeeper: Carol Nemeth
410-939-1845 or 1-800-780-1485
www.spencersilvermansion.com

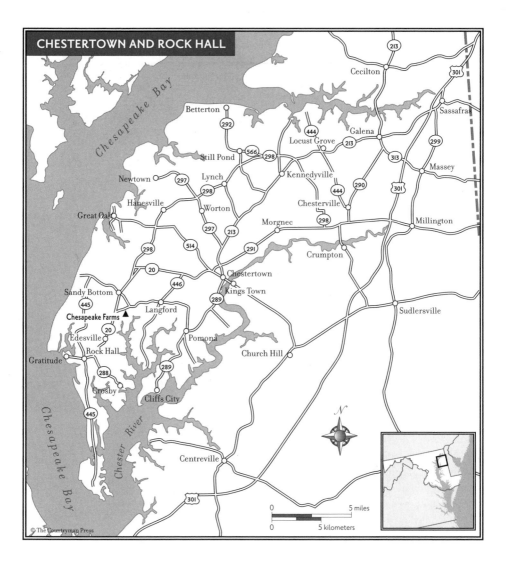

CHESTERTOWN AND ROCK HALL

© The Countryman Press

0 — 5 miles

0 — 5 kilometers

200 S. Union Ave., Havre de Grace, MD 21078
Price: Moderate to Expensive
Handicapped Access: In the carriage house
Special Features: Well-behaved children and pets OK; please speak with innkeeper about house rules regarding pets

"J. N. Spencer, 1896" reads the marble plate surrounding the doorbell at this Victorian, authentic from the turret atop the house to the intricate woodwork in the hallway. A bronze art deco figure even presents itself on the newel post. Original stained glass atop many windows is worth the price of your night's stay, and innkeeper Carol Nemeth has been at it for so many years it's hard to imagine a detail she hasn't foreseen. Not only that, but this is a good bargain. Four rooms, each with amenities such as ironing boards and cable TV and DVDs, are located inside the house and include marble-topped tables or corner cabinets with inset glass. Two enormous front rooms share a bath; two have private baths. Enter one of the private baths, with its two-person whirlpool tub, through stained-glass doors. The stone carriage house out back is cozy enough to spend the winter, with a queen-sized bed and window seat in the wood-stained bedroom at the top of the iron spiral staircase. Downstairs expect a daybed, whirlpool, TV/DVD player, and kitchenette. Breakfast at the Spencer-Silver is served until 10:30 AM. Day-long coffee and tea service and a game closet (including garden games, like bocce) are among the numerous comfortable touches here.

VANDIVER INN

Innkeepers: Susan and John Muldoon
410-939-5200 or 1-800-245-1655
www.vandiverinn.com
301 S. Union Ave., Havre de Grace, MD
21078
Price: Moderate to Expensive
Handicapped Access: Limited

The venerable Vandiver, onetime home to the local mayor and Maryland politician of the same name, offers full breakfast, a "community table" dinner most Mondays, and showcase dinner events monthly. Visitors can stay in the landmark 1886 Victorian's eight rooms, with elaborately tiled fireplaces or twin flues, claw-foot tubs, and antique beds, or head next door for the 10 rooms located in the Kent and Murphy houses. Either way, your old-fashioned-flavored stay comes with modern touches like Wi-Fi. Beds range from queen- to king-sized, and whirlpool suites are available.

The Victorian Vandiver Inn offers lovely accommodations in Havre de Grace.

CHESTERTOWN

BRAMPTON BED & BREAKFAST INN

Owners: Michael and Danielle Hanscom
410-778-1860 or 1-866-305-1860
www.bramptoninn.com
25227 Chestertown Rd., Chestertown, MD
21620
Price: Expensive to Very Expensive
Handicapped Access: Yes (one cottage)

Special features: No children under 12; please call about one pet-friendly room

Century-old trees and boxwoods greet visitors to this gorgeous 1860 house set on 35 acres between the Chester River and Chesapeake Bay. Relax in a rocker on the huge wraparound porch beneath the lazy ceiling fan. Inside, the ceilings are high, the furnishings mix antiques and reproductions, and old wood dominates, from Georgia pine floors to a 3½-story walnut and ash central staircase. Seven smartly decorated guest rooms have private baths, working fireplaces and/or double showers. In addition are five great-looking cottages on the property. "Sunrise" and "Sunset" cottages are located in the old horse barn, and "Russell's Cottage" is the transformed smokehouse. If you and your beloved need to get away, spend a weekend in one of the two highly private cottages with stone fireplaces, a big whirlpool tub inside, and a deep Japanese style overflow tub outside—right next to the outdoor shower. Order breakfast in bed. Brampton's amenity list is long: coffee in the den by 7 AM; drinks, cookies, and biscotti all day; afternoon tea; kayaks available through the Rock Hall Yacht Club, and golf at Chestertown Country Club. Nice. This is a Select Registry, Distinguished Inns of North America member inn.

GREAT OAK MANOR B&B

Innkeepers: Cassandra and John Fedas
410-778-5943 or 1-800-504-3098
www.greatoak.com
10568 Cliff Rd., Chestertown, MD 21620
Price: Expensive to Very Expensive
Handicapped Access: Partial
Special features: Children of all ages welcome with weddings, whole house rentals, and family reunions

A stunning Bay-side inn facing west toward sunset, Great Oak Manor is as handsome a house as you'll see. It's unusual among the many Eastern Shore mansions built in the 1930s because this faithful Georgian reproduction used old brick, probably shipped as ballast in Grace Line ships. Detail and carvings are meticulous, guest rooms are traditionally but smartly furnished—some with antiques—and the public rooms are varied and interesting, with high ceilings and built-in bookshelves. A contemporary conservatory offers an endless lap pool looking out on the grounds. All 12 guest rooms are attractively decorated and spacious, many with Bay views and/or fireplaces. All but one have a king-sized bed; the other has a queen. (The rooms also have landline phones because cell reception gets spotty in this corner of the Bay.) The old third-floor gambling room is spacious and clubby, with a high ceiling, king-sized bed, and knotty pine paneling on some of its walls. Set on 12 acres, Great Oak offers an expansive waterside backyard where the Adirondack chairs

Great Oak Manor near Chestertown features 12 handsomely decorated guest rooms.

beckon. There's even a small beach, and guests have access to bikes, Full breakfast is served, and a light supper can be arranged in advance. Member of Select Registry, Distinguished Inns of North America.

IMPERIAL HOTEL

Owners: Doug and Judy O'Dell
410-778-5000 or 1-800-295-0014
www.imperialchestertown.com
208 High St., Chestertown, MD 21620
Price: Moderate
Handicapped Access: Partial; call to discuss

The circa 1903 Imperial sits in the perfect downtown location for a Chestertown visit, and it's fun to stay in an old place like this. The hotel is high Victorian, perhaps with rosy-pink woodwork and butterflies in the posies on your room's matching wallpaper. On the second floor, you can walk onto a veranda and look over High Street. The 11 rooms and two suites have flat-screen TVs, but the hotel, while renovated, is not brand spanking new. So, your floorboard may creak when you step out of bed or when someone runs up the staircase outside your room. A continental breakfast is served in the fine dining Front Room restaurant, and you gotta admit, the white cloth napkins are a nice touch with the morning's granola. The Imperial's also a relative bargain; you'd easily pay the same in any moderately priced chain motel. Dinner in the Front Room is a local treat, with a menu focused on fresh regional cuisine.

THE INN AT MITCHELL HOUSE

Owners: Jim and Tracy Stone
410-778-6500
www.innatmitchellhouse.com
8796 Maryland Pkwy., Chestertown, MD 21620
Price: Moderate
Handicapped Access: No
Restrictions: Children accepted by prior arrangement

This longtime B&B, an 18th-century manor house, boasts a much older history of welcoming guests. British commander Sir Peter Parker allegedly was brought here after the nearby Battle of Caulk's Field in 1814, fought during the War of 1812. When surgery upon the kitchen table failed to save his life, they pickled Peter Parker in a keg of rum and sent him back to England. You'll find your stay here far more pleasant. Located in the country close to Chestertown, Rock Hall, and the once-bustling resort town of Tolchester, this 1743 manor house sits on 10 acres at the end of a long, tree-lined drive by a pond. Inside are five full rooms with private baths (a sixth room is rented only as part of a suite), four with fireplaces, fire logs provided. Four more fireplaces stand in the house's public areas, which have an outdoor motif of mounted waterfowl, marsh grass, and riding hats. It all makes for a suitable introduction to rural Kent County. A full country breakfast is served in a dining room decorated with china plates, wireless is available, and guests can use the private beach at Tolchester Marina. In addition, the Stones recently built a great new cottage ($239 nightly) at the edge of the property, replete with a kudu trophy over the fireplace, stainless fridge, and a hewn wood breakfast bar. It's rustic in style but modern in comfort.

THE WHITE SWAN TAVERN

Manager: Mary Susan Maisel
410-778-2300
www.whiteswantavern.com
231 High St., Chestertown, MD 21620
Price: Expensive to Very Expensive
Handicapped Access: No
Special Features: No children under 12 unless the family has rented the entire inn

Perhaps the most authentic, meticulous colonial restoration on the Eastern Shore, the 1733 White Swan is a time capsule, handsome, dignified, and well-located on

The White Swan Tavern in Chestertown is a well-known colonial restoration.

downstairs in the parlor. Check the display cabinet to see artifacts found during the 1978 archaeological dig.

ROCK HALL
INN AT HUNTINGFIELD FARM
Innkeepers: Jim and Joanne Rich
410-639-7779
www.huntingfield.com
4928 Eastern Neck Rd., Rock Hall, MD 21661
Price: Moderate to Very Expensive
Handicapped Access: No
Special Features: Pet accommodations available

What a showplace! This telescoping farmhouse, rebuilt after a major 2001 fire, is tucked down a classic tidewater lane. Once inside the front door, it's hard to take your eyes off all the great art, especially the bright still life of, yes, peppers and frogs by local artist Berkeley Ake. The library's comfy leather couch and chairs are perfectly arranged on the brick floor, which is covered in a way-cool hooked rug. The pitch-perfect decor and design go on and on at this 70-acre property, with its wide and private water frontage and a great dock replete with kayaks. You could spend the morning reading in the library, then walk a mown path through the farm (perhaps the sunflower field will be in bloom) to spend an afternoon reading on the dock. The inn's five good-looking rooms are handsome without being fussy, and come with all the amenities. (The reconstruction of the house allowed the Riches to create rooms with large, modern baths and a room arrangement that promotes privacy.) Three cottages include two that are brand new (the Zen Cottage even comes with a bamboo floor) and offer king-sized beds, whirlpool tubs, and pullout couches that make these a good option for traveling families. Dine on a full gourmet country breakfast. Did we mention the saltwater pool? C'mon down!

the Historic District's main street. A collection of people in waistcoats and breeches gathered in its public rooms would create a perfect time warp. Six guest rooms, however, have modern comforts like private baths, nonworking fireplaces (although fires blaze in the common areas), and refrigerators. Accommodations range from the John Lovegrove Kitchen room, with its massive fireplace and exposed beams dating to 1705, to the winding T. W. Eliason Victorian Suite, complete with parlor. Even if you can't stay here, stop by for afternoon tea between 3 and 5 daily. Guests also get a continental breakfast brought to their room on request, a newspaper (so old school!), and a complimentary fruit basket. The TV's

A Tiny Jewel Box

The 14-mile-long Chesapeake & Delaware Canal severs the top of the Delmarva Peninsula from the mainland, linking the Upper Chesapeake Bay with the Delaware River. In so doing, the grand old C&D shaves 300 miles off an otherwise roundabout journey for shipping out of the bustling ports of Baltimore and Philadelphia—small wonder that it's considered the busiest canal in the nation.

And here, along the banks of this waterway where the world's commerce traverses daily on gargantuan cargo ships, there incongruously sits one of the Bay country's most seductively charming hamlets. For the lover of the Victorian-era Main Street of yesteryear vibe, Chesapeake City is likely to inspire fantasies of selling your house, chucking it all, and escaping forever to this Brigadoon by the barges. Rescued from decrepitude by a restoration effort spearheaded in the 1970s by philanthropist Allaire DuPont and a cadre of determined local preservationists,

Victorian accents decorate the Inn at the Canal in Chesapeake City.

Chesapeake City is a unique gem. It is as diminutive as it is picturesque—surely the appellation "city" has never been more outlandishly stretched—but within its few streets there is a rich selection of lodging and dining options.

The **Inn at the Canal,** aka the Brady-Rees House, is a circa-1870 Victorian B&B located in the heart of the Historic District. It sports seven guest rooms, an abundance of antique furnishings, and a memorable breakfast. (410-885-5595; www.innatthecanal.com; 104 Bohemia Ave., Chesapeake City, MD 21915. Moderate to Very Expensive; no handicapped access.) INNtiques, an adjacent antiques shop, is also owned and run by innkeepers Mary and Al Ioppolo.

The **Blue Max Inn** derives its name from former owner Jack Hunter, who dubbed it thusly after his novel of the same name. (Hunter's book, about a World War I flying ace, was made into *The Blue Max,* a 1966 movie starring George Peppard.) Originally built in 1854, the Federal house-turned-B&B enjoys national renown for its luxury-meets-cozy interior design. There are seven rooms and two suites, and the normal B&B accoutrements are augmented by such offerings as murder-mystery weekends and spa packages (410-885-2781; www.bluemaxinn.com; 300 Bohemia Ave., Chesapeake City, MD 21915. Moderate to Very Expensive; handicapped accessible).

If you've come to Chesapeake City to view the canal's maritime parade, then the **Ship Watch Inn** (410-885-5300; www.shipwatchinn.com; 401 First St., Chesapeake City, MD 21915. Moderate to Very Expensive; handicapped accessible), as its name implies, is the clear-cut choice for you. This B&B is situated right along the water's edge, its rooms facing the canal and boasting outdoor decks. Owners Gilda and Gianmarco Martuscelli also operate the nearby **Chesapeake Inn Restaurant and Marina**

(410-885-2040; www.chesapeakeinn.com; 605 Second St., Chesapeake City, MD 21915. Moderate to Expensive; handicapped accessible), a popular presence on the canalfront replete with indoor and outdoor dining options (with separate menus for each), a tiki bar, dancing on the deck, banquet facilities for wedding parties, and more.

The most celebrated dining destination in town is the historic **Bayard House Restaurant** (410-885-5040; www.bayardhouse.com; 11 Bohemia Ave., Chesapeake City, MD 21915. Moderate to Expensive; handicapped accessible), located on the waterfront at the foot of Bohemia Street, the town's main thoroughfare. (The giant, high-arching canal bridge that serves as the town's dramatic visual backdrop is especially prominent here.) The brick structure, which underwent extensive restoration beginning in the 1980s, is said to be the oldest building in Chesapeake City. When the canal-builders patronized it in the 1820s, the town was still known as Bohemia Village and what later became the Bayard House was known as Chick's Tavern. Today, the time-honored establishment is famous for its fine Eastern Shore cuisine, including a Maryland crab soup and Maryland crabcakes for which fans travel from far and wide. Dining

is on two levels, both with prime canal views (the glassed-in patio is the optimum real estate for canal-gazing). For many visitors and revisitors to Chesapeake City, a stop at the Bayard House is standard operating procedure.

Other Chesapeake City highlights include the **C&D Canal Museum** (410-885-5621; 817 Bethel Road, Chesapeake City, MD 21915; free admission). The little museum, located in the pump house for the old canal locks, handily tells the history of the engineering marvel that is the canal. The site is run by the U.S. Army Corps of Engineers, the same outfit that runs the canal. **Miss Clare Cruises** (410-855-5088; www.missclarecruises.com; Town Dock, Chesapeake City, MD 21915) offers a narrated boat tour of the waterway with Capt. Ralph Hazel, scion of a steamboat captain of yore, as your guide. And of course, a stroll through Chesapeake City is an opportunity to poke around in a variety of antique and specialty shops; an exhaustive listing is available at www.chesapeakecity.com /shoplisting.htm.

A view of the C&D Canal from the guest room porches at the Ship Watch Inn.

THE INN AT OSPREY POINT

Owners: Shirley and J. Anthony Messina
410-639-2194
www.ospreypoint.com
20786 Rock Hall Ave., Rock Hall, MD 21661
Price: Moderate to Very Expensive
Handicapped Access: No
Special Features: Children welcome

Newly built in 1993, this Colonial is modeled after the Coke-Garrett House in Williamsburg, Va. It's joined by a renovated farmhouse and a Bay-side annex down the road at the owners' Gratitude Marina, bringing the inn's room total to 15. In the original inn, seven pretty rooms are decorated in colonial style. Family-friendly rooms are large enough to accommodate a pullout couch or a cot. The farmhouse has three guest rooms, although the house layout is such that a fourth may be used if the farmhouse is rented as a whole. The newer annex is literally right on the Chesapeake, and two of its five rooms (all with king-sized beds) have their own balconies. Osprey Point is located on 30 lush Swan Creek acres overlooking a marina. With a swimming pool, volleyball, horseshoes, nature trails, and complimentary bicycles, this is more like a small resort than an inn. Management can arrange sailing, fishing, or horseback riding. The white tablecloth restaurant—with signature dishes like George's Bank Day Boat Scallops—serves dinner Wed.–Sun. and Sunday brunch.

OLD GRATITUDE HOUSE BED & BREAKFAST

Innkeepers: Sandy and Hank Mayer
410-639-7448 or 1-866-846-0724
www.oldgratitudehouse.com
5944 Lawton Ave., Rock Hall, MD 21661
Price: Expensive to Very Expensive
Handicapped Access: No
Restrictions: Children 15 and older only

Gratitude is a community in small Rock Hall named for a steamboat that once docked here. The steamboat's gone but the open Bay it traveled is about 2 feet away if you're in an Adirondack chair at the Old Gratitude House. Why budge? Well, you might want to paddle out in one of the inn's kayaks. You might want to edge into the big whirlpool in the very-old-Orient-meets-British-Colonial "Orient Escape" room. Or you might mosey to the waterfront decks that accompany the inn's four rooms to watch the sun sink over the majestic expanse of Bay as Tchaikovsky's "1812 Overture" plays. A full and fancy breakfast is served at 9 AM on the back deck much of the year, and the rooms have TVs and all the amenities. The Mayers are longtime regional innkeepers.

Hotels/Motels

Comfort Suites (410-810-0555; 160 Scheeler Rd., Chestertown, MD 21620) Located off MD 213 just outside of town. Fifty-three rooms, indoor pool. Moderate to Expensive.

Holiday Inn Express Hotel & Suites (410-778-0778; 150 Scheeler Rd., Chestertown, MD 21620) Also located off MD 213 just outside town. Eighty-one rooms, indoor pool, business center, fitness center, hot breakfast. Moderate.

Mariners Motel (410-639-2291; www.marinersmotel.com; 5681 S. Hawthorne Ave., Rock Hall, MD 21661). Twelve-room local motel offers in-room coffee, bike rentals, horseshoes, use of a nearby pool, and a welcome to your "well-behaved" dogs. Reservations are recommended during hunting seasons and weekends. Located right at Rock Hall Harbor.

RESTAURANTS

As always around the Bay, dining options are varied and the seafood can't be beat. Price ranges, based on dinner entrées (which may include sandwiches or meal-sized salads if that's the appropriate cuisine), are as follows:

Inexpensive: Up to $10
Moderate: $11–20
Expensive: $20–30
Very Expensive: More than $30

The following abbreviations are used to denote meals served:
B = Breakfast; L = Lunch; D = Dinner; SB = Sunday Brunch

HAVRE DE GRACE
LAURRAPIN GRILLE
410-939-FOOD
www.laurrapin.com
209 N. Washington St.
Open: Tues.–Sun. (Sun. 10:30–2:30)
Price: Moderate to Expensive
Cuisine: Eclectic American, Chesapeake
Serving: L, D, SB
Reservations: Recommended on weekends
Handicapped Access: Yes

A mural of Havre de Grace lines the new lounge at Laurrapin, local art covers the two dining rooms' walls, and aioli arrives on the crabcake sandwiches instead of tartar sauce. Fresh and local is the culinary theme here. You can order lamb shank osso bucco or a lobster crabcake entrée. Owner-chef Bruce Clarke has done time in Baltimore's culinary circles, and his Chesapeake chops show with dishes like rockfish sautéed with lump crab. On Saturdays, check out what the kitchen found at the farmer's market that day. Takeout's available at the bar. (Laurrapin, by the way, is an Appalachian colloquialism meaning "tasty.")

PRICE'S SEAFOOD RESTAURANT
410-939-2782
pricesseafood.com
654 Water St.
Open: Daily except Mon.
Price: Inexpensive to Moderate
Cuisine: Chesapeake
Serving: L, D
Reservations: Recommended, especially on weekends
Handicapped Access: Partial

Established in 1944, this is where Havre de Grace cracks steamed crabs. The restaurant bills itself as one of the few original Maryland crabhouses still in operation. Look also for fresh seafood and specials, an appetizer called crabby cheese fries, and Alvin Price, whose parents started the place in 1944. He still works in the steam room.

TIDEWATER GRILLE
410-939-3313
www.thetidewatergrille.com
300 Franklin St.
Open: Daily
Price: Inexpensive to Very Expensive
Cuisine: Authentic regional American
Serving: B 8–11 Sat.–Sun., L, D, SB
Reservations: Only for parties of five or more in the summer
Handicapped Access: Yes

This longtime staple along the upper Susquehanna River reaches of the Chesapeake Bay has changed hands in recent years, but the spectacular views of the river remain. Long windows open the modern dining room onto the Susquehanna and its passing railroad bridge, while an ample enclosed porch and decks accommodate the alfresco crowd. We've always been impressed by the crabcakes. The rest of the extensive menu includes a number of salads, cream of crab soup, seafood dishes, pastas, and beef. There's live entertainment Thurs.–Sat. and bar specials during all NFL games.

CHESTERTOWN
BLUE HERON CAFÉ
410-778-0188
blueheroncafe.com
236 Cannon St.
Open: Daily except Sun.
Price: Moderate to Expensive
Cuisine: Traditional and innovative American
Serving: D
Reservations: Suggested on weekends
Handicapped Access: Yes

Soft music and high ceilings affixed with quietly spinning fans are part of the casual dining atmosphere at this popular restaurant. The menu focuses on fresh local ingredients, with strong emphasis on creative but classic preparation. There's a nice selection of seafood, including Maryland crabcakes and gently sautéed soft-shell crabs in-season. For those desiring heartier fare, entrées such as the roasted rack of lamb fill the bill. For starters, the oyster fritters in a lemon butter sauce are a favorite requested by the loyal patrons—famous enough to get a mention in *Time* magazine some years back. Paul Hanley opened his dining room in 1997, and he and his longtime staff—most with at least a decade's tenure—continue to anchor the downtown.

BRIX TAPAS KITCHEN AND WINE CELLAR
410-810-2749
www.brixtapas.com
337 High St.
Open: Tues.–Sun.
Price: Inexpensive to Moderate
Cuisine: Global-fusion and updated American
Serving: L, D, SB
Reservations: Accepted
Handicapped Access: Yes

Brix landed on the local dining scene like an alien space pod; here, in the Land of Pleasant Living and Crabs and Oysters and More Crabs and Oysters, there now is a venue with a flair for the whole mix-and-match tapas eating aesthetic. The Brix-goer can get creative by combining such offerings as cumin-cured salmon on grilled flatbread with tahini yogurt sauce, Mangalore fried shrimp with yellow curry and green onions, Middle Eastern lamb skewers and garbanzo salad with ginger, soba noodles with spicy peanut sauce and roasted chicken—this is not your father's Eastern Shore restaurant menu. The wine list is extensive, and the atmosphere is relaxed, with tables spilling out onto Chestertown's postcard-picturesque High Street.

BROOKS TAVERN
410-810-0012
www.brookstavern.com
870 High St.
Open: Tues.–Sat.
Price: Moderate to Expensive
Cuisine: Regional American
Serving: L, D
Reservations: Only for parties of six or more
Handicapped Access: Yes

Don't get me wrong, being a travel writer is jolly good fun. But it is (believe it or not) actual work. There are times, though, when you really do feel like you're getting away with something. Like when you're shown to your table at Brooks Tavern. Tucked inside the renovated Radcliffe Mill, the restaurant and its food and decor encourage one long exhale. The old mill's timbers rise to the ceiling. Glass fish sculptures dangle from an overhead pipe. Locals even say hi to you, the stranger in their midst. And then comes dinner. We had a July special, a fat fluke (aka summer flounder) in a light but lemony butter with lots of fresh vegetables like corn and beets, all for $23. Fresh and local is what the beautiful food's about at Brooks Tavern, operated by Kevin McKinney and Barbara Silcox. Long local memories will recall them as the pair who formerly operated the Ironstone Inn and later, the late great Kennedyville Inn. We missed Brooks's three-course Wednesday night prix fixe priced according to the year—in 2012, it'll be $20.12—but are taking an educated guess and suggesting you shouldn't. The restaurant charges $4.50 to share a large plate.

FISH WHISTLE
410-778-3566
fishandwhistle.com
98 Cannon St.
Open: Daily
Price: Moderate to Expensive
Cuisine: Eastern Shore seafood, modern American
Serving: L, D; B Sun. 10–noon
Reservations: Only for parties of six or more
Handicapped Access: Yes

Here's Chestertown's only in-town water-side dining, replete with umbrella-topped tables on a narrow deck along the Chester River. This window-lined building replaced the Old Wharf, an old-style Eastern Shore seafood place that washed out during Tropical Storm Isabel in 2003. In keeping with the update (which includes salmon-colored walls that are anything but old Eastern Shore), the menu offers items such as a big beet and chèvre salad with candied walnuts. For the full Chesapeake experi-ence, top it with a crabcake ($10 extra) and enjoy it while gazing at the bridge stretch-ing from Queen Anne's County across the

river into Chestertown. Look for specials throughout the week, a Sunday breakfast buffet for $11.95, and bar menu options available until midnight.

HARBOR HOUSE RESTAURANT
410-778-0669
www.harborhousewcm.com
Worton Creek Marina, 23145 Buck Neck Rd.
Open: Thurs.–Sun.
Price: Moderate to Expensive
Cuisine: Seafood
Serving: D
Reservations: Accepted
Handicapped Access: No

Worton Creek winds into Kent County from the Upper Chesapeake, creating a natural, and naturally well-trafficked, haven for Bay boaters. To the anchoring yachtsman and the Eastern Shore gourmet alike, Harbor House Restaurant has offered high-quality meals at reasonable rates for years. Rob Jester, a Culinary Institute of America grad, is now the kitchen's guiding hand, serving up an ever-changing menu of classic Eastern Shore delights infused with inter-national nouvelle cuisine flourishes. Those not into such traditionalist-meets-globalist gustatory experiments can take heart in the all-you-can-eat oyster night on Friday and the prime rib night on Saturday. In short, peaceful water views and superlative food.

GEORGETOWN
KITTY KNIGHT HOUSE
Owner: Georgetown Yacht Basin
410-648-5200
www.kittyknight.com
14028 Augustine Herman Hwy.
Price: Moderate
Handicapped Access: Only in the restaurant

This venerable landmark overlooking the Sassafras River at Georgetown Harbor offers stunning river views, a solid menu, and for those so inclined, a heaping helping of history. Kitty Knight (1775–1855) entered the pantheon of local legendry by standing up to fire-happy Admiral Cockburn of the Royal Navy, burning and pillaging his way up the rivers of the Bay during the War of 1812. The two 18th-century brick houses on the hill that eventually were merged into one—today's Kitty Knight House—still stand thanks to Kitty's defiance. Diners will find two options. The interior dining room is low-key but stately, highlighted most of all by its commanding view of the waterway below. For those feeling more festive and outdoorsy, there is the Deck, a popular gathering spot with umbrella'd tables, live music in summer, and a dreamy sunset vantage of the Sassafras stretching into the distance. The same menus serve both dining areas. The cuisine is Chesapeake upscale, the fare inventively prepared but not overly artsy. Certainly repeat visit-worthy. The inn also features 11 moderate to expensive rooms, some with river vistas, one with its own deck. Decor is of the four-poster type, as befits the early American setting.

Rock Hall
BAY WOLF DINING AND SPIRITS
410-639-2000
www.baywolf.com
21270 Rock Hall Ave.
Open: Daily
Price: Expensive
Cuisine: Regional American and Austrian
Serving: L, D
Reservations: Suggested
Handicapped Access: Yes

Austria meets Eastern Shore at this mainstay Rock Hall restaurant, where the Wednesday night all-you-can-eat oyster special draws diners starting in the fall. The building is a converted church and its arched stained glass windows remain, interspersed with watercolors of Salzburg. Chef Larry Sunkler—whose father operated the fabled Shaffer's Canal House in Chesapeake City for 30 years—went to culi-

nary school in Austria. There, he not only met wife Hildegard, but learned to perfect dishes like the menu's schweinsbraten mit knödel. Look for crayons on the tables for the kids, and a large bar that closes at a civilized 9 PM.

HARBOR SHACK WATERFRONT BAR & GRILL
410-639-9996
www.harborshack.net
20895 Bayside Ave.
Open: Daily
Price: Inexpensive to Expensive
Cuisine: Seafood, steaks, Mexican
Serving: L, D
Reservations: For groups of 10 or more
Handicapped Access: Yes

Keep heading east when you reach the Rock Hall harbor and you'll reach the purple front door of this yellow and orange building. Harbor Shack calls itself "a neighborhood hangout," and on summer weekends it's certainly the place to be. Just look at the spacious deck facing Rock Hall Harbor. During inclement weather, the deck's garage-style doors slide shut. Inside the dining room hang lots of signs from long-gone local establishments, giving the place a decidedly neighborhood air. Although you can order steamed crabs in advance, consider checking out some of the unexpected menu options like the grilled and chilled asparagus or the sun-dried tomato pasta. In a pinch, there's always stuffed rockfish. Live music plays on weekends, dialed down a notch come Sunday when acoustic musicians play. Dockage is available.

WATERMAN'S CRAB HOUSE
410-639-2261
www.watermanscrabhouse.com
21055 Sharp St.
Open: Daily (closed Jan.; reopens around Mar., depending on weather)
Price: Inexpensive to Expensive

The bounty of the Bay: there's nothing finer in high summer than crabs and corn. Photo courtesy of Queen Anne's County Department of Economic Development, Agriculture & Tourism

Cuisine: Eastern Shore
Serving: L, D
Reservations: Suggested in the summer
Handicapped Access: Yes

Looking for the perfect waterside crab-pickin' spot? Come here. Red picnic tables line a great big deck and are ready for their butcher paper, your mallet, and as many steamed crabs as you can eat. If you don't feel like spending the afternoon mussing your hands (heresy here in crab country!), the menu provides plenty of seafood options. Don't look for arugula among the greens in your crab- and shrimp-topped salad, but do kick back and enjoy a perfect Chesapeake scene along the busy harbor here in Rock Hall, one of the Bay's few remaining waterman enclaves. Tie up free if you arrive by boat (pay if you stay overnight), check out live music on weekends, and think about indulging during the all-you-can-eat crab feasts held from 4–8 Tues. and Thurs. and 11–4 Sat. and Sun. in summer.

FOOD PURVEYORS

Coffeehouses
Java by the Bay (410-939-0227; 118 N. Washington St., Havre de Grace) Café-style coffeehouse sells teas, frozen concoctions (with or without the coffee), and morning Danish, biscotti, and pastries. It's also easy to find in the tourist shopping district. Open Mon.–Fri. 7–4, Sat. 7–3:30.

Java Rock (410-639-9909; Sharp and Main streets, Rock Hall) Grab a fancy vanilla-English breakfast tea or your espresso here, where you'll also find paninis at lunch, wine, snacks, and offbeat souvenirs.

Play It Again Sam (410-778-2688; 108 S. Cross St., Chestertown) This is a homey local coffee bar serving sandwiches and desserts inside an old store with a wood floor and pressed-tin ceiling. Open Mon.–Thurs. 7–7, Fri. 7–9, Sat. open until 5 and Sun. until 3. Free Wi-Fi, music on Fri. nights, beer and wine available served or to go.

Crabhouses and Seafood Markets
Chester River Seafood (410-639-7018; 4954 Ashley Rd., Rock Hall) Bait, local Chester River crabs (which are usually bigger and better than many others), steamed shrimp, and soft crabs. Carryout, delivery to local marinas.

E&E Seafood (410-778-7995; 504 Morgnec Rd., Chestertown) This seafood market sells soft crabs, Maryland crabmeat, fresh fish, sandwiches, and homemade salads.

J&J Seafood (410-639-2325; 21459 Rock Hall Ave., Rock Hall) Hard-shells, soft-shells, whole fish, and fillets. A wide variety of seafood, plus you can dine in or carry out seafood sandwiches and platters. Open daily year-round. Also sells bait and ice.

Woody's Crab House (410-287-3541; 29 S. Main St., North East) The local crabhouse at the tip of the Bay in North East; other seafood available. Open daily for L, D.

Delis and Takeout

The Feast of Reason (410-778-3828; 203 High St., Chestertown) Bread baked in-house is the star of luncheon sandwiches featured on the changing daily menu here, where you can also get soups, quiches, and salads. PB&J and other nods to kids' taste are also available.

Herb's Soup & Such (410-778-9727; 827 High St., Chestertown) This takeout place is operated by the former chef at Annapolis's late, acclaimed Corinthian Restaurant and the Inn at Osprey Point in Rock Hall. Herb Will makes lunches ranging from muffalettas and double dogs (he has kids; he gets it), as well as soups and salads from 10–3. From 3–5 Wed.–Fri., stop by to pick up dinner.

New York Kosher Style Deli (410-810-0900; 323 High St., Chestertown) Get your genuine New York bagels along with other kosher-style deli eats (salami, brisket) you are highly unlikely to find elsewhere on the Delmarva Peninsula. Eat in, take out, catering.

Ice Cream and Candy

Bomboy's Home Made Candy & Ice Cream (410-939-2924; 322 and 329 Market St., Havre de Grace) Family-owned since 1978, the candy store smells deliciously of chocolate and resides on one side of the street. Ice cream is on the other side, at the original location. Check out the butter crèmes on the candy side, or salty dog (vanilla with pretzels) on the ice cream side.

Durding's Store (410-778-7957; 5742 Main St., Rock Hall) Folks still come for ice cream at the soda fountain installed in this 1872 pharmacy in 1923. Rotating favorites include Moose Track (vanilla with fudge and Reese's peanut butter cups) and Muddy Sneakers (vanilla with chocolate caramel). Also cards and some gift items.

Stam's Drug Store (410-778-3030; 215 High St., Chestertown) Stam's brings the old-fashioned soda fountain and the ice cream to downtown Chestertown.

Natural Foods

Chestertown Natural Foods (410-778-1677; 303 Cannon St., Chestertown) This is a very nice, small grocery stocked with natural foods, organic produce, vitamins and supplements, and the like.

CULTURE

Chestertown's thriving arts scene is showcased during First Fridays, when galleries, studios, and shops stay open from 5–8 PM on the first Friday of each month. For details on this and other Kent County happenings, check the monthly arts and entertainment listings at www.kentcounty.com. To find out about special events at Washington College in Chestertown, check news.washcoll.edu/calendarofevents.php. And mark your calendar for late October/early November, when artists throughout Kent County open their studios for a free tour. Apparently folks have come all the way from Manhattan. For more info: www.artworkschestertown.org/news.htm. Also, note that commercial galleries are listed under the shopping section.

Arts Centers and Galleries

ARTWORKS
410-778-6300
www.artworkschestertown.org
306 Park Row, Chestertown

Artworks features a new exhibit each month, with an opening reception on the first Friday of every month. Classes and workshops are offered, and a gift shop's on-site.

CHESTERTOWN ARTS LEAGUE
410-778-5789
www.chestertownartsleague.org
312 Cannon St., Chestertown
Gallery hours: Thurs.–Fri. 11–4, Sat. and perhaps Sun. 10–4

Established in 1949, the arts league offers classes, exhibits, and workshops in various media. The annual juried show is held at nearby Heron Point Retirement Community each spring, and Art in the Park takes place the Sat. after Labor Day at the distinctive Fountain Park in the middle of Chestertown. Monthly exhibitions are held at the gallery, which showcases the work of a selection of the 150 members.

WASHINGTON COLLEGE ARTS
410-778-7888
www.washcoll.edu
Washington College, 300 Washington Ave., Chestertown

The college's primary performing arts space, the Daniel Z. Gibson Center for the Arts, has undergone a major renovation and expansion. In addition to theater and recital hall space, the center now supplies visual arts-viewing opportunities in Kohl Gallery, which opened to the public in 2009 with an inaugural exhibition of rarely displayed landscapes by Monet, Renoir, and other major 19th-century artists. The center also houses the Decker Theatre for larger concerts and events, the Hotchkiss Recital Hall, and, for drama productions, the Tawes Theatre. Except where otherwise indicated, most events are free and open to the public.

Cinema

Chester 5 Theatres (410-778-2227; 21 Washington Square Shopping Center, MD 213, Chestertown) offers first-run fare at discount prices. Also in town, Washington College offers a weekly film series of first-rate films ("Victor Fleming Weekend") in the **Norman James Theatre** (410-778-7888) at 7:30 PM on Fri., Sun., and Mon. during the school year.

Historic Buildings, Sites, and Schools

CHESTERTOWN
GEDDES-PIPER HOUSE
410-778-3499
www.kentcountyhistory.org
101 Church Alley

Open: Tues.–Fri. 10–4 (house and library); also open Sat. 1–4 (house only) May through Oct.

Admission: Donation requested

Designed in the "Philadelphia style," this 3½-story brick town house was built in 1784 and has long been the museum headquarters of the Historical Society of Kent County. The property was first owned by a customs collector for the Port of Chestertown, William Geddes, who holds an infamous place in local history. His was the brigantine ravaged during the 1774 Chestertown Tea Party, still celebrated at a local festival. He sold his property to merchant James Piper, who built the house. It now features 18th- and 19th-century furnishings, maps, and china, and otherwise represents Chesapeake life during that era. It also has a library for local history and genealogy research. The Tea Time House Tour, formerly the Candlelight Walking Tour, is held on the first Sat. in Oct. Tea, History, and Dessert are served the third Thurs. of every month besides July; History Happy Hour takes place from 4–6 PM on the first Fri. of every month (except July), and a Country Driving Tour is held each year. Check the Web site for details.

WASHINGTON COLLEGE
410-778-2800
www.washcoll.edu
300 Washington Ave.

Our country's father gave express permission for use of his name, contributed 50 guineas to its 1782 founding, and served six years on the Board of Visitors and Governors of Washington College. Now it's known for its creative writing program and the notable undergraduate literary award, the Sophie Kerr Prize (always a healthy sum; more than $60,000 of late). The school also co-sponsors the $50,000 George Washington Book Prize, awarded annually to a new historical work about the founding era. The school, with its beautiful grounds, is a significant presence in Chestertown. From student concerts to highly thoughtful lectures, the campus is full of activities during the school year. Hear the Jazz Band, the Afro-Cuban Ensemble, or the Early Music Consort. Or catch a speech by figures such as Howard Dean, or a lecture on a notable such as Charles Willson Peale. For a monthly listing of activities, contact the Special Events Office (410-778-7849) or check the schedule on the college's Web site.

HAVRE DE GRACE
CONCORD POINT LIGHTHOUSE
410-939-3213
Lafayette and Concord Sts.
Open: Apr.–Oct., 1–5 Sat.–Sun.

The Susquehanna River, the Chesapeake's prehistoric precursor, flows into the Bay at Havre de Grace. Perhaps the best view—though hours are limited—is from here. Visitors to the 1827 lighthouse will notice the boardwalk that ends out front. The half-mile-long promenade rounds the point along the Susquehanna, affording an exhilarating view. Concord Point, a 36-foot light, is the oldest continually operated lighthouse in Maryland. The restored keeper's house, located across the street, tells the story of lighthouse keeper John O'Neil.

The Concord Point Lighthouse is located where the Susquehanna meets the Bay.

EARLEVILLE
MOUNT HARMON PLANTATION
410-275-8819
www.mountharmon.org
699 Mount Harmon Rd.
Open: May–Oct., Thurs.–Sun. 10–3
Admission: Adults $10, seniors $8, children $5

This gorgeous plantation property dates to 1651, when the second Lord Baltimore deeded a 350-acre land grant. Today, the 1730 manor house is open for tours, and it's furnished with antiques to reflect the 1760–1810 period. A "prize house" is also on the property; this is where tobacco was stored, and it's the northernmost extant example. Formal gardens and nature trails through the Sassafras River-side property round out this unique spot.

Museums

HAVRE DE GRACE
HAVRE DE GRACE DECOY MUSEUM
410-939-3739
www.decoymuseum.com
215 Giles St.
Open: Mon.–Sat. 11:30–4:30, Sun. noon–4
Admission: Adults $6, seniors $5, youth 9–18 $2

Fabled Bay decoy carver Madison Mitchell's workshop and the master himself are re-created at the Havre de Grace Decoy Museum.

So you want to know about decoy carving? This is the place, a proud piece of the past in this growing tourist/sailing town that calls itself "The Decoy Capital of the World." The museum is dedicated to preserving the Bay's old "gunning" tradition, the art of hunting with decoys. Works by noted carvers R. Madison Mitchell, Bob McGaw, Paul Gibson, Charlie Joiner, and Charlie Bryan are shown, as well as tools of the trade and displays recalling the early 20th-century days when carvers gathered around the stove. Perhaps most intriguing is a peek into one long-gone reason why conservation measures became so important: the sinkbox. This clever contraption was outlawed in the mid-1930s—"because it was too effective," chuckled a longtime Chesapeake outdoor enthusiast. Shaped like a bathtub with square wings and weighed down with flat-bottomed decoys, the sinkbox held a hunter who took to the duck hunt at the nearby Susquehanna Flats, which drew rich and famous hunters from Baltimore, Washington, D.C., and Philadelphia. In back of the museum stands the workshop of local decoy carver Mitchell.

HAVRE DE GRACE MARITIME MUSEUM
410-939-4800
www.hdgmaritimemuseum.com
100 Lafayette St.
Open: Sept.–May, Mon., and Fri.–Sun. 11–5; Jun.–Aug., daily 10–5
Admission: Adults $3.50, seniors and students $2.50, free for children under 8. Guided tours available by appointment.

First incorporated in 1988, this maritime museum opened its doors early in the new millennium. Visitors will find a recent expansion that showcases life in the region 400 years ago, when Capt. John Smith interacted with the native Susquehannas. Anyone interested in working Bay craft will be delighted by the historic wooden canoes under reconstruction—rib by rib—and the other small craft at the Chesapeake Wooden Boat Builder's School here. Special events are held throughout the year. The museum hosts an annual Marifest in late July, with arts and crafts, children's activities, food, beer, and more.

Canoes in the process of being rebuilt at the Havre de Grace Maritime Museum.

ROCK HALL
ROCK HALL MUSEUM
410-639-7611
www.rockhallmd.com/museum/index.php
Municipal Building, 5585 Main St.
Open Sat.–Sun. 11–3 or by appt.
Admission: Free

Take a down-home look at Rock Hall's long life, from fishing and oystering to decoy carving and boat models depicting Bay workboats.

ROCK HALL WATERMAN'S MUSEUM
410-778-6697
Haven Harbour Marina, 20880 Rock Hall Ave.
Open: Daily; pick up key at the marina's Ditty Bag store
Admission: Free

Rock Hall, a sailing and boating center to many, has roots as a watermen's community, celebrated at this charming museum in an old waterman's

This statue in Rock Hall honors the work of the area's watermen. Tim Tadder, photo courtesy Maryland Office of Tourism

shanty. Inside find tools of the trade for oystering, crabbing, and fishing, along with photographs, local carvings, and boats. Part of the Haven Harbour Marina complex.

TOLCHESTER BEACH REVISITED
410-778-5347
www.rockhallmd.com/tolchester/index.htm
Oyster Court near Sharp and Main Sts.
Open: Sat.–Sun. 11–3
Admission: Free

Homage to the old resorts of the steamship era is paid here. Pennsylvania native William Betts, who used to visit the old Tolchester Beach amusement park in Kent County as a child, opened this small museum after his collection of Tolchester memorabilia outgrew his storage space. Ask your elders who were tots at the time about the kid-sized cars, which, unlike the bumper cars, did not require an adult.

Performing Arts

CHESTERTOWN
PRINCE THEATRE
410-810-2060
www.princetheatre.org
210 High St.

Come hear musicians from far and near (like Maryland favorite Ethel Ennis), see theater, and enjoy all the performances held at this restored 1926 vaudeville theater and movie house. Located on High Street in the center of town.

The Prince Theater and the Imperial Hotel highlight High Street in Chestertown.

WASHINGTON COLLEGE CONCERT SERIES
410-778-7839
news.washcoll.edu/concertandfilmseries.php
Season: Oct.–Mar.
Tickets: Adults $15, youth and students $5

This popular five-concert series, held for nearly 60 yea⌐
groups, string quartets, and even a lutist. Held in the Decker ⌐
Recital Hall of the Daniel Z. Gibson Performing Arts Center.

Church Hill
CHURCH HILL THEATRE
410-758-1331
www.churchhilltheatre.org
103 Walnut St. (MD 19), off MD 213 between Centreville and Chestertown
Tickets: Prices vary

This 1929 building has gone full circle, from town hall to movie theater to decline and,
finally, to rescue. With its restored art deco interior, the Church Hill Players' home has for
nearly 20 years maintained a lively performance schedule of productions ranging from
classics (*The Music Man*) to contemporary (*Jacob Marley's Christmas Carol*). Workshops and
classes, too.

Rock Hall
THE MAINSTAY
410-639-9133
www.mainstayrockhall.org
5753 Main St.

This storefront performance space is home to numerous concerts throughout the year,
including those given by regionally noted musicians like blues/R&B/pianist/vocalist
Deanna Bogart, as well as those from afar, like New Orleans' fabled Preservation Hall Jazz
Band. You may well find classical concerts, and ticket prices are reasonable, often $10–20.

Seasonal Events and Festivals
For information on any of these happenings, see the calendar at www.kentcounty.com or
call 410-778-0416.

Chestertown commemorates its pre–Revolutionary War tea party on the Saturday of
Memorial Day weekend at the **Chestertown Tea Party Festival.** The townwide celebration
features a colonial parade, music, crafts, a 10-mile race, all kinds of activities for children,
food, and a historical re-enactment of the 1774 Chestertown Tea Party, where the townspeople purportedly rose up against port collector William Geddes and plundered his brigantine *Geddes,* Boston style. (Maybe it's apocryphal, but some say that they saved the
shipment's rum.) Did we mention Toss the Tory? It's an event in which a notable local citi-
zen ends up in the Chester River, just like the *Geddes* tea. Free admission; www.chester
townteaparty.com.

Pirates & Wenches Fantasy Weekend, held the second full weekend in August, sees
hundreds come to shiver their timbers, check out music and crafts and street performers,
and otherwise celebrate nouveau pirate life at this relatively new festival that has definitely

Activities all weekend start with the Sea Shanty Sing-Along on Friday, then orated dinghy flotilla and race on Saturday followed by a Pirate Plunder your eye patch. For more: www.rockhallpirates.com.

pt. the Historical Society of Kent County hosts its annual **Chestertown Historic** ur, formerly the Candlelight Walking Tour, in which gorgeous architectural gems n to the public. For information, call 410-778-3499 or check www.kentcounty .y.org.

Blues, bluegrass, and Irish folk music are featured at the **Rock Hall FallFest**, a celebra- on of music and mariners held in late September. Artists, crafts, children's activities, food, including seafood, boats, and regional favorites like oysters shucked before your eyes. Evening concerts at the Mainstay on Main Street. For more, check the Web site at www.kentcounty.com.

Downrigging Weekend sees the tall ships sail into Chestertown to meet the schooner *Sultana* in her homeport, and these are stars like the *Pride of Baltimore II, Amistad,* and the *Kalmar Nyckel* out of Delaware Bay. Come tour them the first weekend of November. On Friday the ships come in. That evening, fireworks burst over the Chester River and the tall ships are illuminated. Beautiful. There's a concert at the Prince Theatre. Public sails are offered on Friday and Saturday, your last chance to check out the boats before the sails and rigs come down for the season. For more: www.sultanaprojects.org. (**Uprigging Weekend**, meantime, marks the season's start. It's a new event at the beginning of April, with music and an opportunity to meet the crew. Check Sultana's Web site for more.)

The **Chestertown Book Festival** is a new event created to celebrate the literary life— authors, books, and literary traditions—of the Eastern Shore. Held in November, it features readings and appearances around town by dozens of authors. Check out www.chestertown bookfestival.org.

Forget about that ball in Times Square. Be in Rock Hall on New Year's Eve for the **Rockfish Drop** at the harbor.

Tours

CHESAPEAKE CITY
Chesapeake Horse Country Tours offers a narrated walking tour of this canal town's Historic District, featuring multicolored 19th-century homes that prospered with the C&D Canal. In addition, the company takes people on a variety of other tours around the area, including van tours of the nearby horse country. A more intimate tour of the thoroughbred horse farms, limited to four people and no children, also is available. For fees and information, contact **Hill Travel** (410-287-2290; 130 S. Main Street, North East, MD 21901).

CHESTERTOWN
Learn about the Georgian, Federal, Italianate, and Queen Anne–style buildings that mark the chapters in the life of pretty Chestertown. "**Chestertown: An Architectural Guide**" is a useful self-guided walking tour that includes more than 70 architectural and his- torical highlights, with stops at the courthouse and the famed White Swan Tavern, where George Washington supposedly supped. Find it at www.chestertown.com/places.
"**History on the Waterfront: A Journey into Chestertown's Past**" (410-810-7161; star- rcenter.washcoll.edu; the Custom House, 101 Water St.) Tour not only Chestertown's circa 1746 riverfront Custom House, but take an audio tour of the town's historic water-

front. Learn about local figures such as Isaac Mason, a young Chestertown slave who escaped through the Underground Railroad. The tour is available Fri. noon–4 and Sat.11–4.

Historic Chestertown Tours (410-778-2829; cliokent@yahoo.com; 530 Kent St.) takes folks on walking tours of the lower Historic District of Chestertown. Tours take 1½ to 2 hours, are priced according to the size of the group, and weave together facts about the town's architectural and overall history.

RECREATION

Baseball

Aberdeen IronBirds and **Ripken Stadium** (IronBirds: 410-297-9292; ironbirdsbase ball.com; 873 Long Dr., Aberdeen) Baseball hero Cal Ripken Jr. hasn't forgotten his home-town. The retired Baltimore Orioles slugger and his brother Bill, also a former major leaguer, co-own a baseball program that includes the Aberdeen IronBirds, a Baltimore Orioles Class A team that plays in the New York–Penn League. The IronBirds play in a great-looking stadium visible from I-95. The complex also houses other baseball programs such as youth camps and clinics. If you're interested in these programs, contact the corpo-rate office of Ripken Baseball (410-823-0808; www.ripkenbaseball.com; 1427 Clarkview Rd., Suite 100, Baltimore, MD 21209).

Bicycling

The Upper Shore's user-friendly topography means pleasantly rolling hills meet generally lightly traveled scenic roads. In Kent County, the tourism office offers a booklet detailing bike-tour options. Distance and difficulty levels range from the 11-mile Pomona Warm-Up to the 81-mile Pump House Primer, which takes in Chesapeake City and Cecil County's rolling horse country. The Baltimore Bicycling Club developed the routes, available at www.kentcounty.com/cycling or by calling 410-778-0416.

Bike Rentals

Rock Hall Landing (410-639-2224; www.rockhalllanding.com; Hawthorne Ave., Rock Hall) Bike rentals are $4 an hour. Open daily 8–5, closed Nov. 15–Apr. 15.

Bird-Watching

Eastern Neck National Wildlife Refuge (410-639-7056; easternneck.fws.gov; 1730 Eastern Neck Rd., Rock Hall) The 2,285-acre refuge lies at the end of the peninsula that includes Chestertown and Rock Hall. It's a favored birding ground, with 230 species recorded here, including a bountiful collection of migratory birds like pintails, old-squaws, and other sea ducks. Tundra swans can be seen Nov.–Mar., since there are both migratory swans and a population that overwinters here. Other times of the year, look for bald eagles, ospreys, terns, gulls, woodcocks, woodpeckers, and other migrants.

Boating

Charters, Cruises, and Boat Rentals

Blue Crab Chesapeake Charters (410-708-1803; www.bluecrabcharters.com; at the foot of Sharp Street, Rock Hall) Don't have tons of time? Not to fret. Capt. Mark Einstein runs a great get-out-on-the-Bay charter that offers sunset cruises and daysails in addition to more ambitious cruises. Up to six guests can head out for a 1½-hour cruise from Rock Hall Harbor for $30 per person.

Gratitude Yachting Center (410-639-7111; www.gratitudeyachting.com; 5990 Lawton Ave., Rock Hall) Bareboat charters of Island Packets available.

Lantern Queen (410-939-1468; www.lanternqueen.com; foot of Congress Ave., Havre de Grace) Take a sunset dinner cruise aboard a Mississippi-style riverboat. Call or check the Web site for prices and times.

Martha Lewis (410-939-4078; www.skipjackmarthalewis.org; Chesapeake Heritage Conservancy, 121 N. Union Ave., Havre de Grace) This skipjack, restored in 1994, offers public cruises in the summer and fall, as well as specialty cruises like sunset cruises, lighthouse cruises, and a "creatures of the Bay" cruise.

Schooner *Sultana* Projects (410-778-5954; www.sultanaprojects.com; 105 S. Cross St., Chestertown) The 97-foot floating classroom *Sultana,* launched in 2001, re-creates a 1767 Boston-built vessel that spent time as a British Royal Navy dispatch boat and revenue cruiser patrolling the Chesapeake Bay. Now, her namesake teaches schoolchildren about history and aquatic science. In addition, there's a famous shallop built by the project that in 2007 retraced the Chesapeake voyage of Capt. John Smith 300 years earlier. Two-hour public sails aboard *Sultana* from Chestertown take place a few times each month. Cost is $30 for adults and $15 for children under 12, but no children under 5 may sail.

The Chestertown-based schooner Sultana *takes to the seas.* Photo courtesy Sultana Projects

Southern Cross Charters (410-778-4460; Great Oak Landing Marina Resort, P.O. Box 426, Chestertown) Day, sunset, and overnight cruises on the Chesapeake Bay aboard *Fantasia*, a 41-foot Morgan Out Island ketch-rigged sail yacht. Food service. Overnight cruises to ports such as Baltimore's Inner Harbor, Rock Hall, Annapolis, and Georgetown.

Marinas

On the **Susquehanna River**, try **Tidewater Marina** (410-939-0950; www.tidewater marina.com) in Havre de Grace, with 160 slips, fuel, haul-outs, repairs, a discount marine store, showers, and a courtesy car.

If you're cruising near **Chesapeake City**, the **Bohemia Bay Yacht Harbor** (410-885-2601; www.bbyh.com) on the eponymous river is a full-service marina with transient slips and lots of amenities (including a private beach). A tad south, along the **Sassafras River**, try **Georgetown Yacht Basin** (410-648-5112; www.gybinc.com). It also has a swimming pool, a marine store, and repairs.

In **Rock Hall**, a popular Bay boating destination with a zillion boat slips, consider the following: **Osprey Point Marina** (410-639-2663; www.ospreypoint.com), located on Swan Creek, has floating docks, a bathhouse, a pool, a full-service restaurant, and an inn (see "Lodging"). The same company owns **Gratitude Marina**, on the Bay in the Gratitude neighborhood, with 80 slips and a fantastic location, fuel dock, bathhouses, and Wi-Fi (1-800-622-7100; www.gmarina.com; 5924 Lawton Ave.).

Also, try **Rock Hall Landing** (410-639-2224; www.rockhalllanding.com), the closest marina to town, in Rock Hall Harbor. They have pump-out facilities, a pool, and bathhouses. The **Sailing Emporium** (410-778-1342; www.sailingemporium.com) on the Chesapeake Bay offers laundry, a library with a liberal lending policy, 150 slips, a pool, a pump-out station, fuel, barbecue grills, and picnic tables. **Lankford Bay Marina** (410-778-1414; www.chesapeake-bay.com/lankfordbay/index.htm) has a working boatyard, pool, bikes, laundry, pump-out, and fuel.

Paddling

The Upper Bay region provides many protected, quiet rivers and creeks. Always check conditions and know your limitations before heading out. Once on the water, you can view ospreys, blue and green herons, kingfishers, and terns, and catch a few perch or rockfish in summer. For local expertise:

Chester River Kayak Adventures (410-639-2001; www.crkayakadventures.com; 5758 Main St., Rock Hall) Here in kayaking country, this outfitter offers eco-tours where the point is to enjoy the ride and the scenery, rather than get there first. Half-day tours (three hours) include stops at a secluded beach or two. Full-day tours (10–4:30), 24-hour, and sunset and moonlight paddles are also offered, as are classes. Single and tandem kayaks.

Sailing and Powerboat Schools

BaySail School on the Chesapeake (410-939-2869; www.baysail.net; Tidewater Marina, 100 Bourbon St., Havre de Grace) American Sailing Association–certified courses, beginner to advanced, aboard boats including Capris, Hunters, Beneteaus, and Catalinas of various sizes. Some can be rented upon certification. A docking course is offered, as well as women-only classes and bareboat chartering certification. Discounts offered for two or more students.

The Maryland School of Sailing & Seamanship (410-639-7030; www.mdschool.com; Lankford Bay Marina, 22978 McKinleyville Road, Rock Hall) American Sailing Association–certified courses aboard Island Packet yachts, including basic sailing, ocean training, and everything in between. Celestial and coastal navigation and docking practice classes offered.

Sassafras Sailing (443-566-2986; www.sassafrassailing.com; Georgetown) Sailing lessons on the Sassafras and Chester rivers on Passagemaker dinghies. Meet at various public landings, by arrangement. Excursions, bird-watching, and fishing trips also available. Open Apr., May, Sept., and Oct., Thurs.–Mon. 8–8; June–Aug., daily 8–8.

Fishing

Boat Ramps
In **Cecil County**, check out www.ccgov.org/tourism/boating3.cfm for a list of public boat ramps, such as the Fredericktown boat launch on the Sassafras River; for information, call **Cecil County Parks and Recreation** (410-392-4537 or 410-658-3000). There's also **Elk Neck State Park** (410-287-5333), which has launching ramps at the Rogues' Harbor Boat Area near the mouth of the Elk River (www.dnr.state.md.us/publiclands/central/elkneck .html). The fee is $10 for Maryland residents and $11 for out-of-staters.

Easy-to-find ramps in downtown **Havre de Grace** include those at **Jean S. Roberts Memorial Park** (410-939-0015) at Ostego and Water streets on the Susquehanna River and at **Tydings Park** at the City Yacht Basin (www.havredegracemd.com/departments _city_yacht.php). Fees for both.

For Kent County, check www.kentcounty.com/recreation/boating for a map and other information. Trailers using public launches must have a permit. Nonresident permits, limited to 50, go on sale the first Friday of December. Three-day permits also available. Call 410-778-7439.

Fishing Charters
Twilight Zone Charters (410-939-2948; tzcharters.com, 113 N. Union Ave., Havre de Grace) Lifelong resident offers guided fishing charters to the Susquehanna Flats region, prime fishery for striped bass. If it's smallmouth bass or shad you're after, guided trips are available on the lower Susquehanna River. Beginners welcome.

ROCK HALL
Known as a place where rockfish lay their eggs, Rock Hall is swimming with fish. And where there's plenty of fish, there's plenty of charters. Here are just a few. A more complete list can be found at www.rockhallmd.com; click on "Marine and Field."

Capt. Bob Gears (410-708-8683) offers half-day and full-day rockfish and blue fish charters aboard the *Virginia II*, a diesel-powered 40-footer equipped with everything you might need. He launches from Bayside Park.

Daddy's Girl Charters (410-778-9424; www.daddysgirlcharters) has two boats available. Besides half- and full-day fishing excursions, they offer photography cruises.

Fish Fear Us Charters (410-639-7063; www.fishfearus.com) welcomes newbies and experienced anglers to fish for blue, rockfish, perch, catfish, sea trout, and more aboard the custom 40-foot *Jennifer II*, located at the Harbor Shack Restaurant.

Fitness

Aqua Fit (410-778-6555; www.ctownaquafit.com; 818 High St., Suite 1, Chestertown) Guest passes are available to this center, which offers classes such as Pilates, yoga, zumba, tai chi, and spinning as well as a 90-plus-degree 30-by-50 saltwater endless swimming pool.

Golf

Bittersweet Golf Course (410-398-8848; 1190 Augustine Herman Hwy., Elkton) 18 holes, par 70; semiprivate. Located on MD 213.

Bulle Rock (1-888-285-5375; www.bullerock.com; 320 Blenheim Ln., Havre de Grace) Named one of the country's top 50 golf courses by Zagat readers. Open to the public, with a locker-room attendant, fine-dining restaurant, Bay views. Tee times can be reserved 30 days in advance. Home to the McDonald's LPGA Championship tournament.

Horseback Riding

Fairwinds Farm & Stables (410-658-8187; www.fairwindsstables.com; 41 Tailwinds Ln., North East) An hour-long ride starts with a 15-minute introductory ride in the outdoor ring before hitting the trails. There are also pony rides, hayrides, horse shows, and special events like a live Nativity at Christmas.

Kent Equestrian Center (410-778-1881; kentequestriancenter.com; 27190 Morgenec Rd., Chestertown) Rides along the 50 acres of wooded trails are available by appointment only.

Hunting

Hopkins Game Farm (410-348-5287; www.hopkinshunting-clays.com; 13003 Turners Creek Rd., Kennedyville) Game, quail, pheasant, deer and goose hunting, as well as sporting clays and five stands. Lodging is available.

NATURAL AREAS: STATE, PRIVATE, AND FEDERAL PARKS

Chesapeake Farms Wildlife Habitat (410-778-8400; 7319 Remington Dr., Chestertown) Free driving tour through 3,300 acres of wildlife and agricultural management demonstration area. Indigo buntings nest here, just one example of the wildlife on-site. Open sunrise to sundown daily from spring through mid-Oct. (Opening and closing dates are weather dependent; call ahead if you're in doubt.)

Eastern Neck National Wildlife Refuge (410-639-7056; 1730 Eastern Neck Rd., Rock Hall) Nearly 2,300 acres of island with walking trails up to 1.2 miles long. The Bay's only undeveloped island with Bay access. Four trails, a boat ramp, an observation deck overlooking the Bay, and a swan lookout ramp to view migratory tundra swans that come through in Nov. or overwinter here. The visitor center is open Mon.–Fri. 7:30–4.

Elk Neck State Park (410-287-5333; 4395 Turkey Point Rd., North East) Swim on a sandy beach, hike or stroll six different trails, launch a boat or canoe, or stay in the campgrounds. Walk to Turkey Point Lighthouse on a bluff that overlooks the C&D Canal and the Bay. Diverse terrain at this 2,000-plus-acre park includes steep bluffs, forests, marshland, and beaches. Nominal fees.

Millington Wildlife Management Area (410-928-3650 or 410-778-1948; www.dnr.state
.md.us/publiclands/eastern/millington.asp; 33626 Maryland Line Rd., Massey) Nature
trails, ponds, woods; 3,800 acres. Hunting in-season, four stocked ponds with bass and
bluegill, mountain biking.

Susquehanna State Park (410-734-9035; 4122 Wilkinson Rd., Havre de Grace) Good for
hiking and mountain biking, with 15 miles of trails; boating and fishing, too. Check out
the Susquehanna River, source of the fresh water in the Bay estuary.

Swimming

Bayside Pool (410-778-1948; Bayside Landing & Park, 20927 Bayside Ave., Rock Hall)
and Millington Pool (410-778-1948; 154 Millington Rd., Millington) Operated by Kent
County Parks and Recreation, both public pools have lifeguards, restrooms, and picnic
area.

Betterton Beach (410-778-1948; MD 292, Betterton) Located deep in the Upper Bay
where freshwater dominates, this is a rare Chesapeake beach and noted for reliable
swimming conditions devoid of stinging nettles. Picnicking, fishing jetty, bathhouse,
beach. Free. Lifeguard only on Sat., Sun., and holidays, Memorial Day–Labor Day.
Picnic pavilion available for rental.

Rock Hall Public Beach (Beach Rd., Rock Hall) From this tiny beach you can watch the
giant container ships make their way from the Bay Bridge up to Baltimore. No lifeguard
at this no-frills, town-owned beach.

SHOPPING

Antiques

Folks with a penchant for antiques (or collectibles) find themselves in fine browsing territory on the Upper Bay, with its antique shops and unique auctions.

Residing on the Upper Shore for decades is a marvel known alternatively as the
Crumpton Auctions or Dixon's Auction (Dixon's Furniture, 410-928-3006; MD 290 and
MD 544, Crumpton). Each Wednesday, an indoor auction selling small items starts at 8 AM,
while the outdoor auction of furniture and larger household items starts at 9.

Or check out the big A. Curtis Andrew Auction (410-754-8826; www.acurtisandrew
auction.com; 25631 Auction Rd. in American Corner, 6 miles north of Federalsburg).
Every Thurs. at 5 PM, buildings full of stuff go on the block. Look for everything from vehicles to furniture.

Bahoukas Antique Mall and Beer Museum (410-939-1290; www.bahoukas.com; 408 N.
Union St., Havre de Grace) What a genius concept: fine antiques like European oil
paintings, art glass, and furniture in a 6,700-square-foot mall. Eight additional antique
vendors join in. What if someone gets tired of looking at the lovelies? Head upstairs to
the Beer MuZeum to spend quality time with the neon signs, beer mirrors, steins, and
glasses. There's even a little NASCAR section. "It's sort of a man cave," says co-owner
Barbara Wagner, who runs Bahoukas with husband George.

Bahoukas Collectibles (410-939-4146; www.bahoukas.com; 467 Franklin St., Havre de
Grace) Collectibles (mostly vintage toys) from the folks with the larger antiques mall
across the street are here in a space shared with the Painted Lady, in which three artists
create an eclectic blend of customized items. Upstairs is a Christmas shop.

Antique shops are legendary in Havre de Grace.

Bayside Antiques (410-939-9397; 232 N. Washington St., Havre de Grace) Multiple dealers and great browsing. Decoys to period antiques. Open daily.

Black Swan Antiques (410-885-5888; 219 Bohemia Ave., Chesapeake City) Particularly good stop for those inclined toward Bay-related items, though they have furniture and other items. Nauticals include old maps, skipjack models, prints, and oyster cans, from Maryland Beauties to the McReady Brothers of Chincoteague. Open Fri.–Sun. and assorted other times—call first.

David H. Ferguson, Inc. (410-810-0603; 241 High St., Chestertown) This is the Eastern Shore's largest selection of Oriental rugs plus antiques, estate jewelry, and Turkish pottery. There's a half-price lot on the second floor.

Fishbones (410-708-3232; 21327 Rock Hall Ave., Rock Hall) Great selection of stained glass panels, midcentury modern furniture, and cool rugs and textiles.

J. R.'s Antique Center (410-827-0555; 6527 Friels Rd., Queenstown) Chestertown antique dealers moved to this 11,000-square-foot space next to the Prime Outlets, where they and the dealers sharing the space sell a little bit of everything, from dining room furniture to country baskets.

Seneca Cannery Antiques (410-942-0701; www.antiquesinhavredegrace.com/seneca; 201 St. John St., Havre de Grace) The enormous stone and brick space, parts of which were once a cannery and a hosiery mill, is almost as interesting as the numerous wares offered by its more than 35 dealers.

Washington Street Books & Antiques (410-939-6215; washingtonstreetbooks.com; 131 N. Washington St., Havre de Grace) Wonderful used bookshop well worth the stop. Includes an impressive number of first editions, as well as a sci-fi collection. Antique items include jewelry, sports memorabilia, and military collectibles.

Books

Bookplate (410-778-4167; www.bookplate.biz; 112 S. Cross St., Chestertown) Focusing on regional history, this shop has a big nautical section, a collection of signed first editions (Seamus Heaney among them), and the musings of Idiots'Books, a Chestertown (or near Chestertown) phenomenon.

The Compleat Bookseller (410-778-1480; 301 High St., Chestertown) This fine independent store has a range of titles that you won't find in the big discount places.

Courtyard Book Shop (410-939-5150; 313 St. John St., Havre de Grace) Terrific, browsable shop.

Clothing

Empty Hangers (410-778-1300; 114 Cross St., Chestertown) Nice-looking consignment shop arranged like a regular store, with clothing, housewares, and children's items.

Mimi's Closet (443-282-0225; www.mimiscloset online.com; 204 High St., Chestertown) Come check out what's here at a "rotating trunk show" where shoppers may find shawls or scarves, shoes or jewelry. Nina McLemore jackets are a mainstay.

Pride & Joy (410-778-2233; 321 High St., Chestertown) Children's apparel and gifts for new arrivals through older children.

Smilin' Jake's (410-639-7280; www.smilinjakes.com; 5745 Main St., Rock Hall) Look for genuine Hawaiian shirts and dresses (including the hibiscus-drenched ones with ruffled sleeves), Maui Jim shades, and Don Ho DVDs.

Galleries

The Artists' Gallery (410-778-2425; www.theartistsgalleryctown.com, 239 High St., Chestertown) Six local artists show at this delightful gallery, which also offers a range of work by other artists and craftspeople.

Capt. Bob Jobes' Decoys (410-939-1843; www.jobesdecoys.com; 721 Otsego St., Havre de Grace) This working decoy shop is, in fact, a gallery. After all, decoys are America's waterfront folk art, and Jobes once earned $1 an hour working under famed Upper Bay carver Madison Mitchell. Folks often stop here after visiting the Havre de Grace Decoy Museum across town. In Jobes' workshop: swans, mallards, canvasbacks, and all manner of shorebirds. He also sells and appraises his forebears' old decoys. Open daily; just stop by.

Rock Hall Gallery (410-639-2494; rockhallgallery.com; 5761 Main St., Rock Hall) Located in the historic Reuben Rodney Building, this cooperative of area artists offers an eclectic range of photography, watercolors, pottery, woodwork, jewelry, and textiles.

Textures Gallery (410-639-7211; 6202 Rock Hall Rd., Rock Hall) Gallery-goers will find rugs and contemporary crafts and art, as well as some vintage and garden stuff.

Vincenti Decoys (410-734-7709; www.vincentidecoys.com; 353 Pennington Ave., Havre de Grace) You'll find not only gorgeous waterfowl carvings here, from pieces by Patrick Vincenti to historic collectibles, but decoy-carving materials, too. Where else are you going to find little plastic packets of glass eyes and pewter duck feet? Vincenti's decoy-making shop is located in nearby Churchville.

Gift Shops and Craft Galleries

The Finishing Touch (1-800-292-0457; finishingtouchshop.com; 311 High St., Chestertown) Framing shop stocking art supplies. Panoramic paintings of the local waterfront by the owner and the work of other local artists are available, as well as interesting old (and huge) maps.

The Hickory Stick (410-639-7980; www.thehickorystickrockhall.com; 5764 Main St., Rock Hall) Vera Bradley bags, jewelry, and other fun stuff.

Marine Supply

Tidewater Marina Store (410-939-0950; www.tidewatermarina.com/supply.asp; 100 Bourbon St., Havre de Grace) Full-service marine store has an ironclad lowest price guarantee and will handle special orders for items not in stock.

Outlets

Perryville Outlet Center (410-378-9399; perryvilleoutletcenter.com; 68 Heather Lane, Perryville) Moderate-sized outlet center with shops including Bass, OshKosh, Jos. A Banks, and Jones New York.

Specialty Shops and General Stores

Back Creek General Store (410-885-5377; 100 Bohemia Ave., Chesapeake City) Circa-1861 general store carrying Vera Bradley, Spartina handbags, Lolita glassware, and more.

Shoppes at Oyster Court (Oyster Court behind Main St., Rock Hall) A cluster of relocated watermen's buildings is home to artists and crafters and some small boutiques. It's open Thurs.–Sun. year-round, more days from spring to fall. Telephone numbers of the artist-shopkeepers are on the doors, so if you come when a store is closed, call.

Twigs & Teacups (410-778-1708; 111 S. Cross St., Chestertown) Specialty bath products, dishes, wind chimes, children's books and toys, clothing, and textiles make this a difficult gift shop to leave.

6

MIDDLE EASTERN SHORE

Time & Tides

KENT ISLAND, WYE MILLS, EASTON, ST. MICHAELS, OXFORD, TILGHMAN ISLAND

There's a genteel, livin'-is-easy mix on the Middle Eastern Shore, where updated trends make careful inroads in a place where old ways stay strong. Traditional oysters, for instance, a declining Bay staple, nonetheless can always be had during their cold-weather season. At old, pine-paneled restaurants, they arrive in thick, milky stews. In fancier dining rooms, with buffed-glass halogen lighting and exposed ductwork, champagne and puff pastries infuse the ol' bivalve.

With its hundreds of miles of snaking shoreline, the Mid-Shore area is less marshy than the Lower Eastern Shore, yet flatter than the upland farther north. We define the area broadly, to include the Shore's gateway, Kent Island. The Mid-Shore extends east to the Delaware line and south to the Choptank River, promising crossroads towns as well as some that are established tourist draws. People come here to relax, rummage, paddle and cycle, dine or do nothing, all in a beautiful setting.

Kent Island ends at the waterway known as Kent Narrows, which is technically on the Eastern Shore, although Kent Island and the Kent Narrows area have become de facto Annapolis suburbs as well as a gateway to the Shore. The powerboat crowd gathers at the Kent Narrows marinas (August's big race: "Thunder on the Narrows"), and a cluster of venerable waterside seafood restaurants hold court along the south end of the Narrows

Heading east along US 50, on the "mainland" Eastern Shore, the village of **Wye Mills** promises peeks at the past via nature and commerce. Schoolchildren gather to hear ground grain clatter through wooden chutes en route to the millstone during flour-making demonstrations at the mid-18th-century mill, which replaced a 1671 forebear. George Washington's troops at Valley Forge even obtained their ground flour from the mill. This is a good stop, with picnic tables behind the mill settled, of course, alongside a lovely stream.

Farther south come the better-known towns of Talbot County: busy **Easton**, the county seat; low-key **Oxford**, with its Tred Avon–side beach known as "The Strand"; **St. Michaels**, the county's biggest tourist town; and **Tilghman Island**, aka "Tilghman," where efforts are under way to launch a local museum to capture the lives of the sturdy but dwindling breed of watermen who have spent generations here.

OPPOSITE: *Talbot Street in St. Michaels is home to many quaint shops.*   Cindy Tunstall, photo courtesy Maryland Office of Tourism

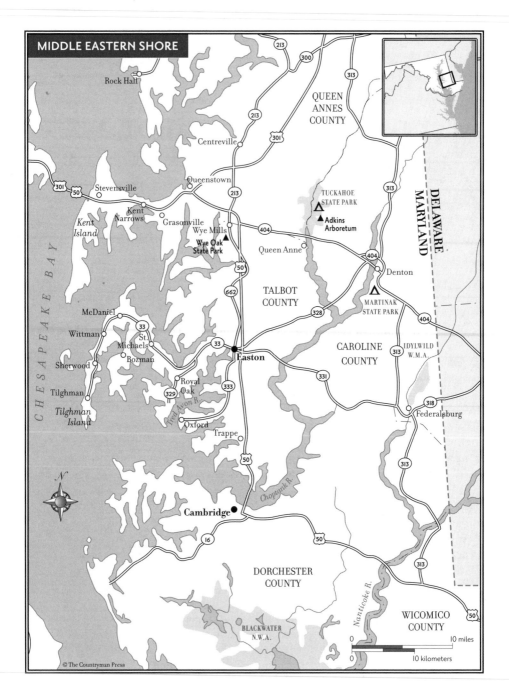

Centered around its 18th-century courthouse, **Easton** is the business center powering this part of Bay Country. The town's roots go back to the late 17th century and construction of the Third Haven Meeting House, an early Quaker structure visited by William Penn that still stands. Highlights here include the renovated art deco Avalon Theatre, with its varied and continuous performance schedule that includes notable touring musicians, the

Academy Art Museum's high-quality exhibitions, antique shops, and the town's contemporary dining establishments. This is a central location with a Federal- and Victorian-filled Historic District—though one without a waterfront. A finger of the Tred Avon River pokes into the southwest corner of town.

South of Easton, via "the Oxford Road," as the locals call MD 333, sits the hamlet of **Oxford**. A prettier waterside village you won't find. White picket fences, clapboard, and grand old manses alternate along Morris Street, the main road into town. This was a colonial deep-water seaport, designated the Eastern Shore's official port of entry in 1694, and an international trade in tobacco and grain bustled here for a time. The so-called financier of the Revolution, Robert Morris, lived in Oxford, his former home a long-standing landmark.

Yet another remnant of that era, the Oxford–Bellevue Ferry, trundles across the Tred Avon River from March through November, providing a considerable shortcut to St. Michaels. Launched in 1683, it is believed to be the nation's oldest privately operated ferry, and it is a favorite of cyclists looping the county's flat roads. The frontage stretching along the Oxford waterfront, known as "The Strand," includes a beach, a good place for visitors of all ages to dip their toes in the water. Afterward, walk up to the Oxford Market & Deli on Morris Street for a hand-dipped ice cream cone. In Oxford come the sweet pleasures of small moments unencumbered by much too much.

Cross the river on the ferry and wind through back roads on the way to St. Michaels. In **Bellevue** sits the kind of surprise explorers often find in the Bay's scratch-in-the-sand-size towns: a weaver's studio and gallery, open during the warm months. Farther on up the road, through **Royal Oak**, an Italian café dwells in the former general store. Businesses increase on the road into **St. Michaels**; Talbot Street is the main drag through this tourist

Watermen work hard on their workboat at Tilghman Island.   Tim Tadder, photo courtesy Maryland Office of Tourism

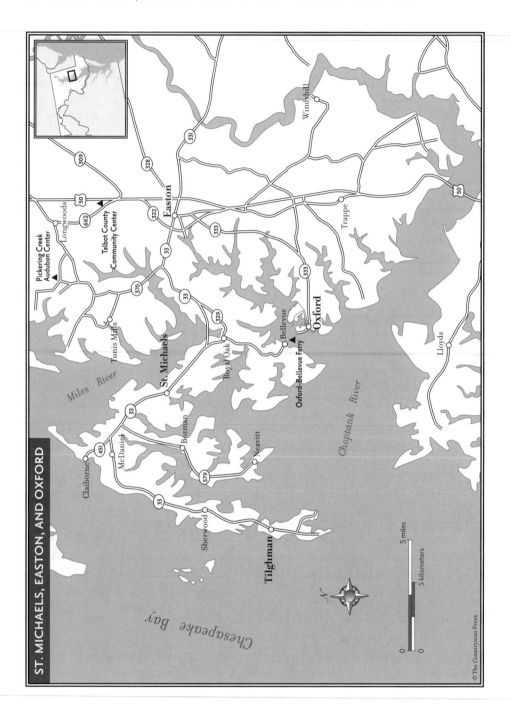

ST. MICHAELS, EASTON, AND OXFORD

Windmill

Easton

Trappe

Longwoods

Pickering Creek
Audubon Center

Talbot County
Community Center

Tunis Mills

St. Michaels

Miles River

Bellevue

Oxford

Oxford-Bellevue Ferry

Royal Oak

Lloyds

Choptank River

Bozman

McDaniel

Neavitt

Claiborne

Sherwood

Tighman

Chesapeake Bay

5 miles

5 kilometers

© The Countryman Press

town, and it's lined with shops selling everything from aromatic candles or Chesapeake T-shirts to fine-crafted gold pins or women's jackets made of handwoven fabric. Fine restaurants and plentiful B&Bs are tucked along the streets.

St. Michaels was first developed in 1778, created from auctioned-off land grants. Its historic claim to fame is the incident during the War of 1812 that led to its reputation as "The Town That Fooled the British." One August night in 1813, as rumor circulated of an impending British attack, the townspeople reportedly darkened their homes, hoisted lit lanterns into the treetops, and tricked the enemy into firing too high.

Now, perhaps its greatest claim to fame emerges from the town's shipbuilding heritage. The extensive Chesapeake Bay Maritime Museum, a multibuilding complex along St. Michaels Harbor, offers a seemingly endless collection of Bay boats, from the skipjack *Rosie Parks* to the *Thor* pilothouse on the museum grounds—a magnet for curious kids. The museum's small-boat collection also shows the evolution of the log canoe, from Native American conveyance to oyster tonger's sailboat to the craft with enormous sails now raced in a popular series involving yacht clubs from many Eastern Shore towns. Given the boat's slender shape—and the springboards that hold crew members balancing them aboard—this can be exciting racing. On a weekend you might get lucky and see the log canoes race along the Miles River in St. Michaels, a tradition stretching back more than 150 years. For information, check www.Tourtalbot.org. And to get around St. Michaels on the water from mid-April to mid-October, consider using the St. Michaels Harbor Shuttle (410-924-2198), located at the foot of Mulberry Street. (Check the schedule at www.stmichaelsmd.org under "boating"—and let the water taxi take you on a 30-minute spin around the harbor as time permits).

For a peek at Bay workboats, continue down MD 33 to **Tilghman Island** and the town of **Tilghman.** Look for the Bay workboats used for crabbing and oystering at Knapp's Narrows, where you cross onto the island, and again at Dogwood Harbor, not far down the island to your left. Although the sailing skipjacks carry the blue-ribbon reputation, there are almost none left out oystering (although some take tourists out). Keep an eye out for the distinctive low sides—"lowboard"—of Bay-built workboats used by crabbers and dredgers, with their pretty lines and sturdy, flat wheelhouse roofs. These are the tools of the working watermen who live on Tilghman and around the Bay. But don't be fooled: There's upscale cuisine to be had and fine lodgings available here. Tilghman mixes old and new Chesapeake.

Additional information for travelers to the Mid-Shore is available through www.tourtalbot.org. Visitor centers are located at 11 S. Harrison St. in Easton and on Talbot Street in the center of St. Michaels. Call 410-770-8000 for more information.

LODGING

From in-town suites with zillion-thread-count sheets and whirlpool tubs to rooms just off the golf course, Mid-Shore visitors will find a range of accommodations. Off long lanes are former farms—and maybe a manse—that have been turned into B&Bs or inns. These offer best-of-both-worlds lodgings, often on the water. Sail in and tie up at the pier, or perhaps launch a kayak. Don't forget your bike!

Prices for the same lodging can vary widely. Typically, prices are highest during summer weekends (when two-night minimums are common). Off-season and midweek rates

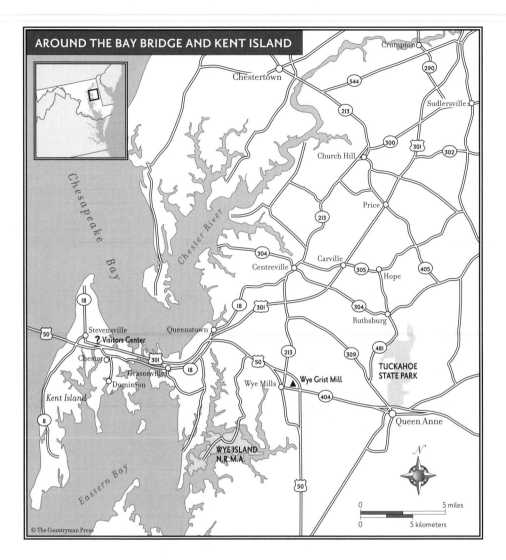

tend to be lower. Rates may be flexible. Check inn Web sites for specials and packages—
which many offer—as well as limitations, including policies regarding the return of deposit
checks if you cancel.

Rates

Lodging rates fall within this scale:

Inexpensive:	Up to $75
Moderate:	$75–150
Expensive:	$150–225
Very Expensive:	$225 and up

KENT ISLAND
KENT MANOR INN
Owners: David Meloy and Alan Michaels
410-643-5757 or 1-800-820-4511
www.kentmanor.com
500 Kent Manor Dr., Stevensville, MD
21666
Price: Expensive to Very Expensive
Handicapped Access: Partial; call to discuss
Special Features: Children welcome

Kent Manor Inn is a faithful restoration of a
large 1820s plantation house set on 226
acres. There's a lovely garden house, a pier
on the shallow headwaters of Thompson
Creek, paddleboats, bicycles, and a 1.5-
mile trail winding through the extensive
property. All 24 rooms are tastefully furnished in period style, some with porches
and French marble fireplaces, with all the
typical amenities like in-room coffee. A
tennis court and pool are available, as well
as a noted restaurant with an outside dining
area serving fine cuisine. This is a quiet,
dignified getaway, located just across the
Bay Bridge from the mainland (and only 45
minutes from BWI Airport).

QUEENSTOWN
THE RIVER PLANTATION
800-697-1777
www.theriverplantation.com
511 Pintail Point Ln., Queenstown, MD
21658
Price: Expensive to Very Expensive
Handicapped Access: No
Special Features: Kennel on-site; children
welcome

This waterside sportsman's paradise on
1,300 acres offers it all. Here guests will
find a nationally ranked sporting clay
range, fishing and yacht charters, and golf.
(The setup goes like this: Pintail Point is
the sporting clay range, Pintail Yachts gets
you out on the water—fishing rod in hand or
not—and Hunter's Oak Golf Club caters to
the golfers.) The spread also features two

B&Bs: the English Tudor–style Manor
House along the Wye River, and a typical
Maryland farmhouse done up in classic "art
ducko" style. The latter, called the
Irishtown Bed & Breakfast, rents as a
whole. The Manor House, built in 1936,
provides finer accommodations, with a
patio open onto the Wye River (one of the
lovelier Bay tributaries) and clubby common rooms. Hunting trophies decorate the
game room, with its pool table, air hockey,
and shuffleboard games. Guest rooms run
from a cottage with floral-covered queen
beds and kitchenette to large, traditional
suites in the house with sitting rooms. A
gourmet breakfast is served. Guests will
find plenty to do here, with complimentary
bikes and tennis courts, a pool at the Manor
House, a pool at Hunter's Oak, and even a
barn where the kids can check out the
horses, cows, and dogs. On-site is a race-
track where guests can watch the standard-
bred horses practice from 6–9 AM. Golf
carts and kayaks are available for a fee.

EASTON
THE BISHOP'S HOUSE
Innkeepers: Diane Laird-Ippolito and John
B. Ippolito
410-820-7290 or 1-800-223-7290
www.bishopshouse.com
214 Goldsborough St./P.O. Box 2217,
Easton, MD 21601
Price: Expensive
Handicapped Access: No
Special features: Children 12 and older wel-
come; bikes (and helmets) available for
guests

Home to the bishop of the Episcopal
Diocese of Easton for much of the 20th
century, this renovated 1880 home serves
up Victorian style of the highest order, from
the plaster ceiling medallions to the claw-
foot tubs. The longtime B&B offers antique
furnishings, vintage hats on the walls, and a
wraparound porch. The five guest rooms all

have private baths with whiz-bang multijet showers (although you'll run up the stairs to reach one), and four of those have a whirlpool tub, too. Rooms with fireplaces are available, and all beds are either king- or queen-sized. Along with the downstairs parlors, guests will find an upstairs sitting room with fridge and microwave. Guests can watch television in their rooms or enjoy the courtyard and fountain. Fancy full breakfast is served, and you're right in downtown Easton.

INN AT 202 DOVER

Innkeepers: Ron and Shelby Mitchell
1-866-450-7600
www.innat202dover.com
202 E. Dover St., Easton, MD 21601
Price: Very Expensive
Handicapped Access: Yes; call to discuss
Special Features: Well-behaved children welcome with prior discussion

An elephant head carved into the vanity, a giant pair of Thai marionettes, and an antique dressing table set. These are a few of the favorite things adorning the elegant, themed, and huge suites at the Inn at 202 Dover. At 10,000 square feet, this is Easton's largest house and its reigning lap of luxury. Nothing appears to have been forgotten at this Select Registry Inn, which features four suites, one bedroom, and a fine-dining restaurant open for dinner Thurs.–Mon. The property was renovated top to bottom in 2005, and you'll have a fine time looking at all the fabulosity. A black baby grand piano inhabits a corner of the welcoming parlor. A stuffed peacock, his tail trailing to the floor, presides over the solarium. Guests inhabit the French, English, Asian, or Safari suites, or a pretty Victorian bedroom. Tumble into your triple-sheeted king bed made up with beautiful linens (ironed after your first night and changed after your second), enjoy a steam shower, or slip into a spacious air

jet tub. Breakfast may include blueberry gazpacho, fancy yogurt parfait, or a crab frittata. Walk to everything in downtown Easton. The inn has Wi-Fi and one room suitable for pets.

TIDEWATER INN

410-822-1300
www.tidewaterinn.com
101 E. Dover St., Easton, MD 21601
Price: Moderate to Very Expensive
Handicapped Access: Yes
Parking: Valet, $10; off-street public parking is available

The venerable Tidewater recently changed hands, and the new owners are looking to return to the traditional Easton inn's roots. First up: The Gold Room will be reopened—probably by the time you read this—and long memories know this was once the town's classic ballroom of choice. With ownership of the Kent Island event venue The Chesapeake Bay Beach Club involved, look for the wedding business to be a focus here. However, those whose nuptials are far in the rearview mirror (or those who have not indulged at all) also will find classic Eastern Shore accommodations. The inn, which was renovated in 2007, offers 101 guest rooms, including seven suites and a bridal suite with classic European-style decor. The suites may include sleeper sofas, fridges, and microwaves, while all accommodations include comfy mattresses and flat-screen TVs. The Tidewater sits right in the center of Easton and its shops, galleries, and restaurants. Hunter's Tavern in-house serves breakfast, lunch, and dinner.

OXFORD
COMBSBERRY

Innkeeper: Mary Alyssa Marvel
410-226-5353
www.combsberry.net
4837 Evergreen Rd., Oxford, MD 21654

Price: Very Expensive
Handicapped Access: No
Special Features: Pets OK in the Oxford
Cottage; children OK for whole-house
rental or reunion

A long colonial lane leads to stately
Combsberry, circa 1730 and centerpiece of
this 35-acre waterside estate, joined by the
brick Carriage House and cute Oxford
Cottage. All are done up in updated English
country style, with the seven guest rooms
inclined toward floral chintz-covered furniture and floral wallpaper, with whirlpool
tubs and water views. The manor house's
downstairs features wood-paneled sitting
rooms with fireplaces where guests relax in
leather chairs. Guest rooms feature such
luxury as the Magnolia Suite, with its huge
second-floor patio and windows onto the
water from the bath, which has a whirlpool
tub. The Carriage House, often leased as a
whole, offers two guest rooms (cathedral
ceilings, whirlpool tubs, luxe bedding, fireplaces) on either end of a broad living/
kitchen area that features TV/DVD, a gas
fireplace, and windows that open onto
Bringman's Cove. Oxford Cottage has a gal-
ley kitchen. Full breakfast is served in the
main house in a contemporary sunroom
with views of the water. Outdoors, brick
patios settle in under magnolias. Two
canoes are available, and guests arriving
via water can tie up at the dock. Bikes are
available.

OXFORD INN & POPE'S TAVERN

Innkeepers: Lisa MacDougal and Dan
Zimbelman
410-226-5220
www.oxfordinn.net
504 S. Morris St., Oxford, MD 21654
Price: Moderate to Expensive
Handicapped Access: No

The old Oxford Inn, built in 1890, acquired
a third floor in 1987 and has been one of

the area's old reliable inns ever since. Its
seven country-style rooms aren't the fanci-
est you'll ever see, nor are they the newest.
They do, however, impart that fading
Eastern Shore fashion—the one that delib-
erately leaves the designer out of the mix
and offers no TV because that's just the way
it is. Rooms are comfortable, too, with thick
towels to go along with the new bathrooms
added in 2005. The inn's rooms come with
their own baths, and the innkeepers
reserve another room as an "add on" if need
be. The beds range from double to king,
there's a suite for traveling companions or
families, and the price is right. See
"Restaurants" to read about the inn's popular restaurant with its French provincial
vibe. Innkeeper Lisa MacDougal pulls double duty as chef.

ROYAL OAK
THE OAKS
410-745-5053
www.the-oaks.com
MD 329 at Acorn Ln./P.O. Box 187, Royal
Oak, MD 21662
Price: Moderate to Very Expensive
Handicapped Access: No
Special Features: Kids OK

Located on the grounds of an original land
grant deeded by Lord Baltimore about
1680, this is a former farm with a long history as a country inn. A swimming pool,
shuffleboard, and a couple of canoes to put
in at Oak Creek set the stage for an easygo-
ing respite off this country road winding
south from St. Michaels. The inn hosts 15
rooms with queen- or king-sized beds, the
former sometimes accompanied by an
antique full-bed headboard. Three rooms
have decks, and some come with gas fireplaces and whirlpool tubs. Settle in on
white wicker furniture on a side screened
porch or at a deckside table along Oak
Creek.

ST. MICHAELS
AIDA'S VICTORIANA INN

Innkeeper: Aida Khalil
410-745-3368 or 1-888-316-1282
www.victorianinn.com
205 Cherry St., St. Michaels, MD 21663
Price: Expensive to Very Expensive
Handicapped Access: No

Victorian this is, but not so high Victorian that you and Grandma's demitasse collection compete for space. Instead, contemporary colors refresh the old waterside inn, which sits across from the Chesapeake Bay Maritime Museum. Its seven guest rooms (one's a suite) come with private baths, and most have water views. Most are queens, although there's a king that converts to twins. A junior suite comes with a gas fireplace, and it's where pets can stay. A welcoming happy hour is held on Fri. evenings, and a full breakfast is served in the pretty dining room.

BAY COTTAGE

Innkeeper: Jackie Fletcher
410-745-9369 or 1-888-558-8008
www.baycottage.com
24640 Yacht Club Rd., St. Michaels, MD 21663
Price: Moderate to Expensive
Handicapped Access: No
Restrictions: No children, no pets

A swimming pool sits alongside Long Haul Creek not far from the deep-water dock where guests arriving by boat tie up. Set right in the slipstream of a long lane leading to the house, the pool makes a perfect spot to catch a breeze on a sultry Eastern Shore day, or to watch the sun set over the water. Lawn chairs, Adirondack or teak, are easy to come by here at Bay Cottage, a well-located hideaway just beyond St. Michaels. The main house is a former hunting lodge and gathering spot for a previous era's Eastern Shore sportsmen and offers plenti-ful water views. A tasteful mix of all-American Ralph Lauren or Drexel furnishings mixed with Asian antiques such as a Ching Dynasty wardrobe decorate the six guest rooms. One room with a single bed connects to another, making them a good option for traveling companions. Breakfast is served out on the porch with yet another view of the water, and the inn is available as a vacation rental.

DR. DODSON HOUSE
BED AND BREAKFAST

Innkeeper: Janet Buck
410-745-3691
www.drdodsonhouse.com
200 Cherry St., St. Michaels, MD 21663
Price: Expensive to Very Expensive
Handicapped Access: No
Special features: Bikes available
Restrictions: Prefer children over 10; call to discuss those who are younger

Victorian decor dominates the dining and guest parlors in this historic home, where service is a focal point. The three-bedroom inn sits close to St. Michaels Harbor and offers spacious, traditionally decorated rooms, including one with an extra daybed. Upstairs is a third bedroom with twin beds, which gives this inn two good accommodations for traveling companions. Guests share a coffee bar. With portions built in 1799 and 1872, the house's signature feature may be the two-story porch lining the facade. But the house also comes with a fascinating past. At one time this was the residence of Louisa Bruff, whose father, Thomas Auld, once owned the slave Frederick Douglass. After the Civil War, Douglass visited the home, where the aging Auld then lived with his daughter and son-in-law, to make amends. Credit cards are not accepted; please pay with cash or checks.

FIVE GABLES INN AND SPA

410-745-0100
www.fivegables.com
209 N. Talbot St., St. Michaels, MD 21663
Price: Expensive to Very Expensive; spa packages available
Handicapped Access: No
Restrictions: Children discouraged

Yellow toile and whimsically painted furniture are among the touches guests will find in the smart, well-appointed rooms here on the main street of St. Michaels. In all, 14 rooms are located in three buildings, each with whirlpool tub. Cobalt blue tiles line the indoor courtyard-style pool. Visitors who want the spa treatment can partake of facials, herbal baths, massage therapy, steam, and sauna. Continental breakfast is served, as well as afternoon refreshments. This is a good-looking inn with a French provincial touch that takes a contemporary approach to Eastern Shore style. Spa packages (featuring Aveda products) range from rosemary mint wraps to Caribbean therapy body treatment to a "Spa & Sail" offering. They're all detailed on the Web site. Spa treatments are not included in room rates.

GEORGE BROOKS HOUSE

Innkeepers: Julia and Will Workman
410-745-8381
www.georgebrookshouse.com
24500 Rolles Range Rd., St. Michaels, MD 21663
Price: Moderate to Very Expensive
Handicapped Access: No

This is a large, historic home revived and renovated some years ago and located at the edge of town near the Chesapeake Bay Maritime Museum. Six handsome, traditionally decorated rooms with pretty Indonesian-made furniture include five with gas fireplaces. You can choose a room with a private porch, and the bathrooms are new and large. Two have whirlpool tubs.

Outside is a pool for lounging and a hot tub, too. Architectural details such as ceiling medallions add to the ambience.

HARBOURTOWNE GOLF RESORT & CONFERENCE CENTER

410-745-9066 or 1-800-446-9066
www.harbourtowne.com
Martingham Dr. (just west of St. Michaels, off MD 33), P.O. Box 126, St. Michaels, MD 21663
Price: Expensive to Very Expensive
Handicapped Access: Yes

Drive through a community surrounding an 18-hole Pete Dye–designed golf course to reach Harbourtowne, with its manicured public areas and 111 rooms, all with water views. Each also comes with a terrace or covered porch. Twenty-four rooms have wood-burning fireplaces. It's a true resort, so there are lawn games, tennis, swimming, trails for walking and jogging, biking, volleyball, badminton, horseshoes, massage services, and a fitness center on its 153 acres. Harbourtowne also has two restaurants, two bars, and a lounge with a pool table and television. The water view from much of the resort is spectacular.

THE INN AT PERRY CABIN

Owner: Orient-Express Hotels
410-745-2200 or 1-800-722-2949 (reservations)
www.perrycabin.com
308 Watkins Ln., St. Michaels, MD 21663
Price: Very Expensive
Handicapped Access: Yes
Special Features: Children and pets welcome; please notify in advance if bringing a pet

Long a showpiece in Talbot County, this luxury 80-room waterside inn has won numerous awards, including five Gold List "Best Places to Stay" commendations from *Condé Nast Traveler*. *Travel & Leisure* named it

The renowned Inn at Perry Cabin has luxurious rooms and a notable restaurant. Photo courtesy of Inn at Perry Cabin

one of the Top 100 Hotels in the U.S. The 40-room historic (circa 1820) section of the inn is a classic. Guests can settle into chintz furniture in the sitting rooms or discover the secret doorway to the "morning room" behind a bookshelf in the salon next door. Rooms are furnished with a mix of traditional and contemporary pieces. This is also home to the upscale restaurant Sherwood's Landing. A newer building hosts the other half of the inn's guest rooms. These rooms have a nautical/British colonial decor that may include an ostrich headboard and a television that rises from a leather "trunk" at the end of the bed. All rooms look out over water and wetlands, and half are suites. Amenities are endless at Perry Cabin: There's a fitness room, a horizon-edge pool, secluded courtyards and porches, attractive gardens, bikes, and concierge service that can arrange guest activities such as boat charters. You can also settle into a nautical bar and lounge. The Linden Spa pampers with herbal treatments and spa cuisine. All in all, it's quite lovely.

THE OLD BRICK INN

410-745-3323 or 1-800-434-2143
www.oldbrickinn.com
401 S. Talbot St., St. Michaels, MD 21663
Price: Moderate to Very Expensive
Handicapped Access: No
Restrictions: Children 12 and older only

This three-building inn is nothing if not diverse. If you don't want to stay in an easy-going room under the eaves, then choose a suite with exposed brick wall and a marble two-person shower with a suit of armor in a corner. Rates vary to reflect the 20 rooms, which are housed in properties on both sides of Talbot Street, including the former B&B known as the Kemp House. It's been remodeled and added to the Old Brick Inn family. Fireplaces light up 19 rooms—some wood and some gas. Two rooms have small balconies, and some have big two-person whirlpool tubs. Different room arrangements create accommodations that work well for families and traveling companions. In the main building, the spacious Chesapeake Suite comes with handsome carved white furniture and enough space to live in. Fridges are available by request if they're not already in the rooms, there's a breakfast buffet, and a small pool is located outside in a brick courtyard.

POINT BREEZE BED & BREAKFAST

Innkeeper: Joan Foster Schneider
410-745-9563
www.pointbreezebandb.com
704 Riverview Terrace, St. Michaels, MD 21663
Price: Moderate to Expensive
Handicapped Access: No

Remember back when B&Bs were more like home stays? Point Breeze tends in that direction because this is the innkeeper's family summer place. Located on St. Michaels Harbor, this B&B provides plenty of room to spread out or to be left alone, whether it's in the house or on the waterside grounds (or waterview screened-in porch, a likely spot to spend a lazy weekend). This place has a lot of space, and everywhere you turn it seems there's another sitting area for guest use. You'll also find a wet bar and a dock for crabbing. There are only two guest rooms, which are comfortable, homey, and not done up in the latest fashion. But when your trusty travel correspondent left the B&B and its warm host, she found herself thinking, "Now, there's a place I'd like to stay."

BETWEEN ST. MICHAELS
AND TILGHMAN ISLAND

WADE'S POINT INN ON THE BAY

Owner: Betsy Feiler
410-745-2500 or 1-888-923-3466
www.wadespoint.com

Wade's Point Rd. (4½ miles south of St. Michaels in McDaniel), P.O. Box 7, St. Michaels, MD 21663
Price: Expensive to Very Expensive
Handicapped Access: Yes
Special Features: Children welcome, but no facilities for infants

A longtime sentimental favorite, this inn sprawls along Eastern Bay 5 miles past St. Michaels. Guests stay in one of several buildings housing a total of 26 rooms. These include the Main House, circa 1890, and the eight-room Victorian Summer Wing, where air-conditioning was added in the early 2000s and the rooms have private baths and water views. In addition, there's the Kemp Guest House, built in 1990, and a farmhouse you can rent as a whole. This is Eastern Shore lodging at its best. Full breakfast. Closes in Dec. and opens again in March.

WATERMARK BED & BREAKFAST

Owners: Mac and Carla Buttrill
410-745-2892 or 1-800-314-7734
www.watermarkinn.com
8956 Tilghman Island Rd./P.O. Box 27, Wittman, MD 21676
Price: Expensive
Handicapped Access: No
Special Features: Kids and pets OK

Yes, that's blue water issuing from the eye-popping fountain/sign announcing the Watermark's long lane. Take it as a fun signal of what's ahead. When last we visited this creative spread, a goat—one of eight—was perched atop a shed not far from Mac's workshop. A fountain sprouts here and there throughout the Bay-side grounds, but wait 'til you see the spectacular mosaic fountain at the edge of the pool. It lights up at night. This secluded log lodging set on 7 acres offers a welcoming front room with a woodstove to keep things warm in winter and a telescope so nature-lovers can peer out at the Bay. Three guest rooms provide a

At the edge of the pool at the Watermark B&B.

whopping 500 square feet of space, with two-person whirlpool tubs set in mosaics, woodstoves, televisions, king-sized beds, minifridges, and Bay views. The downstairs Turtle Cove room is particularly unique, with stained-glass panels inset into logs opening onto the whirlpool tub from the bedroom, and a wet bar area opening onto the porch. Kennel runs are available in the backyard for large dogs, while smaller pets can stay indoors in kennels of their own. If you can subsist on the full breakfast served on weekends (continental during the week) and whatever sustenance you stash in your minifridge, you'll be hard-pressed to leave. The Buttrills do not accept online reservations; call to make your reservations.

TILGHMAN ISLAND
BLACK WALNUT POINT INN
Innkeepers: Tom and Brenda Ward
410-886-2452
www.blackwalnutpoint.com
4417 Black Walnut Rd., Tilghman Island, MD 21671

Price: Moderate to Very Expensive
Handicapped Access: Yes, in the cottages
Restrictions: No children under 12; no pets

On a clear day, you can see Cambridge to the east, and Chesapeake Beach and North Beach to the west from the spread on this spectacular mid-Bay point. There's nothing overly fancy about the rooms in the 1840s house, what with quilts on the beds and basic baths, but that's the point. If you can watch sunset from across the Chesapeake Bay and sunrise from across the Choptank River, swim in the pool, and settle into the hot tub, what more could you want? Maybe just outstanding fishing, especially for migrating rockfish in the fall. This former farmhouse/hunt club complex includes a sitting room with a television and VCR. Three comfy "cottages" (little premade houses) smell of cedar and offer a great get-away, with private screened porches and bedrooms with views of the Bay literally feet away. Continental breakfast is served until 10 AM.

CHESAPEAKE WOOD DUCK INN

Innkeepers: Kimberly and Jeffrey Bushey
410-886-2070 or 1-800-956-2070
www.woodduckinn.com
21490 Gibsontown Rd., Tilghman Island,
MD 21671
Price: Moderate to Very Expensive
Handicapped Access: No
Restrictions: No children under 14

This Dogwood Harbor–side B&B has taken a turn for the culinary with Chef Jeffrey Bushey in residence. The six-room Victorian is comfortably furnished in low-key but upscale Eastern Shore fashion, with queen- or king-sized beds, and there's a great sitting room looking out on the water. Out back stands a contemporary cottage with a CD player and a fun collection of antique doorknobs. And check out breakfast: a pie made from jumbo lump crab, sweet corn, and spinach is just one specialty of the house. Equally inventive dinners are available on Saturday nights as well; call for details. Wi-Fi is available in the house.

LAZYJACK INN

Innkeepers: Mike and Carol Richards
410-886-2215 or 1-800-690-5080
www.lazyjackinn.com
5907 Tilghman Island Rd., Tilghman
Island, MD 21671
Price: Expensive to Very Expensive
Handicapped Access: No
Special features: Children over 12 only

Come to this former waterman's home and enjoy the light flooding in here alongside Dogwood Harbor. The inn has four rooms. A lovely sitting room goes with the Garden Suite, complete with painted furniture and a headboard created from an old piano. The upstairs rooms include the Nellie Byrd Suite, named for a skipjack, with its cool bathroom with a black whirlpool tub and an

Relaxing at Black Walnut Point Inn at the tip of Tilghman Island.

open entryway to the bedroom. You can see the bridge spanning the Choptank River to Cambridge from here. The Richards family also operates lighthouse tours aboard *M/V Sharps Island* (see "Recreation"). Ask about their special packages.

TILGHMAN ISLAND INN
Owners: Jack Redmon and David McCallum
410-886-2141 or 1-800-866-2141
www.tilghmanislandinn.com
21384 Coopertown Rd., Tilghman Island, MD 21671
Price: Expensive to Very Expensive
Handicapped Access: Yes
Special Features: Pets allowed for additional fee; advance arrangements required

With 18 attractive rooms, a terrific restaurant, and Knapp's Narrows flowing alongside, you may decide to settle in for the long run here. The rooms are contemporary, many of them renovated not too long ago, and feature lots of pillows, fluffy duvets, contemporary armchairs, and whirlpool tubs. Many also look out on the water. If you aren't in a waterside room, wander around to the back of the inn and settle into one of the Adirondack chairs lining the Narrows. A pool sits at one end of the inn and an outdoor deck bar is open in summer (see "Restaurants"). The inn also offers spa services, kayak rentals, and is located next door to bike rentals.

Hotels/Motels

Best Western (410-745-3333; for reservations, 1-800-528-1234; 1228 S. Talbot St., St. Michaels, MD 21663) Located before you get to the thick of the town's offerings. Ninety-three rooms, continental breakfast, in-room coffee, pool, free Wi-Fi. Moderate to Expensive.

Comfort Inn Kent Narrows (For reservations, 1-800-828-3361; 3101 Main St., Grasonville, MD 21638) Water-view location next to the Kent Narrows. Indoor pool, hot tub, sauna, exercise room, continental breakfast. In all, 92 rooms and two suites. Moderate to Very Expensive.

Harrison's Chesapeake Country Inn (410-886-2121; www.chesapeakehouse.com; 21551 Chesapeake House Dr., Tilghman, MD 21671) Venerable waterside lodgings renowned among fishers who can eat breakfast early at the inn's fabled restaurant before heading out on a charter boat from the Harrison's fleet. In all, 70 rooms are available. Moderate to Expensive (Inexpensive during the off-season). Packages available. See "Recreation" for fishing details.

Knapp's Narrows Marina & Inn (1-800-322-5181; www.knappsnarrowsmarina.com; 6176 Tilghman Island Road, Tilghman, MD 21671) There's a good chance your room will have a water view here at Knapp's Narrows, the waterway at the drawbridge that crosses to Tilghman Island. Complimentary breakfast, pool, and cabana are among the amenities available to inn and marina guests. Price: Moderate to Expensive.

RESTAURANTS

You won't have a problem finding a great meal in the Mid-Shore area. An haute cuisine chef has taken over a local drugstore luncheon counter, the locals know exactly where to go for great crabs, and fine Northern Italian cuisine is being dished up across from the Talbot County Courthouse. You can even find fried chicken, done up right in a black iron skillet.

Price ranges, based on entrée, are as follows:

Inexpensive: Up to $10
Moderate: $10–20
Expensive: $20–30
Very Expensive: $30 or more

The following abbreviations are used to denote meals served:
B = Breakfast; L = Lunch; D = Dinner; SB = Sunday Brunch

KENT ISLAND/GRASONVILLE/KENT NARROWS

FISHERMAN'S INN & CRAB DECK

410-827-8807 (410-827-6666 for the Crab Deck)
www.fishermansinn.com
3116 Main St., Grasonville
Open: Daily
Price: Moderate to Expensive
Cuisine: Seafood/Eastern Shore
Serving: L, D
Reservations: Not accepted
Handicapped Access: Yes

The same family has operated this popular seafood house on Kent Narrows since 1930. Waterfowl decoys, oyster plates, and duck stamp prints add a nautical air, and a G-scale train circles overhead on 280 feet of track. Like an old friend, you can count on The Fisherman's Inn for standard Eastern Shore fare such as stuffed flounder, broiled or fried catch of the day, combination platters, and crabcakes. Come here for the oyster stew ($5.99 a cup, $6.99 a bowl), or an entrée with two side dishes, bread, and butter. The Chesapeake Bay rockfish stuffed with crabmeat ($29.99) stars and is also the most expensive dish on the menu. Beef, chicken, and vegetarian dishes are available too. For casual outdoor dining you can't beat the adjacent Crab Deck, which features frozen drinks, more than a dozen appetizers, yummy sandwiches and burgers, and a full menu of seafood and non-fishy entrées served with two sides. Prices are lower on the deck than in the inn,

although if you're starved, the Fried Deck Platter with a crabcake, scallops, jumbo gulf shrimp, and flounder fillet is $27.99. Because this is a popular nightspot (and the parking lot is only so big), get here early, especially on weekends, or be prepared to wait.

HARRIS CRAB HOUSE

410-827-9500
www.harriscrabhouse.com
433 N. Kent Narrows Way, Grasonville
Open: Daily
Price: Moderate to Expensive
Cuisine: Seafood
Serving: L, D
Reservations: No
Handicapped Access: Yes
Special Features: Public docking; shops in-season

Follow the sound of mallets on crab shells to Harris Crab House, where diners sit thigh to thigh at long picnic tables to crack steamed blue crabs and drink frosty pitchers of beer. Take your pick of decks—exposed or enclosed. Both overlook the northern end of Kent Narrows and parading sailboats and powerboats. Fresh steamed crabs, soft-shell crabs, shrimp, mussels, and other seafood are on the menu, along with land-and-sea combos. How about the T-bone steak with your choice of fried oysters, shrimp, or scallops? The Stuffed Lobster Platter is a 1¼-pound Maine lobster stuffed with 5 ounces of crab imperial ($32). Not too hungry? A bowl of garlic-laced mussels in a buttery broth is just $7 per pound. Entrées, served with two side dishes, range from $15 to $25. Landlubbers will find steak, barbecued chicken, and ribs. There's a kids' menu for the little ones. Get here early or be prepared to wait on weekends.

HOLLY'S RESTAURANT

410-827-8711
www.hollysrest.com
108 Jackson Creek Rd., Grasonville
Open: Daily
Price: Inexpensive to Moderate
Cuisine: Eastern Shore
Serving: B, L, D
Reservations: No
Handicapped Access: Yes

It's déjà vu every time we settle into a knotty-pine booth at Holly's and my husband repeats the story about his dad bringing him here as a boy for a real chocolate milkshake. Or he waxes over bringing his own daughter when she was a youngster. While waiting for their shakes they would pass the time filling out the placemat quiz, "Can you name the states and their capitals?" More than nostalgia has kept people coming back to Holly's for more than 55 years. Easy access from US 50 helps. Plus, the prices remain reasonable. The standout—other than the shakes, of course—is fried chicken. Hunker down with a three-piece fried chicken platter or half a rotisserie chicken with two side dishes for $8.50. This being Maryland, several seafood dishes are available. The children's menu offers hot dogs, mac and cheese, chicken tenders, and such for $2.95–5.50. Come for breakfast (daily from 7–11:30 AM). Go ahead, have the chocolate milkshake—still delicious and still only $3.

THE JETTY RESTAURANT & DOCK BAR

410-827-4959
www.jettydockbar.com

201 Wells Cove Rd., Grasonville
Open: Daily
Price: Inexpensive to Moderate
Cuisine: Crabs, seafood, light fare
Serving: L, D
Reservations: No
Handicapped Access: Yes

We like to drive here on a pretty day, kick back, and have lunch or dinner outdoors, a stone's throw from the water. Watching the ospreys and gulls searching for their next meals, we always reach the same conclusion: Eastern Shore livin' and dinin' don't get much better than this. Crack crabs or munch on rockfish tenders, a crabcake sandwich, or a particularly tasty hamburger. Tear into an order of steamed shrimp, crabs, mussels, or snow crab legs. Or go for a platter of chicken, fish, or ribs, served with two sides. Two dozen sandwiches and wraps are generous in size, served with chips and a pickle; for $1.50 more you can have french fries or coleslaw. Yes, you can eat inside, but why would you want to?

KENT MANOR INN & RESTAURANT

410-643-7716
www.kentmanor.com
500 Kent Manor Dr., Stevensville
Open: Thurs.–Sun.
Price: Moderate to Expensive
Cuisine: New American/upscale seafood
Serving: L and D Thurs.–Sat., SB
Reservations: Recommended
Handicapped Access: Yes

Only 12 miles from downtown Annapolis and 5 minutes from the US 50, Exit 37 interchange (MD 8 south) lies this gracious inn and restaurant on picturesque Thompson Creek. Come here for lunch en route to the beach or Queenstown shopping, or linger over dinner in a tranquil setting with attentive service—and good value. The restaurant is open for lunch and dinner Thurs.–Sat., and Sun. for the inn's award-winning pull-out-all-the-stops weekend champagne buffet brunch in the glass-enclosed gazebo. The chef turns out mouthwatering dishes utilizing locally grown ingredients. Some recommendations at lunch: the cream of crab soup ($7), outstanding crabcake sandwich ($16), Angus burger, or any entrée salad. Come here to celebrate a special occasion. Dinner entrées ($23–30) include grilled rib-eye steak and filet mignon, crisp-skinned rockfish, crabcakes, cedar-grilled wild salmon, duck, and at least one vegetarian dish. The four-course $40 prix fixe dinner is a bargain. Save room for dessert. When the weather is off and the porch-atrium or waterfront deck are not options, dine in one of the inn's cozy parlor-style rooms with wainscoting, antiques, and fireplaces.

THE NARROWS
410-827-8113
www.thenarrowsrestaurant
3023 Kent Narrows Way S., Grasonville
Open: Daily
Price: Moderate to Very Expensive
Cuisine: Upscale seafood
Serving: L, D
Reservations: Recommended
Handicapped Access: Yes

In an area where restaurants cater mostly to the crab-picking crowd and bare picnic tables are the rule, the Narrows stands out as a bastion of elegant dining—not pretentious, mind you, but this is no crabhouse. The restaurant's cream of crab soup and crabcakes are legendary. So is the three-egg, crab-filled omelet at lunch, a steal at $12. Lunch entrées are $9–15. Besides the Chesapeake staples—crabs, oysters, clams, and rockfish (in season)—you'll find additional seafood dishes along with beef, chicken, and pork entrées (most $23–26). A light supper menu—smaller, well-priced portions ($14.50–18.50) for those watching their waistlines—is available Mon.–Sat.

from 4 PM on, and Sun. from 11 AM to close. Ask for a window table overlooking Kent Narrows when you make a reservation (or arrive early). Then feel your pulse slow as you enjoy your meal and feast on the panorama of passing boats, circling ospreys, low-flying herons, and squawking gulls.

EASTON
GENERAL TANUKI'S
410-819-0707
www.generaltanukis.com
25 Goldsborough St.
Open: Daily
Price: Moderate to Expensive
Cuisine: Pacific Rim and American
Serving: D
Reservations: Recommended
Handicapped Access: Yes

An agreeable mixture of casual and fine dining—and fun—can be found in this popular spot whose namesake (that's Tanuki in the window) symbolizes hospitality and good times. The exposed ductwork and dark gray walls provide the ideal canvas for the colorful food and clientele. How many places feature fish tacos, pizza with sweet Italian sausage, vegetarian red curry, blackened Ahi tuna, and a mile-high burger on the same menu? At General Tanuki's it's easy to build a meal from the appetizers (sushi, crab fondue, veggie spring rolls, or calamari). Libations run from standard cocktails to sake to frosty brewskis that cool the palate after a spicy dish.

MASON'S RESTAURANT
410-822-3204
www.masonsgourmet.com
22–24 S. Harrison St.
Open: Mon.–Sat.
Price: Expensive to Very Expensive (D)
Cuisine: Continental and American, seafood
Serving: L (Mon.–Sat.), D (Tues.–Sat.)

Reservations: Suggested for lunch and dinner
Handicapped Access: Yes

Tucked between antique shops on a handsome historic street in downtown Easton, Mason's is considered one of Easton's best, a very popular local restaurant serving glorified comfort food—at least for lunch. The word is out on both sides of the Bay, making reservations a necessity at lunch and dinner. The bar's jumbo martinis and the kitchen's upscale sandwiches may explain why those in the know like to come here. The seasonal dinner menu is more formal, offering starters such as steamed mussels in Thai lobster sauce, or warm tomato basil tart with carmelized onion. Entrées include seared tuna steak, roasted Australian rack of lamb, and flatiron steak with Gruyère mashed potatoes. Choose from among seven cozy dining rooms, each with its own signature ambience. On your way out, be

sure to stop in the shop portion of the building, which sells chocolates, gourmet food items, and gifts.

OUT OF THE FIRE RESTAURANT & WINE BAR

410-770-4777
www.outofthefire.com
22 Goldsborough St.
Open: Mon.–Sat.
Price: Moderate to Expensive
Cuisine: Mediterranean
Serving: L Mon.–Fri., D Sat.
Reservations: Recommended, particularly on weekends
Handicapped Access: Yes

Chef Michael Roark turns out appetizing dishes that are as attractive as they are delicious. The interior is warm and inviting, reminiscent of a Mediterranean or New York City bistro. Take a break from browsing Easton's downtown area and come here

Fishing boats at Dogwood Harbor on Tilghman Island bring in the fresh seafood served by local restaurants.

for a cup of soup and a sandwich, salad, or hot entrée at lunch. It's easy to understand why the restaurant is a longtime local favorite. At night, settle in for an evening of fine food and great wine. The decor and service are all about making diners feel comfortable, from the sofas off the wine bar to the open kitchen with its wood-burning hearth oven. The menu changes every few weeks to take advantage of local produce. The wood oven–baked pizzas (pear and gorgonzola, for example) are a staple—and not to be missed. We heartily recommend them all. Graze on tapas available at the wine bar.

SCOSSA RESTAURANT AND LOUNGE
410-822-2202
www.scossarestaurant.com
8 N. Washington St.
Open: Daily
Price: Moderate to Very Expensive
Cuisine: Northern Italian
Serving: L, D
Reservations: Not required but recommended
Handicapped Access: yes

Stylish Scossa draws the beautiful people with a tastefully spare and elegant dining room, good service, and Northern Italian cuisine that keeps the locals swooning. Try the risotto with chicken livers or the cannelloni with ground veal, or choose among a pretty list of antipasto (beef carpaccio, sautéed calamari) or salads (beets with fennel and chèvre). French doors front the façade of this renovated former stationer, dividing the front patio tables from the large, modern dining room. Of course they are open during summer, supplying that Italian je ne sais quoi that adds to the atmosphere, as do the oversized La Scala Opera House posters that line the hallway leading to the back lounge, which hosts live music.

SODA FOUNTAIN AT HILL'S
410-822-9751
30 E. Dover St.
Open: Mon.–Sat.
Price: Inexpensive
Cuisine: Haute lunch counter
Serving: B, L
Reservations: No
Handicapped Access: Yes

This beloved, old-fashioned drugstore soda fountain now finds an haute cuisine chef behind the counter, but not to fret. Stephen Mangasarian, known for his late, great Restaurant Columbia nearby, brings his skill to your lunch. Onion rings are properly tempura'd, soups are made from fresh stock ("We don't let the soup sit and cook all day," he says), and hamburgers are made from fresh ground beef. The bread's made every day, too. The most expensive thing on the menu is the $8 crab platter. Belly up. Also: Mangasarian runs a second lunch operation, Lazy Lunch, behind the former Restaurant Columbia. It's takeout except in summer, when a few tables are available.

THAI KI
410-690-3641
www.thai-ki.com
216 East Dover St.
Open: Tues.–Sat.
Price: Inexpensive to Moderate
Cuisine: Thai
Serving: D only Tues.–Thurs.; L, D Fri.–Sat.
Reservations: Recommended
Handicapped Access: Yes

Good karma has surrounded this casual—lots of wood, natural light, and an open kitchen—Thai bistro since it opened about four blocks east of Easton's downtown shopping district. Sharing is a Thai tradition, so have at it. Build a meal from the delectable appetizers (curried samosas or pork and vegetable spring rolls, for example), soups (the hot and sour soup with crab

is awesome), and salads (chicken salad with lemongrass or BBQ pork lettuce wrap, perhaps). You'll dine like Thai royalty while keeping your check in check.
Recommended: chicken with snow peas and cashews, and pad Thai with shrimp. You're sure to find your own favorites.

TRAPPE
MITCHUM'S STEAKHOUSE
410-476-3902
www.mitchumssteakhouse.com
402 Main St.
Open: Restaurant: Tues. through Sun. (D only 5–10)
Café: Mon.–Sat. 10–4 (extended hours in summer). Sun. 11:30 am–3:30 pm
Price: Moderate to very expensive
Cuisine: Beef, seafood
Serving: D (restaurant); B, L (café)
Reservations: Recommended
Handicapped Access: Yes

Voted Maryland's Best New Restaurant in 2008 by the National Restaurant Association, this attractive steakhouse is five minutes from US 50/Ocean Gateway and 9 miles from Easton. It's an excellent refueling spot if you're traveling to or from the Eastern Shore and you're hungry for top-quality, aged beef. The kitchen turns out several seafood dishes, too. From 1958 to 1969 the restaurant's namesake, hunky actor Robert Mitchum, lived on a 333-acre farm in Trappe where he raised quarter horses (and his kids). Who knew? Mitchum's movie posters adorn the smartly sophisticated space where seven cuts of beef ($23–45), seafood, and free-range chicken are served. Sundays the prime rib with a side vegetable is only $20. Check out other specials on Tuesday, Wednesday, and Thursday. Come to the adjacent café for reasonably priced snacks and lunch—sandwiches (grilled steak, perhaps?) and wraps, salads, and the like. Mitchum's is closed Mondays, but the café is open daily.

OXFORD
LATITUDE 38
410-226-5303
www.latitude38.org
26342 Oxford Rd. (MD 333)
Open: Tues.–Sun.
Price: Moderate to Expensive
Cuisine: Creative regional
Serving: D, SB
Reservations: Recommended on weekends
Handicapped Access: Yes

Locals think of Latitude 38 as the Cheers of Oxford. If they don't know your name when you enter, you can be darn sure they will by the time you leave. A haven for locals and weekend sailors, Latitude 38 offers the best of both worlds: multicourse meals for the sit-down crowd and inexpensive bar dinners for those who wish to avoid or escape their own kitchens. For the prices and the camaraderie, you can't beat the light fare menu. Your only obstacle may be finding a spot at this incredibly popular bar, expanded some years ago to accommodate its growing following. Bar dinners change daily, while the regular menu varies biweekly. For small appetites and the budget-conscious, Latitude 38 offers half portions of most dinner entrées.

THE MASTHEAD AT PIER STREET MARINA
410-226-5171
www.latitude38.org/masthead/mh.htm
104 W. Pier St.
Open: Mid-Mar.–Dec.
Price: Moderate to Very Expensive
Cuisine: Eastern Shore seafood, crabs
Serving: L, D
Reservations: Only required for parties of 20 or more
Handicapped Access: Yes

Tropical Storm Isabel dealt this venerable crabhouse a near-fatal blow, but new management rebuilt to create a sturdy tiled dining room as well as the broad deck for covered dining on the Tred Avon River. Casual dress is the order of the day here, where paper tablecloths can be rolled up to discard the mess from feasting on steamed crabs, clams, mussels, and shrimp. Instead of onion rings, look for "onion paddles." The salad croutons are made from corn bread. Nonseafood lovers can settle for burgers and prime rib.

OXFORD INN/POPE'S TAVERN
410-226-5220
www.oxfordinn.net
504 S. Morris St.
Open: Thurs.–Mon.
Price: Moderate to Expensive
Cuisine: Creative American
Serving: D
Reservations: Recommended
Handicapped Access: Yes

The food, service, and ambiance in the intimate Pope's Tavern, in the Oxford Inn, are worth a drive to dine here, as many would agree. Chef/owner Lisa MacDougal oversees the kitchen with an iron whisk and a mother's love. Four nights a week (it may be more when you read this), she and her staff turn out six exquisitely prepared entrées (chicken, fish, crabmeat, beef/veal /pork, pasta) made mostly from local, organically grown ingredients. Not up for a big meal? Enjoy a juicy burger, mac and cheese, meat loaf, or dinner salad from the bar menu ($9–14).

SCHOONER'S
410-226-0160
314 Tilghman St.
Open: Daily spring–Nov.
Price: Inexpensive to moderate
Cuisine: Crabs, pub fare
Serving: L, D
Reservations: Dining room only
Handicapped Access: Yes

Fine dining it is not, but for a decent meal with lots of local color and a water view,

Schooner's is a comfy, casual, fall-into kinda place that attracts transients, locals, and parched sailors in search of grub and grog. The big draw at this crabhouse is the marina setting and waterfront deck (in season). Kick back with a locally produced draft at the deck bar and chill. It's worth the wait for a table if you're not in a hurry, or if you're just off a boat and too grungy to dine in a more formal setting. Not into crabs? The conch fritters, steamed shrimp, burgers, and sandwiches have a following.

ST. MICHAELS
208 TALBOT RESTAURANT & WINE BAR
410-745-3838
www.208talbot.com
208 N. Talbot St.
Open: Tues.–Sun. from 5:30 PM
Price: Expensive to Very Expensive
Cuisine: Innovative American
Serving: D
Reservations: Recommended
Handicapped Access: Yes

208 Talbot is one of those rare restaurants you can always count on for great food and exceptional service. The inventive menu changes at the chef's whim—and it's always a winner, always utilizing fresh, locally produced ingredients. Brothers-in-law Brian Fox and Brendan Keegan (an award-winning chef who previously oversaw O'Learys in Annapolis) reopened 208 in 2008. Since then the restaurant has racked up several national awards. While fish/seafood star, beef and poultry dishes are well represented and prepared with equal flair. We applaud the addition of a tapas menu in the wine bar (all items $4–14), weekday specials (served from 5–6:30 PM), and lunchtime sandwich cart (Fri.–Sun.). A four-course dinner is offered Sat. for $49 per person. Bring someone special here for a romantic evening or to celebrate an occasion. The 1871 dining room radiates enough warmth to melt even the hardest heart.

AVA'S PIZZERIA

410-745-3081
avaspizzeria.com
409 S. Talbot St.
Open: Wed.–Mon. (closed Tues.) 11:30
AM–"the last person leaves"
Price: Inexpensive to Moderate
Cuisine: Pizza/Italian
Serving: L, D
Reservations: No
Handicapped Access: Yes

Since the arrival of Ava's in 2008, we give thanks daily. The popular restaurant, named for co-owner Chris Agharabi's daughter, is conveniently located on St. Michaels' main avenue of boutiques, galleries, and eateries. At lunch we like the pizza (they make the dough daily), wood oven–baked sandwiches on flat bread (served with sensational homemade potato chips), salads, and desserts (tiramisu, cupcake of the day). Sometimes we can't make up our minds and share two or three items. The expanded dinner menu includes the above-mentioned items, as well as several appetizers and a dozen entrées (pasta, beef, chicken, shrimp dishes). Seating is limited and reservations are not taken, so try eating at off times, especially on weekends and holidays.

BISTRO ST. MICHAELS

410-745-9111
www.bistrostmichaels.com
403 S. Talbot St.
Open: Thurs.–Mon.
Price: Expensive
Cuisine: French Provençal meets
Chesapeake seafood
Serving: D
Reservations: Recommended
Handicapped Access: Yes

Conveniently located on the Mid-Shore's left bank in the heart of St. Michaels, this lively and attractive spot features fine dining on tables with crisp, white tablecloths and French theater posters on the wall. The waiting dish of marinated olives, chili, garlic, and olive oil along with crusty French bread will whet your appetite. In the cozy seafood bar you can order a shrimp or crab cocktail, smoked fish plate, or oysters du jour while waiting for your table—or make it a mini-meal. The menu changes seasonally and is limited to six entrées, max. We think of it as a perfect example of less is more. Acclaimed Chef David Stein oversees the open kitchen and staff, and buys locally whenever possible. Everything is done in-house—and done well. So, depending on when you sup, you may find pistou-crusted lamb chops, grilled entrecôte with truffle-madeira vinaigrette, or soft-shell crabs amandine. True to its French roots, the bistro's wine selection is extensive.

THE CRAB CLAW RESTAURANT

410-745-2900
www.thecrabclaw.com
304 Mill St.
Open: Daily, Mar.–early Dec.
Price: Moderate to Expensive
Cuisine: Eastern Shore, crabs
Serving: L, D
Reservations: Recommended on weekends
Handicapped Access: Yes

Settled on prime real estate alongside the Chesapeake Bay Maritime Museum overlooking St. Michaels Harbor, this was originally the Eastern Shore Clam Company, a clam and oyster shucking house. The restaurant was launched in 1965 by the Jones family and is known as the place to crack crabs. Credit cards are not accepted, personal checks are, and there's an ATM on the premises.

FOXY'S MARINA BAR

410-745-4340
foxysstmichaels.com

125 Mulberry St.
Open: Daily, mid-Mar.–Dec.
Price: Inexpensive to Moderate
Cuisine: Seafood/pub fare
Serving: L, D
Reservations: No
Handicapped Access: Yes

Location is everything in real estate, and Foxy's enjoys a primo marina dock location at the end of Mulberry Street. This is the Eastern Shore's answer to Margaritaville. Boaters, locals, and tourists gather 'round umbrella-topped tables to toast the setting sun and each other with giant martinis and frozen drink specials while munching on burgers, crabcakes, and steamed seafood. You can't beat Foxy's for island ambiance in the heart of St. Michaels.

KEY LIME CAFÉ

410-745-3158
www.keylime-cafe.com
207 N. Talbot St.
Open: Daily
Price: Moderate to Expensive
Cuisine: Eclectic American
Serving: L, D, SB
Reservations: Recommended on weekends
Handicapped Access: Partial; call to discuss

Once a barbershop and then an antique shop, this pretty bungalow has housed a St. Michaels favorite since 2005. Key Lime Café keeps it casual, with its signature key lime ribs and burgees as window treatments, but the café also keeps it moving with a dinner menu that changes nearly every week. Look for local ingredients, like the concoction involving a corn cake, sliced tomato, and crab stack. If that dish doesn't get up and scream Eastern Shore, nothing does. And, of course, the café serves up a key lime pie. In winter come the tapas and small plates, or perhaps Chef Randolph Sprinkle's cooking class. This is a locals' place.

ST. MICHAELS CRAB & STEAK HOUSE

410-745-3737
stmichaelscrabhouse.com
305 Mulberry St.
Open: Thurs.–Tues.
Price: Moderate to Expensive
Cuisine: Seafood, steak
Serving: L, D
Reservations: Recommended
Handicapped Access: Yes

You get three for one—a formal dining room, tavern, and waterside deck—at the St. Michaels Crab & Steak House. The building dates back to the 1830s, when it was an oyster-shucking shed. Can't ask for a better pedigree than that. A standout among the dozen and a half appetizers is the seafood pizza ($11.95). Grazing? We recommend the luscious French onion soup, tomato stuffed with shrimp salad, Caesar salad topped with fried oysters or crabmeat, or crabcake sandwich. Entrées showcase crabmeat, fish, and steak selections (New York strip, porterhouse, filet mignon), along with a handful of pasta, chicken, and rib platters. All entrées come with two side dishes.

ROYAL OAK
BELLA LUNA RESTAURANT AND MARKET

410-745-6100
www.bellalunarestaurant.net
25942 Royal Oak Rd.
Open: Daily
Price: Moderate to Very Expensive
Cuisine: Italian
Serving: L, D, SB
Reservations: Recommended
Handicapped Access: Yes

In an old general store near the St. Michaels landing of the Oxford–Bellevue Ferry is a hidden gem touted by travelers from near and far. Two of us stopped for lunch a few years back and owner/chef Barbara Helish greeted us, pulled up a stool, and asked, "What are you in the mood for?" She told us what ingredients were available and then she went to work. The result? A sautéed shrimp/portobello /goat cheese/red pepper sandwich on Italian bread that was unbelievably good. The dinner menu, with a handful of entrées, changes regularly. We're hoping to return soon for the cedar-planked wild king salmon with balsamic reduction and cucumbers—or whatever else is starring that night. Italian wines, homemade mozzarella, artisan cheeses, and other Italian specialties are available for eating in or taking out. It may be off the beaten path, but it is well worth a detour. A second, larger location is open at 305 High St. in the heart of downtown Cambridge.

TILGHMAN ISLAND
TILGHMAN ISLAND INN
410-886-2141
tilghmanislandinn.com
21384 Coopertown Rd.
Open: Daily except Wed.; closed in Jan.
Price: Moderate to Very Expensive
Cuisine: American

Serving: L, D, SB
Reservations: Recommended
Handicapped Access: Yes

After the floodwaters of Tropical Storm Isabel receded in 2003, the owners of the Tilghman Island Inn renovated the inn's first floor and renamed the restaurant for the "once-in-100-year" storm. The decor is spare and sophisticated. Local art adds much but cannot compete with the fantastic views of Knapp's Narrows or the Bay. A longtime star on the menu is the Oysters Choptank, everyone's favorite bivalve in a Pernod-infused champagne sauce and encased in puff pastry. Heaven. The menu changes seasonally to take advantage of what's swimming in the Bay or growing on nearby farms. In addition to seafood, other equally delectable entrées include lamb chops, pork tenderloins, and beef. A five-course tasting menu is available weekends for $60, and the extensive wine list, recognized by *Wine Spectator* for years, includes many half-bottles.

FOOD PURVEYORS

Beer and Wine

Eastern Shore Brewing (410-745-8010; www.easternshorebrewing.com; 605 S. Talbot St., St Michaels) Owned by Adam Moritz and his wife, Lori, this brewing company not only sits right around the corner from the St. Michaels Winery—in case you and yours have different tastes—but provides four year-round beers on tap at all times and one seasonal. For $1, enjoy a sample and ask for a tour. Live local music on weekends; Thurs. evening is open jam night. Open daily in summer and Fri.–Sun. in winter.

St. Michaels Winery (410-745-0808; www.st-michaels-winery.com; 605 S. Talbot St., St. Michaels) Stop by to sample the locally grown wine here at this attractive tasting room.

Coffee Shops

Blue Crab Coffee Company (410-745-4155; 102 Fremont St., St. Michaels) Fresh pastries, coffees, and teas quartered in the historic Freedom's Friends Lodge 1024. Open late Fri. and Sat. in season.

St. Michaels Perk (410-745-8099; 402 S. Talbot St., St. Michaels) Whether it's your computer or your caffeine level, wire up at this coffee shop on St. Michaels' main street and drink in the laid-back vibe. Open daily, although they close in late afternoon come winter.

Gourmet and Specialty Markets

Chesapeake Gourmet (410-827-8686; 189 Outlet Center Dr., Queenstown) A well-supplied store with terrific kitchenware, coffee and tea, wines, microbrews, and specialty food products. Good takeout, too. Located at Prime Outlets on US 50. Open daily.

Flamingo Flats (410-745-2053; 100 S. Talbot St., St. Michaels) An endless collection of hot sauces ("Chesapeake Fire Hot Sauce"), as well as gourmet condiments and sauces like Miles River Dry Goods and Provisions seafood seasoning.

CoffeeCat

(410-690-3662; 5 Goldsborough St., Easton) This is the local coffee bar, with espresso and coffees ready at 9 AM. There's also a full breakfast and lunch menu. Late afternoon brings more lattes, and light fare and a winebar scene arrives at night. This is when NightCat comes alive in an adjoining space, with live music ($10–20 per ticket) booked from all over. Wed. night is trivia night. For schedules: www.night catmusic.com.

Oxford Market & Deli (410-226-0015; 203 S. Morris St., Oxford) All you need, from groceries to ice cream to deli sandwiches, is served here. You can rent DVDs, too. Unless you're staying at an inn, this is the only game in town for breakfast: Try fresh-baked muffins or egg sandwiches. Open by 7 AM in the summer and until 8 or 9 PM in summer, 7 in winter.

Stop in to try the vino at St. Michaels Winery.

Piazza Italian Market (410-820-8281; 218 N. Washington St., Easton) Paninis for lunch, prepared goods, and other great Italian goodies (like olives).

The Railway Market (410-822-4852; www.naturalretail.com; 108 Marlboro Ave #1, Easton) Terrific natural foods grocer originally located in Easton's old-time railway depot. It offers organic groceries, takeout and a café, health and beauty products, books. Open daily.

Ice Cream

Justine's Ice Cream Parlour (410-745-5416; 106 S. Talbot St., St. Michaels) This cute ice cream shop has become a local institution with its array of ice cream goodies. You can't miss it, located in the midst of St. Michaels. Open daily Mar. through Nov.

Olde Town Creamery (410-820-5223; 9B Goldsborough St., Easton) Well-located in the middle of town, this ice cream shop sells everything from malteds to gelati.

Scottish Highland Creamery (410-924-6298; www.scottishhighlandcreamery.com; 314 Tilghman St., Oxford) Located on the water behind Schooner's, the ice creamery makes 600 flavors, a revolving 14 at a time. So if strawberry ice cream isn't working for you, maybe you can try corn ice cream. Even salmon and dill, we're told, which must do something good for one's omega 3 count. Open daily from the beginning of Apr. to the end of Oct., and also selling homemade fudge and candy.

Seafood Markets and Crabhouses

Big Al's Market (410-745-3151; 302 N. Talbot St., St. Michaels) Where St. Michaels buys its hard-shell crabs for summer crab feasts. Fresh fish, groceries, deli, beer, wine, and liquor. Hunting and fishing licenses.

Captain's Ketch Seafood Market (410-820-7177; 316 Glebe Rd., Easton) Picked crabmeat, lobster, and fish, including orange roughy, catfish, and smoked bluefish.

Chesapeake Landing Seafood Market and Restaurant (410-745-9600; 23713 St. Michaels Rd., McDaniel) People drive all the way from Easton to get seafood at this real-deal seafood restaurant between St. Michaels and Tilghman. Chesapeake Landing has its own processing plant; even the crabs shipped in during winter are picked on-site. During oyster season, stop in for the Fri. oyster buffet, or try Angus beef if you aren't a seafood lover.

Fisherman's Seafood Market (410-827-7323; 3032 Kent Narrows Way S., Grasonville) Locals know to stop at the seafood market in the midst of this restaurant complex for fine fresh fish, crabcakes, and more to prepare at home.

CULTURE

When history meets a beautiful landscape, the arts (and their patrons) seem to follow. That's the easy summation of cultural life in this region, which has had its art associations for local painters for years, a wealthy estate society dating back to the Revolution, and gorgeous waterways that draw everyone to a boat. Easton's popular First Friday, in which shops and galleries stay open late, is expanding to a full weekend. That means galleries will be open into Fri. and Sat. evenings, restaurants will offer specials, and entertainment's on tap. For info, check www.eastonmainstreet.com or the Talbot County Office of Tourism at www.tourtalbot.org or 410-770-8000. Also note that commercial galleries are listed under the shopping section.

Cinema

Easton Premier Cinemas (410-822-9950; Tred Avon Shopping Center on Marlboro Rd., Easton) First-run fare.

Museums, Historic Houses, and Arts Centers

STEVENSVILLE
KENT ISLAND FEDERATION OF ARTS

410-643-7424
www.kifa.us
405 Main St.
Open: Wed.–Fri. 1–4; Sat. 10–4

Local and regional artists working in media from oils to photography exhibit at this fine Victorian at the edge of town. Monthly exhibits feature everything from paintings to pottery; a separate member gallery changes its exhibit every two months. Classes and workshops are available.

WYE MILLS
WYE GRIST MILL

410-827-6909 or 410-827-3850
www.oldwyemill.org
14296 Old Wye Rd. (MD 662 off US 50 north of Easton)
Open: Mon.–Sat. 10–4, Sun. 1–4
Admission: $2 donation suggested

A gristmill has been grinding cornmeal and flour in Wye Mills since 1671, and you can still see the great stone turn by water power on the first and third Sat. of every month. An exhibit focuses on the mill's glory days, from 1790 to 1830, when wheat brought prosperity here, where flour for Revolutionary troops was ground. Buy a bag of freshly ground meal or *The Wye Miller's Grind,* a 100-recipe cookbook. Wye Mill is a hotbed of historic sites, all within a few hundred yards of each other. Call 1-888-400-RSVP for information on any of them. On a culinary note, Orrell's Maryland Beaten Biscuits, the world's only commercial beaten biscuit company, makes the small local delights just a stone's throw from the mill. The result is surprisingly flaky and chewy, and certainly worth trying. Call them at 410-827-6244.

EASTON
ACADEMY ART MUSEUM

410-822-ARTS
www.art-academy.org
106 South St.
Open: Mon. and Fri. 10–4; Tues.–Thurs. 10–7; Sat. 10–3
Admission: Free on Wed.; $3 for nonmembers, kids under 12 free

Long the gathering place for the area's artists, this white clapboard former schoolhouse is also known for its fine collection of 20th- and 21st-century American and European drawings and prints. Included are pieces from masters such as James Whistler, John Sloane, Pierre Bonnard, Jim Dine, Robert Motherwell, Richard Diebenkorn, and Chuck Close. Museum exhibits, such as the recent "The Washington Color Painters," change every week

The Academy Art Museum in Easton is central to the Mid-Shore's art scene.

and may be curated by the Smithsonian, the Walters, or other major museums in the region. Catch one of numerous lectures and concerts (Broadway, opera, classical) in the museum's performance space, or take a class ranging from children's art appreciation to printmaking for adults. Watch for the museum's popular juried craft show in October.

HISTORICAL SOCIETY OF TALBOT COUNTY
410-822-0773
www.hstc.org
25 S. Washington St.
Open: Mon.–Sat. 10–4. Tours of the three houses on the property at 11:30 AM Mar.–Nov. or by appt. Walking tours of Easton also can be arranged with advance notice
Admission: Free for museum; $5 for tours

Come learn about Trappe, Cordova, and Tunica Mills, the smaller crossroads towns of Talbot County. They're the focus of the museum here, where you can also catch chapters of local life like that told in the recent exhibit, "World War II: Talbot Supports the Allies." Also on the grounds are three structures you can see via tour. Joseph's Cottage (1795) tells the story of an Easton cabinetmaker. The James Neall House (1810), an excellent example of Federal architecture, shows how life changed for the affluent cabinetmaker and his Quaker family after early 19th-century success. Forman's Studio, a replica of a Colonial home, moved here in 1989 and was created by H. Chandlee Forman, who is well-known among Colonial architectural enthusiasts.

THIRD HAVEN FRIENDS MEETING HOUSE

410-822-0293
www.thirdhaven.org
405 S. Washington St.
Open: Daily 9–5; services Sun. at 10 AM

Built from 1682 to 1684, this is the country's oldest documented wooden building in continuous use for religious purposes. Originally located in virgin timber (Easton was founded
25 years later), the meeting house is now neatly tucked into a residential street on a 7-acre
parcel. Stroll the peaceful grounds and admire a simple building still in use 300 years after
Pennsylvania founder and Quaker William Penn preached here. Friends still meet in the
heated, "new" meeting house next door, circa 1880.

OXFORD
OXFORD MUSEUM

410-226-0191
www.oxfordmuseum.org
101 Morris St.
Open: Mon., Wed., Fri., and Sat. 10–4; Sun. 10–4

This small, free museum reflects the life of this charming white-picket-fence town. You
might see the Oxford class of 1950 roster from the Maryland Military Academy hanging in
the window of this classic storefront museum.

ST. MICHAELS
CHESAPEAKE BAY MARITIME MUSEUM

410-745-2916
www.cbmm.org
Mill St., Navy Point
Open: Daily; summer 9–6, spring/fall 9–5, winter 9–4
Admission: Adults $10, seniors $9, children 6–17 $5

The tale of the Chesapeake Bay is told here, from her shifting shoreline to her watermen
farming a living from her depths to the "come heres" who've made this a recreational
hotspot. Founded in 1965, the museum is home to an endless collection of Bay artifacts,
including the world's largest fleet of indigenous Bay workboats. Among the dozens of vessels here are the famous skipjack *Rosie Parks;* the *Edna E. Lockwood,* the last log-hull bugeye
still plying the Bay; and the *Old Point,* a crab dredger from Virginia. The 18-acre complex
on the shores of Navy Point consists of 23 buildings, nine devoted to exhibits on the Bay's
geological, social, economic, and maritime history, from the age of sail and steamboats to
the advent of gas and diesel engines. The screw-pile Hooper Strait Lighthouse moved here
in 1966. Inside, the lighthouse keeper's late-19th-century life is re-created, and everyone
stops for the prime view of the Miles River. Also displayed are the massive punt guns once
used by the market gunners, as well as a huge collection of decoys used by waterfowl
hunters. Kids love clambering through the interactive skipjack in the "Oystering on the
Chesapeake" exhibit, and Waterman's Wharf lets you into a re-created crab shanty to see if
the crabs are peeling. Changing exhibits such as the recent photographs in "Rising Tide"
starkly depict the Bay's changing shoreline, while the elegant paintings of Louis Fuchter
show old Bay scenes. The museum's calendar of events includes must-do festivals such as

A crowd gathers to watch two people making a skiff at the Chesapeake Bay Maritime Museum's Apprentice for a Day Program. Photo courtesy of the Chesapeake Bay Maritime Museum

Bay Day in Apr. and the Chesapeake Folk Festival on the last Sat. in July (see their Web site or our "Seasonal Events and Festivals"). Also, the gift shop offers a range of nautical items as well as maritime and Chesapeake books. Scholars may be interested in the museum's library, devoted to maritime and Chesapeake writings and history. The vehicle entrance incorporates another Bay artifact: the Knapp's Narrows drawbridge, which served as the gateway to Tilghman Island for 64 years, until 1998. The bridge was moved to St. Michaels and positioned partially open so that motorists could see the same view that boaters saw during the bridge's many years of service.

Nightlife

Kent Narrows, where Kent Island and the Eastern Shore mainland meet in Queen Anne's County, hosts the dock bar night scene, particularly on summer nights when the boating set ties up here. **Red Eye's Dock Bar** (410-827-EYES; www.redeyedockbar.com; Mears Point Marina, 428 Kent Narrows Way North in Grasonville) brings in rock bands and DJs and generally rocks the Narrows on the weekends (and on some weeknights) during the busy season. See bikini contests if it's warm or watch televisions showing NASCAR and NFL if not. On the Narrows' south side, the **Jetty Dock Bar** is the place. Catch live music on weekends, crack a few crabs, and partake of the karaoke jukebox on Thursday nights. The formal address is 201 Wells Cove Rd. in Grasonville; call 410-827-4959 or check www.jettydockbar.com for schedules.

In St. Michaels, locals go to **Carpenter Street Saloon**, aka "C Street" (410-745-5111; 113–115 S. Talbot St.), for conviviality, free popcorn, Thurs. live mike night, and live music on weekends. It's also a good spot for pub fare during the day. Down along the harbor, **Foxy's Marina Bar** (410-745-4340; www.foxysstmichaels.com; 125 Mulberry St.), serves martinis and pub fare along with a heapin' helping of waterfront conviviality. In Tilghman, head for the **Tilghman Island Inn** (410-886-2141; www.tilghmanislandinn.com; 21384 Coopertown Rd.) with its outdoor deck on a summer evening.

In Easton, the live music's at **NightCat** (443-786-2750; www.nightcatmusic.com; 5 Goldsborough St.), with acts from around the region and beyond. **Washington Street Pub** (410-822-9011; 20 N. Washington St.) and **Legal Spirits** (410-820-0765; www.shore boys.com; 42 E. Dover) are the local taverns of choice. The latter shares a lobby with the **Avalon Theatre**, a likely opportunity for a good performance that could even be brilliant— like Wynton Marsalis. The elegant lounge at **Scossa Restaurant** (410-822-2202; www.scossarestaurant.com; 8 N. Washington St.) offers evening music.

Oxford offers a few good spots to stop and have a drink. **Latitude 38** (410-226-5303; www.latitude38.org; 26342 Oxford Rd.) is on the road into town and is also a good place for dinner. **Schooner's** (410-226-0160; 314 Tilghman St.) on Town Creek has a deck bar in-season, a restaurant, and a lounge. **Pope's Tavern** (410-226-5220; www.oxfordinn.net; 504 S. Morris St.) at the Oxford Inn serves its regulars, so get there early to claim a bar stool.

Performing Arts

CENTREVILLE
QUEEN ANNE'S COUNTY ARTS COUNCIL
410-758-2520
www.arts4u.info
206 S. Commerce St.

The Arts Council sponsors a variety of regional events at various locations, including summer Thurs. night "Concerts in the Park" featuring top-grade regional talent. Also, the council hosts classes and events such as the "Members Best" exhibitions displayed throughout Centreville.

EASTON
AVALON THEATRE
410-822-7299
www.avalontheatre.com
40 E. Dover St.

This beautifully restored and renovated 1920s art deco theater is a showplace for all of the performing arts in the area and a well-used community gem. The calendar is packed with classic film screenings, children's theater, poetry gatherings, performances by the Mid-Atlantic Symphony Orchestra, and shows by musicians ranging from Nick Lowe and the Cowboy Junkies to Branford Marsalis and Rita Coolidge. You can also catch lectures and performances by local group such as the Easton Choral Arts Society. All of the seats in this intimate theater are good, but come early to enjoy the architecture or to capture a prime spot in front of the stage.

CHESAPEAKE CHAMBER MUSIC
410-819-0380
www.chesapeakechambermusic.org

The two-week Chesapeake Chamber Music Festival is one of the cultural jewels in the Eastern Shore's summer calendar. The talent roster is always impressive, and a recent fest saw 11 concerts held throughout the Mid-Shore region. Typical venues include the Avalon Theatre, Emmanuel Church in Chestertown, a waterfront estate, or the Aspen Institute in Wye Mills. Chicago Symphony bass clarinetist J. Lawrie Bloom launched the festival in 1986, and continues to serve as artistic director with cellist Marcy Rosen, a member of the Lions Gate Trio. Free concerts include an open rehearsal at the Academy Art Museum. In addition to the festival, Chesapeake Chamber Music hosts a biennial competition for emerging musicians and Interlude Concerts in spring and fall. Check the Web site for event details.

MID-ATLANTIC SYMPHONY ORCHESTRA
410-289-3440 or 1-888-846-8600
www.midatlanticsymphony.org

The Mid-Atlantic Symphony serves both of the Delmarva Peninsula's coasts, performing in Easton, Ocean Pines, and Ocean View, Delaware, and bringing Mozart and Ravel live to the Eastern Shore during the fall/winter performance season. Its (more or less) 40-member company draws from professional musicians hailing from throughout the region, performing under the baton of Maestro Julien Benichou. Check the Web site for schedule details.

OXFORD
TRED AVON PLAYERS
410-226-0061
www.tredavonplayers.org
This established community theater stages musicals, contemporary comedies, and classical dramas featuring thespians from around Talbot County. It's worthwhile to book a ticket for a show like "Damn Yankees" or "Barefoot in the Park" if you're going to be in town. Performances are held at the Oxford Community Center (410-226-5904; 200 Oxford Rd.), which also hosts a variety of events.

Seasonal Events and Festivals
Oxford Day is this town's biggie, held in late April, with a parade, 5K, music, family activities, and more. For info: www.oxfordday.org. In late June comes the Cardboard Boat Races, a zany Strand-side race with lots of creative vessels—with proceeds going to charity.

The Antique and Classic Boat Festival at the Chesapeake Bay Maritime Museum in St. Michaels brings more than 100 old beauties to the Navy Point campus the third weekend of June. For info: 410-745-2916; www.cbmm.org; Mill St., Navy Point, St. Michaels, MD 21663.

July draws artists and observers to Plein Air Easton! with nearly a week of events such as lectures, demonstrations, and opportunities to watch the painters at work in the lovely Talbot County countryside. Usually held the third and fourth weeks in July, festival events are nearly all free and open to the public. (Check out the "Quick Draw" competition in downtown Easton, which fills the streets.) Tickets are required for the Collector's Party and Brunch. For details: 410-822-7297 or www.pleinaireaston.com.

In late July, the **Chesapeake Folk Festival** at the Chesapeake Bay Maritime Museum celebrates high summer on the Bay with food, great music, boat rides, folkways demonstrations, and crafts. For info: www.cbmm.org.

In September, look to the big screen with the arrival of the relatively new but successful **Chesapeake Film Festival**. A recent fest saw screenings of films ranging from *Afghan Star* to the 1936 *After the Thin Man* at venues like the Avalon Theatre and the Oxford Community Center. The festival is primarily centered in Easton. For more: www.chesapeakefilm festival.com or contact the Talbot County Visitors Center at 11 S. Harrison St., Easton, MD 21601.

In October, it's time for the **Mid-Atlantic Small Craft Festival**, which brings tons of folks out to the Chesapeake Bay Maritime Museum in St. Michaels to check out all kinds of small craft, including kayaks and canoes. For info: www.cbmm.org.

The annual **Tilghman Island Day** celebration combines demonstrations of the waterman's way of life with a heaping helping of what that way of life yields: seafood. Crab and oyster aficionados come from afar on the third Sat. in Oct. Boat docking contests (which you must see if you haven't), an oyster shucking contest, crab picking contest, music, and more are offered. The celebration benefits the Tilghman Volunteer Fire Company. For info: www.tilghmanmd.com.

Waterfowl Festival (410-822-4567; www.waterfowlfestival.org; 40 S. Harrison St., Easton, MD 21601) During the second weekend in Nov., Easton undergoes an amazing transformation—and what small town wouldn't if 15,000 to 18,000 visitors showed up? The internationally known, three-day Waterfowl Festival features 300 of the world's finest decoy carvers and wildlife painters. Since its founding in 1971, the festival has raised millions of dollars for conservation organizations devoted to preserving waterfowl. Exhibits spread across town showcase decoy art, paintings, and sculpture. Other events include retriever demonstrations, kids' activities, fly-fishing demonstrations, master classes with artists, a sporting clay tournament, and, always a hit, the World Championship Goose-Calling Contest. A fleet of shuttle buses provides free transportation from the parking areas to the exhibit locations. Admission: $10 per day. Handicapped access.

Tours

Dockside Express (1-888-312-7847; www.docksidexpress.com) Take a one-hour walking tour of St. Michaels, or catch a ghost tour that leaves from the Mill St. info booth. Call for schedules and costs and see "Recreation" for their boat tour information.

Poplar Island Tours (410-770-6503) For a cool experience, take a boat ride out to Poplar Island for a free two-hour bus tour. The island had eroded to 5 acres—next to nothing compared to the 1,147 it was back in 1847—when an ingenious plan went into effect. Dredge material from Baltimore Harbor was recycled to re-create the island. The project's supposed to keep going until the island is 1,715 acres, but in the meantime, the wildlife has moved in and the and habitat is developing. The tours, hosted by the U.S. Army Corps of Engineers, leave from Knapp's Narrows on Tilghman Island. Call about three weeks in advance.

St. Michaels Museum Walking Tours (410-745-9561; www.stmichaelsmuseum.com) The
small St. Michaels Museum in the town's distinctive St. Mary's Square shows some of
the town's history and offers docent-guided tours, including Frederick Douglass in St.
Michaels and a historic tour of the waterfront. There's also a self-guided tour. Call for
prices and times, May–Oct.

RECREATION

Low-lying coastal plains meet gently rolling farmland here along the Bay's Mid-Shore
tributaries, making this perfect territory for biking and kayaking (if you're not already out
on a boat). You'll find flat roads, gear rental options, and cycling maps to help you pedal
for miles. Gentle creeks off the Wye, Miles, Tred Avon, and Choptank rivers create more
than 600 miles for paddling adventures. Then, of course, there's plenty of open water (or
even the aforementioned rivers and creeks) for sailing and powerboating in an area that
has a long and well-respected outdoor tradition. Get outside. Bring a fishing rod or a crab-
dipping net. You'll have fun.

Bicycling

Cyclists have long flocked to the Mid-Shore, so much so that now B&Bs may offer bikes or
bike storage, and long-popular routes are codified on maps for newbies. Many of the main
roads have wide shoulders, but they may also host impatient drivers on busy weekends, so
watch out. US 50 is to be avoided. Favorite rides include the 31-mile Easton-to-St.
Michaels trip, the 10-mile Easton-to-Oxford run, and the 25-mile round-trip from St.
Michaels to Tilghman. Many cyclists make a point of riding the Oxford–Bellevue Ferry,
which costs cyclists $4 one-way and $6 round-trip (and is closed Dec. through Mar.). Pick
up a copy of the Talbot County Bicycle Map, which features six routes, 26.7 to 38.2 miles
long, and is available at visitor centers throughout the county or via www.tourtalbot.org.

Bike Rentals and Guides

Adult Toy Rentals by Tilghman Island Marina Rentals (410-886-2500; www.tilghman
marina.com; 6140 Mariners Ct., Tilghman Island) A sassy name for a serious rental
outfit that offers a variety of bicycles for sale, including mountain, hybrid, and boardwalk cruisers. In addition, they rent mopeds, motor scooters, kayaks, canoes, sailboats,
and a variety of power craft for the water.
Easton Cycle & Sport (410-822-7433; www.eastoncycleandsport.com; 723 Goldsborough
St., Easton) This is a full-service stop for renting bikes, kayaks, canoes, stand-up paddle boards, and Hobie Cats. They can guide trips on a prearranged basis, supply maps
for bike rides or water trails, and provide full sales and service on bikes and kayaks.
St. Michaels Marina Bike Rentals (410-745-2400; www.stmichaelsmarina.com; St.
Michaels Marina, 305 Mulberry St., St. Michaels) Bikes rented for an hour, two hours,
four hours, or all day. Prices start at $7 per hour, and the hourly rate goes down the
longer you ride.

Bird-Watching

Some of the best birding in the Mid-Shore area, with its limited public water access, is
from a boat. Ospreys, bald eagles, herons blue or green, and migratory birds passing

through are often spotted. The area's not far from Blackwater National Wildlife Refuge in Dorchester County on the Lower Eastern Shore and Sandy Point State Park along the Bay Bridge in Annapolis, both favored birding spots.

Boating

Charters and Rentals

Adult Toy Rentals by Tilghman Island Marine Rentals (410-886-2500; www.tilghman marina.com; 6140 Mariners Court, Tilghman) Rentals of every kind: kayaks, small craft, canoes, WaveRunners, small sailboats, and even motor scooters and bikes.

All Aboard Charters (410-745-6022; www.tilghmanislandfishing.com; MD 33, Knapp's Narrows Marina, Tilghman; mailing address: P.O. Box 154, McDaniel, MD 21647) Charter the 46-foot Bay workboat *Nancy Ellen* (custom built to yacht standards) for fishing trips (specializing in light tackle) or three-hour private cruises.

C&C Charters (1-800-733-SAIL; www.cccharters.com; 506 Kent Narrows Way N., Grasonville) This is a longtime charter operation that offers bareboat or captained charters. Power and sailboats are available.

Schnaitman's Boat Rentals (410-827-7663; 12518 Wye Landing Ln., Wye Mills) Crabbers gather at this venerable Wye River spot, where rowboats convertible to motor via a small engine go out on one of the Bay's best crabbing rivers. In all, about forty 16-foot, flat-bottom rowboats are available; you can row out or bring your own small motor (up to 25 hp). Also, six motorboats with 6 hp outboards are available. Crabbing supplies like dip nets are for sale or rent; chicken necks, a favorite crabbing bait, are also for sale. Fishing, too. Mid-May through Oct.

Tred Avon Yacht Sales/Choptank Charters (410-226-5000; www.tays.com 102 S. Morris St., Oxford) If you want to spend time aboard a lovely sail or power boat, here's your opportunity not just to do a bareboat charter, but to arrange a captained day charter.

Excursion and Tour Boats

Chesapeake Lights (410-886-2215 or 1-800-690-5080; www.chesapeakelights.com; P.O. Box 248, Tilghman Island Rd., Tilghman, MD 21671) Check out the Bay's lighthouses—many not easily seen from land—aboard the former U.S. Navy special operations vessel *M/V Sharps Island.* Three tours lasting from all day (10 lights) to two hours (two lights at sunset) are available and priced accordingly. There's also a two-day, 13-light trip down to Virginia. Reservations required. Departs from Bay Hundred Restaurant at Knapp's Narrows.

Dockside Express Cruises & Tours (1-888-312-7847; www.cruisinthebay.com; P.O. Box 122, Tilghman, MD 21671) This multitasking tour operator offers naturalist-narrated ecotours and sunset champagne tours aboard the *Express Royale* from early Apr. to early Nov., and crabbing cruises aboard the smaller *Fun4U* in the early morning every day except Mon. between Memorial and Labor Day or by appointment. Themed cruises and private charters, too.

HM Krenz (410-745-6080; www.oystercatcher.com) The 1955 skipjack, one of the last built, sails on two-hour tours daily from the Chesapeake Maritime Museum, Apr.–Oct. Private charters are also available.

Patriot Cruises (410-745-3100; ticket booth 410-745-5928; www.patriotcruises.com; P.O. Box 1206, St. Michaels, MD 21663) Take a ride on this perennially popular cruise of the

Miles River with narration on local history. The 170-capacity *Patriot* departs at 11, 12:30, 2:30, and 4 daily, Apr.–Oct., from a dock off Mill St. near the Chesapeake Bay Maritime Museum. During the peak summer tourist months, prepare to wait in line. Special lunch cruises and evening charters also available.

Rebecca T. Ruark (Capt. Wade H. Murphy Jr., 410-886-2176 or 410-829-3976; www.skipjack.org; 21308 Phillips Rd., Tilghman, MD 21617) The oldest, prettiest, and fastest skipjack in the Bay's dwindling oyster fleet, captained by Capt. Wade Murphy, a man who has shown a talent for demonstrating dredging and talking about the trade with visitors. Kids of all ages enjoy this two-hour tour. $30 per person, children under 12 are half-price. Longer cruises can be arranged. *Rebecca*, built in 1886, is a National Historic Landmark.

Selina II (410-726-9400; www.sailselina.com) This pretty 42-foot gaff-rigged catboat belonged to the captain's grandfather starting in 1926, and then to her parents, and now it's hers. She brought *Selina* to St. Michaels from her longtime home on Long Island, and now you can go out from St. Michaels five times daily (including for sunset and moonlight cruises) May–Oct. Call for prices; six-passenger limit. Private charters are also available.

Capt. Wade Murphy aboard the Rebecca T. Ruark, *the oldest skipjack on the Bay*

Marinas

On Kent Island, the **Bay Bridge Marina** (410-643-3162; www.baybridgemarina.com) is located hard alongside the east end of the bridge and can't be missed. There, you'll find Hemingway's Restaurant, a bathhouse, laundry, fuel, and a small airport adjacent. Over at Kent Narrows, **Mears Point Marina Kent Narrows** (410-827-8888; www.mearspoint.com) is centrally located, with several restaurants within walking distance, an impressive 540 slips, and amenities including an Olympic-sized pool. Many powerboats live here, where the Chester flows into Eastern Bay.

Across the Bay at St. Michaels, check the **St. Michaels Marina** (410-745-2400 or 1-800-678-8980; www.stmichaelsmarina.com), which has transient slips on the Miles River, a pool, and bike rentals. Also nearby is the **St. Michaels Harbour Inn Marina & Spa** (410-745-9001 or 1-800-955-9001; www.harbourinn.com), with Miles River slips for transients, a water taxi, and bike rentals among the amenities.

The **Oxford Boatyard** (410-226-5101; www.oxfordboatyard.com), which dates to 1866 on the Tred Avon, is open year-round with pump-out station, laundry, and showers. Or check out **Town Creek Marina** (410-226-5747). Mears Yacht Haven (410-226-5157; www.coastal-properties.com/mears.html) located on Town Creek on the Strand, supplies amenities like Wi-Fi, a pool, and cable TV along with a fuel dock and pump-out station.

At Knapp's Narrows along Tilghman Island, the **Knapp's Narrows Marina and Inn** (410-886-2720; www.knappsnarrowsmarina.com) offers a swimming pool, laundry, showers, restaurant, and a 20-room motel. Also consider the **Tilghman Island Marina** (410-886-2500; www.tilghmanmarina.com) along the Narrows. Its amenities include a pool.

Outfitters and Rentals

Adult Toy Rentals by Tilghman Island Marina Rentals (410-886-2500; www.tilghman marina.com; 6140 Mariners Ct., Tilghman Island) A sassy name for a serious rental outfit that offers a variety of bicycles for sale including mountain, hybrid, and board-walk cruisers. In addition, they rent mopeds, motor scooters, kayaks, canoes, sailboats, and a variety of power craft for the water.

Eastern Shore Adventure Company (410-820-8881; www.esadventure.com; P.O. Box 153, Wye Mills) Make arrangements to meet this outfitter at your preferred Mid-Shore tributary to rent a kayak, or hire them to show you the way.

Easton Cycle & Sport (410-822-7433; www.eastoncycleandsport.com; 723 Goldsborough St., Easton) This is a full-service stop for renting bikes, kayaks, canoes, stand-up paddle boards, and Hobie Cats. They can guide trips on a prearranged basis, supply maps for bike rides or water trails, and provide full sales and service on bikes and kayaks.

Fishing

Boat Ramps & Fishing Piers

The state of Maryland makes things easy for anyone looking for a boat ramp. Go to the Department of Natural Resources' Web page, www.dnr.state.md.us, and click on "Find a Boat Ramp" in the column to your right.

Kent Island's **Matapeake Pier** and **Romancoke Pier** cost $10 for 24 hours of fishing. To reach Matapeake, take a right on MD 8 right after crossing the eastbound span of the Bay Bridge and go 3 miles. To reach Romancoke Pier, keep going on MD 8. It's at the southern end of the road. For info: parksnrec.org/landings-a-piers.html.

The bridge that once spanned the **Choptank River** serves as fishing piers from either side of the river, and has been renamed for the late Bill Burton, a well-known Maryland outdoors writer of 50 years who died in 2009. Enjoy crabbing or fishing, or enjoy the 25-acre park with waterside walking path on the Talbot County side. On the Dorchester County side (considered part of the Lower Eastern Shore in this book), the pier remains open and lit year-round. The piers are easy to spot, located alongside US 50 at the Frederick C. Malkus Bridge. Contact: **The Bill Burton Fishing Piers State Park**, 410-820-1668; www.dnr.state.md.us/publiclands/eastern/choptankpier.html; 29761 Bolinbroke Point Dr., Trappe, MD 21673.

Charter Boats and Head Boats

All Aboard Charters (410-745-6022; www.tilghmanislandfishing.com; MD 33, Knapp's Narrows Marina, Tilghman; mailing address: P.O. Box 154, McDaniel, MD 21647) Charter the 46-foot Bay workboat *Nancy Ellen* for fishing trips (specializing in light tackle).

Harrison's Sport Fishing Center (410-886-2121; www.chesapeakehouse.com; 21551 Chesapeake House Dr., Tilghman Island, MD 21671) This is sportfishing central amid a complex that started with an inn opened in 1898. Sportfishers have been coming here since the late 1930s, and the Harrisons are well-known in the region. They operate a 14-boat fleet and can tap into on-call captains. Fishing costs $125 per fisherman for the day. Various packages are available, including a $259-per-person package at the complex that includes dinner, overnight lodging, breakfast, and a box lunch for the boat.

Pintail Point (410-827-7029; www.pintailpoint.com; 511 Pintail Point Farm Ln., Queenstown, MD 21658) Guided charters include cruises on the Chesapeake aboard two 59-foot fishing boats. Or see about having an Orvis guide take you fly-fishing.

Crabbing

Go out with Tilghman's **Capt. Wade Murphy** to trotline for crabs and (hopefully) take home dinner. You can also go fishing for rockfish with him. Call him at 410-829-3976. (If Murphy's name sounds familiar, it's because he also captains the famed skipjack *Rebecca T. Ruark*, which you can also go aboard.)

Capt. Russell Dize takes folks out crabbing aboard the 42-foot *Riley Kat*. Head out from Tilghman Island, and contact Dize at 410-886-2249 or via www.letsgocrabbing.com. First of June through mid- to late-Oct.

Fitness Facilities

Cross Court Athletic Club (410-822-1515; 1180 S. Washington St., Easton) Four indoor and three outdoor tennis courts, exercise classes and equipment, child care, and more. Guest fee is $10.

YMCA (410-822-0566; 202 Peach Blossom Rd., Easton) Two indoor swimming pools, nine tennis courts plus platform tennis, exercise and weight-training equipment (including free weights), Pilates, zumba, yoga classes, racquetball, and squash. One-third of Talbot County belongs to the Y. Day passes cost $10 for a workout ($8 for students and seniors; $15 for a couple; $13 for a senior couple). Child care available.

Golf

Although it's located on the Lower Eastern Shore, the Hyatt River Marsh Golf Course is close enough that it should be on the radar screen of Mid-Shore golfers. See the "Recreation" section of Chapter 7, "Lower Eastern Shore," for information. Otherwise consider:

The Easton Club (410-820-9800 or 1-800-277-9800; 28449 Clubhouse Dr., Easton) Championship 18-hole golf course in a waterfront community. Restaurant, too.

Harbourtown Golf Resort (1-800-446-9066; 9784 Martingham Dr., St. Michaels) Pete Dye–designed 18-hole course with clubhouse.

Hog Neck Golf Course (410-822-6079 or 1-800-280-1790; www.hogneck.com; 10142 Old Cordova Rd., Easton) Owned by Talbot County; 27 holes with an 18-hole championship course and a nine-hole executive course. Daily fee. Golf pros, pro shop, café.

Queenstown Harbor Golf Links (410-827-6611 or 1-800-827-5257; www.mdgolf.com; 310 Links Ln., Queenstown) Two 18-hole courses called the River and the Lakes stay busy. This is a beautiful setting on the Chester River. Fully stocked pro shop, eat-in café, newly updated short game facility, new putting green, and chipping and pitching green. Well-located to both the Eastern and Western shores.

Ice skating

Talbot County Community Center (410-770-8050; www.talbotcountymd.gov/index .php?page=Parks_and_Recreation; 10028 Ocean Gateway, Easton) Newly renovated rink draws teenagers on Fri. nights and families on Sat. and Sun. Open fall to spring.

Natural Areas: Sanctuaries, Parks, Environmental Centers

Visitors trying to contact park management should be aware that some state parks are satellite operations, managed from another park. For camping and picnic shelter reservations, call 1-888-432-CAMP or visit www.dnr.state.md.us.

Adkins Arboretum (410-634-2847; www.adkinsarboretum.org; 12610 Eveland Rd./P.O. Box 100, Ridgely) Those interested in native plants will want to stop at this 400-acre native garden and preserve. Walk more than 4 miles of trails offering over 600 species, or peek at native plants under cultivation. Check the arboretum's Web site for programs that range from guided walks to rotating art shows to spring and fall plant sales. Open daily 10–4; $3 adult admission and $1 for students.

Chesapeake Bay Environmental Center (410-827-6694; www.cbec-wtna.org; 600 Discovery Ln., Grasonville) This is a 501-acre preserve formerly known as Horsehead Wetlands Center. In addition to a variety of programs, including a Restoration Volunteer Corps helping to re-establish Bay habitats, the center provides 4 miles of trails through its property and a 1-mile water trail. The center also rehabilitates birds of prey such as owls, hawks, and bald eagles, providing an opportunity for a great up-close look at these marvelous creatures.

Idylwild Wildlife Management Area (410-376-3236; Houston Branch Rd., Federalsburg) Freshwater marsh and forest mean pileated woodpeckers, owls, and scarlet tanagers live here along Marshyhope Creek. Beavers, too. In all, there are 3,800 acres for hunting, plus trails for biking and paddling access.

Martinak State Park (410-820-1668; www.dnr.maryland.gov/publiclands/eastern /martinak.html; 137 Deep Shore Rd., Denton) A family-oriented, 107-acre area along

Watts Creek and the Choptank River featuring fishing, hiking trails, and playgrounds. Boating access via pier or ramp, campground, camper cabins, one full-service cabin. and riverside picnic pavilions.

Phillips Wharf Environmental Center (1-888-312-7847; pwec.org) With hands-on opportunities to learn about the Bay's plants and animals, this is a good place to take the kids. It's in a Tilghman crab shanty at Knapp's Narrows, and is open Apr.–Oct., Thurs.–Mon 10–4, person power permitting. This is a nonprofit organization associated with the Dockside Express touring operation.

Pickering Creek Audubon Center (410-822-4903; www.pickeringcreek.org; 11450 Audubon Ln., Easton) Forest, fresh and brackish marshes, and about a mile of shoreline along Pickering Creek are part of this 400-acre farm. Walk 3½ miles of trails, check out the kids' garden, or launch a kayak or canoe. Grounds open dawn to dusk daily; office Mon.–Fri. 9–5.

Tuckahoe State Park (410-820-1668; 13070 Crouse Mill Rd., Queen Anne) A pretty 60-acre lake for fishing and boating, and lots of woods, including a marked fitness trail with exercises at each station. In all, 15 miles of trails for hiking or biking. Canoe, kayak, and mountain bike rentals Apr.–Oct. The 51-site campground includes four camper cabins. Picnic pavilions.

Wye Island Natural Resources Management Area (410-827-7577; 632 Wye Island Rd., Queenstown) This is 2,450 acres on a historic island paddlers like to circle. Also, there are 6 miles of trails open sunrise to sunset daily. Information on nearby launch sites and permit fees is available from the Queen Anne's County Department of Parks and Recreation (410-758-0835; www.qac.org) or the Talbot County Parks and Recreation Department (410-770-8050; www.talbotcountymd.gov).

Paddling

Plenty of good paddling can be found throughout the Mid-Shore, with numerous creeks branching from its rivers flowing to the Bay. Many routes have been mapped, among them the Tilghman Island Water Trail, with 10 paddles for varying skill levels covering from 3.3 to 10.2 miles. The St. Michaels Water Trail is four paddles of 2, 3, and 8 miles along Oak and Newcomb creeks; San Domingo Creek to Hamblin Island; St. Michaels Harbor and the Miles River; and Neavitt Landing to Leadenham Creek. Landings and cautions regarding tides, winds, and conditions are included. Tilghman and St. Michaels maps can be obtained via the Talbot County Office of Tourism, 410-770-8000; www.tourtalbot.org; 11 S. Harrison St., Easton, MD 21601; ddodson@talbgov.org. Always check on the weather and bring appropriate gear with you when heading out onto the water.

Sporting Goods and Camping Supply Stores

Albright's Gun Shop (410-820-8811; 36 E. Dover St., Easton) Fishing and hunting gear, gunsmithing on premises. Orvis and other outdoor clothing. You can also book a hunting guide (ducks and geese).

Chesapeake Outdoors (410-604-0446; 1707 Main St., Chester) Hunting, fishing supplies, archery pro shop. Crabbing supplies, too.

Shore Sportsman (410-820-5599 or 1-800-263-2027; 8232 Ocean Gateway, Easton) Hunting, fishing, bait and tackle, archery, clothing, hunting and fishing supplies, as well as info on guides.

Swimming

Public pools are open during the summer in Easton and St. Michaels. Entry fees are nominal and seasonal passes are available. The **George W. Murphy Pool** (410-820-7306) is located at 501 Port St. off the Easton Bypass and includes a smaller "zero-entry" pool for kids. In St. Michaels, check out the **Bay Hundred Community Pool** (410-745-6592) at 911 S. Talbot St. For information including schedules, check www.talbotcountymd.gov/index .php?page=Pools.

SHOPPING

Antiques

Americana Antiques (410-226-5677; *www.americanaantiques.net*; 111 S. Morris St., Oxford) A town fixture for 30 years, offering 17th-, 18th-, and early 19th-century American art and artifacts. Also specializes in carousel art.

Antiques on Talbot (410-745-5208; 211 N. Talbot St., St. Michaels) Nauticals and oyster plates are among the goodies at this shop operated by three partners. Local second-home owners are finding their way here to purchase items such as oars to convert to curtain rods.

Flo-Mir (410-822-2857; 23 E. Dover St., Easton) Popular local antique shop; especially strong on china. Open Mon.–Sat. 10–5; Sun. 11–3 in-season only.

Foxwell's Antiques & Collectibles (410-820-9705; 7793 Ocean Gateway, Easton) Antiques and collectibles fill about 10,000 square feet at this mall at the edge of Easton. Wear comfy shoes, because you've got upward of 60 dealers to work your way through. Open daily 10–5.

Janet K. Fanto Antiques and Rare Books (410-763-9030; 7B Goldsborough St., Easton) Early American silver, rare books, fine art. Mon., Tues., and Thurs.–Sat. 10–5, Sun. noon–3.

London (410-745-4000; www.londonthestore.com; 101 N. Talbot St., St. Michaels) Great shop with lots of antiques direct from London. Furniture, porcelain, paintings.

Oak Creek Sales (410-745-3193; www.oakcreeksales.com; 25939 Royal Oak Rd., Royal Oak, off the road between St. Michaels and Easton) Eclectic selection of antiques and collectibles including wrought iron, urns, lamps, and mirrors. Across the street, an entire barn is devoted to antique and used furniture. Weather vanes also sold here.

Tharpe Antiques and Decorative Arts (410-820-7525; www.hstc.org/tharpeantiques .htm; 30 S. Washington St., Easton) Supports the Talbot County Historical Society Museum, located across the street. Open Tues.–Sat. 10–5.

Apparel and Accessories

Andrea's Papillon (410-820-4925; www.andreaspapillon.com; 21A N. Harrison St., Easton) Handbags from the trendy to the practical.

Bleachers (410-745-5676; 107 S. Talbot St., St. Michaels) Beachy boutique offers colorful, fun clothes for adults.

Charisma Clothing Boutique (410-745-0352; 201 S. Talbot St., St. Michaels) Cool, fun, and/or good-looking clothing for women, including those who are over 25.

Chesapeake Bay Outfitters (410-745-3107; Talbot St. and Railroad Ave., St. Michaels) Look for your Chesapeake T-shirts as well as sportswear, nautical apparel, and shoes.

Lizzy Dee (410-770-4374; 20 Goldsborough St., Easton) Cute and breezy women's clothing.

M. Randall and Company (410-820-4077; www.marcrandall.com; 17 N. Harrison St., Easton) Good-looking women's clothing, including lines like Gant and Blue Willis sweater line.

Art Galleries

Artiste Locale/Frivolous Fibers (410-745-6580; 112 N. Talbot St., St. Michaels) Showcase for artisans from throughout the region, including pottery by Talbot potters The Bogans, Ann Krestensen, and Paul Aspell. The full-service knitting shop on-site features Blue Heron Yarn, which is hand-dyed in Easton. "Sit and Knit" sessions held Tues. 5–8 and Sun. 1–3.

Chesapeake Bay Heritage Gallery (410-770-3663; www.chesapeakebayheritagegallery .com; 5 N. Harrison St., Easton) Devoted to Eastern Shore art, including lots of landscapes.

Gallery by the River & Contemporary Tapestry Weaving (410-745-4303; www.ctw-tapestry.com; 5592 Poplar Lane, Royal Oak, near the Oxford–Bellevue Ferry) Swedish weaver Ulrika Leander's gallery brings expansive, brightly colored tapestry art to the town's old post office. The gallery shows European decorative artists. Open mid-June–Sept., Fri.–Sun. or by appt. Check Web site for details.

The Gregorio Gallery (410-745-0927; www.gregoriogallery.com; 104 N. Talbot St., St. Michaels) Photographer Gregorio's photos of his travels and the Eastern Shore light up his gallery in the middle of town.

Linda Luke Art Gallery & Studio (410-745-2695; 104 N. Talbot St., St. Michaels) Oxford painter Luke shows her regional watercolors.

South Street Art Gallery (410-770-8350; www.southstreetartgallery.com; 5 South St., Easton) Cool artist-owned gallery of regional and national artists housed in 1854 building. Very nice selection of plein air paintings, among others.

Troika Gallery (410-770-9190; www.troikagallery.com; 9 S. Harrison St., Easton) Operated by three local artists, this is a sizable fine arts gallery showcasing regional, national, and international artists. Open Mon.–Sat. 10–5:30, Sun. by appointment.

The Water's Way Art Studio (410-745-3439; 214 Talbot St., St. Michaels) This tiny gallery sells art and pearls. Perfect, eh? Artist Deborah Scales and others show here in exhibits that change every six weeks.

Books

Book Bank: Crawfords Nautical Books (410-886-2230; www.crawfordsnautical.com; 5782 Tilghman Island Rd., Tilghman Island) Thousands of fiction and nonfiction titles on all things nautical, from sailing to shipbuilding to seafaring. The store also buys used books.

Book Cellar (410-827-8474; 431 Outlet Center Dr., Queenstown) Hardcovers and paperbacks below retail, including discounted best sellers. Located at Prime Outlets.

Harrison Street Bookstore (410-819-0000; www.harrisonstreetbooks.com; 27 S. Harrison St., Easton) The local independent bookshop, opened in 2007.

Mystery Loves Company (410-226-0010 or 1-800-538-0042; www.mysterylovescompany .com; 202 S. Morris St., Oxford) Formerly headquartered in Fell's Point and now

Stop in to the Troika Gallery in downtown Easton.

ensconced in a former bank building on Oxford's main street, this bookshop carries mysteries and includes work by local authors, Chesapeake books, and children's books. Local artist openings take place monthly.

The News Center (410-822-7212; Talbottown Shopping Center, 218 N. Washington St., Easton) Large paperback selection and fine section of regional writings. Also stocks the Shore's largest periodicals selection, with more than 1,000 titles.

Unicorn Bookshop (410-476-3838; www.unicornbookshop.com; 3935 Ocean Gateway /US 50, Trappe) Excellent rare and secondhand bookshop; bibliophiles will love this place. Antique map reproductions.

Gift, Home and Lifestyle Shops

Artisans of the World (410-745-6040; www.artisansoftheworld.com; 203 N. Talbot St., St. Michaels) This highly browsable craft shop sells the work of St. Michaels artisans along with pieces from around the globe. Pottery, jewelry, and more is available at reasonable prices.

The Christmas Goose (410-827-5252; www.xmasgoose.com; 4628 US 50, Queenstown) Handcrafted Christmas items like nutcrackers, ornaments, and more. Located across from Prime Outlets.

Coco & Company (410-745-3400; www.cocoandcompany.com; 209 S. Talbot St., St. Michaels) Furniture, candles, antiques, great jewelry, and garden items are among the many goodies in this large and tempting lifestyle and gift shop. Smells terrific, too.

Crackerjacks (410-822-7716; 7 S. Washington St., Easton) Cool toy store in Easton's Historic District selling quality games, dolls, children's books, and stuffed animals. Many imported items. The store carries Playmobile-themed toys.

Hollyhocks (410-745-0555; 500 S. Talbot St., St. Michaels) Traditional and good-looking furniture, nautically inspired paintings, and decoys. Antiques and other fine items for your home.

Hype (410-745-9192; 413 S. Talbot St., St. Michaels) Terrific gift shop with all kinds of cool stuff—including for the garden.

Irish Traditions (410-819-3663; www.irishtranditionsonline.com; 35 N. Harrison St., Easton) Authentic Irish imports include gifts, artwork, apparel, and jewelry. Irish Traditions has also taken to renting kilts, and if you spend much time around the Chesapeake you'll come to appreciate that's a clever market they've gone after. This lovely shop is open daily.

Keepers (1-800-549-1872; www.keepersstmichaels.com; 300 S. Talbot St., St. Michaels) A full-line Orvis dealer with outdoor gear and clothing, plus antique and contemporary decoys.

Maris Elaine Gallery (410-228-0800; www.mariselainegallery.com; 406 S. Talbot St., St. Michaels) This upscale contemporary home store is the smaller counterpart to Maris Elaine's spacious Cambridge store and gallery.

Salisbury Gift and Garden (410-820-5202; www.salisburypewter.com; 650 Old Trappe Rd., Easton) Pewter and silver factory seconds, discontinued and discount items can be found here. The store is located along US 50.

Simpatico (410-745-0345; www.simpaticostmichaels.com; 104 Railroad Ave., St. Michaels) Italian dinnerware, linens, and other luxurious goodies from everyone's favorite country.

South by Southwest (410-745-0077; 310 S. Talbot St., St. Michaels) If you forgot to buy that fabulous turquoise necklace in New Mexico, look for it here.

A Wish Called Wanda (410-745-6762; 110 N. Talbot St., St. Michaels) Wanda herself rules the cash register of this cute shop, which offers a variety of crafts, but be sure to check out the garden sculptures.

Jewelry

Shearer the Jeweler (410-822-2279; www.shearerthejeweler.com; 22 N. Washington St., Easton) Family owned for three generations, featuring diamonds, colored gems, watches, and original designs.

Westphal Jewelers (410-822-7774; www.westphaljewelers.com; 19 N. Harrison St., Easton) Diamonds, gemstones, and custom designs.

Marine Supply
L&B Marine Supply (410-643-3600; 124 Kent Landing, Stevensville) Discount marine supply.

Outlets
Prime Outlets Queenstown (410-827-8699; www.primeoutlets.com; 441 Outlet Center Dr., Queenstown) Notable destination among outlet shoppers, with more than 60 stores such as kate spade and Eddie Bauer. The location, just over the Bay Bridge on the Eastern Shore, makes for a good stop. If you're hungry, the Chesapeake Gourmet has good sandwiches and takeout.

7

Lower Eastern Shore

Water, Water Everywhere

South of the Choptank River: Cambridge, Salisbury, Crisfield, Smith & Tangier Islands

The longest of the Eastern Shore's tributaries, the Choptank River broadens as it reaches the Bay and marks the start of the Lower Eastern Shore. Travelers on US 50 cross its on-and-on bridge, formally known as the Frederick C. Malkus Bridge, to reach **Cambridge**, originally settled in 1684. Alongside the bridge run remnants of its Depression-era predecessor, which are now fishing piers. Sails, wakes, and the typical lowboard of Chesapeake workboats glint white from below, evidence that this is cruising paradise and prime fishing grounds. Creeks detour inland.

Upon arrival in Dorchester County, visitors find Cambridge's Historic District behind the highway's commercial appearance, with grand homes lining a brick street. Wind through the old section of town to Great Marsh Park, look out onto the wide-open Choptank, and you'll get a hint of the Lower Eastern Shore's primary draw. Pure and simple, it's nature.

Marshland blurs the distinction between land and sea in many parts of the Lower Eastern Shore of Maryland. Watermen and farmers live close to the earth, and visitors are perhaps more likely to encounter a more authentic way of life here than in Bay Country's other regions.

Nature lovers who cycle or paddle have found paradise here. Explore the flat "Maryland Everglades," the vast marshland filled with rivers and twisting creeks, called "guts," which run south down the coast from Dorchester County. Loblolly pine, tall green sentinels common to the area, stretch high. The endangered Delmarva fox squirrel lives here, too. Birders find bald eagles along with an abundance of other nesters and avian visitors stopping along the Atlantic Flyway. Put in a boat and fish Bay tributaries, or charter a boat into prime Chesapeake fishing grounds in search of rockfish, croaker, flounder, and spot. From a pier, lower a net or string tied around a chicken neck to catch blue crabs.

Through these blackwater swamps that draw modern-day kayakers passed Harriet Tubman, the escaped slave who led some 300 slaves along the Underground Railroad to freedom through this land. Born in captivity in Dorchester County, "The Moses of Her

OPPOSITE: *The Wintergarden is an indoor-outdoor pool at the Hyatt in Cambridge.*

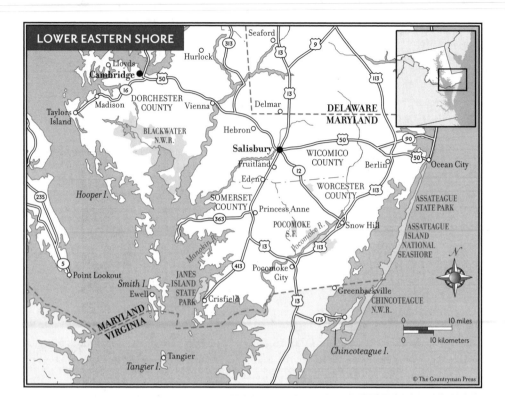

People" is the subject of a local tour, a small museum, and efforts to establish a state park and a national historical park in her honor. The Harriet Tubman Underground Railroad Byway has been named an All-American Road.

Since the arrival of the Hyatt resort high above the Choptank in Cambridge in the early 2000s, life has been starting to look different in this historic town. Old buildings have been gussied up, and galleries and new shops are moving into the old downtown. Overall, the expectation seems to be that Cambridge is ready to boom.

Heading farther south along US 13 through the southern Delmarva Peninsula, you'll pass quaint towns and the bustling burg of Salisbury, as well as long stretches of farmland. Eastern Shore seafood doesn't get any better than what you'll find here, which means the fried soft-shell crabs on potato bread served at local festivals are likely to trump fancier versions in big city cafés.

Salisbury, known as "The Crossroads of the Delmarva Peninsula," lies about 30 miles south of Cambridge. It's home to Salisbury University, the Ward Museum of Wildfowl Art—showcasing the gold standard work of late, great local carvers Lem and Steve Ward and others—and the Salisbury Zoo. From here, many travelers head due east to the ocean beaches.

To stay on a Bay Country course, stay south. Scattered in Somerset and Worcester Counties are historic towns marching toward the Atlantic Ocean. **Princess Anne**, founded in 1733 and named for King George II's daughter, is the Somerset County seat, its streets lined with Federal and Georgian houses.

Snow Hill, a royal port under England's William and Mary, once saw three-masted schooners and steamboats arrive up the Pocomoke River. Now it's a reclaimed historical town drawing paddlers who stay in its updated Victorian B&Bs before heading out on the eminently enjoyable Pocomoke. **Berlin**, near the Atlantic Ocean, descends from colonial Burley Plantation and is stylishly reclaimed.

Maryland's southernmost town is **Crisfield**. It was called Somer's Cove until the mid- to late-1800s railroad arrived via the influence of a local lawyer named John Crisfield. The railroad's arrival touched off a true oyster boom, and by the late 1800s the harbor was thick with watermen's vessels and people were getting rich on oysters. Crisfield was a noisy strip of brothels and saloons and street-brawl recklessness. The oyster boom faded long ago, but Crisfield remains a working watermen's port that calls itself "The Crab Capital of the World." Word has it that oyster shells literally remain a foundation of the town. Today, storefront businesses attend to the working folks, like hardware stores selling commercial crab pots.

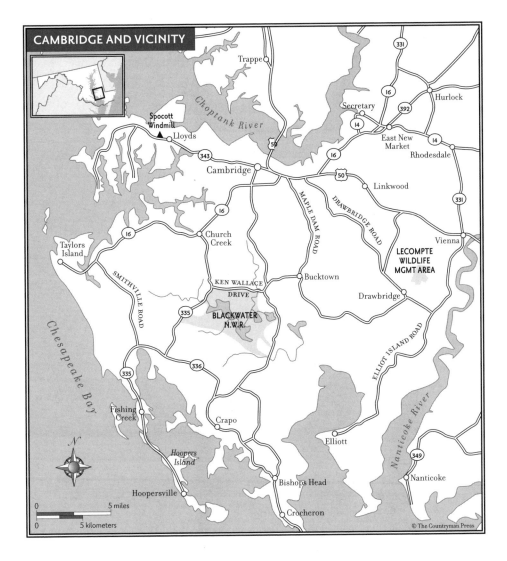

CAMBRIDGE AND VICINITY

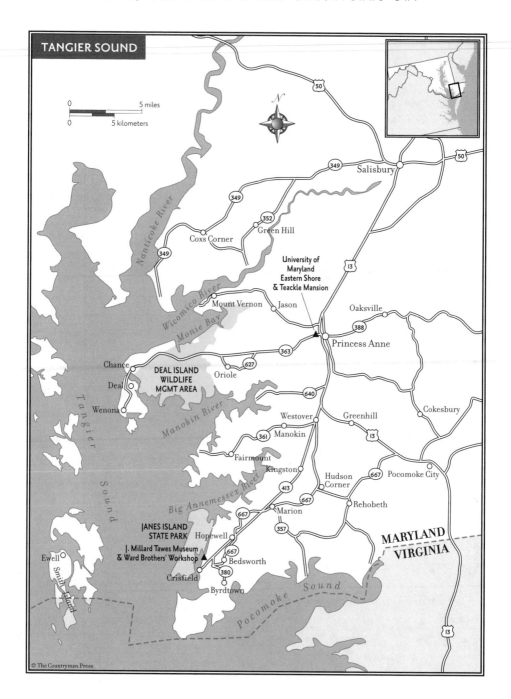

Visitors are well advised to check into one of Crisfield's handful of standard motels or to head out to Janes Island State Park for a cabin—either basic "camper" style (bathhouses nearby in the campground) or full-serve. Crisfield is also the place to take a ferry over to Smith and Tangier islands, those final bastions of Bay island waterman life. If you have only a weekend, plan to visit over Labor Day, when the Crisfield Hard Crab Derby or the nearby Deal Island Skipjack Races and Land Festival (highlighted under "Seasonal Events and Festivals") show folks what the waterman's life is all about.

Smith and Tangier both incubate a disappearing way of life, where crabbers and their families live by the crustacean's life cycle. Tangier, in Virginia, tends to have more for visitors than Maryland's Smith, which, with three towns, is larger. Time and tide erode the shores of both. White crab peeler sheds line Tangier's shores, though they're onshore on Smith. If authentic Chesapeake intrigues, don't miss these islands.

Visitor centers include the Dorchester County Visitor Center at Sailwinds Park East, located on the east side of the Choptank River in Cambridge (and easily visible from the US 50 bridge due to its distinctive sail), which is open 8:30–5 daily. In Delmar (near Salisbury), the Wicomico County Welcome Center at 8480 Ocean Hwy. (aka US 50) is open daily 8–5 from Memorial Day to Labor Day, and 9–5 the rest of the year. Crisfield's Visitor Center, open Mon.–Sat. 10–2 in summer, is open Mon.–Fri. 10–2 in the off-season. You'll find it at 3 Ninth St.

LODGING

The Lower Eastern Shore offers a wide range of accommodations, from fixed-up farmhouses serving as B&Bs to more elegant, renovated Victorians, to rustic cabins with million-dollar water views. Prices can vary widely throughout the week or season; typically, costs are highest during high-season weekends, lower during the week, and even lower in the off-season. Two-night minimums may be in effect during high season. Additional discounts may be offered on an inn's Web site, perhaps in conjunction with other area businesses in a package deal. Additional charges may be made for a third person in a room, and room taxes can add up. Check cancellation policies prior to booking.

Lodging rates fall within this scale:

Inexpensive:	Up to $75
Moderate:	$75–150
Expensive:	$150–225
Very expensive:	$225 and up

CAMBRIDGE

HYATT REGENCY CHESAPEAKE BAY GOLF RESORT, SPA AND MARINA

410-901-1234; reservations 1-800-55-HYATT
www.chesapeakebay.hyatt.com
100 Heron Blvd., Cambridge, MD 21613
Price: Very Expensive
Handicapped Access: Yes

There seems to be little reason to leave this 342-acre luxury spread along the Choptank River, which recently added $7.5 million in new carpets, bedding, TVs, and other such comforts. Guests can find a good time at the 18-hole championship River Marsh Golf Club, in small boats or kayaks rented at the 150-slip River Marsh Marina, or by partaking in a massage at the 18,000-square-foot Stillwater Spa. If it's a cloudy day, perhaps it's time to settle in with a good book in the Michener Library, named for the novelist who wrote his landmark Chesapeake in Cambridge. Four pools plus a hot tub bring different personalities to their hydrotherapeutic functions. An infinity-edge pool sits at the edge of the Choptank, the River's Edge Pool has a waterslide and other fun

The Hyatt Regency in Cambridge features pools, a marina, golf and fine dining. Photo courtesy of Hyatt Regency Chesapeake Bay

stuff for families, and the impressive Wintergarden, glassed-in during the winter but open to river breezes in the summer, beckons. The wide river and the bridge spanning its width dominate views throughout this expansive complex, where the decor hits a tasteful and contemporary Chesapeake note. About 70 percent of the 400 rooms (that includes 58 suites) have water views, and all have private balconies. Bunk beds and pullout sofa beds are available for traveling families who opt for a "petite suite." Nine pet rooms are available. Hungry? Dinner's at the casual Blue Point Provision Company at the marina, breakfast at the Water's Edge Grille, and four other café/market/restaurants are available. Additional amenities include tennis, · two small beaches (netting protects swimmers from sea nettles), a fitness center, and kids' activities. An adjacent parcel is slated for development as the Residences at River Marsh.

MILL STREET INN

Innkeepers: Jen and Skip Rideout
410-901-9144
www.millstinn.com
114 Mill St., Cambridge, MD 21613
Price: Moderate to Very Expensive
Handicapped Access: No
Restrictions: No pets/no children

One of Cambridge's grand old homes was renovated top to bottom in 2006, and it is a beauty. Traditional but stylish and oh so tasteful (but not stuffy), the Mill Street Inn sits two blocks from the water and a walkable few blocks from downtown. A gas fireplace lights up a front parlor, a wood fireplace crackles in another, brown leather club chairs settle before the TV in a guest gathering area, and a beautiful river porch is the place for evening drinks in the summer. For breakfast, you may sample a grit soufflé in the dining room. The three guest rooms have huge bathrooms and queen-sized beds, and are beautifully decorated. The Cambridge Suite has four big windows in the home's multisided Victorian turret, and with its airjet tub, fine fabrics, and large sitting area, you won't want to leave. The toiletries here are even handmade.

PRINCESS ANNE
THE ALEXANDER HOUSE BOOKLOVERS' BED & BREAKFAST
Owner: Elizabeth Alexander
410-651-5195
www.bookloversbnb.com
30535 Linden Ave., Princess Anne, MD 21853
Price: Moderate
Handicapped Access: No
Special Features: Children over age 14 welcome, shoe-free environment; bring slippers

This rambling house on a quiet side street calls itself "The Booklovers' B&B." Owner Elizabeth Alexander, herself an oft-published writer, developed the inn around her favorite authors. You'll find no TVs, Wi-Fi, or phones here. Instead, look for parlors and reading rooms, a wraparound porch with rocking chairs and settees, and a library with a fireplace to spend a day lost in a book. Each room is themed around a different author: the Mark Twain library and reading parlor with its fireplace and well-stocked shelves; the grand Jane Austen Room with its Regency accents; the Robert Louis Stevenson semisuite, with a distinct dressing room, writer's desk, and walls adorned with illustrations from *A Child's Garden of Verses* and NC Wyeth's illustrations of *Treasure Island*. The Langston Hughes room takes guests to the height of the Harlem Renaissance. There's even a faux record player in one corner that's actually a CD/tape deck loaded with recordings of Hughes reading his own works. Breakfast, afternoon tea, and evening refreshments are served in Café Colette, which is the essence of a French country home. If guests tire of reading, there's a supply of board games, including, of course, the Trivial Pursuit Book Lover's Edition.

SNOW HILL
THE CEDARS
Owners: Sherry and Doug Glascox
410-632-2165
www.cedarsnowbnb.com
107 W. Federal St., Snow Hill, MD 21863
Price: Moderate to Expensive
Handicapped Access: No

This beautiful 1850 mansion and its extensive grounds are undergoing a loving restoration by Doug and Sherry Glascox. They've fashioned three elegant suites and several dining and common areas from the original 22 rooms. There is also space for small meetings. The workmanship is impressive: Crown molding hides pipes that couldn't be installed in the plaster walls; research, old photos, and scraps of wallpaper led to details like original paint schemes and furnishings similar to what was once used. Outside there are lovely gardens. The second-floor front porch overlooks the town of Snow Hill, and is a popular spot for sipping mint juleps and reflecting on life. In colder weather, a gas fireplace gives a welcoming glow. It's the perfect time to go through the scrapbooks detailing the building's history. Doug loves to cook. *Really* loves to cook. Breakfasts are not just homemade muffins, but a four-course event—pears sautéed in wine and drizzled with blueberry sauce; pancakes or French toast with lemon zest and rum-flavored syrup; a hearty meat or a lighter tomato and cheese omelet. He's also delighted to prepare dinner if arranged in advance, a nice option for those arriving at night.

RIVER HOUSE INN
Innkeepers: Larry and Susanne Knudsen
410-632-2722
www.riverhouseinn.com
201 E. Market St., Snow Hill, MD 21863

Price: Expensive to Very Expensive
Handicapped Access: Yes, in the River Cottage
Special Features: Children and pets allowed

A profusion of flowers and black wrought-iron gingerbread on the wide veranda greet guests entering this longtime B&B settled alongside the Pocomoke River. The pool and patio only add to the inn's comfort, with two guest buildings on 2 acres of shaded lawn providing accommodations. The charming River Cottage, converted from an 1890 carriage barn, offers a private porch, minifridge, microwave, coffee-maker, and whirlpool tub. The River Hideaway continues the theme of comfort and amenities, and includes wide porches with river views. If you want to get out on the water, the inn operates a pontoon boat. Full breakfast, delivered in a picnic basket to the cottage.

BERLIN
THE ATLANTIC HOTEL
Owners: Michelle and John Fager
410-641-3589
www.atlantichotel.com
2 N. Main St., Berlin, MD 21811
Price: Moderate to Very Expensive
Handicapped Access: Yes
Special note: Not suitable for children

When this hotel closed unexpectedly in early 2009, Berlin was thrown into a panic. For many people, The Atlantic Hotel *is* Berlin. Fortunately, Michelle and John Fager, owners of Fager's Island in nearby Ocean City, purchased it, and by summer the hotel was refreshed and reopened. The grand Victorian entranceway with its elegant staircase and crystal chandelier display all of the charm of that bygone era. The decor of Drummer's Café, just off the main entrance, is also staunchly Victorian (see "Restaurants"). All 18 guest rooms and suites, as well as the ladies' parlor and public areas, have been restored with period furnishings. New feather toppers with down duvet comforters cover the beds, flat-screen TVs are in all rooms, and Wi-Fi's throughout the building. The Gardener's Cottage behind the hotel provides a romantic hideaway. Perfectly situated in the center of Berlin, the Atlantic is convenient to the shops and tea room. Horse-drawn carriage rides start in front of the hotel during the fall and winter holiday season. In the summer, enjoy the occasional breeze from a front porch rocking chair while watching the rest of the world stroll by.

HOLLAND HOUSE B&B
Owners: Jan and Jim Quick
410-641-1956
www.hollandhousebandb.com
5 Bay St., Berlin, MD 21811
Price: Moderate
Handicapped Access: Yes
Special note: Closed Jan.–Mar.

Unlike many B&Bs that overflow with so much antique furniture and lace that you're afraid to touch anything, Holland House is like staying in a particularly comfortable guest room in a good friend's house. Jan and Jim Quick clearly enjoy welcoming visitors to Berlin and the area. The house was the home and office for a long line of country doctors, the first being Dr. Holland. He opened his practice here in 1917. Old diplomas and other artifacts of the house's past line the walls. The hardwood floors in what was once the waiting room still bear the burn marks of cigarettes dropped by waiting patients. When the Quicks bought the property in 1986, they started renovating the examination and treatment rooms on the first floor into large bedrooms, each with a private bath. The couple continued the renovations upstairs, eventually adding two more bedrooms and a private suite. The house is on a quiet side street, only about a block from Main Street with its shops and restaurants. The only TV you'll find is in the common room on the first floor. A very secluded and private outdoor shower is located just beside the back entrance to the house. Jan is a baker and Jim is a trained chef, so it's worth staying here just for the full breakfast.

MERRY SHERWOOD PLANTATION

Owner: Cynthia Burbage
410-641-2112 or 1-800-660-0358
www.merrysherwood.com
8909 Worcester Hwy. (US 113), Berlin, MD 21811
Price: Moderate to Expensive
Handicapped Access: No
Special Features: Children OK

Standing more than 50 feet tall, comprising 27 rooms in more than 8,500 square feet, the Merry Sherwood Plantation house is as impressive today as when it was completed in 1859. A jewel in classic Italianate style, it's set amid 22 acres of gardens featuring roses, topiaries, and perennials. These grounds, designed by Southern Living magazine, are almost enough to make you forget the rush of modern life. Inside the three-story house are seven rooms and one suite; two rooms share a bath in order to retain the building's integrity. Rooms are elegant and large, and the antique furnishings (including the Vanderbilts' former carved rosewood furniture) honor the mid-19th-century Philadelphia affluence that created the house. A gourmet breakfast is served under an enormous chandelier. For a well-rounded visit, spend time on the fabulous sunporch perusing the photo album, which reveals the full marvel of the restoration that readied Merry Sherwood for guests in the mid-1990s.

Motels/Hotels

Captain Tyler Motel (410-968-2220; 701 W. Main St., Crisfield, MD 21817) Located in the middle of town, four blocks from City Dock, with 28 rooms, including nine with whirlpool tubs. Inexpensive to Moderate. Formerly called the Paddlewheel.

Hampton Inn & Suites, Fruitland-Salisbury South (410-548-1282; Prosperity Ln., Fruitland, MD 21826) Let your head hit a soft or "hard" pillow, whichever it prefers, at this new hotel. A continental breakfast is served in a very nice dining room and the service here comes with a smile. A good central location from which to venture out. Prices vary seasonally, Moderate to Expensive.

Somer's Cove Motel (410-968-1900; Somer's Cove Marina, 700 Norris Harbor Dr., Crisfield, MD 21817) Forty rooms with balconies or patios. Outdoor pool. Inexpensive to Moderate.

The Washington Hotel (410-651-2525; 11784 Somerset Ave., Princess Anne, MD 21853) Owned by the same family since 1936, this inn was built in 1744. Check out the double staircase: one for gentlemen and one for ladies in hoop skirts. There's a restaurant, Hotel Inn, available for meals, and 12 rooms are available for overnight guests. Inexpensive.

RESTAURANTS

Two words to travelers of the Lower Eastern Shore: local seafood. Blue crabs—soft-shells, crabcakes, hard-shells—oysters, rockfish, clams. Indulge in these Bay delights while you're on the Lower Shore, where they're as fresh as you'll ever find and the prices tend to be quite reasonable.

Price ranges, based on entrée, are as follows:

Inexpensive: Up to $10
Moderate: $10–20
Expensive: $20–30
Very expensive: $30 or more

The following abbreviations are used to denote meals served:
B = Breakfast; L = Lunch; D = Dinner; SB = Sunday Brunch

CAMBRIDGE
BELLA LUNA

410-745-6100
www.bellalunarestaurant.net
25942 Royal Oak Rd.
Open: Tues.–Sun.
Price: Moderate to Expensive
Cuisine: Italian
Serving: L, D, SB
Reservations: Highly recommended on weekends
Handicapped Access: Yes

An offshoot of Bella Luna in Royal Oak, and under the same capable ownership, this Bella Luna in re-emerging/gentrifying downtown Cambridge serves the same mouthwatering regional Italian fare served up in the original location. Pasta with seafood marinara sauce, homemade gnocchi, lasagna, and grilled double-cut pork chops keep patrons—and food critics—coming back for more. Owner/chef Barbara Helish has developed quite a following—for good reason. The restaurant has won national awards and is in the Zagat guide for Washington and Baltimore. Barbara takes pride in making everything from scratch (salad dressings, pastas, desserts), using locally grown, organic produce. The dining room is tasteful and warm, with fresh flowers topping the red tablecloths.

JIMMIE & SOOK'S RAW BAR AND GRILL

443-225-4115
jimmieandsooks.com
421 Race St.
Open: Daily

Price: Inexpensive to Moderate
Cuisine: Eastern Shore, comfort food done to order
Serving: L, D
Reservations: Accepted only for five or more, and recommended in summer
Handicapped Access: Yes

This is a comfortable and casual eatery downtown where you can get a glass of iced tea to go, old-fashioned but updated Eastern Shore food (which includes chicken and dumplings in addition to voluminous seafood offerings), or something a tad more contemporary like a warm goat cheese and crab spinach salad. Owner Amanda Bramble's a Cambridge local who says she designed her restaurant thinking of herself in the present with her grandmother's memory—and Grandma was from the country, out in Bishop's Head on the other side of Hooper's Island. So, Amanda put her grandfather's oyster tongs in her restaurant. A picture of a lady—one of many depicting local life lining the walls—turns out to be Amanda's great-aunt. This is a good place to get a feel for Dorchester County, as Tom Brokaw himself discovered when touring through for a TV special on US 50. Monthly fundraisers are held for local charities, and live acoustic music plays Wed.–Sat. evenings. Here's one local who's bringing her contemporary eye to her hometown.

PORTSIDE SEAFOOD RESTAURANT

410-228-9007
www.portsideseafood.com
201 Trenton St.

Open: Daily
Price: Inexpensive to Expensive
Cuisine: Eastern Shore seafood and steaks
Serving: L, D
Reservations: Accepted
Handicapped Access: Yes

Located hard alongside the drawbridge through Cambridge's town center, Portside features a big deck overlooking Cambridge Creek that's warmed by heat lamps to allow for winter waterside dining. With its old-style Eastern Shore restaurant feel, one is tempted to take full advantage of crab and oyster dishes here in crab and oyster country, but don't overlook the prime rib (queen or king cut), a popular alternative. The Chicken Chesapeake, a chicken breast topped with crab imperial, ham, and melted cheese, is $18.95. Less expensive offerings include sandwiches, salads, baskets (fried chicken or fish with fries), and steamed seafood.

HURLOCK
SUICIDE BRIDGE RESTAURANT
410-943-4689
www.suicidebridge.com
6304 Suicide Bridge Road
Open: Tues.–Sun.
Price: Inexpensive to Very Expensive
Cuisine: Seafood, Eastern Shore
Serving: L, D
Reservations: For parties of 10 or more only. Priority seating for groups; call ahead
Handicapped Access: Yes

Located on a sturdy bit of rare upland in Dorchester County not far from Cambridge, this seemingly remote waterside restaurant draws the locals and offers a deck, open dining rooms, and a menu featuring terrific seafood, although meat-lovers will find plenty to enjoy. (The owner also operates Kool Ice and Seafood in Cambridge, which explains menu items named "Kool," like Kool's Crab Cake). The Choptank Riverboat Company operates the 80-foot reproduc-

tion paddle-wheelers *Dorothy-Megan* and the *Choptank River Queen*, which depart from here (call for departure times), and boaters ducking in from the Choptank River a half-mile away can find dockage. As for the legend of Suicide Bridge: The restaurant tells of devastated locals who flung themselves from this remote locale. A local we know once demurred, explaining that the bridge's natural curve, to accommodate the channel, had something to do with drivers failing to stay on course.

FISHING CREEK NEAR HOOPERS ISLAND
OLD SALTY'S RESTAURANT
410-397-3752
2560 Hoopers Island Rd.; from Cambridge, MD 16 west to MD 335 south to Hoopers Island
Open: Wed.–Sun.
Price: Inexpensive to Moderate
Cuisine: Eastern Shore
Serving: L, D
Reservations: Recommended
Handicapped Access: Yes

Drive through miles of winding marshland to reach Old Salty's, which recently changed hands and was renovated. (A friend who was a pupil at this former elementary school fondly recalls roller-skating in what is now the nautically themed main dining room.) Among the changes: If you don't want your seafood fried, you can now have it steamed or broiled. Also, alcohol is now served here. Breads are made fresh daily—look forward to the bread pudding—as are meringue pies like lemon, chocolate, and banana. The popular prime rib special on Fri. and Sat. nights remains. Operated by Dorchester natives.

SALISBURY
THE BACK STREET GRILL
410-548-1588
www.backstreetgrillandpizzeria.com
401 Snow Hill Road
Open: Mon.–Sat.

Price: Inexpensive
Cuisine: Updated pub fare
Serving: L, D
Reservations: Not required
Handicapped Access: Yes

Located just a couple of blocks from the Ward Museum and the Salisbury Zoo, Back Street provides the best kind of local hang-out. The wait staff knows most of the regulars by name, and you're treated like the neighborhood's newest arrival. The best daytime seats in the spacious restaurant are in the sunny, enclosed garden room. It's hugely popular for casual business lunches or folks taking the afternoon off. You can order from a good selection of salads, soups, and sandwiches, but the best way to go is to try the "build your own sandwich" option. Check off the ingredients of your dream sandwich—half a dozen different breads, at least that many meat and cheese options, and condiments—and the kitchen will take it from there. The chicken tortilla soup and Popeye salad (spinach, apples, and apple-wood smoked bacon) are both treats. Back Street can get a bit noisy in the evenings, particularly on the weekends, but it's still a good choice for a glass of wine or a beer and an easy meal spent working through the appetizer menu with some friends.

SOBO'S WINE BEERSTRO

410-219-1117
www.soboswinebistro.com
1015 Eastern Shore Dr.
Open: Mon.–Sat.
Price: Moderate to Very Expensive
Cuisine: American
Serving: L, D
Reservations: Accepted
Handicapped Access: Yes

SoBo's is an example of tweaking a good idea to make it even better. The restaurant started off as a moderately upscale bistro, serving new American cuisine and wines from a list of 100 non-European labels. A women's wine night and monthly wine pairing dinner solidified its reputation as the "go-to" spot for after-hours decompression and finer dining. Then owners John and Tom Knorr (who also own Boonie's and Red Roost) opened a micro-brewery in Delaware. Now, beer joins wine among aficionados: In addition to its own "Evolution" label, SoBo's serves 30 different microbrews, a monthly beer-pairing dinner, and $1 off microbrews on Thurs. night. Chef Patrick Fanning's strength is creative and fun use of local, seasonal ingredients to make comfortably sophisticated entrées. The Summer Veggie Bisque blends squash, zucchini, and smoked bacon. Avocado, sweet corn, and a grape salsa saffron crème give a fresh take to the de rigueur crab salad. The salmon entrée is herbal tea–cured and served with purple sticky rice, edamame, and a micro green salad. Even the meat-and-potatoes selections have a spin; filet mignon that's twice cooked in red chili sauce, chèvre cream, whipped mash, and grilled asparagus. Bar food gets a similar adventurous treatment.

VINNY'S LA ROMA

410-742-2380
www.vinnyslaroma.com
934 S. Salisbury Blvd.
Open: Daily
Price: Inexpensive to Expensive
Cuisine: Italian
Serving: L, D
Reservations: For large parties
Handicapped Access: Yes

This is a casual Italian restaurant with good food and a surprisingly excellent wine list. Vinny is the sort of host who visits each table, greets new customers like old friends, and sits down to chat with regulars. All of the usual entrées are here—the lasagna you compare to Grandmom's, chicken and veal Parmesan, baked ziti. There are a lot of lighter entrées, too.

Chicken Florentine with a boneless broiled chicken breast over sautéed spinach with a light lemon sauce is always good. The kitchen is excellent about playing "Iron Chef"; tell them what you are in the mood for (or your dietary needs), and they will take care of you. A word of warning—don't fill up on the warm Italian bread that arrives while you wait for your main course. Their pizzas are baked in a separate kitchen off to one side of the restaurant. They are equally popular for carryout as for eat-in.

VIVA ESPRESSO
410-749-8482
www.vivaespressosby.com
105 E. College Ave.
Open: Mon.–Sat.
Price: Inexpensive
Cuisine: American
Serving: B, L, D
Reservations: Not required
Handicapped Access: Yes

Nancy Dix opened her coffee shop in the deepest trough of the recession, right after Starbuck's closed 600 of its stores. Within a year, she'd expanded her seating by 50 percent and extended her hours to stay open through dinner. How did she pull that off? Excellent coffees from around the world and a staff knowledgeable about them, freshly made pastries, an ever-changing menu of interesting sandwiches and salads, a seating area designed to encourage lingering, and a calendar that includes Monday night movies, coffee tastings, and "listenable" live music. There's a fireplace and bookcase with volumes for browsing and borrowing. In addition to tempting breakfast muffins and pastries, look for a choice of two quiches. Paninis are the lunch specialty, such as portobello and mozzarella, or brie, bacon, and mango chutney. Their signature panini is a hearty combination of Italian salami, prosciutto, provolone, arugula, basil, and pepperoncino

peppers. The staff is constantly working on new sandwich ideas. Early morning customers are sometimes asked to taste-test.

TYASKIN (NEAR WHITEHAVEN)
BOONIES
410-873-2244
www.booniesrestaurant.com
21438 Nanticoke Rd.
Open: Daily except Mon.
Price: Moderate to Expensive
Cuisine: Eastern Shore
Serving: D, L on Sat.–Sun., SB
Reservations: For large parties and on holidays
Handicapped Access: Yes

"It's not the end of the world, but you sure can see it." That's the slogan for this popular, albeit somewhat remote, restaurant on the outskirt of the tiny hamlet of Tyaskin. (Thirteen miles down Nanticoke Road (MD 349) from the west end of Salisbury, Tyaskin is too small to warrant the S on outskirts.) The menu focuses on seafood and chicken, the mainstays of Eastern Shore cuisine, and often in combination. This is the place to experience what's arguably the most sublimely delicious dish of the Chesapeake: stuffed rockfish. It's a broiled filet of the iconic fish, topped with a mound of lightly browned crab imperial. Ribs here are marinated and slow roasted, about as good as you will find outside a dedicated ribs joint. The ahi tuna appetizer is prepared by a chef who understands the delicate difference between rare and raw. Sunday brunch is a recent addition that's proving to be a popular kickoff for the week. Some folks linger for most of the afternoon. There's live entertainment on weekends. In summer, that means sitting at the outdoor tiki bar. Try the watermelon margarita on a muggy evening, or anything from their long, inventive list of martinis. The desserts are equally wonderful; warm cobblers with ice cream, derby pie, and decadent things involving chocolate.

Tiny Whitehaven

The **Whitehaven Hotel** (410-873-2000; whitehaven.tripod.com/beta2.htm; 2685 Whitehaven Rd., Whitehaven, MD 21865; Moderate prices) has been settled near the Whitehaven Ferry landing since 1810. That tells you something about how old this tiny settlement is, but in truth it goes back even further. One of its early developers, Col. George Gale, was the second husband of George Washington's grandmother, Mildred Warner Washington. Today, you can cross into "town" via the Whitehaven Ferry. Make a reservation for the old hotel, which is fully restored and has eight attractive rooms on

The restored Whitehaven Hotel at the ferry southeast of Salisbury.

three floors and views of the river. For dinner—at least from mid-Mar. through Oct. 31—you must head over to the fabled Red Roost (410-546-5443; www.theredroost.com; 2760 Clara Rd.). It's a couple of miles away, serves awesome all-you-can east feasts that include hard crabs, and is famous for its Wed. night sing-alongs with the Backfin Banjo Band starting at 6 PM. In addition to the conviviality, the **Red Roost** is famous because it's a crabhouse in, no kidding, a converted chicken house. If you're coming from Salisbury, about 25 miles away, plan on a nice, scenic drive.

SNOW HILL
THE PALETTE
410-632-0055
104 Green St.
Open: Daily, except Mon.
Price: Inexpensive to Expensive
Cuisine: American
Serving: L, D, SB
Reservations: Accepted for dinner
Handicapped Access: Yes

As Snow Hill establishes itself as an arts town, this trendy eatery is rapidly becoming the "in" spot. The former storefront's hardwood floors, soft jazz, and streamlined furnishings create a comfortably sophisticated atmosphere, but purple and aquamarine window trim keeps it from becoming pretentious. This is a small place with only about 30 seats, so guests can spy on what others are eating before ordering. There's a lot to consider. Try the cream of onion soup, whisper-thin slices of sweet onion and carrots softened in a delicately rich cream broth accented with the tang of fresh ground pepper. Sandwiches come on a choice of breads: sesame seed bun, olive rosemary bread, sundried tomato foccacia, or whole wheat with warm tortilla chips. A choice of either homemade salsa or hummus comes on the side. Sandwiches run from crabcakes and nice burgers to fancier fare, like a BLT with avocado and garlic aioli or a scallop wrap with field greens and pickled ginger. Full entrées include a catch of the day over sautéed spinach and shallots with a sweet lemon vinaigrette, and an Angus fillet over fried tomatoes and chipotle hollandaise sauce. Thurs. nights from 4–8 is tapas night. Sunday brunch is worth trying for the citrus cinnamon French toast with warm maple syrup, if nothing else, although Mom's Savannah, spicy blackened shrimp and tomatoes on creamy hominy, would make a Southerner out of a die-hard Yankee.

BERLIN
DRUMMER'S CAFÉ IN THE ATLANTIC HOTEL
410-641-3589
www.atlantichotel.com
2 N. Main St.
Open: Daily
Price: Moderate to Very Expensive
Cuisine: Maryland American
Serving: L, D, SB
Reservations: Accepted
Handicapped Access: Yes

Drummer's Café in the historic (1895) Atlantic Hotel focuses on fresh, seasonal ingredients and beyond-generous portions. It is nearly impossible to eat the sandwiches without using a knife and fork. The grilled wild salmon BLT with roasted red peppers, applewood smoked bacon, and pesto mayo is big enough to share. Try the fish tacos, featuring grilled fish with Havarti cheese, cabbage, and cilantro avocado sauce. The combination may sound a little avant-garde, but the tastes blend wonderfully. There are organic and vegetarian selections, too. The menu expands slightly at dinner with a half dozen or so additional items, like the herbed blue cheese–crusted all-natural Angus New York strip steak, or free-range chicken breast stuffed with a seasonal dressing. "Fish Four Ways" lets you enjoy the catch of the day grilled, broiled, blackened, or sautéed with a caper lemon beurre blanc, sweet and hot onions. Add the optional topping of crab imperial, and you've got fish five ways. The interior dining area reflects the building's Victorian history and architecture. It's worth stopping in just to admire the massive wooden bar. The enclosed porch is less historic, but very bright, even in winter.

PRINCESS ANNE
THE OLNEY MARKET
410-621-5643
11779 Somerset Ave.
Open: Mon.–Sat.
Price: Inexpensive
Cuisine: American
Serving: L
Reservations: Not required
Handicapped Access: No

This tiny shop serves ambitious sandwiches, the sort you plan to make yourself before reaching instead for the PB&J. The menu offers only five or six choices, but they change every week and reflect the owner's whims. A typical week might include the red, white, and green panini (thin slices of ham, salami, spinach, provolone, and pesto grilled to melting inside a foccacia), Eastern Shore pork BBQ wrap with coleslaw, or a substantial turkey club on wheat. Everything comes with a bag of chips or fresh apple slices. There's usually one hot "meal" like Indian butter chicken with garlic rice, cucumber salad, and naan bread. The cookies and dessert pastries are all made on-site. The shop also has a small selection of foodie gifts, teas, and snacks.

CRISFIELD
LINTON'S SEAFOOD
410-968-3707
www.lintonsseafood.com
4500 Crisfield Hwy.
Open: Daily
Price: Moderate to Expensive
Cuisine: Crabs and seafood
Serving: L, D
Reservations: For large parties
Handicapped Access: Yes

Where else but Crisfield, "The Crab Capital of the World," for a Chesapeake crab feast? Linton's isn't on the water, but it's close enough that any crab escaping from the kitchen has a good chance of scrabbling back to the Bay. The retail store, which has

THE GLOBE

410-641-0784
www.globetheater.com
12 Broad St.
Open: Daily
Price: Inexpensive to Expensive

Cuisine: American with Asian overtones
Serving: L, D, SB
Reservations: For most shows
Handicapped Access: Yes
Special Features: Balcony art gallery

This art deco movie theater has a new life, or—to be more accurate—new lives, as a restaurant, theater, art gallery, and epicenter of Berlin's nightlife. The menu is pleasantly eclectic. In a move that is considered nearly sacrilegious to crabcake purists, the appetizer Global Crabcakes are mini, cashew–encrusted, and served on strawberry horseradish sauce with a honey wasabi drizzle. At the other end of the culinary spectrum, you'll find comfort food entrées like bacon-wrapped homemade meat loaf or pork chops with applesauce. Soups are treated with respect here. The sweet onion soup is light and flavorful, while the Brazilian black bean soup is a vegetarian mélange of coconut milk, hearts of palm, and roasted red pepper, garnished with cilantro sour cream. Sandwiches take the standard ingredients and upgrade them. Chicken salad is made with diced bacon, scallions, and a hint of BBQ sauce, for example. There's also a range of pastas and steaks; seafood includes two different treatments of tuna steaks. The rest of The Globe's operation is equally interesting. The theater has been restructured to create an intimate dining area by a small stage. Live entertainment takes place very weekend, with local and regional favorites like Deanna Bogart or frequent "tribute" shows to stars like Elvis and Johnny Cash. Seating is available several hours before the show, or you can enjoy dinner during the show. Look for something happening every night, like free family-friendly movies on Mon. or wine tastings and team trivia contests alternating on Wed. The mezzanine gallery has regular shows highlighting regional artists—and more seating for dining.

been selling anything edible from the Chesapeake for 40 years, has a large, screened porch with picnic tables protected from the marshes' bugs. There's also one table indoors for days when the weather is just too hot and muggy to be outside. On weekends during the season, which runs from "May to November or whenever it gets too cold," the separate adjacent crabhouse is open. With air-conditioning and a big-screen TV, it's the perfect place to spend an afternoon picking hot crabs and drinking cold beer with friends. You can get crabs in any quantity—single, by the dozen, half-bushel, bushel—at market price, with the usual accompaniments of corn on the cob and slaw. Be sure to order a slice of Smith Island cake for dessert. This locally invented creation of seven to 10 dime-thin layers of cake is Maryland's official state dessert. If you get a hankering for seafood when you get home, they ship nationwide.

WATERMEN'S INN

410-968-2119
crisfield.com/watermens
901 W. Main St.
Open: Thurs.–Sun. (also Wed. in July and Aug.)
Price: Moderate to Expensive
Cuisine: American with heavy Eastern Shore emphasis
Serving: L, D
Reservations: Recommended for dinner

Handicapped Access: Yes

For 20 years, Watermen's has been Crisfield's "night out" place—brick walls, pendant lights, soft jazz in the background. The ingredients are fresh and local. Crabs are delivered from workboats, and co-owner Kathy Berezoski is a familiar face at area farmer's and organic markets. The crabcakes are all backfin lump; salad lovers should order the Caesar topped with a crabcake. Both crab soups are on offer: the Baltimore style with a tomato-based broth and vegetables, or the incredibly thick and rich cream of crab that's served with a decanter of sherry. Finishing the soup with a drizzle (or more) of sherry is the classic final ingredient. The rest of the menu raises what might otherwise be basic fare—pork chops, shrimp, grilled chicken breast—several notches by the skillful application of just enough innovation. Said pork chops are treated to a brown sugar and bourbon marinade before being grilled and served with a balsamic jus. Shrimp are sautéed in garlic butter and wine and served with wilted spinach, Kalamata olives, sun-dried tomatoes, and pine nuts over linguini; salmon is grilled with a lingonberry glaze. Lunches serve much more casual fare, concentrating on a large selection of salads, clubs, and Reubens. If you've never tried a soft-shell crab sandwich or an open-face crab bruschetta, here's your chance. Desserts are decadent; Kathy's a Johnson & Wales–trained pastry chef.

Raw bars await diners at many Eastern-Shore restaurants.

FOOD PURVEYORS

Cafés and Specialty Markets and Shops

A Few of My Favorite Things (410-221-1960; 414 Race St., Cambridge) Look for good wines, good chocolates, good cheeses, and amusing culinary accompaniments.

Health Store and More (410-749-1997; 720 E. College Ave., Suite 7, Salisbury) Organic and natural foods, gluten-free and bulk products, herbs, and specialty items. Closed Sun.

Pusey's Country Store (410-632-1992; 5313 Snow Hill Rd., Snow Hill) Once the general store selling provisions to the tiny town, it now focuses on specialty foods while keeping the old ambiance with weathered plank floors, exposed beams, and an old soda machine that still works. More than 60 microbrews and regional wines are here, as well as all sorts of regional brand foods—cheeses, condiments, soups, honey, and some baked goods. A good place to get local information. Closed Sun.

Scoop Station (443-477-0232; www.thescoopstation.com; 400 Muir St., Cambridge) Coffee, ice cream, and sandwiches and wraps. Tuck in, connect to the Wi-Fi and sit a spell—maybe even on the patio. Live music ranging from reggae to bluegrass plays in the adjacent café at night.

Ice Cream

Ice Cream Gallery (410-968-0809; 5 Goodsell Alley, between the city and county docks in Crisfield) Open daily Apr. through Oct., serving 26 flavors and sugar-free ice cream. One scoop costs $1.98 plus tax.

Seafood and Fish Markets

The J. M. Clayton Company (410-228-1661; www.jmclayton.com; 108 Commerce St., Cambridge) Come see the world's oldest working crab processing plant, founded in 1890 by Capt. John Morgan Clayton and operated by his descendants. You can tour the plant and see jimmies and sooks being picked and steamed if you and nine of your buddies make advance plans. It costs $5 per person. If you can't do that, stop by the retail market Mon.–Fri. 8–5 and pick up your Epicure crabmeat. It's an old-fashioned experience where you get to watch them pack up your seafood fresh off the production tables. If that doesn't work, call 1-800-652-6931 to place your order and have it shipped.

Kool Ice and Seafood (410-228-2300 or 1-800-437-2417; 110 Washington St., Cambridge) Dorchester-caught crabs and a fine selection of oysters, clams, lobsters, and fresh fish. Frozen seafood, too.

Metompkin Bay Oyster Company (410-968-0660; 101 11th St., Crisfield) This wholesale operation that runs crab and oyster processing plants also sells retail, so check out the crabmeat, soft crabs, and oysters. In addition, you can tour the plant with the Tawes Museum (see "Culture," below).

Smith Island Crabmeat Co-op (410-968-1344; 21128 Wharf St., Tylerton) The co-op was born after times changed and the women of Smith Island could no longer pick crabmeat in their kitchens. Now, they sit at stainless-steel tables at the co-op and pick a bushel basket of crabs—something on the order of 7 to 9 pounds of crabmeat—in two or three hours. Stop by if you see the co-op is open; late afternoon is probably best.

Southern Connections (1-888-340-3977; www.crabsandseafood.com; 4884 Crisfield

Vines by the River

Grapes are growing along the Chesapeake. For an adventure via land—and if you know the right person, sea—head for the Bordeleau Vineyards & Winery at water's edge.

It's a beautiful spot with or without the II varieties of purple and pale green clusters dripping from the vines. Set on Wicomico Creek, the vineyard is the brainchild of Tom Shelton, who has made a name for himself in the region's poultry business. Now, with his sights set on wines, he spends time in the lab and overseeing the operation in order to bring quality control to his product.

The tasting room is a treat. Open and convivial, visitors can sample Wicomico Red or Vidal Blanc. Wander down to the banks of the creek to catch the breeze that seems to gently blow even in the heat of summer.

Bordeleau is a terrific bike destination along country roads from Salisbury, but you'll reach it most easily if you check www.bordeleauwine.com for directions. If you want to see it by kayak, contact Adrenaline High tours: www.adrenalinehigh.com. As for the larger picture: www.chesapeake winetrails.com.

Hwy., Crisfield) Wholesale operation also offers hard crabs, Chesapeake and Atlantic fish retail. Shipping available.

CULTURE

Art Galleries and Centers

To find out about the region's commercial arts and crafts galleries—many of them showing local artists—check out "Galleries" in the "Shopping" section at the end of this chapter.

CAMBRIDGE
DORCHESTER CENTER FOR THE ARTS
410-228-7782
www.dorchesterartscenter.org
321 High St.
Open: Mon.–Thurs. 10–5, Fri.–Sat. 10–4

The rehabilitation of Cambridge's pretty Historic District took yet another step forward when the former Nathan's Furniture Store was renovated. Into the first floor moved the DAC, and voila! The center more than tripled in size. Hand-in-hand with the physical expansion has come a parade of activity. In addition to monthly exhibitions of local and regional artists are gallery receptions on the second Saturday of the month; art classes ranging from stained glass to mosaics to painting; and an expanded clay program complete with kiln. The Dorchester Drama Guide and their performances are based here, and regional talent performs from time to time. The annual holiday concert features the Chorus of Dorchester, and the last Sun. in Sept. usually brings the Dorchester Showcase, a street festival with entertainment, a juried fine arts and crafts show, and food the length of High Street. For class and entertainment schedules, check the Web site.

ART INSTITUTE AND GALLERY
410-546-4748
www.aiandg.com
212 W. Main St., Suite 101
Open: Mon.–Fri. 11–3

The beautifully renovated former Woolworth's store on the Downtown Plaza is called the
Gallery Building, and among its fine tenants is The Art Institute and Gallery, showing
works by local, mid-Atlantic, and national artists in all media. In Sept., the institute holds
its annual national juried exhibition. Look for a wide range of Delmarva artists in various
media, classes, a fine gift shop, and even a pottery studio.

SALISBURY UNIVERSITY GALLERIES
410-548-2547
www.salisbury.edu

View traveling exhibitions and student shows at Fulton Hall, the university's fine arts
building, or in the Atrium Gallery in the Guerrieri University Center. The former has mid-
day hours except mid-July through Aug., while the latter closes Mon. and weekends year-
round. Exhibitions may include cultural events. Fulton Hall is located off Camden Avenue,
the main street along the campus's eastern edge, while Guerriera is off Dogwood Drive to
the south.

Cinema
Cambridge Premiere Cinemas (410-221-8688; 2759 Dorchester Square), located next to
    Wal-Mart off US 50 in Cambridge, offers first-run films and bargain matinees. Down
    Salisbury way, check out **Regal Salisbury Stadium 16** (410-860-0211; 2322 N. Salisbury
    Blvd.).

Museums & Historic Buildings

LAGRANGE PLANTATION
410-228-7953
www.dorchesterhistory.org
902 LaGrange Ave.
www.dorchesterhistory.org
Open: Tues.–Sat. 10–4 year-round
Admission: Free; donation requested. Group rates upon request

Home to the Dorchester County Historical Society, this property includes Meredith House,
a circa-1760 Georgian house with Greek Revival ornamentation that is noted for its
Flemish-bond brickwork. Inside, see local period artifacts as well as a salute to Dorchester
County's seven Maryland governors (including Thomas Holiday Hicks, who managed to
suppress the state's strong secessionist element to maintain Maryland's Union status).
Also on the grounds are the Neild Museum, displaying the sickles, scythes, and yokes of
the Lower Shore's yeoman class, as well as maritime tools used in oystering and crabbing.
Look also for memorabilia from onetime Cambridge resident Annie Oakley. The brick

Goldsborough Stable (circa 1790) houses a transportation exhibit. The most recent addition to the complex came in 2007, when an exhibit celebrating Chesapeake decoy carving opened in the Robbins Heritage Center. Classes and workshops, many centering on the site's colonial-style herb garden, are ongoing. Check the Web site for schedules, and check out the genealogy department if you're interested in your roots.

RICHARDSON MARITIME MUSEUM
410-221-1871
www.richardsonmuseum.org
401 High St.
Open Wed. and Sun. 1–4, Sat. 10–4
Admission: Donations accepted; $3 per person for tour groups, $5 for boatworks, too

Dorchester County's maritime history and the accomplishments of the late, legendary local boatbuilder "Mr. Jim" Richardson are celebrated at this brick building that once was a bank. Mr. Richardson built the Spocott Windmill and the re-created *Dove* docked at St. Marys City. Also here: a waterman's dock exhibit, workboat models built by their captains, examples of Bay boats, and a photo history on the building of the skipjack *Nathan of Dorchester*. Folks at the museum are knowledgeable and eager to educate visitors. Plans are afoot for significant expansion to create a maritime heritage complex, which will incorporate the regional maritime history archive known as the Brannock Education and Research Center (which was not yet open at deadline) as well as the Ruark Boatworks. The latter, now operating at the Maryland Avenue site that will house the complex, is a boatworks devoted to restoring traditional wooden craft. It, too, is named for a local boatbuilding legend: "Mr. Jim's" protégé, Howard Ruark, who is often working in the shop on Wednesday.

LLOYDS
SPOCOTT WINDMILL
For info: www.tourdorchester.org
Located on MD 343 6 miles west of Cambridge
Open: Daily 8–5
Admission: Donations accepted

One of the region's most enduring residents, the late great boatbuilder James B. "Mr. Jim" Richardson took it upon himself to build this reproduction of a windmill destroyed here during the blizzard of 1888. "Mr. Jim," who passed away in 1989, kept his master builder's wooden boat workshop at his LeCompte Creek boatyard. His windmill, the only post windmill in Maryland, commemorates the 23 post windmills that once towered over the marshy countryside. Also open to the public on the property are a colonial tenant house (circa 1800) and the 1870 one-room schoolhouse called Castle Haven. Lloyd's Country Store Museum opens on special occasions or by appointment. In addition, there's an 1850 smokehouse here.

SALISBURY
PEMBERTON HISTORICAL PARK
410-860-2447
www.pembertonpark.org
Pemberton Dr., about 2 miles southwest of MD 349 and US 50
Open: House tours are Sun. 2–4 May 1–Oct. 1 or by appt; park hours are 8 AM to dusk daily

One of the oldest brick gambrel-roofed houses in the Chesapeake region, Pemberton Hall was built in 1741 for Col. Isaac Handy, a plantation owner and shipping magnate who helped found what would become the city of Salisbury. Col. Handy's home is the center-piece of a 262-acre park and museum complex that includes an education center designed to look like a colonial tobacco barn. This is also the Wicomico Historical Society headquarters, with a permanent collection of local historic memorabilia and rotating exhibits. Don't skip Pemberton even if the museums are closed. The park features 4.5 miles of nature trails through woods and along the Wicomico River, as well as a lovely picnic area. Handy's Wharf here is the oldest wharf in Maryland, if not the U.S. Look for special events on the park's Web site calendar.

WARD MUSEUM OF WILDFOWL ART
410-742-4988
www.wardmuseum.org
909 S. Schumaker Dr.
Open: Mon.–Sat. 10–5, Sun. noon–5
Admission: Adults $7, seniors $5, students $3

The legendary Ward brothers, Lem and Steve, elevated the pragmatic craft of decoy carving to artistry, and their name symbolizes the decoy-as-art-form. Their namesake museum may be the region's most extensive public collection of antique decoys, and it houses a showcase of wildfowl art as well. The evolution of decoys is traced from the Native American's functional, twisted-reed renderings to the latest lifelike wooden sculpture. View the "Ward Brothers Workshop," an exhibition that looks at the Crisfield brothers' work. The museum, affiliated with Salisbury University, also hosts a folklore and folklife archive. Annual events include the World Championship Carving Competition and Art Festival in Apr. and the Chesapeake Wildfowl Expo in Oct., in addition to quarterly exhibitions such as the recent "Clever Corvids: In the Company of Crows." The building and gift shop are set on a 4-acre site overlooking Schumaker Pond. A must-see for decoy lovers.

Snow Hill
FURNACE TOWN LIVING HERITAGE MUSEUM
410-632-2032
www.furnacetown.com
3816 Old Furnace Rd., off MD 12 (Snow Hill Rd.)
Open: Apr.–Oct., daily 10–5
Admission: Adults $5, over 60 $4.50, children 2–18 $3; does not include entry to special events

The imposing Nassawango Iron Furnace looms over a swamp, a forest, and a small collection of buildings at this quiet echo of the bustling 19th-century village that once stood here. From 1832 to 1847, hundreds of people lived and worked around this 35-foot-high, hot-blast furnace in the forest, digging up bog ore and smelting it into pig iron. Around its remnants stand re-creations of the old ways, including broom-making, printing, black-smithing, weaving, and gardening. Visit the museum, a gift shop, a picnic area, exhibit buildings, and many nature trails and boardwalks over the Nassawango Cypress Swamp. Come midweek to have the place to yourself, or visit when Furnace Town hosts one of many events, including the Chesapeake Celtic Festival in Oct. This is a captivating spot.

JULIA A. PURNELL MUSEUM
410-632-0515
www.purnellmuseum.com
208 W. Market St.
Open: Apr.–Oct., Tues.–Sat. 10–4,
Sun. 1–4; tours by appt. in off-
season
Admission: Adults $2, children
50 cents

At the age of 85, Snow Hill's Julia
A. Purnell (1843–1943) fell and
broke her hip. In place of her
formerly active lifestyle, she
completed more than 2,000
needlepoint pieces documenting
Worcester County's homes,
churches, and gardens. Her son
William was so proud that he
opened a museum of her work one
year before her death. The place is
informally known as "The Attic of
Worcester County" for all of the
period everyday items and artifacts here. A textile festival called
Fiberfest is held each Oct.

POCOMOKE CITY
DELMARVA
DISCOVERY CENTER
410-957-9933
delmarvadiscoverycenter.org
2 Market St.
Open: Wed.–Sat. 10–4, Sun.
noon–4

*Typical of many small Bay museums is the Julia A. Purnell
Museum in Snow Hill. It contains thousands of needlepoint
pieces documenting the sights of Worcester County.*

Cost: Adults $10; seniors and students $8; kids $5; members free (annual membership is
$25 for individuals and $40 for families)

Tiny Pocomoke City, founded along the dark and deep waters of its namesake river, started
out as a 19th-century ferry landing. For much of the past few decades, the pretty town
seemed mostly to drowse in the humidity and sun. Now, a burst of civic enthusiasm seems
to have arrived, the strongest evidence of which is this very attractive museum. Surprisingly
attractive, even, if (like your trusty correspondent) you didn't expect to find it here. A black
bear, the likes of which once lived on the Delmarva Peninsula, greets visitors who'll learn
about the river ecology and American Indians who once lived on the Delmarva Peninsula.
Clamber through a re-created steamship that teaches about that era. Check out fishing and
decoy exhibits, too. A 7,000-gallon aquarium devoted to river ecology is soon to be joined
by a smaller aquarium devoted to the Bay.

The Delmarva Discovery Center in Pocomoke City explores the Delmarva Peninsula.

Princess Anne
TEACKLE MANSION
410-651-2238
www.teacklemansion.org
Mansion St.
Open: Apr.–Nov., Wed., Sat., and Sun. 1–3; group tours by appt.
Admission: Adults $5, children $2.50

Back before the Manokin River became so shallow, its deep water encouraged ships to travel upriver toward Princess Anne. Plantations and ports thrived along its banks, and Teackle Mansion is a well-preserved holdover. Probably the best example of neoclassical architecture on the Lower Eastern Shore, the 1801 mansion dominates the town with its 10,000 square feet and stylish symmetry. Built by Littleton Dennis Teackle, who moved from the Eastern Shore of Virginia with his wife, the house boasts his-and-her dressing rooms on either side of a central high ceiling, multiple stairways, and entrances by river or land. Outside are beautiful gardens. Teackle fell on hard times and lost nearly everything in the depression of 1821, but his mansion stands as testament to his onetime wealth.

CRISFIELD
J. MILLARD TAWES MUSEUM
410-968-2501
crisfieldheritagefoundation.org
3 Ninth St. and Somer's Cove Marina
Open: Mon.–Sat. 10–4
Admission: Adults $3, children 6–12 $1

A Maryland governor and famous decoy-carving brothers Lem and Steve Ward hailed
from Crisfield, known for a rakish late-19th-century oyster gold rush and a bustling crab
industry. Learn about them at the J. Millard Tawes Museum, named for the Crisfielder who
ascended to the statehouse in the 1960s. Visitors find Native American artifacts and learn
about the Tangier Sound area as well as the Wards of the mid-20th century. The carvers
lived and worked "Down Neck" on Sackertown Road, and visitors can see their restored
workshop by appointment. The museum also offers the Port of Crisfield Walking Tour
that gives visitors a peek at a crabhouse operation with a stop at Metompkin Bay Oyster
Company. That tour leaves at 10 AM Mon.–Sat. from late May through Sept. Nominal fees
are charged. Special tours can be arranged by appointment.

Performing Arts

SALISBURY
COMMUNITY PLAYERS OF SALISBURY
410-543-ARTS
www.communityplayersofsalisbury.org
Tickets: Prices vary

Noteworthy among the Lower Eastern Shore's community troupes, this one dates to 1937.
Each season typically includes a musical, a drama, and a comedy performed at locations in
and around Salisbury.

SALISBURY SYMPHONY ORCHESTRA AT SALISBURY UNIVERSITY
410-548-5587
www.salisbury.edu/sso
c/o Salisbury University Fulton Hall, Room 100, 1101 Camden Ave.

Based at Salisbury University, the symphony typically performs a children's performance
during its winter–spring performance season at Holloway Hall Auditorium. The SSO
membership includes faculty, students, professionals, and community players, and enjoys
enthusiastic regional support.

SALISBURY UNIVERSITY PERFORMANCES
410-543-6000
www.salisbury.edu
1101 Camden Ave.

The theater stage in Fulton Hall hosts drama, comedy, dance, and musical productions
throughout the school year. Think Joffrey, Juilliard, and the campus theater department.
Performances in Holloway Hall Auditorium may include musicians like those from the

Chamber Orchestra Kremlin. To find out what's happening and where, check the calendar at www.salisbury.edu.

Pocomoke City
MAR-VA THEATER PERFORMING ARTS CENTER
410-957-4230
www.marvatheater.com
103 Market St.

This former vaudeville theater opened in 1927, closed in 1993, and has seen a major renaissance in recent years, including a renovation to return it to its 1937 art deco glory (but with modern technology). Movies, performances by the Mar-Va Theater Academy, singers, and other events. Ticket prices vary, but average about $10. Check the Web site for details.

Seasonal Events and Festivals

You'll find no more hard-core celebration of Lower Eastern Shore living than the 60-plus-year-old **National Outdoor Show,** held at the South Dorchester School deep in the marshy countryside south of Cambridge. You can compete in the muskrat-cooking contest if you bring your own 'rat, or stand back and watch the natives vie for honors in the muskrat-skinning contest. Come Fri. night to watch the crowning of Miss Outdoors; Sat. brings exhibits, local crafters, food, and log-sawing races. It's always held the last full weekend in Feb. at the school in Golden Hill. Take MD 16 south from Cambridge; at Church Creek turn left onto MD 335; proceed 2 miles to school on the left. For information, call 410-397-8535 or 1-800-522-TOUR, or check www.tourdorchester.org or www.nationaloutdoorshow.org. Admission fee.

For nearly a century, powerboaters have converged on Hambrooks Bay in the wide-open Choptank River for the **Cambridge Classic Power Boat Regatta.** Watch the hydroplanes and runabouts race in the country's oldest active regatta. Held the fourth weekend in July at Great Marsh Park, the regatta hits its century mark in 2010 with a burst of activity: the World Championships, the U.S. Championships, and the Canadian Championships will all be held that very weekend in Cambridge. Make your reservations yesterday. For info, check www.cpbra.com or call 410-228-3575.

Launched in 1948, the **National Hard Crab Derby & Fair** is held in Crisfield over Labor Day weekend. Top billing tends to go to the annual Governor's Cup Race and the National Derby—the crab races have drawn entrants from as far away as Hawaii—but we'd also recommend the workboat-docking contest on Sun. at the Crisfield City Dock. Smith and Tangier Island watermen come over to participate, and fans come by boat from all over the place. Also featured: a crab-picking contest, a crab-cooking contest, the "Miss Crustacean" beauty contest, a carnival with rides and games, a 10K race, a parade, live entertainment, and, of course, plenty of excellent eating. It all ends Sun. night with fireworks over the harbor. Held at Somer's Cove Marina. Call 410-968-2500 or check www.crisfieldchamber.com.

Also held over Labor Day weekend, the **Deal Island-Chance Lions Club's Skipjack Races and Land Festival** provides a double-dip of authentic Bay life. On deck are rides, food (five-star soft-shell crabs), Smith Island skiff races, fly-fishing demonstrations, and even a pole-climbing contest. At 9:30 AM Mon. comes the marquee event. Skipjacks races, dating to 1959, take place in Tangier Sound. Bring binoculars. In the afternoon, catch

"The Moses of Her People"

The Underground Railroad operated throughout the plantations of the Delmarva Peninsula, where its notable conductor, Harriet Tubman, was born south of Cambridge. Known as "The Moses of Her People," Tubman was born at Bucktown in a house that's no longer standing. It's about 2 miles from the renovated Bucktown Store, which holds artifacts (like an old "wanted" newspaper advertisement for Tubman, which was rescued from a dumpster) and is also used as an outfitter's headquarters. Tubman operated in and around these murky creeks and rivers near Blackwater National Wildlife Refuge. The store is notable in her story because that's where a young Tubman, known then as Araminta Ross, suffered a head injury after a weight was thrown at her. This caused her to suffer a sleeping disorder. After she escaped slavery, Tubman went back and forth to Dorchester 19 times and led more than 300 people to freedom.

Today, efforts are well under way to celebrate this hero. The Harriet Tubman Underground Railroad National Historical Park is expected to be established in Dorchester, Caroline and Talbot counties. (Legislation was working its way through Congress at deadline.) The Harriet Tubman Underground Railroad State Park is under development adjacent to the Blackwater refuge at Key Wallace Drive and MD 335. Once the park is developed, a visitor center is expected to share the Underground Railroad story. To keep up with progress, check www.tourdorchester.org. And in the meantime, partake of the small museum operated by the Harriet Tubman Organization at 424 Race St.; 410-228-0401. It's open Tues.–Fri. 10–3, Sat. noon–4. They can make arrangements for bus tours so you can see where Tubman and the Underground Railroad passed through the region. You can also learn more about the Underground Railroad in the area at the Dorchester County Visitor Center at Sailwinds Park in Cambridge, located on the east end of the US 50 bridge over the Choptank River (look for the giant sail).

another round of workboat-docking contests. For information, call Somerset County Tourism at 410-784-2785 or check www.skipjack.net.

Legend says Assateague Island's wild ponies descended from Spanish horses that swam ashore after a long-ago shipwreck. Scientists suggest that they descended from ponies that grazed on this outpost island in centuries past. Whatever the case, in Virginia, Chincoteague's annual **Pony Penning** is an event to see. Always held the last Wed. and Thurs. of July, it starts when members of the sponsoring Chincoteague Volunteer Fire Company corral the ponies and send them swimming across the channel from Chincoteague National Wildlife Refuge to town. The swim attracts tens of thousands of visitors; for a more intimate experience, preview the ponies in a corral on Assateague Island on Tues. or stick around for the return swim on Fri. The pony sale, held on Thurs., is a long tradition to raise funds for the local fire company, which officially owns the ponies in Virginia. A Firemen's Festival stretches for a couple of weeks leading up to Pony Penning. If you really want to attend, make reservations well in advance. For information, contact the Chincoteague Chamber of Commerce (757-336-6161; www.chincoteague chamber.com; P.O. Box 258., Chincoteague Island, VA 23336).

The last Sun. in Sept., check out the popular **Dorchester Showcase**, a street festival on Cambridge's High Street featuring music, dance, antique boats, juried fine arts and crafts, and plenty of good local food. It starts at noon and runs all afternoon. For info, visit dorchesterartscenter.org.

In mid-Oct., visit Princess Anne for **Olde Princess Anne Days**, now more than a half-century old. The event, held at Teackle Mansion, includes an 1812 Heritage Festival with music, children's activities, craft demos, and a military encampment. For info: 410-651-2238.

Zoos

Hailed as one of America's finest small zoos, the **Salisbury Zoo & Park** (410-548-3188; www.salisburyzoo.org; 755 S. Park Dr.) has distinctive and well-conceived animal exhibits. Free. Picnicking area and concessions outside. Open year-round. Located east of US 13 and south of US 50.

RECREATION

Baseball

The **Delmarva Shorebirds** play at Arthur W. Perdue Stadium (named for poultry magnate Frank Perdue's father) at 6400 Hobbs Rd., just east of US 50 and the US 13 bypass in Salisbury. The Class-A Baltimore Orioles affiliate draws a crowd during its Apr.–early Sept. season, particularly for Sat. fireworks in the summer. While you're here, check out the Eastern Shore Baseball Hall of Fame, a salute to the old Eastern Shore baseball leagues and local heroes like Princess Anne's Jimmy Fox and St. Michaels's Harold Baines who made it to the big leagues. Contact 410-219-3112 for tickets or www.theshorebirds.com for tickets, directions, schedules, and special events.

Bicycling

The flat country roads through Chesapeake's tidewater make bicycling a favorite pastime. There are miles of back roads to explore. Serious cyclists mark their calendars for early Oct., when the 100-mile Sea Gull Century takes 7,000 riders from Salisbury to the ocean and back in the largest century in the East. In addition, the event hosts easier rides, like a trip to the Ward Museum, local crabhouses, or Bordeleau Vineyards, a highly pleasant Wicomico Creek-side locale that's a mere 24 miles from the start. For a registration packet: 410-548-2772; www.seagullcentury.org.

In Worcester County, relatively light traffic makes for some good riding on the main roads. (Beware the overcast day, however; heavy traffic often heads inland from the Atlantic beaches.) A good ride starts in Berlin, a historic town with some interesting shops and worthy cafés, then heads down Evans Road. Wander west along Bethards Road to Patey Woods Road, then pedal down Basket Switch Road to Taylor Road. This route is about 19 miles long and brings you to a good choice of destinations: Go left and head to Chincoteague Bay, or go another 4 miles west to Snow Hill, a pretty, historic town along the Pocomoke River.

Bicycling Outfitters & Guides

Adrenaline High (410-749-2886; www.adrenalinehigh.com; 107 Morris Mill Road, Salisbury) Stan Sheddaker founded the popular Seagull Century, and now he's turned his attention to leading custom bike and paddle trips.

To obtain the **Great Delmarva Bicycle Trail** map, which covers more than 2,000 miles of trail in varying habitat (including cypress swamps), go to www.dliteonline.net/misc/bicycling-trail.html. Biking trail guides of Dorchester County can be obtained by contacting Dorchester County Tourism, www.tourdorchester.org, or stopping at the Visitor's Center (I-800-522-TOUR; 203 Sunburst Hwy., Cambridge). The latter includes trails through Blackwater National Wildlife Refuge, a popular cycling spot and interesting lowlands with bald eagles and hawks.

Blackwater Paddle & Pedal Adventures (410-901-9255; www.blackwaterpaddleand pedal.com; 4303 Bucktown Rd., Cambridge) This local family business offers guided trips in the Dorchester County area as well as rentals, which come with a bottle of water, helmet, and map. Plan on a 20-mile nature tour and see eagles and turtles, or do a 12-mile trip to check out Blackwater National Wildlife Refuge and local spots of historic interest. You'll begin your trip at one, because the outfitter is headquartered at the Bucktown Village Store. This is where Underground Railroad conductor Harriet Tubman famously hit her head as a young woman, leading to blackouts later in life.

Bird-Watching

The parade of good birding sites on the Lower Shore is equal to the long list of parks and recreational areas along this portion of the Delmarva Peninsula. You won't have trouble seeing eagles, who dwell in their largest nesting colony north of Florida at Blackwater National Wildlife Refuge. Black rails nest at Fishing Bay National Wildlife Management Area south of Blackwater in Dorchester County. Other possible sightings: yellow-billed cuckoos, Bewick's wrens, and northern goshawks near Hoopers Island in Dorchester. See everything from hummingbirds to woodpeckers at Assateague Island, where parts of the beach are closed for piping plover nesting season in early summer. The Delmarva Peninsula is on the Atlantic Flyway, so suit up for fall migration. Hawks, songbirds, and numerous others end up at the peninsula's tip in early Oct., which the faithful celebrate at the Eastern Shore Birding & Wildlife Festival. For info, contact the Eastern Shore Chamber of Commerce (www.esvachamber.org). For more about these parks and sites, "Natural Preserves."

Boating

The *Nathan* of Dorchester (410-228-7141; www.skipjack-nathan.org; Dorchester Skipjack Committee, P.O. Box 1224, Cambridge, MD 21613) This sailing ambassador, a skipjack built in 1994—a project helmed by legendary local boatbuilder Harold Ruark, namesake of the Ruark Boatworks), sails the Chesapeake. However, on Sat. from May–Oct. *Nathan* is in port at Long Wharf to take the public out for a two-hour sail. One-hour sails on Sun. are available monthly. Check the Web site for schedules.

Marinas

Cambridge Municipal Yacht Basin (410-228-4031), next to the Historic District in an area known as Port of Cambridge. Facilities include gas, diesel, pump-outs, Wi-Fi, gas, and grills. Borrow a bicycle to get around town.

Workboats docked at Crisfield. Maryland Office of Tourism

Hyatt River Marsh Marina (410-901-1234 or 1-800-233-1234; www.chesapeakebay
.hyatt.com) offers 150 slips, water, power, marina store, and all of the luxurious amenities offered by the Hyatt Regency Chesapeake Bay Golf Resort, Spa and Marina.

Somers Cove Marina (410-968-0925 or 1-800-967-3474; www.dnr.state.md.us/public
lands/eastern/somerscove.html) is a huge marina right in Crisfield on Tangier Sound
with 100 transient slips that can hold boats up to 150 feet. Facilities include seven comfort stations, pump-out station, fuel, and a swimming pool. It's owned and operated by
the state Department of Natural Resources.

Boat Ramps

No more wondering where to put your boat in: Go to www.dnr.state.md.us and click on
"Find a Boat Ramp" in the menu.

Charter Boats & Head Boats

Double A Charter Fishing (410-493-1707 or gibbydean@yahoo.com; 6311 Suicide Bridge
Rd., Hurlock) Fish out of remote Fishing Creek on Hoopers Island aboard the 42-foot
Double A. Capt. Gibby Dean, who has more than 20 years' experience, was raised in the
area and departs from the marina his grandfather used to own. He fishes mid- and
lower Bay.

Sawyer Fishing Charters & Tours (410-397-3743; www.sawyercharters.com; 1345
Hoopers Island Rd., Church Creek) This Hoopers Island resident takes anglers out
into the Bay between Smith Point and the Patuxent River, or maybe into the Honga
River or Tangier Sound aboard *Sawyer*, a 48-foot Chesapeake deadrise-style fishing

boat. The base rate is $600 for six people, but check the Web site for specials and kids' promotions.

Tide Runner Fishing Charters (410-397-FISH; www.captmikemurphy.com; P.O. Box 55, Fishing Creek, MD 21634) Light tackle and fly-fishing out of Hoopers Island. Fish the mid-Chesapeake, the lower part of Maryland, as far as Choptank, and as far south as Smith Island. Capt. Murphy's been at it since 1989.

For a list of the many charter boat captains operating out of the fine fishing grounds near Crisfield, contact the Somerset County Tourism office at 1-800-521-9189.

Fishing

Fish or crab along the piers that once were the Choptank River Bridge, located alongside US 50 and the current bridge in Cambridge. They're now named for a beloved late Maryland outdoor writer: the Bill Burton Fishing Piers State Park. Lit at night, parking, and open 24/7. For info: www.dnr.state.md.us/publiclands/eastern/choptankpier.html.

Golf

Great Hope Golf Course (1-800-537-8009; www.greathopegolf.com; 8380 Crisfield Hwy., Westover) 2,047-yard, links-style championship golf course. Pro shop, restaurant, PGA instruction.

Nassawango Golf Course and River View Restaurant (410-632-3114; www.nassawango .com; 3940 Nassawango Rd., Snow Hill) Semiprivate 18-hole championship course. Driving range, pro shop. Located along the Pocomoke River.

Nutters Crossing Golf Course & Driving Range (410-860-4653; 30287 Southampton Bridge Rd., Salisbury) Bermuda fairways at this 18-hole championship golf course with special rates for members and locals. There's an on-site restaurant.

River Marsh Golf Club (410-901-1234; Hyatt Regency Chesapeake Bay Golf Resort, Spa and Marina, 100 Heron Blvd., Cambridge) An 18-hole championship golf course designed by Keith Foster. Pretty holes along the Choptank River. Instruction, pro shop, driving range, Eagle's Nest Bar and Grille.

Winter Quarters Golf Course (410-957-1171; 355 Winter Quarters Dr., Pocomoke City) Public course. Two separate sets of tees make a front nine and a back nine.

Natural Preserves: State and National Parks and Refuges

The Lower Eastern Shore's many expansive natural areas are a huge draw to the region. Endangered Delmarva fox squirrels reside here and the exotic sika deer can be spotted. These large-dog-sized deer, which got loose decades back, now provide intriguing animal sightings alongside plentiful bird species. During summer? Expect bugs, and we mean flies, mosquitos, and all the other insects that provide dinner for all the cool bird species you hope you'll see. Be prepared.

Assateague Island National Seashore (410-641-3030 for the Sinepuxent District Ranger Station; 410-641-1441 for the Barrier Island Visitor Center; www.nps.gov/asis; 7206 National Seashore Ln., Berlin) This 13-mile barrier island along the Atlantic Ocean straddles the Maryland-Virginia border. The spectacular seashore wilderness offers stretches of isolated beach, a lifeguarded beach, shellfishing, crabbing, paddling, and hiking. Visitors can also camp in the backcountry with a permit, and rent canoes or bikes. Lifeguards are stationed at portions of the beach. There's a nature center, too.

There are 44 mammal species here, including gray seals, born at the southernmost point in their birthing range, and bottlenose dolphins offshore. Birds include northern bobwhites, least bitterns, indigo buntings, and more exotic seagoing passers-by. This is also home to the famous wild ponies, who live on the Maryland side of the island and most likely descended from horses grazed here by 17th-century settlers. They're generally mild-tempered and will leave you alone if you leave them alone.

Assateague State Park (410-641-2918; 7307 Stephen Decatur Hwy., Berlin) The sun worshippers, families, and beachcombers gather here, where there are two lifeguarded areas. There's also a nature center, seasonal programs like guided kayak and canoe tours, Bay-side clamming, nature-oriented arts and crafts, and yoga on the beach. The park is open from the end of Apr. to the end of Oct.

Blackwater National Wildlife Refuge (410-228-2677; 2145 Key Wallace Dr., Cambridge) More than 25,000 acres south of the tiny town of Church Creek include lowlands, forests, flat roads for cycling, 1 and 2-mile hiking trails, and creeks for paddling (bring a water trail map). Birds aplenty, and you might even glimpse the Chesapeake's endangered Delmarva fox squirrel, as Blackwater has the highest natural concentration of the small creature. It also has the East Coast's largest nesting population of bald eagles north of Florida. Take the 6-mile driving loop, with its minimal cost for cars and cyclists. There's a nature center and gift shop; the visitor center is open 8–4 weekdays and 9–5 weekends.

Fishing Bay Wildlife Management Area (410-376-3236; 4220 Steele Neck Rd., Vienna) A total of 28,903 acres with paddlers' trails (see "Paddling" for water trail information),

Golfers playing at the Hyatt Regency in Cambridge enjoy beautiful views of the Choptank River.

boating, in-season hunting, bird-watching, and boat ramp. Habitat supports the Asian sika deer, bald eagles, ospreys, ibis, wintering short-eared owls, shorebirds, and waterfowl. Fishing and crabbing. The WMA's entrance is located down Bestpitch Ferry Rd., 14 miles south of Cambridge. Watch out for summertime bugs (flies, ticks, chiggers), and wear something tough if you're going to be in the wooded sections that can get quite wet (sneakers may not cut it). Expect the unexpected here, where there are no rangers and the state workers are in and out on their own schedules.

Janes Island State Park (410-968-1565; 26280 Alfred Lawson Dr., Crisfield) One of the coolest parks anywhere, composed of a mainland portion with marina, camping, and cabins, and a 2,800-acre island. Rent a small kayak/boat to explore the guts of the island, marked into its fabled water trails. Boasts a lovely beach on the island's far side along Tangier Sound. GPS tracking for the trails can be downloaded.

Pocomoke River State Park (410-632-2566; dnr.maryland.gov/publiclands/eastern /pocomokeriver.html; 3461 Worcester Hwy., Snow Hill) Two discrete areas make up this intriguing, 1,000-ish-acre park, with its cypress swamp and blackwater paddling on the Pocomoke River. The Milburn Landing area is 7 miles north of Pocomoke City; the Shad Landing area is 3.5 miles south of Snow Hill. Visitors will find cabins, boating, paddling, fishing, trails for walking, a 23-slip marina, a 191-site campground with camphouse/facilities, and a swimming pool at Shad Landing. In addition, the area has a nature center open daily during its seasonal operation and weekends in fall and spring. Check out the free camper programs from Memorial Day to Labor Day. Athletic fields have recently been revamped, so there's volleyball, a new playground, and a new baseball field. Also consider staying at one of eight mini-cabins at Shad. Milburn Landing provides a 32-site campground, four mini-cabins, recycled tire playground, two pavilions (for rent), hiking trails (no biking), fishing pier, and boat launch area (soft launch for paddling, plus boat ramp—no fees) Call to ask about pets. Biking on paved trails only.

Pocomoke State Forest (410-632-3732; dnr.maryland.gov/publiclands/eastern/pocomoke forest.asp; 6572 Snow Hill Rd., Snow Hill) Stands of loblolly pine, cypress swamps, and the Pocomoke River can be found in this 14,753-acre property. Activities include fishing, hunting, paddling, and hiking/mountain biking along its trails.

Paddling

The Lower Shore's rivers, creeks, swamps, and bays are as wild as you'll find even though they're within reasonable driving distance of big cities. With literally thousands of miles of shoreline passing through fresh- and saltwater, the region has become a mecca for paddlers. Water trails mark an increasing number of those miles, and that's a good thing since it's quite easy to get turned around in the "guts" that pass through marshy lowlands. A water trail guide is available via Dorchester County Tourism at www.tourdorchester.org or 1-800-522-TOUR. Or, you can stop at the Visitor's Center (1-800-522-TOUR; 203 Sunburst Hwy., Cambridge).

Always keep safety in mind when paddling. Check on weather and tides before heading out, and know the depth of the stream you're about to paddle. Outfitters can be an invaluable resource for paddlers of all abilities, and the Maryland Department of Natural Resources also may have more information you can use: www.dnr.state.md.us.

Assateague Island National Seashore (410-641-3030 for the ranger station and camper registration; 410-641-1441 for the visitor center; 7206 National Seashore Ln., Berlin)

This is a good place to poke around marshes and interior bays, although wildlife protection regulations must be followed. Canoe, kayak, and boat rentals are available.

Blackwater National Wildlife Refuge (410-228-2677; www.friendsofblackwater.org /paddling.html; 2145 Key Wallace Dr., Cambridge) Three color-coded trails mark your passage through Blackwater and are 7.6, 8, and 9 miles long. Maps are available at a nominal fee and are advised for the 9-mile trail (aka the "purple" trail) due to the long stretches of open water. This particular trail also is closed Oct.-Mar. due to waterfowl migrations.

Fishing Bay Wildlife Management Area (410-376-3236; 4220 Steele Neck Rd., Vienna) Keep an eye on winds and tides in this 28,500-acre area that abuts Blackwater. Obtain the guides for the Island Creek Trail and Transquaking River Loop Trail here in the management area or the waters of Taylor's Island via 1-800-522-TOUR or www.tour dorchester.org.

Janes Island State Park (410-968-1565; 26280 Alfred J. Lawson Drive, Crisfield, MD 21817) Color-coded water trails meander through the island "guts," or channels, of this wonderful lowland paradise, trails that Paddler Magazine rated in its national top 10. Backcountry camping available.

Outfitters & Rentals

Adrenaline High (410-749-2886; www.adrenalinehigh.com; 107 Morris Mill Road, Salisbury) Stan Sheddaker founded the popular Seagull Century bike ride and now he's turned his attention to leading custom paddle and/or biking trips with all your needs taken care of. By this we mean he designs the trip (which can be multi-day) makes lodging arrangements (which might well be in one of his own rustic properties in the area) and feeds you (which could include, say, soup made from butternut squash grown in his garden). He also provides a variety of specialized trips like the one where folks stay in remote Whitehaven at the restored Whitehaven Hotel and paddle to the Bourdeleau Vineyard for a nice little tasting. He also knows his way around Virginia's barrier islands and combines paddles with dinner out. Call for prices.

Blackwater Paddle & Pedal Adventures (410-901-9255; www.blackwaterpaddleandpedal .com; 4303 Bucktown Rd., Cambridge) This local family business offers guided trips in the Dorchester County area as well as kayak and canoe rentals. Its headquarters is interesting, too. The Bucktown Village Store is located en route to Blackwater National Wildlife Refuge, and it's historically significant as the place where Underground Railroad conductor Harriet Tubman famously hit her head as a young woman, which led to blackouts later in life. BPPA can guide you through the Blackwater area. They also run the waterfront at the nearby Hyatt resort. Call or check the Web site for prices.

Pocomoke River Canoe Company (410-632-3971; 2 River St., Snow Hill) This knowledge-able outfitter of more than a quarter-century rents canoes, kayaks, and tandem kayaks every day, Apr.–Oct. The company can provide livery service and is well worth contacting, even if you're going out with your own canoe. They specialize in Pocomoke River and Nassawango Creek areas, where a pleasant half-day, self-guided trip leads paddlers back to the canoe company location. Maps are provided. Cost is $40 for kayaks and $45 per canoe. Weekly rentals are also available, as are occasional eco-paddles with naturalists.

Survival Products (410-543-1244; www.survivalproducts.com; 1116 N. Salisbury Blvd. (US 13) Salisbury) Canoe and kayak sales and rentals from knowledgeable people who cruise

A kayak trip yields a wonderful sight: a bald eagle. Photo courtesy of Adrenaline High

area waterways. They can even tie down the craft to your car before you head out, and can recommend area guides. Cost is $50 per day for a solo kayak; $75 for tandem kayaks and canoes, complete with life vest, paddle, and tie-down kit.

Sporting Clays

Delmarva Sporting Clays (410-742-2023; 23501 Marsh Rd., Mardella Springs) A 55-station sporting clay range located on 60 acres. Open daily year-round, 9 AM–6 PM. $15 for 50 targets or $30 for 100. The facility also offers a rifle range with rifle and pistol rentals, as well as an archery range. $15 per shooter per day. Instruction offered.

Swimming

Dorchester County Pool (410-228-5578; 107 Virginia Ave., Cambridge) Where the locals go, especially after the sea nettles arrive in the Bay. Open daily, Memorial Day–Labor Day.

Great Marsh Park (contact Dorchester County Tourism, 410-228-1000; Somerset Ave., Cambridge) Boat ramp, picnicking, pier, and playground. Swim in early summer, before the sea nettles arrive.

Pocomoke River State Park (410-632-2566; 3461 Worcester Hwy., Snow Hill) Swimming pool at the Shad Landing portion of the park, 3.5 miles south of Snow Hill.

Tennis

Salisbury City Park (410-548-3177; E. Main St. and S. Park Dr., Salisbury) A few public courts located in a tree-shaded park that also features a bandstand where concerts are held on summer Sun. Park also has a playground, paddleboats, and riverside walking trails.

SHOPPING

Antiques

Dark Horse Antiques & Collectibles (410-221-1505; www.darkhorseantiques.com; 2923 Ocean Gateway (US 50), Cambridge) Furniture, primitives, regional items like oyster cans, knives, and plates. Paintings, prints. Multidealer, lots of local advertising, decoys.

Packing House Antiques (410-221-8544; 411 Dorchester Ave., Cambridge) Recommended by those in the know; more than 60,000 square feet.

A Step Above (410-629-1595; www.astepabovegalleryandgifts.com; 27 N. Main St., Berlin) Local artists, jewelry, fountains, metalwork. High-end art and crafts.

Stuart's Antiques (410-641-0435; 5 Pitts St., Berlin) A delightful shop, half antiques focusing on china dinnerware, silver services, and furniture; half designer accessories like Mary Frances handbags and Italian shirts and ties. Not large, but still one of the best browsing places on the Shore.

Town Center Antiques I (410-629-1895; 1 N. Main St., Berlin) Antiques and collectibles from more than 70 dealers are spread out in a big building. If you want to browse the whole thing, plan on two hours. A nearby, second location at 113 N. Main St. showcases even more dealers.

Nearby Recreation

Ocean City is within easy driving distance of Salisbury, Berlin, and Assateague—in fact, these are a natural and worthy grouping of travel destinations. The sprawling beach town's major attraction is a 10-mile-long strip of golden sand that often is packed blanket-to-blanket on summer weekends.

Visitors come for the sun, the sand, the boardwalk, the carnival rides, the "World Famous French Fries," the shops and restaurants, the golf, and the fishing that includes a big-money white marlin tournament in August.

You can reach Ocean City, or "O.C.," from the Bay via three routes: Enter the oldest, southern-most part of the city on US 50 from the west. Or take MD 90 across the Assawoman Bay Bridge to what has become the city's center. Or from the north, from the Delaware towns of Rehoboth Beach, Dewey Beach, and Bethany Beach (highly worthwhile destinations), take DE 1, which becomes the Coastal Hwy., MD 528, once you reach Maryland. For information, contact the Ocean City Convention and Visitors Bureau (410-289-8181 or 1-800-OC-OCEAN; www.ococean.com).

Apparel

Dragonfly Boutique (410-228-6825; www.dragonflyboutique.biz; 406 Race St., Cambridge) This place smells great and is full of stylish (and maybe saucy) summer apparel during the season. Look for Life is Good and Spanx, too.

Sunnyside Shop (410-901-9001; 500 Poplar St., Cambridge) This large store seems kinda like an eco-friendly department store, with a little of this and a little of that. Ladies, look for your Flax clothing right here, or pick up some fair-trade finger puppets for the kids.

Books

Henrietta's Attic (410-546-3700 or 1-800-546-3744; 205 Maryland Ave., Salisbury) Aisles of antiques and used books watched over by bookseller Henrietta Moore. Browse as long as you like, or ask for Moore's help. Collectibles, glassware, china, and geneal-ogy materials are also packed into this "anything goes" place five blocks south of the hospital, west of US 13.

Maggie's of Snow Hill (410-632-4050, 312 N. Washington St.) An independent book-store with a great selection of books on regional topics and history. They carry best-sellers, but the focus is on lesser-known titles that the staff knows and recommends. Maggie's Café, the coffeehouse in the rear of the shop, sells good brews and baked goods. Closed Mon.

Galleries

Artiques (410-632-3885; www.artiquescollection.com; 310 N. Washington St., Snow Hill) Connected to the bookshop Maggie's through an open wall, this is a spacious gallery with European and Eastern antiques and work by the Eastern Shore's most highly regarded artists. Closed Mon.

Bishop's Stock (410-632-3555; www.bishopsstock.com; 202 W. Green St., Snow Hill) Generally regarded as one of the premier galleries on the Eastern Shore. Ann and Randy Coates' goal is to promote Delmarva artists and stimulate interest in the region's creative community. All manner of media is represented here, with very reasonable prices as part of the strategy to get people started collecting Eastern Shore artists. Closed Tues. and Wed.

Chesapeake East/Lakeside Gallery (410-546-1534; www.chesapeakeast.com; 510 W. Main St.) Not the easiest place to find, but worth the effort. Dana Simson's large shop is filled with joyous ceramics, prints, custom tiles, hooked rugs, painted furniture, and children's books—all her works. Her designs are sought by national textile and home decor companies. She also runs a "paint your own ceramics" workshop in the gallery. Closed Sun.

The Gallery (410-742-2880; 625 S. Division St., Salisbury) Originally focused on ceramics, this co-op of about 40 regional artists and artisans now displays regional works in many media. Regular one-person shows and an annual Dec. exhibit featuring four or five local artists. Custom framing and a range of gifts and crafts, including functional pottery and handcrafted jewelry. Closed Sun.

j.j.Fish Studio (410-641-4805; jjfishstudio.com; 14 N. Main St., Berlin) John and Judy Fisher call their 750-square-foot space "A Gallery of Friends." It consistently ranks highly in surveys of galleries exhibiting American handicrafts. In addition to their own highly regarded jewelry, they display glass, quilts, pottery, wood, metal, and more from over 60 regional and national artists. Open daily.

Joie de Vivre Gallery (410-228-7000; www.joiedevivregallery.com; 410 Race St., Cambridge) A good cross-section of local artists show here, such as Mexican-born resident Victor Abarca, whose fiery paintings mix his here and now (herons and fish) with his heritage (cacti).

Perfect Touch Gallery (410-641-2373; 4 Bay St., Berlin) Full of interesting, unusual home decor accessories. Many items are handcrafted. This is one of the dealers for Leaf Leather handbags—intricate, hand-tooled works showing every rib and vein of leafs and twigs. Closed Sun. and Tues.

Salisbury Art & Framing (410-742-9522; www.salisburyartandframing.com; 213 North Blvd., Waverly Plaza, Salisbury) Much more than a framing store, this shop features a nice selection of crafts and fine art pieces, both decorative and functional. Ceramics are a specialty. Owner Marilyn Bookmyer is a walking reference on the subject and is glad to share her knowledge. South of downtown and west of US 13. Closed Sun.

Gift Stores and Specialty Shops

Bay Country Shop (410-221-0700; 2709 Ocean Gateway, Cambridge) Rustic and goose-oriented Shore items. Lots of gifts as well as men's and women's clothing and jewelry. Limited edition prints. Open daily year-round, Mon.–Sat. 10–5, Sun. 1–5.

The Country House (410-749-1959; www.thecountryhouse.com; 805 E. Main St., Salisbury) The largest store selling "country" items on the East Coast. Well laid out by departments (kitchen items, bath, candles, Christmas, furniture). Customers have been known to get lost for hours. Closed Sun.

Specialty Shops

Pear Tree South (410-221-1777; 412 Race St., Cambridge) Jewelry, local soaps, and unique clocks are among the finds at Kate Huntington's store. Her sister owns the Pear Tree to the north—in Vermont.

Petite Fleur (410-651-4999; www.la-petitefleur.com; 11779 Somerset Ave., Princess Anne) Wonderful shop for elegant, European-inspired home decor: pottery from Hungary, Garnier-Thiebaut French linens, Mistral toiletries, Pillivuyt porcelain cookware and tableware. Closed Sun.

Ta-Da (410-641-4430, 18 William St., Berlin) Features hand-painted glass and tableware by owner/artist Patty Falck. Everything from elegant floral designs to whimsical things like olives on Martini glasses. Also here: B.B. Becker's line of inspirational jewelry, with each piece engraved with a quote from Ghandi, Longfellow, or The Talmud. Open daily.

Jewelry

Bailey Jewelers (410-251-0394, www.chesapeakejewelers.com; 30400 Mount Vernon Road, Princess Anne) Jonathan Bailey used the lost wax process to create 14K charms of Chesapeake icons like crabs, skipjacks, and workboats. More than souvenirs, these merit being worn and seen every day. There is a second shop open seasonally in St. Michaels. Open daily.

G. B. Heron & Company (410-860-0221; 1307 Mt. Hermon Rd., Salisbury) Custom-designed jewelry and a store full of high-quality pieces. Jewelry repair by goldsmiths on the premises.

Kuhn's Jewelers (410-742-3256; www.kuhnsjewelers.com; 107 Downtown Plaza, Salisbury) Diamonds and watches; full line of quality jewelry from a company established in 1853. This is the sixth-oldest independent jewelry store in America.

Malls and Outlets

The Centre at Salisbury (410-548-1600; www.centreatsalisbury.com; 2300 N. Salisbury Blvd., Salisbury) This is the region's major local mall, with four anchor department stores (Boscov's, Macy's, Sears, and J. C. Penney), a Dick's Sporting Goods, dozens of specialty stores, a food court, and a 16-screen stadium-style cinema.

SMITH AND TANGIER ISLANDS

The boat schedule rules the time visitors can spend rambling on Chesapeake's last two inhabited islands, the remote crabbing communities on Smith Island in Maryland and Tangier Island in Virginia. Promptly, the boats depart Crisfield, and just as promptly, the boats pull away from the island docks, 12 miles away, to return to the mainland.

Visitors who want a true-blue peek at old Chesapeake life should visit one or both of these islands. There's no ATM, and the islands, bastions of an old-style brand of Methodism, are dry. For many, an afternoon peek at island life via the tourist ferries may be enough. If you're staying overnight, make reservations.

Part of a chain of shifting, sinking, eroding islands, Tangier and Smith lie only a few feet above sea level—and sometimes far less. On Tangier, half of the 3-mile island is livable; the rest is tidal marsh. At 8 miles by 4 miles, Smith Island is far larger.

The two share similarities, but they are different, too. Erosion threatens their lives, and precarious crab populations their livelihoods. After a day or two cycling the narrow streets where grave markers in front yards repeat old names like Crockett or Parks, outsiders know this isn't a place where people forget their past. The islanders' distinct accents reportedly descend from Elizabethan forebears who settled here.

The white crab shanties that once lined Smith's "Big Gut," the channel into Ewell, have come ashore, but they still line the channel into Tangier. Just as you wouldn't waltz into a businessman's private office without an invitation, so a visit to a Tangierman's crab shanty comes only at his invitation. Shallow wooden "tanks" line the interior, filled with crabs moving toward a molt, the final step toward producing a valuable soft-shell.

Three towns are settled on Smith Island: Ewell, Rhode's Point, and Tylerton. Tylerton, reputedly the most devout of the three, is separated from the island proper by a channel, and therefore accessed only by boat. It is fronted by docks, with well-kept houses and its own general store. A bike ride out the main road from Ewell takes visitors into tiny Rhode's Point, teetering on the edge of the Bay. Upon finishing a ride, only a stop at Ewell's nearly century-old general store, called Ruke's for the current owner of more than 40 years, will do. Order up soft-shell crabs; you won't find finer in any fancy city restaurant. And, of course, indulge in a slice of Smith Island layer cake. It's become Maryland's official state dessert, and you can buy it off-island now, but this is your real-deal opportunity to indulge in the multilayer treat.

Tangier hosts just one town, but visitors immediately see its bustle. Golf carts manned by tour guides line up to meet the tour boats, and a "tour buggy" excursion is quick but thorough, covering the gift shops lining the main road, the school, and the Methodist church. On poles are containers akin to bluebird boxes, welcoming those honest enough to plop in a couple of quarters in exchange for an island recipe, often featuring crab. In recent years, Tangier has built the Tangier History Museum and Interpretive Cultural Center, which tells its story. Smith Island built a similar center some years back.

Travelers should understand that the islands are not Chesapeake Disneyland, nor are they well-developed second-home tourist meccas like Nantucket and the Vineyard. Tangier has a bit more for tourists to do, including a 3-mile beach on the far side of the island and an airstrip. But Smith draws visitors as well, including those who want to visit the fabled Ruke's General Store or the lovely Inn of Silent Music in Tylerton, the ultimate getaway.

GETTING TO THE ISLANDS

Take a seasonal ferry for tourists, or travel year-round, as the locals do, via mail boat, usually from Crisfield. Be sure to leave enough time to secure parking—especially if you're going to be gone overnight—and note that not all boats departing Crisfield leave from the City Dock. For general questions about the boats and their schedules, contact the Somerset County tourism office at 1-800-521-9189 or check www.visitsomerset.com, www.smith island.org, or www.tangierisland-va.com.

The *Captain Jason I* (410-425-5931; 4132 Smith Island Rd., Ewell, MD 21824) travels year-round between Ewell and Crisfield. The *Captain Jason II* (410-425-4471; 21162 Tuff St., Tylerton, MD 21866) travels between Tylerton and Crisfield. The two boats are operated by the Laird brothers. Depart 12:30 daily, return at 4. Leave Crisfield again for the night at 5 PM. $25 per person; $20 each way if you're staying overnight.

Mail Boat to Tangier Island (757-891-2240; 16458 W. Ridge Rd., Tangier, VA 23440) The *Courtney Thomas* travels year-round between Crisfield and Tangier. Leaves Tangier at 8 AM and Crisfield at 12:30 PM Mon.–Sat.

Smith Island Cruises (410-425-2771; www.smithislandcruises.com/main.htm; 14065 Smith Island Rd., Ewell, MD 21824) Sail from Crisfield's Somer's Cove Marina from Memorial Day–Oct. 15. À la carte lunch available at the Bayside Inn at the dock in Ewell. Departs Crisfield 12:30 PM, returns 4:30; adults $22. The company also operates a ferry from Point Lookout at the mouth of the Potomac River in St. Marys County (see Chapter 4, "Annapolis & Points South").

Tangier Island Cruises (410-968-2338; www.tangierislandcruises.com; 1001 W. Main St., Crisfield, MD 21817) The *Steven Thomas* runs daily, May 15–Oct. 15, departing from 10th and Main streets in Crisfield at 12:30 PM, leaving the island at 4 PM, and returning about 5:15 PM. Adults $25, ages 7–12 $12. It's $35 if you're staying overnight and $20 for a one-way trip. Advance tickets available via Web site.

A crowded harbor is a typical Chesapeake sight in the summer.

WHAT TO DO, WHERE TO STAY

Smith Island

Orient yourself to island life at the Smith Island Center (410-425-3351; www.smithisland
.org; Caleb Jones Rd. at the county dock), which tells of boats, oystering, crabbing, and
Joshua Thomas, the famed "Parson of the Islands" who spread Methodism here in the 19th
century. Open May–Oct., noon–4 daily.

Food and Lodging

Bayside Inn Restaurant (410-425-2771; 4065 Smith Island Rd., at the dock in Ewell)
Open Memorial Day–Oct. 15, daily 11–4. Family-style by reservation, or à la carte.
Serves up big platters of Southern-style seafood, as well as famed Smith Island layer
cake—up to 10 layers!—for dessert.

Drum Point Market (410-425-2108; Union Church St., Tylerton) The grocery store and
lunch stop at this end of the island. Open year-round, Mon., Tues., and Thurs.–Sat.
10–3 and 6–8; Wed. 10–3. Soft crabs, crabcakes. The only store in Tylerton, and it's
open all winter.

Ewell Tide Inn (410-425-2141; www.smithisland.net; 4063 Tyler Rd., Ewell, MD 21824)
Reasonably priced and very homey, located in a former captain's house. Four rooms;
some share a bath. Owner Wayne Gaither will take you on a tour, show you where the
pelican colony is (7,500 birds at peak), cook you a crabcake, and otherwise show you
around the island. The crabcakes are $4—even if you're not staying at the inn, which is
inexpensive to moderately priced.

Inn of Silent Music (410-425-3541; www.innofsilentmusic.com; 2955 Tylerton Rd.,
Tylerton, MD 21866) This unique and seasonal waterside getaway, surrounded by water
and with soft colors and peaceful ambience, offers three guest rooms with private baths.
Gourmet breakfast is included, and a seafood dinner may be available by advance
arrangement. Canoes, a kayak, bikes. Moderate. No credit cards. No handicapped
access.

Ruke's (410-425-2311; 20840 Caleb Jones Rd., Ewell) Don't pass up the opportunity to eat
a crabcake, seafood platter, or soft-shell crab here at Ewell's longtime general store,
maybe even out on the deck. Locals drop by for coffee, and you can find a few antiques
and ice cream, too. And, of course, the famous Smith Island layer cake. Open Memorial
Day to the end of Oct.

Tangier Island

Clamber aboard a "tour buggy," one of the fleet of golf carts lined up to meet the tour boats,
and take a tour of the island, which includes a 3-mile beach on the far side.

A handful of gift shops with sensible names like Jim's and Wanda's reside along
Tangier's main street, where visitors can buy souvenirs like T-shirts and shell wreaths.
Hours conform to the tour boat schedule: about 10:30–4 from spring through fall, when
tour boats operate. They reopen in the evening so the townspeople can shop.

For bike rentals, stop by **Ruby Dize's** (757-891-2308). She lives next door to the
Chesapeake House, and rentals—$2 an hour, $7 overnight—are handled via the honor system. Look for the jar in the yard.

Tangier Island Museum & Interpretive Cultural Center (302-234-1660; www.tangier historymuseum.org; 16215 Main Ridge) This is a relatively new museum that showcases the unique life here, where watermen have crabbed for generations. They also can help you out with nature trails, a history walking trail, and water trails—explored with free kayaks and canoes. While you're out on the water, you might see black skimmers or clapper rails. Download the water trails from the Web site.

Food and Lodging

Bay View Inn (757-891-2396; www.tangierisland.net; P.O. Box 309, Tangier Island, VA 23440) Walking distance to gift shops, beach, and airport. In all, nine "cottages" in back and two rooms in the main house. Two cottages are family cottages, with one full, one twin, and bunk beds. Enjoy the gazebo and look out toward the water. Full breakfast. Moderate to expensive; Internet access; pet-friendly cabins available. The innkeepers will pick you up at the boat.

Fisherman's Corner Restaurant (757-891-2900; www.fishermanscornerrestaurant.com; 4419 Long Bridge Rd., Tangier Island) Operated by local island women, this homey restaurant serves the kind of indigenous seafood people travel a lifetime to find. Soft-shells, crab claws, crabcakes, and other Bay specialties are available, and dessert's homemade. Inexpensive to expensive. Open May–Sept.

Hilda Crockett's Chesapeake House (757-891-2331; 16243 Main Ridge Rd., Tangier Island) Family-style seating at this island institution, open daily 11:30–5 from Apr. 15–Oct. 15. Breakfast is available 7–9. Inexpensive. Also, there's lodging here, eight rooms that have recently been updated. Prices are moderate, and including breakfast and dinner. No alcohol served. No pets. One golf cart's available for guest rental.

Sunset Inn (757-891-2535; www.tangierislandsunset.com; P.O. Box 261, Tangier Island, VA 23440) Next to the island's 3-mile beach. Ten cottages with fridges, open Apr.–Oct. for the general public, and Nov. and Dec. to hunters. Continental breakfast. Moderate prices; one three-bedroom apartment is very expensive.

Waterfront Restaurant (757-891-2248; 16125 Main Ridge Rd., Tangier Island) You can't miss it, right where the tour boats come in. Sit at a picnic table and enjoy soft-shells and crabcakes or a sub sandwich. Open May through Oct. Inexpensive. Personal checks OK.

8

Information

The Right Connections

Consider this an abbreviated encyclopedia of Bay-related information that will help you move more easily through the area. This chapter provides guidance on the following:

AREA CODES

In Maryland, you must dial the area code to make any phone call, even if it's not long-distance. Most Chesapeake area codes—including Baltimore—are 410 or 443, except for St. Marys County, in Southern Maryland, where it's 301.

Bicycling Basics

Cyclists can't cross major bridges in the region. These include the Bay Bridge near Annapolis (formally called the William Preston Lane Jr. Memorial Bridge); the Harry W. Nice Bridge where US 301 divides Maryland and Virginia, or the Thomas J. Hatem Bridge at Havre de Grace, where US 40 crosses the Susquehanna River. Nor can they ride through

OPPOSITE: *Sailing into Baltimore's Inner Harbor.*

Both Maryland and Virginia offer roadways and bicycle routes to suit cyclists of all abilities.
McAllen Photography, photo courtesy Maryland Office of Tourism

the Chesapeake Bay Bridge–Tunnel at the Bay's southern end in Virginia. Here's what to do:

- Make arrangements to be transported across the Bay Bridge at least 12 hours in advance for a fee. Call 410-974-0341 for info.
- If they have time and staff, Maryland Transportation Administration officials may be able to give you a lift across the Harry Nice Bridge or the Thomas J. Hatem Memorial Bridge. Call 301-259-4444 a full day (24 hours) in advance to find out about the Nice Bridge, and call 410-575-7162 for the Hatem Bridge.
- If you call the Bay Bridge–Tunnel in advance at 757-331-2960, authorities will transport you and your bike. Expect to pay the $12 vehicle toll.

For maps and other cycling-centric info, check "Explore Maryland" at www.maryland roads.com, or contact the state's Bicycle and Pedestrian Advisory Coordinator at 410-545-5656; 707 N. Calvert St., C 502, Baltimore, MD 21203.

CLIMATE AND WEATHER

Expect relatively mild weather in Chesapeake Country. In the winter, Chesapeake City near the top of the Bay sees January highs of 40 degrees and lows of 22. Nearly 240 miles to the south, at the mouth of the Bay in Norfolk, Va., average highs hit 47 degrees and lows are 30 degrees. Chesapeake snowfall averages fewer than 10 inches, but watch out for wind chills near the water.

Summer temperatures rise into the upper 80s and 90s, usually with high humidity in July and August. This can spur furious afternoon and evening thunderstorms, which you should take seriously—especially if you're out on the Bay. Even on the calmest day, boaters need to keep an eye on the windward sky and an ear on the marine weather forecast.

By early September, humidity often has dropped, although temperatures in the 80-degree range may continue into the month. Chesapeake's average fall temperature is 62 degrees. Sailors love it; a steady breeze blows in the 10- to 15-knot range.

On the open Bay, rays are magnified by the water's surface, increasing the risk of sunburn and sunstroke. A hat, lip balm, and sunscreen are always recommended. Also, keep in mind that alcoholic beverages are best consumed after your voyage. Enforcement of drunken-boater laws can be stringent.

EMERGENCY INFORMATION

For police, fire, and ambulance emergencies, dial 911. On the water, the U.S. Coast Guard responds to VHF marine radio Channel 16.

Maryland Department of Natural Resources Police: 410-260-8888 or 1-877-620-8DNR.
Maryland State Police: 410-486-3101 or 1-800-525-5555.
U.S. Coast Guard Activities Baltimore: 410-576-2561, general information; 410-576-2693, emergency.
U.S. Coast Guard Station Annapolis: 410-267-8108.

ENVIRONMENTAL ORGANIZATIONS

"Save the Bay" is a rallying cry around the Chesapeake Bay, the focus of a massive cleanup effort by state and federal agencies since the late 1970s. If you really want to get into the issue, there's plenty of information. Here are some places to start:

The **Chesapeake Bay Foundation** (410-268-8816; www.cbf.org; 6 Herndon Ave., Annapolis, MD 21403) is headquartered out of a notable "green" building in Annapolis, with other offices throughout the Chesapeake watershed region. This is the major "Save the Bay" organization and actively educates the public about a range of Bay-related environmental issues. Check the Web site for details on its myriad programs.

The Bay Journal is online at www.bayjournal.com and is published by the **Alliance for the Chesapeake Bay** (410-377-6270; www.alliancechesbay.org). They work with local watershed organizations.

FARMS AND PRODUCE MARKETS

The fabled "Bounty of the Bay" includes crops ashore as well as those from the water. When the tomatoes come in, you'd be hard-pressed to find better. Not to mention the sweet corn, cantaloupe, and all the rest of the fresh produce spilling from numerous roadside stands from spring well into fall. You can't miss 'em, but if you'd like more information about finding farm stands, farms, and farmer's markets, contact the tourism departments listed at the end of this chapter, or check www.marylandsbest.net, brought to you by the Maryland Department of Agriculture.

Getting Outside: Boating, Fishing, Hunting, Parks

Here's a Web site to memorize: www.dnr.md.us. It's headquarters for the Maryland Department of Natural Resources and can point you toward boat landings, hunting and fishing regulations, and details about parks. Some things you should know:

- Maryland requires anyone born on or after July 1, 1972, to have a Certificate of Boating Safety Education to operate a powerboat on state waters.
- Reserve your cabins and campsites at state parks online or by calling 888-432-2267.
- Good sources of information for boaters in the Bay region include the freebies *Spinsheet* for sailors and *PropTalk* for powerboaters (www.spinsheet.com; www.proptalk.com; 301 Fourth St., Annapolis, MD 21403). For marine services, the "PortBook" is available at www.portbook.net.
- This is outdoor sportsman country, so hunters are out from spring until fall. Check hunting seasons because you should know when hunters are out if you're going hiking or kayaking. If you're a hunter, likewise check with the DNR for regulations.

The Chesapeake and its tributaries create a terrific destination for anglers. Seventeen species of game fish live in the Bay, and are pursued from riverbanks, piers, skiffs, head boats, and charter boats. Among the favorite finfish: bluefish, striped bass (known locally as rockfish), sea trout, white and yellow perch, spot, catfish, and summer flounder. There's also the Maryland blue crab, wildly popular and the focus of considerable political attention as both Maryland and Virginia wrestle with how to manage the tasty and lucrative crab population. Decreases are blamed on overharvesting, the natural cycle of any species, loss of key grass-bed habitat, and predation by finfish, Whatever the reason, be kind and resist the urge to catch more crabs than you'll eat. (Some believe it would be best to ban the catch of females, which have rounded, U-shaped aprons—like the U.S. Capitol dome—unlike the pointed aprons of the males, which resemble the Washington Monument.)

Fishing licenses are widely available at fishing and sporting goods stores. Here's what you need to know:

- Licenses are not required for fishers under age 16 in Maryland.
- A saltwater fishing license issued by Maryland or Virginia is good in either state.
- You won't need a license in Maryland if you are fishing from a chartered boat or if you are fishing as a nonpaying guest from private property.
- Ask about nonresident licenses for consecutive days of fishing. Prices are generally reduced for anglers older than 65.
- Usually, you don't need a fishing license on July 4.
- In Maryland, recreational crabbers must get a license if they are using a trotline, if they plan to catch more than two dozen crabs, or if they're using more than 10 traps.

Hospitals and Health Care

Should a serious health problem arise, you are, fortunately, near some of the nation's top medical facilities.

Baltimore
The Johns Hopkins Hospital (410-955-5000 main number, 410-955-2280 emergency room; www.hopkinsmedicine.org; 600 N. Wolfe St.)
University of Maryland Medical Center (410-328-8667; www.umm.edu; 22 S. Greene St.)

Annapolis
Anne Arundel Medical Center (443-481-1000; 443-481-1200 emergency room; www .aahs.org; 2001 Medical Parkway, off US 50)

The Upper Bay
Chester River Hospital Center (410-778-3300; www.chesterriverhealth.org; 100 Brown St., Chestertown)
Harford Memorial Hospital (443-843-5000 main number, 443-643-2000 emergency; www.uchs.org; 501 S. Union Ave., Havre de Grace).
Union Hospital (410-398-4000; www.uhcc.com; 106 Bow St., Elkton)

Middle Eastern Shore
Memorial Hospital at Easton (410-822-1000; www.shorehealth.org; 219 S. Washington St., Easton)

Lower Eastern Shore
Dorchester General Hospital (410-228-5511; www.shorehealth.org; 300 Byrn St., Cambridge)
Edward W. McCready Memorial Hospital (410-968-1044; www.mccreadyfoundation.org; 201 Hall Hwy., Crisfield)
Peninsula Regional Medical Center (410-546-6400; www.peninsula.org; 100 E. Carroll St., Salisbury)

LATE-NIGHT FOOD AND FUEL

Annapolis
Chesapeake Exxon (410-266-7475; 2101 West St.) Open 24 hours; fuel and towing.
Double T Diner (410-571-9070, 12 Defense St.) On a side road easily seen from West St. near the MD 2 exit off US 50. Open 24 hours.

The Upper Bay and Middle Eastern Shore
Fast Stop (410-822-3333; 9543 Ocean Gateway Dr., Easton) Open 24 hours; food and fuel.
Royal Farm Store (410-778-0646; 301 Maple Ave., Chestertown) Open 24 hours. No gas.
Trailways Truck Stop (410-758-2444; US 301 E and MD 304 E, Centreville) Open 24 hours; food and fuel. Centrally located on the Eastern Shore.

Lower Eastern Shore
Cambridge Diner (410-228-8898; 2924 Old US 50) Located just south of the bridge spanning the Choptank River. Open seven days a week, 6 AM to 11 PM.
Dunkin' Donuts (410-228-6197; 213 Sunburst Hwy., Cambridge) Open 24 hours.

NEWSPAPERS AND MAGAZINES

The Chesapeake's proximity to major cities means that folks deep in Chesapeake Country are likely to read *The Washington Post* as their local paper. Still, the local papers are filled with information about everything from tides to VFW oyster roasts.

Maryland

Bay Weekly (410-867-0304; www.bayweekly.com; 1629 Forest Dr., Annapolis) Eclectic free weekly features entertainment, nature, and other topics of interest to Bay readers. Look for it around Maryland's Western Shore. Published Thurs.

The Capital (410-268-5000; www.hometownannapolis.com; 2000 Capital Dr., Annapolis) The state capital's daily newspaper. Also publishes a comprehensive Thurs. entertainment section focusing on Annapolis-area events.

Chesapeake Bay Magazine (410-263-2662; www.chesapeakeboating.net; 1819 Bay Ridge Ave., Annapolis) A monthly magazine featuring stories about the Bay, boating, fishing, and other water-related issues.

City Paper (410-523-2300; www.citypaper.com; 812 Park Ave., Baltimore) Baltimore's alternative weekly is a must-have for nightlife info and good local cultural coverage. It's available free around town.

The Daily Banner (410-228-3131; www.newszap.com; 103 Cedar St., Cambridge) Published Wed. and Fri.

The Daily Times (410-749-7171; www.delmarvanow.com; 618 Beam St., Salisbury)

Kent County News (410-778-2011; www.kentcountynews.com; 217 High St., Chestertown) Published Thurs.

The Star-Democrat (410-822-1500; www.stardem.com; P.O. Box 600, Easton) Published Sun. through Fri.

The Sun (410-332-6000 or 1-800-829-8000; www.baltimoresun.com; 501 N. Calvert St., Baltimore) Blanket coverage of Maryland, great source of info on Baltimore.

What's Up? Annapolis and *What's Up? Eastern Shore* (410-267-9390; www.whats upmag.com; 929 West St., Suite 208A, Annapolis) This is a good monthly that covers activities and events in two publications: one for Annapolis and one for the Eastern Shore. Look for it in stands throughout the area.

Washington, D.C.

The Washington Post (202-334-6000; www.washingtonpost.com; 1150 15th St. N.W., Washington, DC 20005) The national morning daily includes "Weekend," a Fri. section focusing on events in and around Washington, D.C., and often on the Bay.

The Washington Times (202-636-3000; www.washingtontimes.com; 3600 New York Ave. N.E., Washington, DC 20018) Morning daily.

ROAD SERVICE

The Upper Bay: Morgan's Auto Repair & Tow Service (410-398-1288; www.morgans autorepair.com; 668 W. Pulaski Hwy., Elkton) Towing 24 hours.

Middle Eastern Shore: Mullikin's Auto Body (410-820-8676; 9277 Ocean Gateway Dr., Easton) 24-hour towing.

Lower Eastern Shore: Adkins Towing (410-749-7712; 2207 Northwood Dr., Unit 8A, Salisbury) 24-hour towing.

TIDES

If you're going for a sail or leaving your crab pot in the water for a few hours, you may want to check the tide. Typical Chesapeake tide falls are only 1.5–2 feet, but that can make a big difference in the Bay's shallow waters. Keep an eye out for extra-high tides if a storm is forecast. For information, check local newspapers, broadcast weather reports, or the many monthly freebies that publish tide schedules. Information also is available at any marina or bait and tackle shop.

TOURIST INFORMATION

The Chesapeake Bay Gateways network is an effort to tie together the range of historic sites, sailing ships, parks, refuges, paddling trails, and other related sites—including visitor's centers—that tell the full story of the Chesapeake Bay. Look for signs, a map, and a guide at visitor's centers, or check www.baygateways.net.

Civil War Trails in both Virginia and Maryland can be followed, including John Wilkes Booth's escape from Ford's Theatre in Washington, D.C., to points east at the edge of Bay Country. Watch for signs and brochures, and for additional information go online to www.civilwartrails.com.

Although this book does not cover Virginia as it has in the past (except for Tangier Island—we just couldn't bear to leave out that Chesapeake icon!), the mouth of the Bay is indeed in Virginia and explorers may be interested in the Eastern Shore of Virginia or the Northern Neck/Middle Peninsula region on the Western Shore east of Richmond. So, contact the Virginia Tourism Corp. (804-786-4484 or 1-800-VISITVA; www.virginia.org; 901 E. Byrd St., Richmond, VA 23219) if you want to explore farther south. Otherwise:

Maryland Office of Tourism Development (1-866-639-3526; www.visitmaryland.org; 401 E. Pratt St., 14th Floor, Baltimore, MD 21202)

Annapolis South to the Potomac River

Annapolis and Anne Arundel County Conference and Visitors Bureau (410-280-0445 or 1-888-302-2850; www.visitannaplis.org; 26 West St., Annapolis, MD 21401)

Calvert County Tourism (1-800-331-9771; www.co.cal.md.us/visitors; Courthouse, 175 Main St., Prince Frederick, MD 20678)

St. Mary's County Tourism (1-800-327-9023; tour.co.saint-marys.md.us; 23115 Leonard Hall Dr., Leonardtown, MD 20650)

The Upper Bay

Cecil County Office of Tourism (1-800-CECIL95; www.ccgov.org/tourism; 68 Heather La., Suite 43, Perryville, MD 21903)

Following in Smith's footsteps

Capt. John Smith famously explored the Bay and tributaries in 1607, 1608 and 1609, and hoped to find the Northwest Passage to China. Alas, he never found it, but the map and journals he left behind shaped colonial-era development in the region and thus, the place you see today.

Commemorating Smith's historic journeys is the 3,000-mile Capt. John Smith Chesapeake National Historic Trail, authorized by Congress in 2006. The following year, sailors departed in a re-created shallop like Smith and his crew would have sailed (built, incidentally, by the Chestertown-based Sultana Projects). The closely watched tale of the modern-day voyage captured the region's imagination, and now efforts by the National Park Service are well under way to create ways for you, too, to follow Smith's routes. Or, perhaps more realistically, parts of them.

For instance, you can check out the Woodland Village at Jefferson Patterson Park north of Solomons to see how the American Indians lived.

You can also plan your own journey via www.smithtrail.net. Under "Visit the Trail," click through historic vs. present-day map overlays to plot your own trail through John Smith's Chesapeake. Water trails were under development at deadline.

To arrange a paddle up the Sassafras (or the nearby Chester) that reflects Smith's journey, contact Sultana Projects at www.sultanaprojects.org. And keep an eye out around the region for the distinctive NPS John Smith Trail logo at trail sites, which are going up as the project moves ahead.

Harford County Office of Tourism (410-638-3327; www.harfordmd.com; 220 S. Main St., Bel Air, MD 21014)

Kent County Tourism Development Office (410-778-0416; www.kentcounty.com /tourism; 400 High St., Chestertown, MD 21620)

Middle Eastern Shore

Caroline County Office of Tourism (410-479-0655; www.tourcaroline.com; 15 S. Third St., Denton, MD 21625)

Queen Anne's County Office of Tourism (410-604-2100 or 1-888-400-RSVP; www.qac .org; 425 Piney Narrows Rd., Chester, MD 21619)

Talbot County Office of Tourism (410-770-8000; www.tourtalbot.org; 11 S. Harrison St., Easton, MD 21601)

Lower Eastern Shore

Dorchester County Office of Tourism (410-228-1000 or 1-800-522-TOUR; www.tour dorchester.org; 2 Rose Hill Pl., Dorchester, MD 21613)

Wicomico County Convention & Visitors Association (1-800-332-TOUR; www.wicomico tourism.org; 8480 Ocean Hwy., Delmar, MD 21875)

Somerset County Tourism (410-651-2968 or 1-800-521-9189; www.visitsomerset.com; P.O. Box 243, Princess Anne, MD 21853)

IF TIME IS SHORT

It's hard to pick and choose among the Bay's many activities, but here are some best bets.

IN BALTIMORE

Head over to the **American Visionary Art Museum** (410-244-1900; www.avam.org) at 800 Key Hwy. to take in the truly visionary art in this unusual and nice-sized museum. When you're finished, visit the nearby **Baltimore Museum of Industry** (410-727-4808; www.thebmi.org) at 1415 Key Hwy. to learn about Baltimore's many industrial firsts. Then go over to the other side of the Inner Harbor and tour the *USS Constellation* (410-539-1797; www.historicships.org) at Pier 1, and the nearby **Seven Foot Knoll Lighthouse** (which is free) to get a feel for Baltimore's maritime past. From here, either rummage around Fell's Point's cobblestone streets (consider a tour), or go north to Mount Vernon Square and the **Walters Art Museum** (410-547-9000; www.thewalters.org; 600 N. Charles St.), the **George Peabody Library** (410-516-8335; www.georgepeabodylibrary.jhu.edu; 21 E. Mount Vernon Place) and, farther to the north, the **Baltimore Museum of Art** (443-573-1700; www.artbma.org; 10 Art Museum Dr.). A wonderful evening would include dinner at **Sotto Sopra** (410-625-0534; www.sottosoprainc.com; 405 N. Charles St.) followed by a performance at the nearby **An Die Musik** (410-385-2638; www.andiemusiklive.com; 409 N. Charles St.).

IN ANNAPOLIS

Sit in the gardens at the **William Paca House** (410-267-7619; 186 Prince George St.), perhaps the best spot in the Historic District. Dine at **O'Learys Restaurant** (410-263-0884; 310 Third St., Eastport), the **Wild Orchid Café** (410-268-8009; 909 Bay Ridge Ave., Eastport), or Joss for sushi (410-263-4688; 195 Main St.). Check to see if **Watermark Cruises** (410-268-7600; www.watermarkcruises.com; Annapolis City Dock) is running a music cruise one evening and plan on that. Or, take one of their walking tours through the colonial downtown. Rent a kayak from **Annapolis Canoe and Kayak** (410-263-2303, www.annapoliscanoeandkayak.com; 311 Third St.) about 4 PM on a summer weekday and take a paddle before heading over to dinner at the **Boatyard Bar and Grill** (410-216-6206; 400 Fourth St.).

ON THE UPPER SHORE

Wander Chestertown's historic streets. Go to the **Eastern Neck Wildlife Refuge** (410-639-7056; 1730 Eastern Neck Rd.), a peninsula past Rock Hall, to look for good birds. For a meal? **Brooks Tavern** (410-810-0012; www.brookstavern.com; 870 High St.) gets the enthusiastic nod.

ON THE MIDDLE EASTERN SHORE

Go out aboard the *Rebecca T. Ruark,* the Bay's oldest skipjack, with Capt. Wade Murphy (410-886-2176; 21308 Phillips Rd., Tilghman) out of Tilghman's Dogwood Harbor. Or save the third weekend of July for **Plein Air Easton** (www.pleinaireaston.com) and watch the painters at work. Plan on dinner at **Scossa** in Easton (410-822-2202; www.scossa restaurant.com; 8 N. Washington St.), where you can sit outside and enjoy Northern Italian cuisine.

On the Lower Eastern Shore

Rent a camper cabin at **Janes Island State Park** near Crisfield (410-968-1565; 26280 Alfred Lawson Dr.). Canoe, kayak, or motor through the marshy guts. Ferry over to **Tangier Island,** take a nickel tour of the watermen's village aboard a golf cart, then stop at any restaurant to eat the only truly great (except if you're on Smith Island) soft-shells mere mortals ever find.

General Index

Lodging by Price

Inexpensive: up to $75
Moderate: $75 to 150
Expensive: $150 to 225
Very Expensive: over $225

Baltimore

Moderate to Expensive
Fairfield Inn & Suites, 46–47

Moderate to Very Expensive
Baltimore Marriott Inner Harbor Camden Yards, 45
Celie's Waterfront Bed and Breakfast, 46
Doubletree Inn and Spa at the Colonnade Baltimore, 46
Homewood Suites/Hilton Garden Inn, 48
Hotel Monaco, 48–49
Peabody Court, 50
Tremont Plaza Hotel, 52

Expensive
The Inn at Henderson's Wharf, 49–50
Inn at 2920, 49

Expensive to Very Expensive
The Admiral Fell Inn, 44–45
Baltimore Marriott Waterfront, 45–46
Hampton Inn & Suites Baltimore Inner Harbor, 47
Hilton Baltimore, 48
Hyatt Regency Baltimore, 49
Intercontinental Harbor Court Baltimore, 50
Pier 5 Hotel, 50–51
Scarborough Fair Bed & Breakfast, 51–52
Sheraton Inner Harbor Hotel, 52

Annapolis

Moderate
Back Creek Inn B & B (Solomons Island), 151

Moderate to Expensive
The Barn on Howard's Cove, 106
O'Callaghan Hotel Annapolis, 110

Expensive
Butterfly Fields B & B, 106–107

Expensive to Very Expensive
The Inn at 30 Maryland Avenue, 109
1908 William Page Inn, 105
Blue Heron B & B (Solomons Island), 151
Flag House Inn, 107
Harbor View Inn, 107
Historic Inns of Annapolis, 107–109
Inn at Horn Point, 109–110
Loews Annapolis Hotel, 110
Two-O-One Bed & Breakfast, 110–111

Very Expensive
Annapolis Inn, 105
Annapolis Marriott Waterfront, 105
Schooner *Woodwind*, 110
Westin Annapolis, 111

The Upper Bay

Moderate
The Inn at Mitchell House (Chestertown), 164
Holiday Inn Express Hotel & Suites (Chestertown), 168
Imperial Hotel (Chestertown), 164

Moderate to Expensive
Comfort Suites (Chestertown), 168
La Cle D'Or Guesthouse (Havre de Grace), 160
Spencer-Silver Mansion (Havre de Grace), 160–162
Vandiver Inn (Havre de Grace), 162

Moderate to Very Expensive
The Inn at Osprey Point (Rock Hall), 168
Inn at Huntingfield Farm (Rock Hall), 164–165

Expensive to Very Expensive
The White Swan Tavern (Chestertown), 164–165
Brampton Bed & Breakfast Inn (Chestertown), 162–163
Great Oak Manor B&B (Chestertown), 163–164
Old Gratitude House Bed & Breakfast (Rock Hall), 168

Middle Eastern Shore

Moderate to Expensive
Bay Cottage (St. Michaels), 202
Best Western (St. Michaels), 208
Harrison's Chesapeake Country Inn (Tilghman Island), 208
Knapp's Narrows Marina & Inn (Tilghman Island), 208
Oxford Inn & Pope's Tavern (Oxford), 201
Point Breeze Bed & Breakfast (St. Michaels), 205

Moderate to Very Expensive
The Oaks (Royal Oak), 201
The Old Brick Inn (St. Michaels), 204–205
Black Walnut Point Inn (Tilghman Island), 206
Chesapeake Wood Duck Inn (Tilghman Island), 207
Comfort Inn Kent Narrows (Grasonville), 208
George Brooks House (St. Michaels), 203
Tidewater Inn (Easton), 200

Expensive
The Bishop's House (Easton), 199–200
Watermark Bed & Breakfast (St. Michaels), 205–206

Expensive to Very Expensive
The River Plantation (Queenstown), 199
Aida's Victoriana Inn (St. Michaels), 202
Dr. Dodson House Bed & Breakfast (St. Michaels), 202
Five Gables Inn and Spa (St. Michaels), 203
Harbourtowne Golf Resort & Conference Center (St. Michaels), 203
Kent Manor Inn (Kent Island), 199
Lazyjack Inn (Tilghman Island), 207–208
Tilghman Island Inn (Tilghman Island), 208
Wade's Point Inn on the Bay (St. Michaels), 205

Dining by Price

Inexpensive:	up to $10
Moderate:	$10 to 20
Expensive:	$20 to 30
Very Expensive:	over $30

Baltimore

Inexpensive
Matthew's Pizza (Patterson Park), 58–59

Inexpensive to Moderate
Harborque (Locust Point), 58
Jimmy's (Fell's Point), 60

Inexpensive to Expensive
Café Hon (Hampden), 63

Moderate
The Brewer's Art (Mount Vernon), 62
The Helmand (Mount Vernon), 62
The Wine Market (Locust Point), 58
Abbey Burger Bistro (Federal Hill), 57
Café Gia (Little Italy), 61
Frank and Nic's West End Grille (Inner Harbor), 53–54
Jack's Bistro (Canton), 56
Joe Squared (Station North), 64
Miss Shirley's Cafe—Downtown (Inner Harbor), 54
Nacho Mama's/Mama's on the Half Shell (Canton), 56–57
Pazo (Harbor East), 56
Regi's American Bistro (Federal Hill), 57
Ryleigh's Oyster (Federal Hill), 57–58
Ze Mean Bean Cafe (Fell's Point), 60–61

Moderate to Expensive
Diamond Tavern (Inner Harbor), 53
Kali's Court (Fell's Point), 60
La Scala (Little Italy), 61–62
Salt Tavern (Patterson Park), 59–60
Sotto Sopra (Mount Vernon), 63
Woodberry Kitchen (Hampden), 63–64

Expensive
Della Notte (Little Italy), 61

Expensive to Very Expensive
Charleston (Harbor East), 54–56

Annapolis

Inexpensive to Moderate
49 West Coffee House, Winebar & Gallery, 112
Boatyard Bar and Grill, 112
Chick & Ruth's Delly, 114
Davis' Pub, 115
Lemongrass, 117

Inexpensive to Expensive
Café Normandie, 112–113

Rams Head Tavern, 119–120
Reynolds Tavern, 121
Skipper's Pier Restaurant & Dock Bar, 120

Inexpensive to Very Expensive
Middleton Tavern, 118
Mike's Restaurant & Crab House, 118
Tsunami, 120

Moderate
Joss Café & Sushi Bar, 116–117

Moderate to Expensive
The Wild Orchid Café, 121–122
Cantler's Riverside Inn, 113–114
Carrol's Creek Waterfront Restaurant, 114
Galway Bay Irish Restaurant and Pub, 115
McGarvey's Saloon & Oyster Bar, 117–118

Moderate to Very Expensive
Harry Browne's Restaurant, 115–116
Osteria 177, 119

Expensive to Very Expensive
Lewnes' Steakhouse, 117
O'Learys, 118–119

The Upper Bay

Inexpensive to Moderate
Brix Tapas Kitchen and Wine Cellar (Chestertown), 170
Price's Seafood Restaurant (Havre de Grace), 169

Inexpensive to Expensive
Harbor Shack Waterfront Bar & Grill (Rock Hall), 172
Waterman's Crab House (Rock Hall), 172–173

Inexpensive to Very Expensive
Tidewater Grille (Havre de Grace), 169–170

Moderate
Kitty Knight House (Georgetown), 171–172

Moderate to Expensive
Brooks Tavern (Chestertown), 170–171
Fish Whistle (Chestertown), 171
Harbor House Restaurant (Chestertown), 171
Laurrapin Grille (Havre de Grace), 169

Moderate to Very Expensive
Blue Heron Café (Chestertown), 170

Expensive
Bay Wolf Dining and Spirits (Rock Hall), 172

Middle Eastern Shore

Inexpensive
Soda Fountain at Hill's (Easton), 213

Inexpensive to Moderate
The Jetty Restaurant & Dock Bar (Grasonville), 210
Ava's Pizzeria (St. Michaels), 216
Foxy's Marina Bar (St. Michaels), 216–217
Holly's Restaurant (Grasonville), 210
Schooner's (Oxford), 215
Thai Ki (Easton), 213–214

Moderate to Expensive
The Crab Claw Restaurant (St. Michaels), 216
Fisherman's Inn & Crab Deck (Grasonville), 209
General Tanuki's (Easton), 211
Harris Crab House (Grasonville), 209–210
Kent Manor Inn & Restaurant (Stevensville), 210–211
Key Lime Café (St. Michaels), 217
Latitude 38 (Oxford), 214
Out of the Fire Restaurant & Wine Bar (Easton),
   212–213
Oxford Inn/Pope's Tavern (Oxford), 215
St. Michaels Crab & Steak House (St. Michaels), 217

Moderate to Very Expensive
The Masthead at Pier Street Marina (Oxford), 214–215
The Narrows (Grasonville), 211
Bella Luna Restaurant and Market (Royal Oak),
   217–218
Mitchum's Steakhouse (Trappe), 214
Scossa Restaurant and Lounge (Easton), 213
Tilghman Island Inn (Tilghman Island), 218

Expensive
Bistro St. Michaels (St. Michaels), 216

Expensive to Very Expensive
208 Talbot Restaurant & Wine Bar (St. Michaels), 215
Mason's Restaurant (Easton), 211–212

Lower Eastern Shore

Inexpensive
The Back Street Grill (Salisbury), 251–252
The Olney Market (Princess Anne), 255
Viva Espresso (Salisbury), 253

Inexpensive to Moderate
Jimmie & Sook's Raw Bar and Grill (Cambridge), 250
Old Salty's Restaurant (Hoopers Island), 251

Inexpensive to Expensive
The Globe (Crisfield), 256
The Palette (Snow Hill), 254–255
Portside Seafood Restaurant (Cambridge), 250–251
Vinny's La Roma (Salisbury), 252–253

Inexpensive to Very Expensive
Suicide Bridge Restaurant (Hurlock), 251

Moderate to Expensive
Bella Luna (Cambridge), 250
Boonies (Tyaskin), 253
Linton's Seafood (Crisfield), 255–256
Watermen's Inn (Crisfield), 256–257

Moderate to Very Expensive
Drummer's Café in the Atlantic Hotel (Berlin), 255
Sobo's Wine Beerstro (Salisbury), 252

Dining by Cuisine

Baltimore

Afghan
The Helmand (Mount Vernon), 62

American
Frank and Nic's West End Grille (Inner Harbor), 53–54

Bistro fare
Regi's American Bistro (Federal Hill), 57

Breakfast, sandwiches
Jimmy's (Fell's Point), 60

Burgers
Abbey Burger Bistro (Federal Hill), 57

Comfort Food
Café Hon (Hampden), 63

Eastern European
Ze Mean Bean Cafe (Fell's Point), 60–61

Eclectic
Jack's Bistro (Canton), 56

Farm to table
Woodberry Kitchen (Hampden), 63–64

Italian
Café Gia (Little Italy), 61
Della Notte (Little Italy), 61
La Scala (Little Italy), 61–62

Low-country Southern
Charleston (Harbor East), 54–56

Mediterranean, seafood
Kali's Court (Fell's Point), 60

New American
The Brewer's Art (Mount Vernon), 62
The Wine Market (Locust Point), 58
Diamond Tavern (Inner Harbor), 53
Salt Tavern (Patterson Park), 59–60

Northern Italian
Sotto Sopra (Mount Vernon), 63

Oysters and seafood
Ryleigh's Oyster (Federal Hill), 57–58

Pizza
Matthew's Pizza (Patterson Park), 58–59

Pizza, risotto, sandwiches
Harborque (Locust Point), 58
Joe Squared (Station North), 64

Southern-style Comfort Food
Miss Shirley's Cafe—Downtown (Inner Harbor), 54

Tapas
Pazo (Harbor East), 56

Tex-Mex
Nacho Mama's (Canton), 56–57

Annapolis

American, kosher
Chick & Ruth's Delly, 114

American, pub fare
Rams Head Tavern, 119–120

American, seafood, pub fare
McGarvey's Saloon & Oyster Bar, 117–118

Asian fusion
Tsunami, 120

Authentic Irish
Galway Bay Irish Restaurant and Pub, 115

Contemporary American, seafood
Carrol's Creek Waterfront Restaurant, 114

English, regional Chesapeake, and light fare
Reynolds Tavern, 121

Farm to table
The Wild Orchid Café, 121–122

French
Café Normandie, 112–113

French-influenced, light American
49 West Coffee House, Winebar & Gallery, 112

Italian-Mediterranean
Osteria 177, 119

Japanese
Joss Café & Sushi Bar, 116–117

New American, regional
Harry Browne's Restaurant, 115–116

Seafood
Cantler's Riverside Inn, 113–114
Mike's Restaurant & Crab House, 118
Skipper's Pier Restaurant & Dock Bar, 120

Seafood, American, tavern fare
Middleton Tavern, 118

Seafood, casual American
Boatyard Bar and Grill, 112

Seafood, nouveau
O'Learys, 118–119

Seafood, pub fare
Davis' Pub, 115

Steakhouse
Lewnes' Steakhouse, 117

Thai
Lemongrass, 117